42

42

Inside the Presidency of Bill Clinton

Edited by Michael Nelson,
Barbara A. Perry, and
Russell L. Riley

CORNELL UNIVERSITY PRESS   ITHACA AND LONDON

PUBLISHED IN ASSOCIATION WITH
THE UNIVERSITY OF VIRGINIA'S MILLER CENTER

Frontispiece: President Bill Clinton, January 11, 1993. National Archives & Records Administration, Courtesy, William J. Clinton Presidential Library

First published 2016 by Cornell University Press
First printing, Cornell Paperbacks, 2016

Printed in the United States of America

Library of Congress Cataloging-in-Publication Data

Names: Nelson, Michael, 1949– editor. | Perry, Barbara A. (Barbara Ann), 1956–
    editor. | Riley, Russell L. (Russell Lynn), 1958– editor.
Title: 42 : inside the Presidency of Bill Clinton / edited by Michael Nelson,
    Barbara A. Perry, and Russell L. Riley.
Other titles: 42 (Nelson, Perry and Riley) | Forty-two
Description: Ithaca ; London : Cornell University Press, published in association
    with the University of Virginia's Miller Center, 2016. | "This book is based
    on papers presented at the 2014 conference that accompanied the release of the
    Clinton oral histories at the William J. Clinton Presidential Library"—
    Foreword. | Includes bibliographical references and index.
Identifiers: LCCN 2016010308
ISBN 9780801454066 (cloth : alk. paper)
ISBN 9780801456893 (pbk. : alk. paper)
Subjects: LCSH: Clinton, Bill, 1946– —Congresses. | United States—Politics and
    government—1993–2001—Congresses.
Classification: LCC E885 .A125 2016 | DDC 973.929092—dc23
LC record available at http://lccn.loc.gov/2016010308

| Cloth printing | 10 | 9 | 8 | 7 | 6 | 5 | 4 | 3 | 2 | 1 |
| Paperback printing | 10 | 9 | 8 | 7 | 6 | 5 | 4 | 3 | 2 | 1 |

Contents

Foreword

In the fall of 1996, I was on a campaign bus trip with President Bill Clinton and my boss, Vice President Al Gore. The enormous motorcade consisted of buses for the candidates, buses for the staff, buses for the press, and buses for the secret service. It also contained police motorcycles, ambulances, and fire trucks, making it seem like the row of vehicles went on for miles. As the motorcade snaked through towns between Seattle, Washington, and Portland, Oregon, it stopped every fifty miles or so. Some of the stops along the 175-mile trip were in small towns such as Roy, Fenino, and Longvic. Others were unscheduled. At each stop, Clinton and Gore would bound off the bus, climb onto a quickly constructed plywood stage with a sound system, and be introduced by a local notable or two. The president would launch into a short version of his stump speech and the vice president would weigh in with an even shorter one. The entire event would sometimes take less than thirty minutes.

With the message discipline that only a seasoned politician could have, Clinton delivered the core of his campaign speech at every single stop. In his first term he had created 11 million new jobs and attained the smallest federal government since John F. Kennedy was president. Like all messages from incumbent presidents, it worked not because of the rhetoric or the delivery but also because it was real and people felt it. America in 1996 was employed and at peace. The budget deficit was getting smaller and so was the government. Clinton had given his vice president the job of "reinventing government," a task that signaled he understood the frustration Americans felt with bureaucracy. There had been ups and downs during Clinton's first term, but by and large Americans were happy with his performance, and in November they made him the first Democratic president to be elected to a second term since Franklin Roosevelt.

The end of Clinton's second term stood in stark contrast to the end of his first term. To be sure, America was still prosperous and at peace. The federal budget was balanced for the first time in more than a quarter-century. But as Clinton left the White House amid nasty stories about deals for pardons and whether or not he was taking the furniture, the country seemed ready to see him go. He had spent two of the precious four years of his second term hunkered down defending himself against accusations that he'd had a sexual relationship with a young White House intern. This had led to a vote to impeach in the House, although the Senate did not convict him. So in addition to being the only Democratic president elected to a second term since FDR, Clinton became the only president to be impeached since Andrew Johnson in 1868.

And there you have it—the incongruity at the heart of the Clinton presidency. For most Americans, his personal behavior, from his philandering to his obfuscation and oh-so-careful parsing of words, left a lot to be desired. Older people and married women were especially appalled. But the American people can be pretty smart when they want to be and they had no trouble embracing the paradox that was Bill Clinton.

Nothing sums this up better than the fact that, as Andrew Rudalevige points out in his chapter in this volume, in 1998, while Clinton was being publicly excoriated for a sexual relationship and subjected to near-daily embarrassing revelations and impending impeachment by the House of Representatives, his approval numbers never dropped below 60 percent. Moreover, to the surprise of many, Clinton was not an albatross on Democrats running in the 1998 midterm elections. In fact, the Republicans lost five House seats and merely broke even in the Senate. This was only the second time since Reconstruction that the president's party had gained strength at midterm.

Clinton was, simply, an incredibly gifted president and Americans knew it, whether they agreed with him or not. He had it all: policy expertise that never failed to amaze the experts in the room; an ability to communicate on the all-important medium of television that rivaled that of President Ronald Reagan, and an instinct for politics and strategy that allowed him, more often than not, to run rings around his adversaries.

One of the earliest indications of this superb instinct was his choice of Senator Al Gore of Tennessee to be his running mate in 1992. Clinton's choice broke the mold and has been repeated by successful presidential candidates ever since. As Michael Nelson points out, the choice "defied all the traditional canons of ticket-balancing." Like Clinton, Gore was a southerner and a moderate, an early member of the Democratic Leadership Council. In choosing Gore, Clinton understood that he would be reinforcing, not confusing, his "New Democrat" label. He also understood that he would be getting a helpmate in the two areas where he had little direct experience, foreign policy and technology.

The other early indication of Clinton's political savvy was his pursuit of the 1993 budget deal. Like Reagan, he understood macro-economic timing. There are always long lags between the passage of a piece of legislation and its effect on the economy. Although the budget deal was costly to Democrats in the short run, in the long run it paved the way for the "virtuous circle" that Clinton's economic team was so fond of talking about—lower federal debt, higher growth, more jobs and tax revenue, and then lower debt again. That deal led to Clinton's biggest domestic accomplishment—the first balanced budget in decades—and reflected his political judgment that he had been elected, in part, as a result of deficit hawks deserting the Republican Party to vote for Ross Perot. Although the 1993 budget deal wasn't the only contributing factor in achieving a balanced budget (Republican cuts in discretionary domestic spending were also important), the pursuit of a balanced budget was an example of Clinton's propensity to take on his own party. Other first term accomplishments that fell into that category included fulfilling his campaign pledges to "end welfare as we know it" and pass the North American Free Trade Agreement (NAFTA).

The one exception was the failure of comprehensive health care legislation, an initiative that, for all the attention paid to it in the first term, was probably doomed from the start. Unlike welfare reform, which, as Nelson points out, was the subject of the most frequently run issue-related television commercial of the 1992 campaign, no campaign mandate sought health care reform. And, as Hillary Rodham Clinton herself admitted, by taking on such a substantive and public role in the development of the Clinton's health care plan, she placed herself in uncharted territory for a presidential spouse. As quoted in Barbara Perry's chapter, Hillary said: "I knew I had contributed to our failure, both because of my own missteps and because I underestimated the resistance I would meet as a first lady with a policy mission."[1]

But another factor, perhaps more powerful, was at work here. As Brendan Doherty points out in his chapter, Democrats on the Hill were simply not accustomed to taking the lead from a president of their own party. Until the huge upset in the 1994 midterm elections, in which Democrats lost control of Congress for the first time in a generation, congressional Democrats had been accustomed to going their own way. I remember an early trip to Capitol Hill to discuss the future of the Federal Aviation Administration and being told by a Democratic staffer that they would have to "check with the Executive Branch." I thought that by representing the president and the vice president in this matter, I was representing the Executive Branch. Apparently that not was not the case!

On foreign policy, Clinton had many fewer challenges. But as Deputy National Security Advisor Nancy Soderberg points out in the chapter by Russell Riley, there was no post–Cold War rule book. Clinton had to write it, as he did in the Balkans and in his late but intense efforts at peace in the Middle East. As Robert A. Strong writes, "Maybe his final year push for a Middle East agreement was an effort to make amends for a second term that was dominated by scandal and impeachment." But by and large, the Clinton presidency was not a foreign policy presidency, especially compared to the two Bush presidencies that bracketed it.

Much of Clinton's second term can be characterized as a huge lost opportunity. The once-in-a-generation prospect of a balanced budget and even budget surpluses opened the possibility for big pieces of legislation. At the top of the list for everyone looking forward to a second term was the prospect of revamping the frayed social safety net. Budget surpluses provided the unique opportunity to do some big things with Social Security and Medicare because in every reform of large programs, the transition costs are enormous and budget surpluses would be able to pay for at least some of these costs. But once the Monica Lewinsky scandal broke and the Republicans moved toward impeachment, all hope of large-scale reform was gone. Clinton needed every bit of political capital he had just to survive, and he could not challenge the system. The tragedy of that scandal is that for all practical purposes, the second term ended almost before it began.

In the years since the end of the Clinton presidency, his popularity has increased, albeit in fits and starts. He has become the most popular politician in America. After years of stalemate in the political system, slow growth in the economy, and disappointments in foreign policy, President Clinton is looking better than ever. His personal moral failures seem to have faded into the past and been forgiven by a public that is hungry for competence in the job. And that Clinton had.

Elaine Kamarck

Preface

So impressed was former president Bill Clinton with the University of Virginia Miller Center's oral history of his presidency that in remarks at the tenth anniversary of his presidential library in Little Rock, he told the assembled administration alumni that if they had not done an interview for the project yet, they needed to do so.

42 offers scholarly analysis of the many oral history interviews that were conducted and that, taken together, expand our understanding of the Clinton presidency and the final decade of the second millennium. As a cooperative effort of the Miller Center and the Clinton Foundation, the Clinton oral history project consists of more than 130 interviews with senior White House and cabinet officials, leaders of Congress, world leaders, campaign aides, and others. In sessions normally running seven to ten hours, teams of scholars conducted confidential interviews. Typically, each interview explored officials' memories of their service with and for President Clinton, along with their careers prior to joining the administration. Interviewees also offered political and leadership lessons they gleaned as eyewitnesses to, and often shapers of, history.

The Miller Center has conducted the authorized oral history of every president since Jimmy Carter. No questions are off limits; officials are encouraged to speak candidly to history. Each interview's audio recording is transcribed by the Center, and then edited by the subject, following standard oral history protocols. The transcript becomes the authoritative record of the interview. In November 2014, the Miller Center released all cleared Clinton project transcripts. They can be accessed at www.millercenter.org/president/clinton/oralhistory.

This book is based on papers presented at the 2014 conference that accompanied the release of the Clinton oral histories at the William J. Clinton Presidential Library. Knowing that by their nature most of the oral histories would present a generally friendly view of Clinton, each author drew on but did not rely exclusively, or even mainly, on the interviews to produce new and illuminating interpretations of his presidency.

The conference included panels covering the Clinton administration's foreign policy, domestic policy, and economic policy. Each panel included scholars and Clinton alumni, notably Wesley Clark, Sandy Berger, Nancy Soderberg, and Mara Rudman (foreign policy); Alexis Herman and Bruce Reed (domestic policy); and Erskine Bowles and Gene Sperling (economic policy). Closing remarks were offered by former Virginia governor Gerald L. Baliles, director of the Miller Center, and President Clinton.

In Chapter 1, Michael Nelson discusses Clinton's election and reelection to the presidency, along with the intervening midterm election in which the opposition Republican Party gained control of Congress. Chapter 2, by Bruce F. Nesmith and Paul J. Quirk, places Clinton's "triangulation" (or "third way") approach to public policy in the context of other modern presidencies. In Chapter 3, Sean M. Theriault, Patrick Hickey, and Megan Moeller assess Clinton's relationship with Congress as one that included elements of compromise and confrontation. Brendan J. Doherty focuses on one successful aspect of that relationship in Chapter 4: the enactment of Clinton's landmark economic plan in 1993. Andrew F. Rudalevige examines an unhappier aspect in Chapter 5: the controversy in Congress over Clinton's impeachment.

In Chapter 6, Nelson draws almost entirely on excerpts from the oral histories to construct a narrative account of welfare reform in the Clinton administration. Barbara A. Perry assesses the unusually influential role played by First Lady Hillary Rodham Clinton in Chapter 7. The Clinton administration's foreign policy is the subject of Chapter 8, by Spencer D. Bakich (Bosnia and Serbia), and Chapter 9, by Robert A. Strong (Northern Ireland, the Middle East).

Forming bookends for these nine chapters are Russell Riley's introduction and Sidney Milkis's conclusion. Riley combines his overview of the Clinton oral history project, which he directed, with his analysis of how it refines our knowledge of the presidency. Milkis's conclusion synthesizes the theories and evidence presented in each chapter into a portrait of presidential politics, policy making, and leadership in the twentieth century's last decade. Elaine Kamarck, both a scholar and a participant in the Clinton presidency, has written a foreword for the book that is itself a contribution to scholarship.

Our profound gratitude goes to those who were instrumental in making the Clinton Project possible: Philip Zelikow, the former director of the Miller Center, both for establishing an ongoing program in presidential oral history at the Center and for his leadership in securing the Clinton Project; the late James Sterling Young for coming out of retirement to head the new program and for his direction in getting the Clinton Project started; the members of the Miller Center's Governing Council for supporting the execution of the project; and subsequent director Gerald Baliles for his support and leadership in bringing the project to a successful conclusion. We thank President Bill Clinton for his endorsement of the project and, accordingly, the extraordinary cooperation of the Clinton alumni network for making the project the success that it was. Special thanks also go to Bruce Lindsey and Stephanie Streett at the Clinton Foundation for being so patient and cooperative and for the financial support of the Foundation, which covered the substantial transactions costs of these interviews. Historian Taylor Branch commended the Miller Center's work to President Clinton, and Ted Widmer and Karen Tramontano at the very earliest stages of the project's design gave critical staff support to him as well, all helping bring the project to life. Similarly, we wish to thank colleagues at the University of Arkansas-Fayetteville, who worked with the Miller Center to design a two-part project, making use of the comparative advantages of the two universities in recording a comprehensive oral history of the life of Bill Clinton. Leading the Arkansas effort were Jeannie Whayne, Andrew Dowdle, Michael Pierce, and Kris Katrosh. The project benefited from the external guidance of a superb advisory board, named jointly by the two university partners and President Clinton. For their guidance, especially in the design phase of the project, we thank Taylor Branch, Thomas Donilon, Jacquelyn D. Hall, Charles V. Hamilton, Darlene Clark Hine, David Levering Lewis, Bruce Lindsey, Sylvia Mathews, Richard E. Neustadt (deceased), Skip Rutherford, and Randall B. Woods.

Two other groups of people also should be acknowledged as absolutely indispensable to the effort: the more than 130 interviewees, who freely gave of their time to be interviewed; and the fifty-nine scholars from thirty-five institutions who volunteered their time to help with the questioning. In no instance was a single cent spent in honoraria—all of these participants, on both sides of the interview table, freely contributed their time to this endeavor.

At Cornell University Press, we are especially grateful to Senior Acquisitions Editor Michael J. McGandy, Senior Production Editor Karen M. Laun, and Copy Editor Kate Babbit for their excellent work on 42. We also thank the Press' two anonymous reviewers for their helpful comments on the manuscript.

Finally, the project would have been impossible without the support of the highly talented staff at the Miller Center. Chief among these were Beatriz Lee Swerdlow, Katrina Kuhn, Keri Matthews, and Bonnie Burns, who handled the scheduling and logistical arrangements for the interviews, and Jane Rafal Wilson, who directed a staff of professional editors who turned the spoken words in the interviews into clear transcripts. Former Miller Center faculty Stephen Knott, Darby Morrisroe, and Paul Martin helped provide leadership for the project and also conducted interviews. Information director Mike Greco and librarian Sheila Blackford led the Miller Center's talented technology team in digitally preparing and posting the transcripts online. And no interview could have been conducted without the detailed briefing books prepared by our skilled researchers, especially Bryan Craig and Rob Martin.

Michael Nelson, Barbara A. Perry, and Russell L. Riley

Bill Clinton's Road to the White House

Anyone interested in the possibilities for upward mobility in American society would do well to consult the story of Bill Blythe. Blythe, a vagabond Texan, was one of nine children raised by two transplanted Mississippians trying to forge a Depression-era existence from a small dirt farm sixty miles north of Dallas. At thirteen, when his father fell ill, Blythe took work in a dairy, later becoming an auto mechanic after his father's early death. He subsequently assumed the life of a traveling salesman, which—perhaps intentionally, perhaps fortuitously—fostered a careless existence, including an impetuous series of marriages, divorces, and abandoned children, all before he turned twenty-five.

During a 1943 visit to a Shreveport hospital with a female companion suffering from appendicitis, Blythe struck up a flirtatious acquaintance with a young nurse. The two were married only weeks later, shortly before Blythe was shipped overseas to service engines used by American soldiers then liberating Europe. His new bride knew virtually nothing of her husband's checkered past. In 1946, less than a year after returning to his wife and another job on the road, Blythe was found dead, drowned in a ditch alongside Route 60 in Missouri, the victim of a late-night car accident. He never knew financial success—or the child his wife was carrying at the time. That child would grow up to become president of the United States.

Young Billy Blythe later took the last name of his stepfather: Roger Clinton, a struggling car dealer who drank and gambled to excess. From these meager beginnings Bill Clinton rose to the highest political station in American life—testament in part to the love of a single mother and the devotion of extended families, but also to his own exceptional personal attributes.[2]

The future president was born in Hope, Arkansas, on August 19, 1946. When Bill was six, his family moved to Hot Springs, where he spent the remainder of his school years. There Clinton established himself as a stellar student and an accomplished member of the high school band. He was, in the words of biographer David Maraniss, "the school's golden boy"—quite an accomplishment for a southern teen bereft of athletic talent. Not only did he attend Arkansas Boys State after his junior year, he was elected by the assembled delegates as one of two Arkansas senators, entitling him to a trip to Washington in the summer of 1963. On that occasion he shook hands with President John F. Kennedy, a moment captured on film and recovered by diligent researchers working for Clinton's presidential campaign in 1992.

His interest in national politics stoked by this experience, Clinton earned admission to Georgetown University, where he enrolled in the School of Foreign Service in the fall of 1964. To support his studies, he worked for the Senate Foreign Relations Committee, then chaired by Arkansas senator J. William Fulbright. When discussing the terms of his employment, Clinton was told that there were two jobs available—a part-time position paying $3,500 a year, and a full-time one paying $5,000. "Well, how about two part-time jobs?" he reportedly answered.

By the late 1960s, college campuses across America were cauldrons of turmoil. Clinton had openly embraced the civil rights movement, but the Vietnam War left him greatly conflicted. He was by most accounts a peripheral figure in antiwar efforts, which fully engaged many of his closest friends. But his own struggles, morally, intellectually, and with what he himself termed his "political viability," created an ambiguous record on the war that would come back to haunt him as a presidential candidate more than two decades later.

After he graduated from Georgetown in 1968, Clinton won a Rhodes Scholarship to study in England. Clinton "went up" to Oxford—an English phrasing perfectly suited in this instance—at a time when, in the United States, student deferments from military induction were in a state of flux. Ultimately Clinton benefited from having a high draft lottery number—a fact he would emphasize in later years to explain how he had avoided military service legitimately. But the reality was far more complicated and less exculpatory.

Clinton was expected to report to the University of Arkansas Law School to begin ROTC training—an arrangement that had been made to save him from an already-scheduled draft induction. Returning instead to Oxford, he had second thoughts about ROTC and asked to be placed back into the draft pool—where, in December 1969, he drew number 311, virtually assuring that he would not be drafted. Although fortune smiled on Clinton, exceptions had been made, and liberties taken, to delay his service until the first lottery was held. Clinton was hardly alone among Rhodes Scholars in getting special treatment, but his simple story of good luck did not bear up under scrutiny. This subjected Clinton to lingering charges of draft dodging for the rest of his public career.

Among his cohort of Rhodes Scholars at Oxford, Clinton was a famously quick study and favored companion. He spent much of his time using Oxford as a point of departure for travels further abroad, even going to the Soviet Union at a time when few Americans were making that trip. He did not, however, earn a degree.

It was clear to all who knew Clinton that he wanted a political career—and to those who knew him well that he intended to return to Arkansas for this purpose. First, however, he studied law at Yale, where he met a fellow student, Hillary Rodham. They were so taken with each other that Rodham, whose Wellesley commencement address had been featured in *Life* magazine, decided to leave behind a promising East Coast–based legal career to follow Clinton home. They both worked as law professors at the University of Arkansas in Fayetteville and were married in 1975.

Clinton's first attempt to win public office was a well-fought failure. In 1974, he challenged incumbent Republican John Paul Hammerschmidt for a congressional seat in northwest Arkansas. Although the first post-Watergate election was a terrific one for Democrats nationally, Clinton lost narrowly, by 52 to 48 percent. Undaunted, he ran statewide for attorney general two years later, this time winning the office. Only two years later, in 1978, he was elected governor of Arkansas, becoming the youngest governor in the United States.

In 1980, Clinton became the youngest *ex*-governor in the country. That election—dominated at the national level by the presidential contest between Jimmy Carter and Ronald Reagan—was a terrible one for Democrats. But Clinton had amply contributed to his own troubles, including his decision to increase taxes on car tags, and, by his own accounting, the fact that he had hired "too many young beards and out-of-staters in important positions."[3] Concerns were also raised by some Arkansans about a liberal wife who was unwilling to take her husband's last name. Clinton claims that he spent the months after the election asking everybody he saw why they thought he lost. Defeat, and his reaction to it, was a crucial learning experience for a politician with bigger ambitions.

Chastened, Clinton ran again for governor in 1982 and won. He was successfully reelected three more times and became known as a rising star within the national Democratic Party, especially for his efforts to improve education in his poor state. During the 1980s, Clinton began to seriously consider making a run for the presidency. He understood that the starting point for a successful candidacy was a record of accomplishment in Arkansas. But there were two additional factors in the national political environment that had to be right before he could mount a plausible campaign.

The first was the creation of a broad network of supporters he could rely on to build a national organization. To some extent Clinton had been working on this his entire life. A vast network of Friends of Bill (or FOBs) had been accumulating since at least his days at Boys Nation, and it was a natural part of his personality to remain in touch with them. These were people who expected him to run for president at some point, the only question being when. The second factor was the receptivity of the national Democratic Party to the kind of centrist leadership Clinton intended to provide. The national trends were increasingly favorable. The party's losses at the presidential level, by staggering margins in 1980, 1984, and 1988, created a hunger for victory, making it receptive to new ideas and departures from established party orthodoxies. Clinton fit the bill as a moderate, successful governor of a southern state.

Clinton was not, however, merely a passive beneficiary of these national trends. After the failed Michael Dukakis campaign in 1988, he allowed himself to be recruited by centrist activist Al From to take the helm of the Democratic Leadership Council (DLC), a group created expressly to move the party's center of gravity away from the political left. The DLC was a crucial element in Clinton's subsequent rise to the presidency. From that perch From and Clinton mutually exploited one another. From's organization benefited from its association with a creative and energetic political talent. Clinton received a platform for developing and expounding his moderate policy ideas and a network of like-minded political figures eager to win.

Clinton came very close to running for president in 1988. But he decided a presidential campaign would be too disruptive for his family—especially for a very young daughter Chelsea, who was only seven at the time. Close associates have also admitted that rumors of Clinton's womanizing made him vulnerable to scandal during an election campaign in which Coloradan Gary Hart had already dropped out after being caught in an affair.

These concerns remained active into 1991, as were Clinton's continuing worries about how his draft history might harm him in a race against an incumbent with impeccable foreign policy credentials. Indeed George H. W. Bush's approval rating had soared to nearly 90 percent in the immediate aftermath of the Gulf War, causing some of the Democratic Party's strongest figures to forgo a challenge. Clinton was convinced, however, that Bush was vulnerable on domestic and economic policy, and some of his advisors, including longtime friend and Russia expert Strobe Talbott, assured him that the end of the Cold War meant that Bush's advantages in foreign policy had become politically unimportant. Clinton announced his candidacy in October 1991.

Although Democrats Paul Tsongas (Massachusetts), Bob Kerrey (Nebraska), Tom Harkin (Iowa), and Jerry Brown (California) each challenged Clinton's candidacy, the greatest obstacles to the nomination arose from his own past. The campaign suffered what pollster Stanley Greenberg called a "meltdown" in January during the New Hampshire primary, the result of revelations, in close succession, by lounge singer Gennifer Flowers that she had engaged in an affair with him (seemingly supported by taped telephone calls) and by the former director of the University of Arkansas ROTC program that Clinton had gamed the draft system to avoid service in Vietnam. Clinton survived both, in part by focusing his attention on the economic plight of New Hampshire residents, promising to stand by them "'till the last dog dies." Finishing second in New Hampshire to the neighboring Tsongas, Clinton declared himself the "comeback kid." Quick primary victories after that in the South and Illinois made Clinton the prohibitive favorite. No serious challenge for the Democratic nomination arose thereafter.

The general election in 1992, however, was complicated by the presence of one of the most popular third-party challengers in the annals of American elections: Texas billionaire H. Ross Perot. Indeed, in the late spring, even though he had secured the nomination, Clinton was reportedly despondent because he was running third in the national polls behind Bush and Perot. Perot's campaign was built on an outsider's distrust of Washington and a commitment to getting the nation's financial house in order.

Yet Clinton reversed his fortunes in relatively short order. First, his campaign staff discovered during an intensive internal audit of the campaign, dubbed the "Manhattan Project," that the public had a fundamental misunderstanding of who Bill Clinton was. Through a series of focus groups, they found that the popular conception of Clinton, based on his education at Georgetown, Oxford, and Yale and on his marriage to an independent professional, was that he came from a life of privilege. The main thrust of the 1992 Democratic Convention became to focus on Clinton's biography, which had the effect of resetting his basic public image. Next, Clinton defied conventional thinking about ticket balancing and named Tennessee Senator Al Gore as his running mate. The result energized the campaign as a generational changing of the guard and reinforced the image of Clinton as a political centrist.

Finally, Ross Perot announced in the middle of the Democratic convention that he was leaving the race—apparently satisfied that the Democrats were embracing his reform agenda. Perot reentered the race in October but never regained the heights of popular support he enjoyed at the time of his departure.

The positive momentum of the convention was extended by the decision to put the candidates and their wives onto buses immediately for an unprecedented tour of the vote-rich American heartland. The bus trip drew massive crowds at all hours of the day and night. After these events, Clinton secured a firm lead in the polls he would never relinquish.

As always, the presidential debates held out the prospect of shaking up the race, but the two most memorable debate moments that year both worked in Clinton's favor: his own (planned) decision in a town hall-style debate to leave his seat and engage, face to face, with an African American questioner, as a way of establishing a personal connection with her through body language; and President Bush's unfortunate decision to look at his watch while on camera, suggesting to viewers an impatience with having to be there.

The substance of Clinton's campaign was captured on a whiteboard posted in the Little Rock headquarters. These three items served as a constant reminder of the central focus of the campaign, above and beyond the skirmishes of each 24-hour news cycle:

Change vs. More of the Same

The Economy, stupid

Don't forget health care.

Clinton won the presidency with 370 electoral votes, swamping Bush's 168. The popular vote totals, however, were far less definitive: 43 percent for Clinton, 37.5 percent for Bush, and 19 percent for Perot. Although the pollsters generally agreed that Perot drew support equally from Clinton and for Bush, the fact that Clinton ran behind so many members of Congress in their districts created lingering problems for the new president when he came to Washington. Clinton found himself leading a nominally unified government of Democrats, but he was yoked to congressional parties at once habituated to opposing the White House and strongly inclined to question whether this president had the political muscle to lead them where they did not always want to go.

Introduction

HISTORY AND BILL CLINTON

Russell L. Riley

No American president has courted Clio, the muse of history, more assiduously than the 42nd, Bill Clinton. In part, President Clinton's fascination with his forebears in the White House was the continuation of a lifelong passion for history, the product of a relentless and prehensile intellect. On the evidence of the oral history interviews conducted among those who worked most closely with him, Clinton refused to allow even the vast burdens of the presidency to intrude on that obsession. One of his personal aides, Kris Engskov, who was often the first staff member to see the president each day, reported that Clinton commonly stayed up reading history while the rest of Washington slept. "He finished books so quickly," reflected Engskov, that "I think he spent half the night reading. . . . He'd get engrossed in a book and just not go to bed. The next morning, I'd say, 'Good morning, Mr. President. . . . Are you tired?' He'd say, 'Yes, I spent the whole night reading this book on Alexander Hamilton,' or whoever it was. It would almost always be biography, almost always something in relation to the Presidency."[1]

Clinton's extraordinary reading habits clearly were not the nonfiction equivalent of Ronald Reagan's fondness for Louis L'Amour westerns—a mental refuge from the excruciating load it is the president's duty to carry. Rather, Clinton was a purposive reader, an active seeker of lessons from the past that might help illuminate a path ahead for him or at a minimum help him develop a coherent narrative about the forces and institutions around him. Nancy Soderberg, a key member of his foreign policy team from the earliest days of the 1992 campaign, reported in her interview that Clinton "took a lot of solace in history, because you realize that the politics of some of these guys were a lot more brutal than what he

1

was going through." His nighttime reading wasn't recreation, it was research: an attempt to discover his own place in time.

Clinton was particularly motivated to immerse himself in the history of presidencies past because of an inconvenient truth. He openly aspired to greatness in the office, to do big, consequential things with his powers, but he recognized that one of the most fundamental laws of American politics is that big presidencies typically grow from big moments. War or a domestic crisis were the necessary predicates for the kinds of presidencies Clinton most admired: those of Abraham Lincoln, Woodrow Wilson, Franklin D. Roosevelt, even John F. Kennedy. Yet there was no empowering crisis to rally the nation to the White House after 1993, depriving Clinton of the circumstances normally required for transformational leadership in the office. Perhaps, however, purposive reading would yield more subtle lessons in presidential history.

Clinton's frustration with the fundamentals of his own incumbency was an open secret. Bob Woodward reported that during his first term, Clinton "yearned for an obvious call to action or even a crisis. He was looking for that extraordinary challenge which he could define and then rally people to the cause." He reportedly voiced to White House intimates irritation with his inability to identify "a big, clear task" and exclaimed, "I would have much preferred being president during World War II. *I'm a person out of my time.*" Biographer David Maraniss echoed this point, noting that "Clinton has long lamented that he was born in the wrong era." And although Clinton later dismissed the comment as a joke, he said privately during the 1992 transition, "Gosh, I miss the Cold War," an era when Americans did not have to be convinced about the threats to their security and thus the need for strong presidential direction.[2]

Vexed by the constraints of tranquility, Clinton began to ponder the kinds of political conditions that have allowed for vigorous leadership from the White House apart from war or domestic crisis. If he could not reasonably aspire to be a Lincoln or an FDR, perhaps there were examples among other strong presidents he could emulate. By 1996, he believed he had found a model: Theodore Roosevelt. During the course of his reelection campaign, Clinton began to identify himself publicly with TR, who did not lead during a major war or other national emergency but still managed to earn a place next to Lincoln on Mount Rushmore. More complicated, however, was the question of whether the parallels between Roosevelt's time and his own might provide Clinton with the occasion for neo-Rooseveltian leadership in the 1990s. Clinton thought the answer was yes and explained why in an August 1996 interview with the *Washington Post*.

"This is an unusual moment in history," Clinton observed. The nation was experiencing a rare and "major change in the way people worked, lived, and related to each other and the rest of the world" that, in his view, bore striking similarities to the *fin de siècle* tremors of a century before, characterized by mass relocations "from farm to factory . . . from country to city." The disruptions of Clinton's time were caused by the end of the Cold War and "the growth of [a] global economy and a global information age . . . with rapid movement of ideas, of information, people and money . . . and [thus] the rapid movement of problems across national borders."[3] In Clinton's reading, Theodore Roosevelt's greatest achievement was to lead the nation from the White House through that earlier transition successfully. Clinton's challenge—his opportunity—was to replicate Roosevelt's peacetime success. Clinton repeated his thinking in a second interview for the *Post* in early 1997, one that led to a front-page story on the day of his second inauguration with a headline that emphasized his choice of "T. Roosevelt" as a model for his second term.[4]

The mainstream press pointedly failed to see the resemblance. That *Post* headline finished with a boldface disclaimer: Clinton's "Style Is More Like McKinley's." A Harvard historian sniped in a *Los Angeles Times* op-ed that "Clinton earns a D– as a student of the Old Bull Moose's savvy." And Roosevelt's celebrated biographer, Edmund Morris, took to the *New York Times* to dismiss Clinton's logic in an essay acerbically headed "The Rough Rider and the Easy One."[5] The perceived differences between TR and Clinton were simply too profound for these critics to treat seriously the possibility that there might be meaningful similarities between the two.

Although Clinton's assessment of Roosevelt's presidency was plainly self-serving, his grasp of the broad historical forces of his time was, in retrospect, remarkably acute. Clinton's first national security advisor, Tony Lake, credits him with being far ahead of his foreign policy team in his ability to see the changes emerging in the world. "[Right] from the start, in fact, he understood something that none of us foreign policy nerds did, and that was what later became called globalization. . . . [He] loved talking about the connection of economics and politics and the lessening importance of borders. He understood this in a way that none of us did . . . and was trying to tutor all of us in that." Nancy Soderberg echoed this observation. "I think the way he understood the challenges of globalization was pretty brilliant and prescient." And Lake's successor at the NSC, Sandy Berger, extended the point to include Clinton's superior grasp of terrorism, the "dark side of globalization." But in the end, precisely how Clinton might use his advanced understanding of these global challenges to rally the nation with Roosevelt-like leadership remained unclear.

Theodore Roosevelt was not the only product of Clinton's search for relevant forebears. At times Clinton also took a special interest in Harry Truman. Truman's star ascended in the public mind during the 1992 presidential campaign because of the celebrated publication that summer of David McCullough's biography of the 33rd president.[6] Indeed, that campaign sometimes featured a three-way competition among Clinton and his two opponents, incumbent Republican George H.W. Bush and independent Ross Perot, to claim the mantle of the blunt-spoken Missourian.[7] Soderberg suggests that sometime during Clinton's presidency he went back to McCullough's Pulitzer Prize–winning volume and discovered there a helpful parallel. As Clinton worried over the chaotic world left by the collapse of Soviet communism, that book "put him in . . . a good mood, because he realized it took Truman two or three years to figure out how to shape the Cold War, the post–World War II era. He said, 'Okay, I'm on par with Truman.' That made him feel good."

The relevance of Truman's experience to Bill Clinton's was undeniable. Both served at a time when the inherited ways of dealing with American foreign relations had been upended, when new realities required new relationships, new ways of thinking, and new institutions. Clinton and his foreign policy team clearly struggled in the early years of his presidency with how to address these problems. As General John Shalikashvili, chair of the Joint Chiefs of Staff under Clinton, said of the foreign policy establishment, "We had never thought about what would happen if the Cold War ended." This meant that Clinton and his team were practically starting from scratch. Soderberg later admitted, "In effect, what happened with foreign policy is that there was no rule book after the Cold War. . . . It took us two and a half years, essentially, to figure out the new rules of the post–Cold War era. . . . The world had fundamentally changed. The way you do business has to change, but how you do it took a while." In this environment, it is not surprising that Clinton took comfort from Truman's experience.

There was, however, a darker side to the Truman parallel that Clinton either missed or chose to ignore. And this analogue, properly recognized, helps generate a radical revision in how the Clinton presidency should be understood.

Usually forgotten in our shorthand histories of Harry Truman—epitomized by the beaming victor of 1948 holding aloft the edition of the *Chicago Daily Tribune* that wrongly announced his political demise—are the grim years of 1945 and 1946. The trajectory of Truman's presidency had changed dramatically by early 1947, when the beginnings of the Cold War gave him the kind of "obvious call to action" that Bill Clinton sought but did not find. Yet it is those early, neglected Truman years that are especially relevant to understanding the Clinton presidency, because it was during that interval that President Truman was subject to the distinctive and powerful forces of postwar political contraction that later engulfed Clinton. Truman's experience, like that of other presidents at similar junctures, sheds light on the troubled times in which Clinton governed—as a post–Cold War president.

"For President Truman the postwar period did not simply arrive," observed his biographer Robert J. Donovan. It "broke about his head with thunder, lightning, hail, rain, sleet, dead cats, howls, tantrums, and palpitations of panic. The storm of war had passed. But the turbulence in its wake . . . all but capsized the Truman administration."[8] Only a fraction of what Truman endured was occasioned by the new and unique requirement that the president assume global leadership in the nuclear age. More to the point, Truman was grappling with unrelenting public pressure to demobilize the armed forces and convert the economy and the state commanding it back to its peacetime standing after years of wartime sacrifice. Moreover, he was dealing with these multiple demands for action at a historic moment when his institutional standing as president was tottering. The foundations of the president's powers were being rapidly eroded by an extraordinary undertow of political and constitutional currents, the natural ebb to the wartime enlargement of presidential authority. What Truman experienced was not anomalous; it is a common experience of presidents who govern when a major war has ended.[9]

The dynamic of this postwar counterpoint, the return to something approaching the political *status quo antebellum*, is not as widely understood as the forces that typically give rise to emergency presidential leadership. Although there are no formal provisions in the U.S. Constitution for emergency government, as there are in some democratic charters—what Clinton Rossiter famously called "constitutional dictatorship"—Americans have treated their Constitution as sufficiently malleable to allow for a different practice of government when a genuine crisis arises.[10] Under such circumstances, the standard norms of separated institutions sharing power and the usual protections of the Bill of Rights have been relaxed to give the president extraordinary latitude to fight the good fight. As Rossiter (and others) have detailed, Presidents Lincoln, Wilson, and Franklin Roosevelt all were empowered by the American people—with the active support or quiescent consent of the other two branches of government, as well as of the Fourth Estate—to take exceptional actions to lead the nation to victory against the forces that threatened its existence. This pattern was so well established that the expansive contours of the post-9/11 presidency under George W. Bush could easily have been foreseen by anyone with a basic grasp of this history.

The rest of the story, however, has been little recognized. Because the powers of the wartime presidency have not lasted forever and because there has been no visible master narrative to define clearly what happens to these institutions in the aftermath of conflict, the common tendency is to assume that the restoration of normal peacetime governance will occur smoothly and without incident. Indeed the president most closely associated with this phenomenon, Warren Harding, who proclaimed his intent after World War I to preside over a "return to nor-malcy," has such an anodyne historical image as to invite this erroneous assump-tion.[11] Scholars are hardly immune to such logic. Cambridge political scientist David Runciman, for example, has written, "In war . . . democratic governments have often had to resort to emergency powers, but when the war is over, those powers get given back."[12] *Get given back.* That passive characterization is com-monly assumed. Yet the evidence shows that it is deeply flawed.

The history of restoration politics in the United States—that is, the return to something approaching constitutional normalcy after a temporary reliance on emergency government—includes some of the most bitterly contested political fights in the annals of the republic. Consider the three presidents who served in the immediate aftermath of the biggest wars in American history: Andrew Johnson, Woodrow Wilson, and Harry Truman. All three initially experienced the presidency when it enjoyed extraordinary latitude to act and could count on other political actors to volunteer unusual deference to the president's lead-ership. Small wonder that each would see the virtues of perpetuating that ar-rangement after the war. But in each instance, others beyond the White House saw things differently. They took the end of war as the occasion to reclaim, without delay, their equal constitutional right to set the nation's direction, to restore, for all its demonstrated inefficiencies, a government of opposite and rival interests.[13]

For seeking to exercise a fraction of the power Lincoln had unilaterally de-ployed just years earlier, Andrew Johnson was impeached by a Congress intent on reasserting its constitutional independence. Johnson's impeachment was oc-casioned by his violation of the Tenure of Office Act, which regulated appoint-ment authority that Lincoln had routinely exercised without incident as the wartime commander-in-chief.[14] More to the point, Johnson was charged in the impeachment articles with bringing "into disgrace, ridicule, hatred, contempt and reproach the Congress of the United States," both in his speechmaking and in his attempts to set the nation's peacetime path without giving due deference to legislative prerogatives.[15] Congress telegraphed its intentions to reclaim its role at the end of the war even while President Lincoln was still alive. When Lincoln began developing ideas in 1863 for the postwar return of rebellious southern states to the union, he met with vigorous opposition in Congress, which for-mally passed a much harsher plan. After Lincoln pocket-vetoed the measure, its two main co-sponsors issued the Wade-Davis Manifesto, charging Lincoln with gratuitously extending his reach into peacetime policy. The manifesto asserted about Lincoln's veto that "a more studied outrage on the legislative authority of the people has never been perpetrated."[16]

Wilson confronted the same pressures. He watched with alarm in 1918 as the Great War wound down at almost the same time that Americans would be voting on a new Congress and decided to nationalize that midterm election over control of peacetime policy. He desperately wanted to perpetuate into the postwar period his wartime leadership advantages over the forces of Republican isolationism. To this end, in mid-October he issued to the American public "An Appeal for a Democratic Congress," explaining that "the return of a Republican majority to either House of Congress would . . . certainly be interpreted on the other side of the water as a repudiation of my leadership."[17] The results were disastrous for the president, whose party lost control of both chambers to the Republicans, an almost unprecedented development. Clearly postwar politics would be very different from those of a wartime presidency, which had allowed Wilson unprecedented powers, including the authority to regulate how much sugar Americans could use in their morning coffee.[18] Congress was now intent on reestablishing its primacy in the practice of peacetime governance. An indignant Wilson sent himself to an early grave raging against these forces, fighting for a postwar global order through the League of Nations that the resurgent Congress would not indulge. This was the early and painful part of the return to normalcy that Harding was elected to complete in 1920.

Truman's postwar maelstrom merely repeated the pattern. Only one week after the Japanese formally surrendered in September 1945, the New York Times reported: "It appears that now there's another war on—in Congress. President Truman is no longer, to the whole Congress, the Commander in Chief of the armed forces at war, but . . . the titular head of the opposition (the head man and the target, so to speak). . . . [From] here on there will be rather ruthless battle."[19] That battle was fought not only in Washington but also in the country beyond—in the mines and factories, in the boardrooms and on the rails. With the wartime emergency ended, labor and industry both reasserted their rights to independence, seeking to escape the constraints of a controlled economy after years of feeling compelled to submit to a wartime president's lead. The resulting epidemic of strikes nearly brought the economy to its knees. At a Gridiron Dinner late in 1945, Truman was moved to observe, in the semi-serious tone typical of the event, "Sherman was wrong. I'm telling you I find peace is hell."[20] In his formal message to Congress laying out the challenges confronting them, Truman emphasized a new emergency—demobilization—in the hope that the characterization might afford him the constitutional high ground.[21] It did not.

Times columnist Arthur Krock, surveying the political landscape one year into Truman's tenure, readily identified the root cause of the president's problems.

"Mr. Truman is a post-war President, and when the shooting ends wartime combinations for political action fall apart."[22] Relegated to junior-partner status for most of the preceding twelve years, Congress sought ways after the war to regain its constitutional vitality. Emblematic of these efforts was the Legislative Reorganization Act of 1946, which political scientist Roger H. Davidson characterized as "the most ambitious, comprehensive, and publicized reorganization in the history of Congress." It was largely motivated by the desire of Congress "to maintain its place as an equal partner in the constitutional scheme of things."[23] The American electorate then voted to increase this restored congressional independence in the November midterm election by transferring majority control of both the House and the Senate from the Democrats to the Republicans, just as they had in 1918. Shortly thereafter, the new speaker of the House, Joseph Martin, announced that "our American concept of government rests upon the idea of a dominant Congress."[24]

However, Truman's return to normalcy was interrupted by the onset of the Cold War. By 1947, Americans were confronted with a new kind of threat that seemed to require a government in a perpetual state of readiness. The exact place of the presidency in this new order was not entirely apparent, but it more nearly followed the example of Franklin Roosevelt than that of Warren Harding. This was true for the remainder of the Cold War. Although the power of the presidency fluctuated during this long era, depending on perceptions of the proximity of the threat and the emergence of hot wars in Korea and Vietnam, the baseline standing of the presidency during the entire run of the Cold War remained elevated. It was the president, after all, who was followed everywhere by a military aide carrying the "football," a code-protected communications briefcase that gave the president the power to decide, instantaneously and without consultation, whether a foreign threat was sufficient to order the earth's descent into nuclear winter.

The Cold War ended dramatically and unexpectedly, beginning with the collapse of the Berlin Wall in November 1989. Did presidential power follow suit? Some have suggested otherwise, claiming that a nation long acclimated to deviating from the Founders' checks and balances had decided that an empowered presidency was necessary in the modern world whether the Soviet Union survived or not. For these, who cite as evidence such things as the White House–directed military interventions in Bosnia and Kosovo, Bill Clinton inherited an imperial presidency that was still imperial when he left it.[25]

In truth, however, the presidency of the 1990s looks anything but imperial. Five major pieces of evidence from the immediate post–Cold War era can best be understood as part of the larger, repeating pattern of severe postwar contraction of the presidency's standing in the political order.

The 1992 Election

In 1992, the American electorate voted to replace the celebrated victor of the Persian Gulf War, whose public approval ratings had once approached 90 percent, with the youthful governor of a small southern state whose greatest accomplishments were in a backwater of federal government policy: education. Times had changed.

Indeed Bill Clinton probably would never have become president in the first place had it not been for the end of the Cold War. Strobe Talbott, his longtime friend and later deputy secretary of state, reported in his oral history that Clinton "knew that one reason he had his chance to knock off Bush was because the Cold War was over." That postwar dynamic shaped the 1992 election in two fundamental ways, one easily seen, the other less so.

First, the end of a protracted conflict that had given shape to American politics domestically and abroad for nearly half a century effectively removed foreign policy as a salient issue in 1992. George H. W. Bush would have entered that contest bearing the burdens of any candidate who was standing for his party's fourth consecutive term. But his unparalleled foreign policy credentials were rendered practically meaningless by the Cold War's end. Foreign affairs all but disappeared from the national discourse. Popular attitudes about the need for a foreign policy leader had so shifted that Bush's reelection campaign did not advertise his many successes abroad that staff had spent four years video recording. "In Moscow, in the Ukraine, in Czechoslovakia, in Turkey, in South America, on our visits to Venezuela, to Uruguay, to Argentina, Mexico, Japan, Australia, Korea, all that footage was assembled, all the pictures of the President actively working with world leaders, and we didn't use any of it," reported Bush's media advisor Sig Rogich in his oral history of the Bush presidency. "The pollsters said that no one cared about foreign policy and yet we had a President with among the greatest records in foreign policy in my lifetime. But we didn't do one commercial on foreign policy."[26]

The nation's indifference to foreign policy created space for a governor with few international credentials (and questions about his lack of military service) to win favor with the American electorate. Some of Bill Clinton's advisors have objected to this characterization, observing that Clinton was not a run-of-the-mill Arkansas politician. Talbott recalls that while at Georgetown in the School of Foreign Service, Clinton worked for the chair of the Senate Foreign Relations Committee, "was always interested in Russia," and that as a Rhodes Scholar he focused his thesis on "alternative futures for the USSR." But Clinton's main campaign mantra, scrawled on a whiteboard in the national headquarters in Little Rock, was "The economy, stupid!" And a June 1992 Associated Press poll found that only 1 percent of those surveyed identified foreign policy as important in their choice of a presidential candidate.[27] Clinton gave them what they wanted in his Democratic convention acceptance address in July, when he devoted only 6 percent of the text to foreign policy—a low for either party's presidential nominee since at least 1960.[28] And, as speechwriter David Kusnet notes in his oral history, "the first drafts [of the Clinton inaugural address] had nothing specifically about the rest of the world except the discussion of the imperatives of the global economy," requiring the intervention of Nancy Soderberg on behalf of the foreign policy team to make sure that their issues got another few lines. Simply put, 1992 was not a year conducive to reelecting a man who first won the presidency as a decorated World War II veteran, an ambassador to the United Nations, an envoy to China, and a former director of central intelligence.

Equally important, but less visibly so, the tides of postwar restoration politics had already engulfed Bush before the reelection campaign began.[29] At home, his much-reported troubles with the federal budget, which in 1990 led him to renege on his "Read my lips—no new taxes!" pledge, were exacerbated by the impatience of the public to enjoy some kind of "peace dividend" after years of giving the Pentagon the first fruits of the nation's tax dollars. Cognizant of ongoing threats to national security, Bush labored to avoid what he saw as damaging cuts to the defense budget, angering congressional Democrats who wanted more domestic spending and congressional Republicans who sought new tax cuts. The chair of Bush's Council of Economic Advisers, Michael Boskin, later remarked that "What isn't appreciated is how much of the [1990] budget agreement was Bush protecting defense . . . for another couple of years while he did what he had to do diplomatically and geopolitically."[30] Abroad, the familiar stability of the Cold War world had given way to a "new world order," which created new and unfamiliar perils for the United States. Instability in the Balkans and in the neighborhood of Iraq had been unlikely in the days of bipolar conflict. As Joseph Nye observed, Kuwait, which Iraq invaded in 1990, was "the first victim of the end of the Cold War world order."[31]

Although Bush's approval ratings had risen to extraordinary highs in the successful glow of the Desert Storm campaign to liberate Kuwait, even that great success had little currency with voters as Bush contemplated another term. Some members of the president's campaign team expressed worries that his one-dimensional association with foreign policy would sink his chances for reelection. Bush pollster Frederick T. Steeper circulated a prescient internal memorandum entitled "1992 Presidential Campaign: The Churchill Parallel," in which he voiced worries about the road ahead, based on the fact that "leaders are not necessarily reelected for their foreign policy and wartime successes, even when monumental." He briefly outlined the similarities between British prime minister Winston Churchill's political standing in 1945 and Bush's in 1992. "Historians concluded," according to Steeper, "that the British voters felt Churchill was needed for war time, but he was not appropriate to rebuild Britain's economy during peace time."[32] Some of Bush's aides accordingly urged on him a "domestic desert storm" to compensate for these perceived deficiencies. That effort failed, as did the 1992 campaign, by a historic margin.

Misreading the Times: Health Care Reform

"War," American social critic Randolph Bourne pronounced in 1918, "is the health of the State."[33] The mass mobilization of human and economic resources necessary to wage war has typically required a commensurate increase in the size of the administrative state to direct the mustering and deployment of these resources. The national government has accordingly grown massively during each major war, mainly to generate an effective military force that is well fed and well-armed through the extraordinary devices of a command economy. This growth has also greatly enlarged the job description of the nation's chief executive.

Once the war effort has succeeded, however, equally strong countervailing pressures to demobilize arise, both to return the national government to an approximation of its former size and to reinstitute taxing and spending policies appropriate for a nation at peace. In 1917, for example, government purchases of goods and services as a percent of the gross national product was 8.9 percent. During World War I it peaked at 21.3 percent, then fell off precipitously in 1920 to 6.6 percent. A similar pattern attended World War II: 14.2 percent in 1940, 46.3 percent in 1943, 13.1 percent in 1946.[34] The final figures in these sequences are simple numerical indicators of the powerful politics of retrenchment that made life miserable for Woodrow Wilson and Harry Truman, respectively.

The government Bill Clinton inherited in January of 1993 was in a similar state of transition, still experiencing the contracting pressures common to immediate postwar eras. As was the case with his predecessors, Clinton did not suffer easily the institutional constraints of his time. In defiance of them, he produced and promoted as a core of his agenda in 1993 a health care reform package that hearkened back to the New Deal and the Great Society. Thus, at a moment when the historical currents of American politics were favoring retrenchment and government demobilization, Clinton decided to commit his presidency to an initiative that placed nearly one-sixth of the U.S. economy more fully in the government's orbit. That initiative met with the defeat of an anachronism.

In fairness to Clinton, the reform program he helped design was largely shaped to avoid charges that the national government would be running the American health care system. As pollster Stanley Greenberg noted, the complexity of the Clinton reform effort was a product of the desire for a proposal that preserved free market mechanisms while guaranteeing basic coverage to everyone: "It was complicated, ironically, because it *wasn't* a government-run healthcare plan." In the end, however, the particulars mattered much less than the proposition that the government was extending its reach where it had not been before, at a historic moment that was singularly inauspicious for this kind of initiative. The Clinton effort inadvertently replicated Harry Truman's own ill-fated effort to promote universal health care in 1945, during a similar juncture of political time.

It is striking in retrospect how often those close to Clinton look back on health care reform as a quixotic endeavor that was doomed by unfavorable fundamentals rather than by transactional failures that might have been remedied by better people or tweaks in policy. "It's hard to conceive of a set of tactics that would have produced the desired result," observed Senate majority leader George Mitchell, who noted that Republican senators were so opposed to the basic idea of reform that they eventually could not be counted on even to vote for the alternative bill they originally co-sponsored. Media advisor Frank Greer found himself having to remind the president that contrary to his own recollections, "You didn't get elected on healthcare. You didn't run one spot on healthcare [during the general election]. . . . And the reason was, we [produced] a lot of health care spots and we never could find a message that worked." Greenberg concurred. "There were many, many, many polls on trying to figure out the case for healthcare," none of which succeeded. "It was vulnerable because of its design to be attacked that it was big government. . . . But it would have been attacked as a big-government takeover of healthcare, whatever its content." The reform ultimately failed, then, because of its mismatch with the times. The White House congressional liaison during this period, Patrick Griffin, observed that the Clintons' willingness to pursue the effort in the face of such overwhelming odds was quite admirable. It "was one of the truly most visionary things that they were trying to do. Mrs. Clinton and the President were really not following polls. They really were trying to get ahead of something and I thought it was very courageous in that regard."

It is instructive to contrast the administration's failure on health care reform with one of the major accomplishments of the first term—the controversial decision to "end welfare as we know it." If health care suffered from running against the prevailing political currents of the postwar period, welfare reform was the exact opposite. The core idea of shrinking the size of the welfare state fit neatly within the routine popular impulses typical of such times. Indeed, in retrospect many Clinton insiders—including Greer; Greenberg; Chief of Staff Mack McLarty; and his deputy, Roy Neel—asserted in their interviews that the administration would have been well advised to have reversed the order of the two, sequencing welfare reform first as a way of building political capital on an issue that was at least as central to Clinton's 1992 victory. Greenberg reports that nothing polled higher as a potential administration priority. Moreover, Clinton's successes with public volunteerism, reinventing government, and a raft of so-called "small ball" domestic initiatives late in his first term all benefited from their consistency with popular impulses for a leaner government.

Similarly, Clinton's most highly lauded domestic accomplishment—the federal budget surpluses that marked the final years of his presidency—surely would not have happened without the end of the Cold War and its effects on defense spending. According to historical tables compiled by the Office of Management and Budget, the Clinton administration achieved two years of surpluses, amounting to just under $2 billion in 1999 and nearly $90 billion in 2000, before the long-standing pattern of federal deficit spending returned in 2001.[35] For most of the Clinton presidency, the defense budget was $270 to $280 billion, down from the Cold War high of $303 billion in 1989.[36] Assuming that a continuation of the Cold War would have led to annual increases in defense spending from 1989 at roughly the same levels seen under Jimmy Carter, Ronald Reagan, and George H. W. Bush, the Clinton-year surpluses would not have occurred.[37] Without question the president pursued a difficult and politically painful course of fiscal restraint, especially in 1993. But the end of the Cold War created the conditions without which the benchmark of a balanced budget would probably have been impossible to reach. This was a case where Clinton's yielding to the political realities of his time paid political and economic dividends—later.

The 1994 Midterm Elections

Nothing more clearly identifies the Clinton presidency with the bitter politics of postwar demobilization than the 1994 midterm elections, when a "Republican Revolution" brought GOP control to both houses of Congress for the first time in forty years. The catastrophic loss by a president of both congressional chambers at a single midterm election is a very rare event, and one that is effectively a signature of postwar contraction in executive power.

In all of American constitutional history, only seven times did a president lose both chambers of Congress at midterm. At least four of them were immediate postwar midterm elections: Wilson in 1918, Truman in 1946, Dwight Eisenhower in 1954 (the first national election after the signing of the Korean armistice), and Clinton in 1994. (Arguably the 2006 election during George W. Bush's second term is a fifth.)[38] The same general trend—voters reestablishing congressional independence from a war-empowered president—appears prominently in two other postwar elections without producing a change in partisan control. The midterm of 1866 during Andrew Johnson's administration sent to Washington a famously oppositional Republican Congress that was openly aligned against Johnson, a former Democrat who had been elected vice president with Lincoln as a Unionist. And the 1974 midterm, immediately after direct U.S. involvement in the Vietnam War ended, did not produce a change in party control in either chamber of Congress, but it did strongly reinforce congressional opposition to a Republican White House by extending Democratic Party majorities in both chambers with a class of legendarily activist "Watergate babies." The signature pattern in these cases is of voters accentuating the postwar return to normalcy by reinvigorating the independence of Congress from the White House. And in the cases of Johnson, Wilson, and Truman, the election returns were a direct rebuke to presidential efforts to sustain the institution's wartime leadership capacity during peacetime.

The 1994 case is, however, puzzling in several ways, notwithstanding the fact that the partisan outcome perfectly fits the pattern of typical postwar behavior. If conventional postwar political impulses run so strongly against presidential power, why did the electorate send Clinton to Washington with Democratic majorities in both houses of Congress in the first place? Political strategist Al From, a founder of the centrist Democratic Leadership Council, suggests in his oral history that the 1992 congressional returns were the last, inertial vestige of a dying system—as much a product of habit as of logic. He argues that Clinton gets a "bum rap" for losing Congress at his first midterm: "I think the '92 and the '94 elections to the Congress were what I call truth-in-packaging elections. . . . What happened is that the South caught up with its real politics and the white South went Republican." The tipping point was reached in 1994.

It is also true that the congressional Democrats joining Clinton in 1993 were anything but a presidential party in the waiting. Indeed, the Democrats were in some ways as troublesome for Clinton as the Republicans. The party in Congress had little experience dealing with a Democratic president and thus entered the Clinton era habituated to obstruction. Congressional liaison John Hilley, who was still on the Hill at this time, admitted that the Democrats "were good at fighting things. They weren't particularly good at thinking about how to get things done." Thus, according to deputy domestic policy advisor William Galston, "Bill Clinton ran, and won [in 1992], on the basis of ideas that enjoyed widespread support in the country, but much less widespread support within his own party. You can write the history of the first two years of the Clinton administration around that proposition." Congressional Democrats were none too happy with Clinton's interest in campaign finance reform, education policy, crime, and NAFTA—the last of which Chief of Staff Mack McLarty felt compelled to check on three times with the president to make sure he really wanted to move ahead. (Clinton "was slightly terse . . . and said, 'Well, Mack, I told you this twice.'") Clinton and the 103rd Congress offered no textbook exercise in the practice of responsible party government.

Also, however striking the parallel to earlier postwar elections, it is harder to read the intent of the 1994 midterms as another rejection of wartime leadership. That said, Clinton's willingness to raise taxes in his first year, his embrace of a perceived "big government" guarantee for personal health care, and, perhaps, public concerns about a raft of alleged personal improprieties suggested to many American voters that this president was too eager to maintain an imperial presidency when it was no longer needed.

Although the voters' intent in 1994 remains somewhat ambiguous, the actual effect of the election on Washington was perfectly clear. The immediate focus of public attention shifted to Capitol Hill, where a remarkable exercise in congressional government soon emerged. For a time in 1995–1996—until the point at which Clinton was able to goad the Republicans into overreach with shutdowns of the government—the nation's eyes were fixed on Speaker Newt Gingrich, who surely agreed with his predecessor Joseph Martin about the virtues of congressional dominance. During that interval, the center of gravity in the national government shifted from 1600 Pennsylvania Avenue to the south wing of the Capitol. Galston called this "an amazing political feat . . . to marginalize a President in an off-year election." And the mission of the 104th Congress was clear. In the words of a chief aide to education secretary Richard Riley, 1994 produced a "kind of anti-government, cut back, trim back, smaller government, government doesn't do much for you attitude . . . in Congress" that required Clinton to move strongly in that direction or risk being marginalized for the remainder of his presidency.[39]

The turn to congressional government under Gingrich followed closely the traditional pattern of postwar behavior in the United States, in which Congress returns to center stage after a protracted displacement. The 1994 election was effectively nationalized, this time by the Republican opposition in the form of its Contract with America. Clinton, like his postwar predecessors, was subsequently left to deal with a Congress that believed itself invested with the authority of the American people to retake the reins of the national government.[40] In a revealing signal of his low estate, Clinton was reduced to publicly pleading for his own relevance.[41] And in what sounds to be, in this context, a concession, he announced in his 1996 state of the union message that "The era of big government is over."

Foreign Policy and the Comprehensive Nuclear-Test-Ban Treaty

Although the Clinton presidency is not recalled mostly for its record in foreign policy, the international problems the administration did confront were largely the product of the new world order that had begun emerging under George H. W. Bush. The troublesome conflicts in Bosnia and Kosovo were directly attributable to the entropic ethnic rivalries released by the collapse of the Soviet empire. Other major developments in foreign affairs were also traceable to the end of the Cold War, most prominently the issue of NATO expansion. Even American policy toward the developing world was shaped indirectly by the new and unfamiliar absence of bipolar global politics. National Security Advisor Tony Lake reported in his oral history, for example, that the administration's approach toward Africa was "absolutely" shaped by the end of the Cold War. "If I could have argued that Rwanda was about to go communist, we've got an interest [for Washington policymakers]. . . . But no Cold War, less attention."

Little remembered from the Clinton years is a major foreign policy defeat that comports perfectly with typical postwar patterns: the Senate's refusal in October 1999 to ratify the Comprehensive Nuclear-Test-Ban Treaty. Three years earlier, the president had signed the treaty, thereby pledging American compliance with an international effort to secure a total ban on the testing of nuclear devices. After the severe deterioration in Clinton's political standing that accompanied public revelations about his affair with Monica Lewinsky, the treaty failed by a wide margin to get the necessary two-thirds vote for ratification. The public nature of the defeat—a floor-vote rejection orchestrated by the Republican majority when other, quieter means of burying the treaty were available—strongly suggests an intent among the opposition to repudiate openly presidential leadership in the field of foreign affairs.[42] This was certainly the prevailing interpretation in the press. The *New York Times* recognized the extraordinary nature of the vote against Clinton in an area of traditional presidential strength and called it "the bluntest rebuff of a President on a major international agreement since it voted down Woodrow Wilson's Treaty of Versailles in 1919." A *Newsday* editorial announced, "We are in a period of congressional hegemony."[43]

The obscurity of this defeat in chronicles of the Clinton presidency—it merits not a single mention in John F. Harris's stellar *The Survivor: Bill Clinton in the White House*[44]—is evidence of how far the nation had moved away from its Cold War preoccupations with security and "the bomb." And this change is an indispensable predicate for understanding fully Clinton's greatest defeat.

The Clinton Impeachment

The most prominent mark of decline in presidential standing during the post–Cold War era came with the impeachment of President Clinton. Yet the connection between trend and event is not readily apparent. What did the collapse of

Soviet communism have to do with Clinton's personal indiscretions with Monica Lewinsky and what that affair wrought? The answer is to be found in the vagaries of constitutional jurisprudence.

The pathway to Clinton's impeachment was actually opened through a civil lawsuit filed in 1994 by another woman, Paula Jones, who alleged that Clinton had sexually harassed her in 1991, when he was still governor of Arkansas and she was a low-level state employee. Under oath in a deposition in the *Jones* case, Clinton offered dubious testimony about his relationship with Lewinsky, following which a flurry of activity arose by Clinton and his associates (dealing with Lewinsky-related evidence) that led to suspicions of obstruction of justice. That alleged pattern of illegal behavior gave independent counsel Kenneth Starr a basis for expanding his investigation, which had begun years earlier over completely unrelated questions about an Arkansas land deal, into the realm of the president's sexual conduct. And it was Starr's detailed and graphic report to Congress about Clinton's liaisons with Lewinsky, contradicting the president's sworn testimony, that set the impeachment process into motion on Capitol Hill.[45] The Supreme Court's 1997 decision in *Clinton v. Jones*, which allowed Jones's lawsuit to proceed during Clinton's presidency, was thus a pivotal event.[46] It created the conditions that elevated the Lewinsky matter from a private indiscretion to a legal and public scandal.[47] It is also a decision that would have been almost inconceivable under Cold War conditions.

When Jones initially filed the lawsuit against Clinton, the president's legal team had moved to have it delayed until after Clinton left office by invoking the concept of presidential immunity. Their central claim was that the responsibilities of the presidency are so momentous that the distractions of a civil lawsuit would be detrimental to the public good. Seemingly in their favor was what federal district judge Susan Webber Wright called "the case most applicable to this one," *Nixon v. Fitzgerald*, a Cold War–era decision in 1982 in which the Warren Burger court granted absolute and perpetual immunity to former president Richard Nixon against charges that while he was president, he had improperly fired an Air Force employee.[48] By contrast, Clinton, a sitting president, was requesting temporary immunity. Yet he did not get it. Why?

The conventional understanding about the reason the Rehnquist court did not fall in line with the Burger court has focused on the difference between the kinds of activity involved in the two cases. Nixon was sued for an official act as president, Clinton for private behavior before he came to the White House. The Rehnquist court determined that this distinction made a difference constitutionally in whether immunity should be afforded to the president. By its interpretation, the main basis for extending immunity to the president for official acts in *Nixon v. Fitzgerald* was the need to avoid unnecessary and damaging distortions regarding executive decision making. A president should not be worried in the conduct of official business about whether decisions taken in the public interest might create vulnerabilities to private lawsuits filed by aggrieved parties. That consideration, of course, would not be at issue in private decisions.

Although the Supreme Court's ruling in *Clinton v. Jones* is commonly reported as 9–0, Justice Stephen Breyer wrote a concurring opinion revealing significant differences between his judgment on the case and that of the rest of the Court.[49] Breyer argued that his colleagues actually misunderstood the basic logic of the earlier ruling. While Justice Lewis Powell, as author of the majority opinion in *Nixon*, had, in fact, addressed the distorting effects of exposure to civil litigation on presidential decision making, the majority in *Nixon* had actually been more concerned about the adverse effects of legal vulnerability on the president's time, attention, and energies. Breyer held that the earlier court was less concerned about distortions than about distractions—a worrisome factor whether the legal action pursued against the president was based on official or unofficial acts.[50] Accordingly, his proposed solution was to return the case to the district court, as the majority ruled, but to instruct the lower court to ask the president "to provide . . . a more reasoned explanation of why immunity is needed"—to which the lower court was to provide due deference, as the separation of powers doctrine demands. Breyer wrote that "the [Burger] Court rested its conclusion in important part upon the fact that civil lawsuits 'could distract a President from his public duties, to the detriment not only of the President and his office but also the Nation that the Presidency was designed to serve.'"[51]

As he wrote his concurring opinion, Breyer no doubt had in mind the Court's demonstrably cavalier regard for the president's time during oral argument. Justice Antonin Scalia had openly belittled the possible intrusions, noting, to laughter, that he had often seen "Presidents riding horseback, chopping firewood, fishing for stick fish, playing golf and so forth and so on," surmising that there must be time in the president's schedule to deal with the modest intrusions of private civil litigation. Perhaps even more revealing, the sole reference to foreign policy during oral arguments was a set of occasionally lighthearted exchanges about what might happen if the trial court scheduled a date that conflicted with a NATO meeting.

This was a far cry from acknowledging the kinds of nuclear-age foreign policy demands on the president's time that were typical of the Cold War and that formed the backdrop of the Nixon decision. One simple metric illustrates the point. On the day in 1982 that the Court issued its ruling in *Nixon v. Fitzgerald*, the front page of the *Washington Post* included a photograph of Ronald Reagan meeting with British prime minister Margaret Thatcher to discuss the sovereignty of the Falkland Islands with an accompanying story; three articles on eruptions of violence in the Middle East, including one about how Israel's military success was benefiting the United States in the superpower conflict with the Soviet Union; a story about the congressional vote on a potential nuclear freeze; and an account of armed U.S. agents raiding a ship in international waters to end a hostage situation. The only stories about American foreign policy on the front page of the *Post* on the day in 1997 the *Jones* decision was issued were one about Indonesian donors allegedly buying influence with the Democratic National Committee and one on Boris Yeltsin's evolved acceptance of NATO expansion.[52] Moreover, if General Hugh Shelton's memoir is accurate, Clinton served at a time when he could misplace for months the "biscuit," the pocket card containing the top-secret codes needed to activate the "football," without generating any special alarm.[53]

Indeed, the gravity of the Cold War is essential for understanding why the Burger court ruled as it did in a case that Justice Harry Blackmun privately observed to his colleagues "stinks." Five justices voted to extend absolute immunity in *Nixon v. Fitzgerald* even though (a) the recipient of that immunity was a *former* president, and not just any former president, but the one who had resigned in disgrace; (b) the case involved the ham-handed termination of a senior Defense Department whistleblower who was openly proclaimed "disloyal" by the Nixon White House; and (c) attorneys for the contending parties had previously reached a private contingency settlement that looked suspiciously to several justices like the lawyers were wagering on the Court's decision. Notwithstanding the case's singular odor, however, the majority of the Court was moved by "the singular importance of the President's duties" to extend immunity. They concluded, as the Rehnquist court did not, that "concern with private lawsuits would raise unique risks to the effective functioning of government."

In sum, it is almost impossible to see a Cold War–era court, focused, deferentially, on the extraordinary value of the president's time, issuing the decision made in 1997 by the Rehnquist court. Far more likely, the majority would have signed onto an opinion like that authored by Judge Donald Ross, one of three appellate judges who heard the *Jones* case before it came to the Supreme Court.[54] Judge Ross wrote (in dissent) that separation-of-powers concerns, which were embedded in the "language, logic, and intent of *Nixon v. Fitzgerald*," obliged him to rule that "private civil actions against a sitting President for unofficial acts must be stayed during the President's term in office," including all aspects of discovery and trial.[55]

> When the President is called upon to defend himself during his term of office, even in actions wholly unrelated to his official responsibilities, the dangers of intrusion on the authority and functions of the Executive

Branch are both real and obvious. The burdens and demands of civil litigation can be expected to impinge on the President's discharge of his constitutional office by forcing him to divert his energy and attention from the rigorous demands of his office to the task of protecting himself against personal liability. That result would disserve the substantial public interest in the President's unhindered execution of his duties and would impair the integrity of the role assigned to the President by Article II of the Constitution.[56]

In recalling the *Jones* decision in his oral history years later, Commerce Secretary Mickey Kantor voiced the opinion of the case typical of most Clinton insiders, confirming the prescience of Judge Ross's opinion. "[The] whole thing created chaos and took away from the ability of the U.S. government to function. The ability of the presidency and the White House to function—it is not even arguable. . . . I watched it happen and it was devastating to see." On Capitol Hill Republicans pressed ahead with attempts to remove Clinton from office, notwithstanding the popular rebuke administered by the voters in November 1998, when the party, remarkably, lost seats in Congress at Clinton's six-year midterm. Congressional liaison Lawrence Stein recounts that House Republicans decided to proceed immediately against the president anyway and that the leadership would "break the elbows of anyone [in the House Republican caucus] who was going to oppose it." Weeks later, for only the second time in American history, a president was impeached. Both happened in the aftermath of war.[57]

Conclusion

It is still too soon to know how history will judge the Clinton presidency. In the few surveys of scholars conducted after Clinton left office, he has tended to finish near the middle of the pack, although a 2010 Sienna College survey rated Clinton the thirteenth best.[58] These early evaluations are inevitably skewed, for better and for worse, by the recency of the Clinton years (and thus the firsthand impressions that over time will pass) and by our inability to know yet what about Clinton's legacy is ephemeral and what is enduring.

One factor too often overlooked, however, in making evaluations of presidents past is the question of how receptive their basic governing environment was to presidential direction. Some presidents serve when the political system is aligned perfectly to follow their leadership. Some serve during times when the playing field is level, inviting an even competition with Congress and other political actors in the direction of the nation's affairs. And others, such as Clinton, serve when presidential leadership is endlessly confounded. Wartime presidents have been required to make terrible decisions involving life and death, but they have typically done so at historic moments when they could count on others in the American system to rally to an unusual degree behind their leadership. This is decidedly not the case for postwar presidents, who confront less often the awfulness of mass mortality but who typically find themselves deeply entangled in the messy politics of constitutional restoration while the former glories of presidential leadership are still fresh in the public mind. How we measure the success (and failure) of a president in this frustrating environment would seem to require a special acknowledgement of that profound difficulty. Presidents, ultimately, should be graded on a curve.

A clear realization of the historical forces at work as the Cold War ended should give us a deeper understanding of the institution in which Bill Clinton served and thus a more complete appreciation of what actually happened during his presidency. That kind of understanding may also help illuminate in advance the perils that the nation's next postwar president will confront. Properly understood, the problems of the Clinton presidency become a cautionary tale about something greater than the personal temptations of power.

Part I
POLITICS

REDIVIDING GOVERNMENT

National Elections in the Clinton
Years and Beyond

Michael Nelson

Republicans emerged from the 1988 election as confident of their supremacy in presidential politics as Democrats were of their dominance of Congress.[1] Republican vice president George Bush's 40-state, 426-electoral vote triumph over the Democratic nominee, Massachusetts governor Michael Dukakis, was the GOP's third victory in a row and its fifth in the last six elections, all but one of them by a landslide. From 1968 to 1988, Republican candidates for president outscored their Democratic opponents by a cumulative 2,501 electoral votes to 679 electoral votes and by 265 million to 215 million in the national popular vote. The Democrats' sole victory came in 1976 when former Georgia governor Jimmy Carter narrowly defeated President Gerald R. Ford in the post-Watergate depths of Republican unpopularity. Entering the 1992 contest, some even speculated that Republican control of the presidency was so strong as to amount to an Electoral College "lock." Twenty-one states with 191 electoral votes had voted Republican in each of the six most recent elections. Another twelve states, with 142 electoral votes, had gone Republican in every election but one. Only Minnesota, with 10 electoral votes, and the District of Columbia, with 3, had been comparably loyal to the Democrats.

The Democrats' primacy in Congress in this period was just as impressive as the GOP's hold on the White House. The House of Representatives had been a Democratic preserve since 1954, never once going Republican. In 1988, the Democrats added three seats to their majority, raising it to 260 to 175. They added one to their ranks in the Senate, giving them 55 of 100 seats in that chamber, which they had controlled for all but six of the last thirty-four years. Bush's election made him only the third newly elected president in history, after Zachary Taylor in 1849 and Richard Nixon in 1969, to take office with a Congress controlled by the opposition party. No new president ever had faced a Congress that included so small a fraction of fellow partisans.

Divided government, in which the political party that controls the White House does not also control Congress, long had been the exception in American politics, especially during the first two-thirds of the twentieth century. Nearly always the voters gave the president a Congress controlled by his own party and then assigned credit or blame for the government's subsequent performance to that party in the next election. From 1901 to 1969, divided government prevailed only 21 percent of the time, just fourteen years out of sixty-eight. Starting with Nixon's election in 1968, however, divided government became the rule, with Carter's four years of united party government the single exception through the end of Bush's tenure in 1993. In every instance, divided government in this period entailed a Republican president and a wholly or partially Democratic Congress.

Bill Clinton's eight years as president marked not the end of divided government but rather its redividing. In a mirror image of the previous twenty-four years, Clinton's election in 1992 began a quarter-century in which Democrats presidential nominees handily won four of six elections (carrying the national popular vote in five) and lost the other two narrowly. In 1996, he became not only the first Democratic president in sixty years to be reelected to a second term, but the first in history to be elected with a Republican Congress—which in turn was the first since 1928 to remain in Republican control for more than two years. From 1992 to 2012, the Democrats bested the Republicans by 1,963 electoral votes to 1,263 electoral votes and by 337 million to 311 million in the national popular vote. In late 1996, Clinton White House political director Douglas Sosnik even declared "the beginning of a Democratic electoral college advantage" based on Clinton's having carried twenty-nine states with 346 electoral votes both times he ran, including eighteen states that had gone Republican in all or all but one of the six previous presidential elections.[2]

In congressional elections, however, the Democrats soon became the minority party. Although Clinton enjoyed a Democratic Congress during his first two years as president, in 1994, the first midterm election of his presidency, the Republicans won control of both chambers and maintained it for nearly all of the next twelve years. Never before had a Democratic president had to serve more than two years with a Republican House and Senate, but Clinton faced such a Congress for six of his eight years in office. The Democrats won back both chambers in 2006, only to lose the House to the GOP in 2010 and the Senate in 2014, the two midterm elections of Barack Obama's presidency. The result was that the pre-Clinton era of Republican presidents and Democratic congresses was succeeded by one in which Democratic presidents and Republican congresses were the norm. What remained nearly constant was divided government.

What happened during Clinton's two elections as president and the midterm election that occurred during his first term to help explain this reversal of fortune for the two parties? What accounts for the persistence of divided government during the past half-century and for the change in its partisan makeup that began during the Clinton years? In addressing these questions, I draw not just on published accounts of the elections and their consequences, but also on two oral history projects: the William J. Clinton Presidential History Project conducted by the University of Virginia's Miller Center and the Diane D. Blair Project, archived at the Pryor Center for Arkansas Oral and Visual History at the University of Arkansas. The Miller Center interviews, more than fifty of which have been released since 2014, were conducted after Clinton left office by teams of political scientists and historians and cover his entire presidency. The sixty-four cleared Blair interviews of Clinton campaign staffers were conducted by Professor Blair during and immediately after the 1992 election and released in 2010.[3]

1992

The Republican ascendancy in presidential elections that began in 1968 followed a period in which they usually lost. In nine elections from 1932 to 1964, the GOP won just twice, and then mostly because Dwight D. Eisenhower headed the ticket, a war hero whose personal popularity transcended the party's. Starting in 1968, however, Republicans worked hard, steadily, and successfully to attract groups of voters that previously had been either Democratic (southern whites; blue-collar northern Catholics) or politically dormant (evangelical Christians) to their national coalition with a host of racial, religious, cultural, and economic appeals.[4] The Republicans' perceived toughness on national security issues, which historically had little effect in elections, also was important during the height of the Cold War between the United States and the Soviet Union. The Democrats usually played into their hands by nominating candidates for president whom most voters perceived as being more concerned about racial minorities than the white majority; squeamish on matters of security, whether against criminals at home or communism abroad; insufficiently respectful of religion and traditional values; and determined to protect every domestic federal program regardless of effectiveness or cost to the taxpayers. The lesson from the Democrats' shrinking vote in recent elections, chief Clinton speechwriter David Kusnet observes, "was that if all the groups in the Democratic coalition, including labor, liberals, minorities, and women's rights advocates, were in the same tent, we could still get clobbered."[5]

During the Nixon and Ronald Reagan years, the GOP grew at the national level while becoming more homogeneous: white, conservative, Christian, employed (or retired). Its quadrennial national conventions were united, confident, even scripted gatherings that conveyed a sense of competence to the country. The Democrats, in contrast, were raucously heterogeneous: white, black, and Latino; liberal and conservative; Catholic, Protestant, Jewish, and nonreligious; working and on welfare; uneducated and professionally educated. Its conventions often revealed these divisions in ways that were contentious and therefore far from confidence-inspiring.

In a presidential election, a party chooses one identity—one nominee, one platform. This proved an advantage to the less-conflicted Republicans. In congressional elections, however, a party can be almost as many things as there are states and districts. Consequently, in fielding candidates for Congress, the Democrats' diversity, far from being the obstacle to success that it was in presidential contests, was advantageous. The party was able to offer liberal candidates in the North and conservative candidates in the South; pro-gun candidates in rural areas and pro–gun control candidates in the cities; blacks, Latinos, or whites depending on each district's ethnic composition; and so on. Republican candidates, in contrast, seemed everywhere to have been cut from roughly the same cloth.[6]

A final source of divided government in this era was, in political scientist Gary Jacobson's phrase, "the electorate's unwavering attempt to have its cake and eat it too."[7] Pro-government Democratic candidates for Congress promised the voters that they would protect popular but expensive social programs while anti-tax Republican presidential candidates promised not to make voters pay for them, and both were elected.

As a young man and then as governor of Arkansas, Clinton was immersed in the divided politics that these differences in the parties produced. From 1946, the year of his birth, through the 1980s, Arkansas regularly sent Democrats to Congress. But from 1968 to 1988 it voted Democratic for president just once.

In 1978, Clinton was elected governor at age thirty-two, only to be defeated in 1980 at age thirty-four, making him the youngest governor in the country at that time and the youngest ex-governor, all within a two-year span.[8] He was returned to office in 1982 and then was reelected in 1984, 1986, and 1990 (making him the nation's longest-serving governor). Of all these elections, the defeat in 1980 made the greatest impression on Clinton. Determined to transform his state in the progressive manner he had embraced as a student at Georgetown, Oxford, and Yale and as the Texas co-coordinator of the George McGovern presidential campaign in 1972, Clinton staffed his first administration with bearded out-of-state liberals and raised taxes on motor vehicles. Hillary Rodham's decision to keep her last name rather than take her husband's added to Arkansans' sense that Clinton was no longer one of them. So did his apparent acquiescence in President Carter's decision to take in more than 100,000 Cuban deportees from the communist Fidel Castro regime, many of them criminals or mental patients, and house about 20,000 of them at Fort Chaffee in northwest Arkansas.

Clinton learned from his mistakes, taking to heart advice from a friend ("They just thought you were an arrogant son of a bitch") and an Arkansas state legislator ("Hillary's going to have to change her name and shave her legs").[9] He jettisoned the bearded aides, apologized for raising the car tax, reintroduced Hillary Rodham to the voters as Hillary Clinton, and won back his office in 1982. Proud of what he then was able to accomplish in Arkansas, with Hillary's help, in the areas of education reform and economic development, Clinton's ambitions turned national. To pursue them successfully, he would have to persuade his party that a small-state governor could be elected president, something that had not happened since Franklin Pierce of New Hampshire won in 1852. Working in his favor was that the Democrats' only recent victory had come when, acknowledging its leaking southern base and the voters' growing estrangement from Washington, the party nominated southern governor Jimmy Carter in 1976.

In addition to making his candidacy plausible, Clinton knew, he would also have to remake the party to free it from its losing ways. He found national homes in the National Governors Association, of which his long tenure leading Arkansas eventually made him the senior member, and the Democratic Leadership Council (DLC), a group formed in 1985 to help make the party more acceptable to middle-class voters in presidential elections by proposing innovative centrist policies that transcended orthodox conservatism and liberalism.[10] As a "New Democrat," Clinton became the leader of both organizations, a natural pairing because, as his chief domestic policy advisor, Bruce Reed, points out, "The DLC essentially represented the governors' wing of the Democratic Party." In contrast to congressional Democrats, governors "had to solve problems all the time. . . . They actually had to balance a budget every year, make progress on schools and health care. . . . And as it turned out, the Governors after whom we modeled ourselves had figured out pretty much what the country wanted: a less ideological, more pragmatic, approach to policy and politics that appealed because it worked."

The DLC's emphasis on winning presidential elections rather than appeasing the party's varied and conflicting constituencies was consistent with this approach. "We had done a whole lot of work on a whole bunch of ideas," says DLC executive director Al From: "national service, charter schools, welfare reform, community policing, reinventing government, our [nonprotectionist] position on trade—a whole host of those ideas, which later became the policies of the Clinton administration." The "watchword" for Clinton and the DLC, according to veteran media consultant Frank Greer, was "new common sense solutions, putting aside false choices, being different in the sense of having values, having religious faith, and having a sense of patriotism and love of country," all of which "Democrats too often have run from." "Liberal passions, but conservative governing values" (Reed) and "a shift of Democratic economic policy from redistribution to growth" (From) were hallmarks of the DLC approach. In addition, DLC-affiliated scholar William Galston observes, as the organization's chair in 1990–1991, Clinton reaped a collateral benefit: he "could move around the country on somebody else's dime in the guise—a legitimate guise—of establishing chapters in various states, but also plant his own political flag" as a future presidential candidate.

The highlight of Clinton's time at the DLC's helm came at the organization's May 1991 convention in Cleveland. A showcase for several better-known potential candidates for the 1992 Democratic presidential nomination, including Senator Al Gore of Tennessee, the convention became a pep rally for Clinton, who gave a stunningly effective keynote address. "He put 'opportunity, responsibility, community' into the lexicon on that day," says From. "What he convinced a lot of people of is that you could be a centrist with passion." "Democrats have been talking about opportunity since [Franklin D.] Roosevelt, if not longer," adds Reed, "and community since [Lyndon B.] Johnson. But they'd gone a long time without talking about responsibility, and that was Clinton's obsession over the course of our search for ideas at the DLC." At the 1991 convention not just the delegates but also "the national press corps was blown away . . . ," Reed recalls. "In that speech he laid out the basic themes of his [1992] campaign: that for too long Democrats had failed to represent the economic interests, defend the values, and stand up for the security of the forgotten middle class."

Although Clinton's political philosophy was shaped by the National Governors Association and the DLC, it was not limited by them. He also embraced the "investment" economics articulated by his longtime friend Robert Reich. In his 1991 book *The Work of Nations*, Reich argued that in an increasingly international economy in which jobs and capital flow easily from one country to another, a nation's only viable strategy for long-term prosperity is to enhance the value of its fixed assets, especially its work force. To Clinton, the implication was clear: the federal government should invest public funds to improve the productivity of workers through education and training—an investment that eventually would yield high returns in the form of accelerated economic growth.[11]

Clinton's decision to seek the Democratic nomination in 1992 was not an easy one. Other prominent Democrats looked at President Bush's post–Gulf War job approval rating, which peaked at 89 percent in March 1991 and did not fall below 70 percent until September, and decided not to run. Clinton himself, recalls Greer, "pointed out to me that a sitting president who had won a war had never lost an election." He worried that longstanding rumors about adulterous relations with women might sink his candidacy, as they sank Colorado senator Gary Hart's bid in 1988, or at a minimum embarrass him before his family.[12] And he feared that breaking his pledge to the voters of Arkansas to serve a full four-year term in 1990—a pledge "he had to make—polling indicated that he did" to win that election, according to campaign congressional liaison Gloria Cabe—might make it impossible for him to win another term if a bid for the presidency fell short.[13]

But Clinton also believed that by Election Day, voters' dissatisfaction with the weakening economy would eclipse their appreciation of Bush's international triumphs. Indeed, he hoped, the victory in the Cold War over which the president had presided and the defeat of Iraq he had engineered might have the perverse effect of removing foreign policy, the incumbent's greatest strength, from the public agenda. The unwillingness of prominent Democrats to run cleared the field of the party's most popular figure, Governor Mario Cuomo of New York, as well as others who would have competed with Clinton for the southern and DLC vote, especially Gore, House Democratic leader Richard Gephardt of Missouri, and Senator Sam Nunn of Georgia. In addition, Clinton counted on political reporters being so chastened by adverse public reaction to the "feeding frenzy" they had engaged in against Hart that they would tread lightly on similar matters in the coming election. Finally, speaking before audiences that aides secretly seeded with supporters who urged him not to be bound by his 1990 pledge, Clinton was pleased to conclude that Arkansans would be proud rather than angry if he ran for president.

What decided the matter for Clinton was his certainty that a campaign based on ideas would overcome all obstacles. "He had a better idea of what he wanted to do as president," says Reed, which offered "a good contrast with Bush, who didn't have much of an agenda, and with the other Democrats, who hadn't thought it through." In his October 3, 1991, announcement speech and in three subsequent policy addresses at Georgetown University, Clinton built his campaign on a work-centered platform. Government would foster opportunities for people seeking employment, and those without jobs would be responsible for taking them. At the heart of this appeal was the promise to "end welfare as we know it" by limiting welfare payments to two years at a time and five years in a lifetime. As Clinton said in his announcement speech, "Government's responsibility is to create more opportunity. The people's responsibility is to make the most of it."[14]

"Welfare was the best example of what Clinton would prove to be a master of," says Reed: "taking an issue that Republicans had demagogued for years and turning it into an affirmative political and substantive agenda for Democrats." Although Clinton's agenda placed him at odds with many traditional Democrats, who thought more in terms of public sector jobs than private sector jobs and resisted any change in welfare policy, he counted on them caring more about breaking their long losing streak in presidential elections than about preserving ideological purity. Making a virtue of his status as a Democratic outsider, Clinton based his campaign in Little Rock; staffed it with young, energetic professionals rather than traditional Washington power brokers; and organized his team non-hierarchically to facilitate innovation and coordination. The Clintons brought to bear "a lot of management lessons they learned from Arkansas corporations," says communications director George Stephanopoulos. "We kept hearing about Wal-Mart" and its "flattening out" approach to decision making.[15] Describing the Clinton campaign, co-field director John Monahan adds, "It's more like a basketball team than like an army because you really need people who are playing well individually as well as a group."[16] Clinton raised more early money than the other candidates, including $2.6 million from Arkansas donors, well above what any opponent received from his home state.

In all, Clinton won what campaign manager David Wilhelm calls the "pre-primary primary" and emerged from 1991 as the front runner for his party's nomination heading into the February 18 New Hampshire primary.[17] His campaign's ideas-based rationale, deep pockets, and effective organization surpassed those of any other Democratic candidate. In an effort to dissuade national political reporters from pursuing allegations about his marital infidelity, Clinton even met in September with the "Sperling Breakfast"—which Greer described as "a kind of political reporter insider group"—to declare, "What you need to know about Hillary and me is that we've been together nearly twenty years. It has not been perfect or free from problems, but we're committed to our marriage."[18] As a consequence, the issue vanished from the mainstream media for several months. Reporters barely acknowledged a January 16, 1992, story that appeared in *The Star*, a supermarket tabloid, with the headline: "Dems' Front Runner Bill Clinton Cheated with Miss America and Four Other Beauties."

Ignoring these allegations was no longer possible, however, when one week later *The Star*'s front page blared "They Made Love All over Her Apartment." The story was based on public testimony, loosely supported by taped telephone conversations, from Little Rock lounge singer Gennifer Flowers that she "was Bill Clinton's lover for twelve years." He and Hillary Clinton did much to defuse the charge when they appeared before a massive television audience on CBS's *60 Minutes*, which aired right after the January 26 Super Bowl. "You're looking at two people who love each other . . . ," Clinton declared. "This is a marriage."[19] But eight days later a second allegation was published in the widely respected *Wall Street Journal* recounting Clinton's apparent efforts to avoid military service during the Vietnam War. Pollster Stanley Greenberg told Clinton that in New Hampshire his candidacy suffered a "melt-down," noting "that's my phrase about what happened in the polls" right after the *Journal* story was published. In Washington, Gore "bet me Clinton would not be the nominee," recalls Gore's chief of staff, Roy Neel.

What enabled Clinton to survive the Gennifer Flowers and draft controversies with a solid second-place finish in New Hampshire behind Paul Tsongas, a former senator from neighboring Massachusetts? Part of the answer is personal. "He had the tenacity and the courage to stand up and take it," says Greer, "when a Gary Hart or somebody—I mean the tradition in American politics has been, Let's just collapse, let's walk away." Clinton translated his own adversity into the idiom of a small state whose economy was suffering. "That's when he said [to the voters], 'The hits I've taken are nothing compared to the hits that you've taken,'" Reed points out. "They loved that about him." A second part is organizational. Well-funded, the Clinton campaign not only proposed a detailed economic plan but also had the money to publicize it in multiple ads and televised town meetings, which gave him "the strength to withstand two major bits of scandal, largely on the strength of his plan . . . ," according to Greer. "Even the national press corps said, 'We may be a little carried away on this'" and backed off for a couple of weeks. Finally, the DLC's From credits the substantive nature of Clinton's entire campaign for his comeback, based on the new centrist policies the candidate had embraced. "A lot of the people were engaged in this process to redefine the party."

After New Hampshire voted, the terrain grew more favorable for Clinton, with primaries in Georgia on March 3, South Carolina on March 7, and six additional southern states on March 10. Clinton swept them handily, even prevailing in Colorado on the same day Georgia voted. Tsongas and Clinton's other major rival for the nomination, Senator Bob Kerrey of Nebraska, lacked the organization and funding to compete effectively on a national or even regional basis. After the election, Greenberg recalls, "the Kerrey people said, 'We were bewildered, we had no data,'" which explains why, playing a hunch, Kerrey made his stand against Clinton in Georgia instead of Colorado, only to finish a distant third. According to Greenberg, "We had data that said Kerrey could have won Colorado."[20]

Endowed with the money, organization, and message to compete next in Illinois and Michigan, Clinton effectively wrapped up the nomination on March 17 with landslide victories in both states. In further demonstration that Clinton was not a traditional liberal Democrat, says deputy communications director Robert Boorstin, "We went to an AFL-CIO hall in Flint and we said we are for NAFTA [the North American Free Trade Agreement]. Heretical. We went to [white working-class] Macomb County and we talked about race. Heretical. Then the next morning we went to the black church [in Detroit] and we gave the exact same talk."[21]

Clinton ran out the string, winning every one of the remaining twenty-two primaries except Connecticut—"more primaries than anybody who'd ever run," notes strategy consultant Paul Begala. Yet "[n]o one cared."[22] Although he defeated former California governor Jerry Brown in his own state on June 2, the last day of primary voting, polls showed Clinton running second or even third in the general election. He trailed Bush, whose own political standing was tarnished by declining popularity and a nettlesome primary challenge from conservative media pundit Pat Buchanan. "Buchanan was in no way a true challenger to President Bush," says *Washington Post* national political correspondent Dan Balz, "and yet it was clear that this was a disruptive candidacy, partly because it sapped them of some resources, partly because it drew attention to things about President George H.W. Bush that the Democrats wanted to emphasize. That he was inattentive to the economy, that he was out of touch with people."[23] In some polls Clinton also ran behind the wealthy, self-financed independent candidate, Texas businessman Ross Perot, whose folksy demeanor on television talk shows made his promise to reduce the soaring national debt by "taking out the trash and cleaning out the barn" sound appealing.[24]

Polls aside, Clinton's problems were fixable in a way that Bush's and Perot's were not. Two of the president's three most recent predecessors—Gerald R. Ford in 1976 and Carter in 1980—had faced renomination battles that unleashed ideological animosities within their parties. Bloodied, both then lost the general election. Bush's domestic agenda as president, which mattered most politically now that victory in the Cold War against the Soviet Union and the hot war against Iraq had reduced voters' concern about foreign policy, was disdained by Republican conservatives as too moderate—especially his willingness to raise taxes after famously pledging in his 1988 campaign to tell Congress: "Read my lips. No new taxes." Perot was congenitally testy and suspicious, qualities that were bound to diminish his appeal when voters and the media began scrutinizing him as a potential president instead of as an entertaining iconoclast.

In contrast to his two rivals, Clinton's main weakness as a candidate was grounded as much in misperception as in accurate perception. This conclusion emerged from the "Manhattan Project," a study by Greenberg, Greer, senior strategist James Carville, and advertising director Mandy Grunwald, who stepped off the campaign trail late in the primary season in a secret effort to figure out why Clinton was not more popular. According to David Kusnet, focus group research revealed that many people "assumed he was a rich kid whose family were big shots in Arkansas and who had bought his way into government or inherited it or something. Yale, Georgetown, Oxford . . . people assumed he had grown up in very different circumstances from how he actually had grown up—the son of a single mother who worked as a nurse anesthetist." This finding meant "our main task was biography," says Greenberg, and so "we went to popular culture shows" such as *The Arsenio Hall Show, Donahue, Good Morning America*, and MTV "because we could talk about biography, which is hard to do in newsrooms."[25] These appearances reintroduced Clinton to voters and "changed their opinion of him," says Grunwald. "And it also changed their opinions of everything he was proposing. They put it in a totally different context because it came from somebody who was one of them."[26]

Along with the Manhattan Project, three other events, the latter two outside Clinton's control, broke in his favor during the summer. First, on July 9, four days before the Democrats gathered in convention, Clinton tapped Gore as his running mate. Months earlier, Clinton had told campaign chair Mickey Kantor, who helped run the vice presidential search, to "throw out all notions of what the criteria politically had been in the past and think about this from a new perspective." Although Clinton and Gore "had been natural rivals" (Reed) and "had virtually no relationship" (Neel), they had a professional respect for each other and hit it off personally in a three-hour, late-night meeting. Clinton's choice of Gore defied all the traditional canons of ticket balancing: both men were southerners, both were Southern Baptists, both were baby boomers with young families, both were policy "wonks," and both were ideological centrists. In these obvious ways, Gore reinforced rather than offset Clinton's most visible qualities. In more subtle ways, however, Gore did bring balance to the ticket. Clinton's potential vulnerabilities as a foreign policy novice, a pro-industry governor, a skirt chaser, and a draft avoider were counterbalanced by Gore's Senate experience, environmentalist credentials, stable family life, and service in the Vietnam War.

To most voters, Gore also provided a welcome contrast to Bush's gaffe-prone vice president, Dan Quayle. A July poll found that voters thought that Gore was "more qualified to be president" than Quayle by 63 percent to 21 percent.[27] Secretary of State James Baker, former president Gerald R. Ford, and Bush's son George were among those who advised the president to replace Quayle on the ticket but, as Bush dictated to his diary, "The bottom line on Quayle is, if he is dumped, I'm attacked for not keeping my word, 'Read My Lips'; no loyalty." Bush also underestimated Gore's appeal. "I've always thought Gore was kind of fragile and surreal, very liberal," he told his dairy; "and on the environment, he's [a] far-out extremist."[28]

Second, Perot, besieged by critical news stories about his naval service, business dealings, and temperament, withdrew from the race on July 15, the third day of the Democratic convention. Even more important, he halfway endorsed Clinton, saying that "the Democratic party has revitalized itself" by moving toward the center.[29] Although Perot resumed his candidacy on October 1, his initial withdrawal contributed to Clinton's emergence from the convention with a 55 percent to 37 percent lead over Bush in the Gallup Poll.

Third, the mid-August Republican convention focused on social, not economic issues, and in a severely conservative way. More than by Bush's acceptance speech, the convention was dominated by Buchanan's opening-night address, in which he declared, "There is a religious war going on in our country. . . . And in that struggle for the soul of America, Clinton and Clinton are on the other side and George Bush is on our side."[30] The convention ended on August 20, recalls Clinton's campaign chief of staff, Eli Segal, and "in the course of the next five days . . . I got a phone call [every day], direct and indirect, from a prominent Republican leader, announcing that they wanted me to know that they were going to make a six-figure gift, which was still legal at the time, to the Democratic National Committee." The callers "included people like Augie Busch, the beer tycoon, Ernest Gallo, the wine man, Thomas Watson, Dwayne Andreas and one or two others. One a day, it was like clockwork." Bush's post-convention bounce was modest, lifting him only to 39 percent.

Part of the prevailing lore of American politics in 1992 was that to be elected president a candidate had to run to the party's ideological extreme to get the nomination and then tack toward the center to win the general election. Clinton did not do that. From October 1991 to November 1992, his centrist message hardly changed at all. Clinton "kept saying to me, 'I need a new stump speech,'" says Begala. "I would give him one and he would say, 'There's nothing in here that wasn't in my announcement speech.' And I would say, 'That's because on announcement day you knew why you wanted to be president.'"[31] The campaign's "workhorse" ad all year, according to Grunwald, was "the first spot we did on welfare. . . . It was a really boring spot."[32] But Clinton's promise to move people "from welfare to work" continued to air because the campaign's research showed that the message connected with voters.

Ironically, the real temptation for the Clinton campaign after he won the primaries but still trailed Bush and Perot badly in the polls was to adopt what Reed disparagingly calls "the 34 percent solution"—namely, to run left in the fall campaign to motivate the Democratic base and thereby win a plurality election. Clinton rejected this strategy and, according to deputy political director Nancy McFadden, "traditional Democratic constituencies," desperately tired of losing presidential elections, accepted his centrist approach, acknowledging that "this election is bigger than them. It is bigger than a labor union. It is bigger than the Sierra Club. It is bigger than the Gray Panthers. It is bigger than the choice issue alone."[33]

Reelection-seeking presidents invariably order from a strategic menu with only two entrees: "Wasn't my first term great?" (the preferred appeal of popular presidents such as Eisenhower and Reagan) and, if that option is not available (as it wasn't for Bush), "Whatever you think of me, my opponent is worse." Bush's international triumphs notwithstanding, domestic policy motivated most of the electorate in post–Cold War, recessionary 1992. In the Election Day exit poll, only 8 percent of the voters said that foreign policy was an important consideration in their choice of a candidate. Eighty-seven percent of them voted for Bush, but many more resented what they regarded as his concern for the world's problems at the expense of their own. To be sure, Bush could have done differently. In March 1991, riding high in the polls after the triumph in Iraq, he had enjoyed a rare opportunity to mobilize Congress in support of a domestic agenda. But Bush had no such agenda. As his chief of staff, John Sununu, told a conservative audience the previous November, "There's not another single piece of legislation that needs to be passed in the next two years for this president. In fact, if Congress wants to come together, adjourn, and leave, it's all right with us."[34]

To the extent that Bush dealt with domestic affairs, he was unsuccessful politically. In September 1990, he abandoned his "no new taxes" pledge in return for Congress's agreement to reduce federal spending over a five-year period, proclaiming, "It is balanced, it is fair, and in my view, it is what the United States of America needs," A month later, inundated by criticism from conservative Republicans and from voters outraged that he had violated his main campaign promise in 1988, Bush told reporters that the agreement made him "gag," a line he maintained through the end of the 1992 election.[35] Arguably, Bush's patient approach to economic recovery worked. The economy grew rapidly in the fourth quarter. But growth accelerated too late for most voters to notice. Politically, Mickey Kantor points out, "in '92 it was the perception of the economy, not the actual."

Attacking Clinton was Bush's best available strategy, but he executed it badly. The Clinton campaign's own research revealed that if Bush "had done a solid six-week campaign attacking Arkansas, we would have been meat," says Robert Boorstin. "We would have been on the defensive the whole time."[36] But even when the Bush campaign tried, "the way they did [Clinton's gubernatorial record on] the environment was dead wrong because they were trying to do two things at once. They were saying 'He's the pits' and then they were saying, 'He's too green.'" Even tactically, the Bush campaign erred. Clinton was able "to outspend the Republicans in every state that was a battleground because they were buying national time," according to Grunwald. "So if you lived in [solidly Democratic states like] Massachusetts, you were seeing Bush ads every day."[37] Clinton confined his advertising to states he was neither certain to win nor certain to lose.

Perot's candidacy vexed both major party nominees when he reentered the race in October. Unlike previous prominent independent candidates, Perot was a businessman who spent lavishly from his own wealth, not an established political leader running on a shoestring. As a Texas entrepreneur, he drained votes from Bush, but as a candidate of change he also cut into Clinton's support. The exit poll showed that in the final tally Perot drew equally from both major party candidates. Despite receiving 19 percent of the national popular vote, he carried no states and received no electoral votes. Perot's supporters, many of whom said they would have stayed home if he had not been on the ballot, helped raise voter turnout from 50 percent in 1988 to 55 percent in 1992. But his popular vote—the largest for any independent candidate since former president Theodore Roosevelt in 1912—meant that Clinton was elected with the support of only 43 percent of the voters and 24 percent of the voting age population, the smallest share for any president since John Quincy Adams in 1824.

In the 1992 congressional elections, Clinton's party made no gains in the Senate and actually lost ten seats in the House while still remaining the majority party in both chambers. Most victorious Democrats ran in safe constituencies and therefore had no incentive to abandon their party's traditional liberalism in favor of Clinton's centrist strategy. Virtually all won a higher share of the vote than Clinton, providing them with further confirmation that no change in approach was necessary. The ranks of Democratic women and ethnic and racial minorities rose substantially, moving the Democratic caucus several degrees to the left.

These developments, added to the new president's lack of a popular vote majority, "left Clinton without the strength of his own convictions to govern from a majority standpoint," according to Reed. Instead, he ceded control of his first-term agenda to conventionally liberal Democratic congressional leaders, putting welfare reform aside in pursuit of his failed proposal for national health insurance. Although James Carville had famously posted a sign in the "war room" of Clinton's Little Rock headquarters listing "Don't forget health care" as one of the campaign's three major themes, in reality Clinton had downplayed the issue in his campaign advertising. After his health care proposal failed in Congress, recalls Greer:

> I go to this dinner in the small dining room upstairs at the White House. Clinton is saying, "I just don't understand, we ran on health care and we tried to do the right thing. I know there are a lot of interest groups that we're up against and—" I turned to him and I said, "Mr. President, how many spots do you think you ran on health care in the general election?" He said, "I don't know, four or five. We ran a lot on health care." I said,

"Zero. You didn't get elected on health care. You didn't run one spot on health care. You ran on welfare reform and you might have been better off if you'd started with that.

1996

In the midterm election of 1994, Republicans gained control of both houses of Congress for the first time in forty years. United by House Republican leader Newt Gingrich of Georgia behind a ten-point Contract with America that it pledged to honor with new conservative legislation, the GOP gained fifty-four seats to secure a 226–208 majority in the lower chamber. In Senate elections, Republicans added eight new seats, which gave them a 53–47 majority. Gingrich was elected speaker of the House and Robert J. Dole of Kansas became the Senate majority leader.

The seeds of Clinton's 1996 reelection strategy were sown in the aftermath of the Democrats' heavy losses in 1994, which restored divided government but in a new form: Democratic president, Republican Congress. "It was clear by the fall of 1994 that the American people had decided that the '92 campaign had been a bait-and-switch operation," according to deputy domestic policy advisor William Galston—baiting with innovative centrist promises and then switching to conventional liberal policies. "He'd been listening to advice from advisors who were oriented toward congressional Democrats. . . . The fact that the New Democratic strategic course had never gotten a careful examination during the first two years was not lost on the president. I don't think he felt very happy about it."

During the first half of 1995, Clinton gradually adopted a three-pronged strategy for reelection, all the elements of which were firmly in place by the end of the year.[38] The first prong was to preempt any challenge to his renomination at the Democratic convention by raising so much money (about $35 million in 1995 alone) that no serious opponent would dare take him on. Among those who thought about running before backing off were Senator Kerrey of Nebraska, Senator Bill Bradley of New Jersey, Senator Robert Casey of Pennsylvania, House Majority Leader Richard Gephardt, and Rev. Jesse Jackson. Clinton's success in this effort made him the first Democratic presidential candidate since FDR in 1936 not to face opposition for his party's nomination.

The other two prongs of Clinton's strategy were aimed more directly at winning the general election against the Republican nominee. One of these was to regain his centrist appeal by pursuing a version of campaign advisor Dick Morris's goal of "triangulation."[39] Morris, along with Reed, Galston, and eventually

Clinton himself, thought that it was important for the president not only to stake out a position at the political center, midway between liberal congressional Democrats and conservative congressional Republicans, but also to find new issues that would allow him to rise above the conventional left-right political spectrum. The three points of the new political triangle would then be occupied by orthodox Democrats and Republicans at opposite ends of its baseline, with Clinton hovering at a point above and between them. Part of the strategy's appeal was that the midterm election had made the baseline longer. GOP gains in 1994 were concentrated in the South, which added to the party's conservative ranks while draining moderate "Blue Dogs" from the Democratic caucus, thereby making the Democrats' congressional party more liberal.

Triangulation (Clinton's preferred term was the "third way") explains, for example, the president's approach to the defining controversy of his third year in office—the budget battle with the Republican Congress. Fresh from their midterm triumph, the Republicans went beyond the promises of the Contract with America by vowing to balance the budget by 2002 while cutting taxes. Congressional Democrats opposed them on both counts, aiming most of their fire at the spending reductions in popular federal programs that would be required to achieve these purposes. In mid-1995, Clinton angered Democrats by boldly embracing the Republican goal of a balanced budget but infuriated Republicans by insisting that Democratic mainstays such as Medicare, Medicaid, support for education, and enforcement of environmental legislation be left substantially unaltered.

The public, prompted in part by $18 million worth of pro-administration television commercials paid for by the Democratic National Committee, supported the president on both counts. Then, when the Republicans tried to impose their own budget on Clinton, he refused to yield. More than that, Clinton persuaded the voters that Gingrich, Dole, and the Republican Congress, not he, were responsible for the two federal government shutdowns, totaling twenty-seven days, that occurred in late 1995 and early 1996 in the absence of a budget agreement. He vetoed two Republican welfare reform bills but fulfilled his 1992 campaign promise by signing the third, which included his proposed time limits on welfare while providing additional funds to help recipients move into the work force. He also persuaded Congress to expand the earned income tax credit to increase the economic value of low-income jobs. "We knew most of the Republicans, especially Dole, who at this point was in the heat of the Republican presidential primaries, didn't want the president to sign welfare reform," says Reed. "They wanted it as an issue for the '96 campaign." Public support for Clinton, who had consistently trailed Dole in the early polls, increased dramatically. He opened up a solid lead against the Republican frontrunner in January 1996 and never lost it.

The remaining prong of Clinton's strategy for winning the general election was to present himself to the voters as a presidential rather than a partisan or political figure. The terrorist bombing of the Oklahoma City federal building in April 1995 gave him his first opportunity after the midterm election to do so. His effort was successful. As one observer recorded in the aftermath of the traumatic bombing, Clinton "exhibited the take-charge determination as well as the on-key rhetoric that Americans expect of their president in times of trouble."[40] In November 1995, Clinton learned something else about presidential behavior. When he overruled public opinion by sending 20,000 American troops on a peacekeeping mission to Bosnia, the voters' approval of his overall handling of foreign policy went up. Privately, Clinton likened it to "telling your children to go to the dentist—they don't want to go, but they know you're right."[41]

Clinton's strategy of triangulation and acting presidential had clear implications for the way he conducted his general election campaign in the fall of 1996. In dozens of appearances around the country, Clinton pointed with retrospective pride to the economic progress of his first term: four consecutive years of low inflation, a drop in the unemployment rate from 7 percent in 1992 to 5 percent in 1996, steady economic growth, and a reduction in the annual budget deficit from $290 billion the year before he became president to $106 billion in the fourth year of his term. He struck unifying presidential poses for the television cameras, signing legislation at the Grand Canyon and presiding over an Arab-Israeli summit conference at the White House. He also celebrated the first-term enactment of laws such as the Family and Medical Leave Act, funding for more police officers, and welfare reform, along with his successful defense of "Medicare, Medicaid, education, and the environment" (a litany that frequent hearers recast as M^2E^2) against alleged Republican assaults.

But Clinton's discussion of the future was nearly content free. Standing under banners that proclaimed "Building America's Bridge to the 21st Century," Clinton repeatedly offered empty "bridge" rhetoric to the voters. He promised (in language later echoed in his inaugural address) a bridge "big enough, strong enough, and wide enough for everybody to walk across" and asserted that "everyone has a right to walk on the bridge." By one count he used the word an average of more than nine times per speech.[42] Aside from some specific promises concerning tax credits for education, Clinton's campaign was short on proposals for the second term. Although "Aren't things great?" was a more positive appeal than "My opponent is worse," Clinton nonetheless proposed little in the way of a policy agenda. "Never asking for a specific mandate," wrote political scientist Gerald M. Pomper, "it was inevitable that he would not receive one, regardless of his popular vote."[43]

Nor did Clinton tie his campaign to the fortunes of congressional Democrats, even as his lead in the polls remained consistently in double digits. Determined to win 51 percent of the national popular vote even though Perot was once again on the ballot and wary of alienating voters who might fear giving him too coopera-tive a Congress, Clinton never called for the restoration of a Democratic House and Senate. When endorsing individual candidates, White House press secretary Michael McCurry noted, "the president does not make this appeal solely on par-tisanship."[44] Only late in the campaign did Clinton raise significant amounts of money for congressional Democrats and adjust his campaign schedule to help them out. Even more concentrated in safe districts than before the 1994 midterm, the Senate and especially the House Democratic caucuses remained as wedded as ever to the party's traditional liberalism.

Dole, who in three previous runs for national office had never displayed strong gifts as a campaigner, showed little improvement in 1996. Lacking a strategy, he lurched from tactic to tactic, stressing variously his economic plan, his support for family values, and his opposition to affirmative action and illegal immigra-tion. He had an equally hard time settling on a line of attack against Clinton, claiming variously that the president was responsible for an increase in teenage drug use, that he was too liberal, that his administration was corrupt, or that he could not be trusted. In one speech, inadvertently underscoring his campaign's themelessness, Dole proclaimed, "It all boils down to one word. Trust." He then added: "It's about leadership. It's about family. It's about business. It's about the next century."[45] Dole's speaking skills, whether on television or at campaign ral-lies, were limited. Departing from carefully crafted speech texts, he often lapsed into shorthand legislative terminology that Washington insiders understood but that left most voters baffled.

Compared with his performance in 1992, Clinton's biggest gains in 1996 were among women, Latinos, liberals, moderates, union households, and young vot-ers. He lost support among white men, older voters, and Protestants.[46] Clinton won 49 percent of the popular vote to Dole's 41 percent and Perot's 8 percent, along with 379 electoral votes to Dole's 159. To that extent, his reelection strategy was effective. It certainly was the safest strategy he could have pursued. But the low-risk, light-on-substance campaign that Clinton conducted prevented him from securing an achievement-style victory based on a change-oriented agenda and long congressional coattails.[47] Indeed, the Democrats lost two seats in the Senate, outweighing their modest gain of nine seats in the House, and failed to regain control of either legislative body.

Voter turnout in 1996 fell to 49 percent, the lowest share of the electorate since 1924, a year when many women, newly enfranchised by the Nineteenth Amendment, were unfamiliar with voting and many states had registration laws that discriminated against recent immigrants and African Americans. The decline was especially noteworthy in light of the passage in 1993 of the National Voter Registration Act. The so-called motor-voter bill required all the states to allow registration by mail and at motor vehicle, welfare, unemployment, and other state offices. With registering to vote easier, turnout should have been up, not down.

Redivided Government

Nineteen ninety-six was the last time Bill Clinton appeared on the ballot but not the last election of his presidency. At Gingrich's direction, Republicans fought the 1998 midterm election on the issue of Clinton's fitness to remain in office in light of his affair with Monica Lewinsky, which had been revealed in January. Gingrich was confident of success, especially considering that midterm elections at the six-year mark of a president's tenure historically have been punishing affairs for his party. Yet Democrats gained five seats in the House and broke even in the Senate, a remarkable outcome that prompted Gingrich to resign both as speaker and as a member of the House. The results were largely a measure of Clinton's unflaggingly high job approval ratings in polls of voters. Despite this public endorsement of his performance as president, however, Republicans continued to control both chambers. Taken together, Clinton's popularity and the large number of politically safe, mostly urban, and traditionally liberal legislative constituencies placed a high floor on congressional Democratic success. But House and Senate Democrats' unwillingness to embrace Clinton-style centrism also left them with a low ceiling.

Clinton showed Democrats that the way to win presidential elections was by moving toward the political center in creative—that is, more than split-the-difference—ways, such as welfare reform joined to an increased earned income tax credit to encourage and reward work and a budget that was balanced while preserving long-standing Democratic commitments to the poor, the elderly, public school teachers, and the environment. The strategies the Democratic presidential candidates who followed in his wake pursued, like their success in elections, have been more variable. Of the three Democratic nominees since Clinton, two—Gore in 2000 and John Kerry in 2004—ran traditional liberal Democratic campaigns and lost and one, Barack Obama in 2008 and 2012, took a more centrist approach and won. Although Gore was Clinton's vice president for eight years, he ran a populist-style, "people, not the powerful" campaign more appropriate for a candidate challenging an incumbent in economic hard times than for a vice president seeking to extend his party's control of the presidency in good times. Kerry centered his campaign on opposition to the Iraq War, a popular position in its own right but one that resurrected voters' old concerns that Democrats are too dovish to forcefully defend America against foreign enemies, whether in the Cold War or the war on terrorism. Obama, in contrast, offered himself as a unifying candidate who, like Clinton, transcended conventional divisions between Democratic liberalism and Republican conservatism. In foreign policy, Obama balanced his opposition to the Iraq War with a promise to pursue the war in Afghanistan aggressively.

Yet Clinton's success in reversing long-standing Republican control of the presidency coincided with a reversal of the even longer-standing Democratic control of Congress, a countertrend that began two years into his administration. This was partly because of Clinton's own actions. In pursuit of a personal mandate, he did little to help his party's down-ballot candidates. Indeed, in his bid for renomination and reelection in 1996 he soaked up most of the available Democratic political money and fund-raising talent, leaving slim pickings for the rest of the ticket. In Daniel Galvin's stern judgment, Clinton was a thoroughgoing "party predator" during his first term; "he either ignored [the Democratic Party] or exploited it for his short-term political benefit."[48]

Clinton's centrist policies, which were popular among the national electorate, also fostered the creation of an ideological divide between him and the congressional Democratic Party. To be sure, it was hardly Clinton's responsibility that the party's core constituencies—minorities, singles, young adults, secular voters, and gays and lesbians—were (and still are) both strongly liberal and "inefficiently" concentrated in a relatively small number of urban House districts and in large states that, like the less populous and generally more conservative ones, elect only two members of the Senate.[49] But when he moved rightward toward the center, Clinton stranded the majority of these Congress members, for whom a similar ideological move would have invited primary challenges from the left.

Republicans have not been bystanders in recent political developments. The redividing of government also may be attributed in part to the recent southernization of the GOP. Although Clinton was a southern governor and his running mate a southern Democrat in both 1992 and 1996, he lost the South to Bush and Dole by a combined 90 electoral votes to 204 electoral votes while winning the rest of the country by a combined 659 to 123. In the presidential elections of 2008 and 2012, Midwesterner Obama's balance of regional support was quite similar: 97 electoral votes to 208 electoral votes in the South, 600 to 171 outside the region.

In congressional elections, trends under way since the 1960s that culminated in the 1990s left Clinton's party a disheartening southern legacy. As recently as 1992, Democrats won 77 of 112 southern seats in the House and held 13 of 22 in the Senate. In 1994, however, as much a watershed in congressional elections as 1992 was in presidential elections, Republicans gained twenty-one seats in the eleven southern states, giving the GOP a majority in the region of 66–59. Even though only six southern Senate seats were on the ballot in 1994, Republicans also added four to their ranks, which gave the party a 13–9 majority. By 2014, Republican representatives outnumbered Democrats by 101 to 37 in the South and Republicans held 19 of 22 southern Senate seats. The proliferation of "majority-minority" House districts in the 1990s, the result of an alliance between Republican and African American politicians, now accounts for most of the thirty-seven southern House seats held by Democrats, including sixteen blacks and four Latinos (all Texans). Each of the eight House Democrats from the Deep South is African American.

In presidential elections, the result of these Republican gains has been to make the GOP seem more a regional than a national party. In the 114th Congress, for example, their southern-based majority status in both chambers sharply contrasted with their minority status outside the South, where they were outnumbered by 35 to 43 in the Senate and by 144 to 172 in the House. The result has been to undermine the party's appeal in contests for the presidency, of which it won only two of six from 1992 to 2012, none by a margin of more than one state. Like the Democrats who dominated the South but lost most presidential elections a century ago, the Republicans' growing identity as a southern party has made it harder for their presidential candidates to compete successfully in the rest of the country.

Irony abounds in this account of redivided government. When Clinton won the presidency in 1992, Democrats rejoiced that the era of divided control had ended in their favor. Arthur M. Schlesinger Jr. heralded the arrival of a new turn of his father's famous cycle of alternating periods of "public purpose" and "private interest" in a liberal direction.[50] No pundit or political scientist foresaw that the Republicans would capture control of Congress in 1994, much less hold onto it. Compounding the irony, Clinton's success in forging a centrist Democratic path to victory in national elections proved unavailable to (and unsought by) his party in the state-by-state, district-by-district elections that constitute Congress. The Democratic Party's Moses made it to the Promised Land, but his party's people were expelled from it.

TRIANGULATION

Positioning and Leadership in Clinton's Domestic Policy

Bruce F. Nesmith and Paul J. Quirk

In March, 2015, a relatively obscure potential candidate for the 2016 Democratic presidential nomination, former Maryland governor Martin O'Malley, sought to identify front runner Hillary Clinton with a political strategy for which her husband, President Bill Clinton, had been known. O'Malley declared that "triangulation is not a strategy that will move America forward." He added, "History celebrates profiles in courage, not profiles in convenience."[1] We leave aside the question of whether O'Malley had Hillary Clinton right. Did he have Bill Clinton and triangulation right?

As a political term, *triangulation* is a Clinton-era neologism that has not passed into general use, even though it has broad potential application. After the Democrats' disastrous defeat in the 1994 midterm congressional elections, Clinton hired Dick Morris, a Republican political strategist whom he had consulted while governor of Arkansas, to provide political advice on how to deal with the new Republican Congress. Morris concocted a highly instrumental approach, taking into account the Republicans' extreme conservative positions on a variety of domestic issues, and proposed the name *triangulation* to identify it—a reference to the geometric methods surveyors use to find the location of a point. In this strategy, Clinton would stand firm on partisan Democratic positions when they were popular. On issues where Republican positions were more popular, however, Clinton would take advantage of the current Republican Congress's tendency to overreach: he would make major concessions from conventional Democratic policies and adopt centrist positions that would have broader support than the Republicans' offerings. By such systematic, instrumental positioning, Clinton hoped to win politically on most issues, no matter which party had the initial advantage in public opinion.

In many ways Clinton was successful. Aided by a booming economy, he cruised to a reelection victory in 1996 and managed to ride out the Monica Lewinsky scandal and Republican impeachment effort of his second term—ending up a popular president.

Morris's hard-core instrumental approach was only part of the story of Clinton's centrist positions. An active member of the centrist Democratic Leadership Council, Clinton had portrayed himself as a moderate "New Democrat" on some issues in the 1992 presidential election campaign. At least ostensibly, the purpose of New Democrat politics was to transcend conflicts between rigid liberal and conservative ideological positions, recognize the requirements for both a thriving private economy and social needs, and adopt policies that would benefit all Americans. In his most notable departure from mainstream Democratic policies, Clinton promised to "end welfare as we know it." Thus, Clinton's centrism had roots in principled policy judgments—that is, judgments reflecting ideological, policy-analytic, or other public-interest goals—as well as in political calculation. William Galston, who served as deputy assistant for domestic policy during Clinton's first two years in office, made such a claim about his budget moderation: "I think that the tough decisions he made—particularly in 1993 that cost him dearly in 1994—were not poll-driven. They were conviction-driven, and he understood very well that the short-term politics of fiscal restraint were not positive."[2]

Along with having these centrist dispositions, Clinton may have adapted his orientation to the changing opportunities and challenges Congress presented. In effect, Congress sometimes invites the president to pursue substantive policy goals and other times renders such goals impractical or outlandishly costly in political terms and pushes electoral competition to the forefront of attention. In the words of his health and human services secretary, Donna Shalala, Clinton "tries to make decisions on evidence but shifts to politics when it's absolutely necessary."

The lessons of the Clinton presidency about the nature and consequences of centrist positions may be relevant for a wide range of presidencies—those in which the president makes a sustained or recurring move toward the political center and those in which divided party control makes the president's relations with the opposing party central to his political success. Such circumstances include at least parts of the two succeeding two-term presidencies—those of George W. Bush and Barack Obama. Indeed, because a successful campaign for the presidency requires winning highly competitive pivotal states, centrist positions and some form of triangulation are likely to be common features of presidential politics in any period.

We begin with the most basic question: In making policy decisions, do presidents mainly pursue substantive policy goals (peace, prosperity, ideological goals, social or environmental gains, and so on) or do they instead pursue political goals (popularity, interest-group support, or election victories for the president, his party, or a successor)? How are these choices affected by political circumstances? And in particular, what do they have to do with centrist or moderate policies? Is triangulation a politics of political expediency that ill serves the country's interests or is the capacity for moderation and centrist positioning a vital element of constructive presidential leadership?

We address these questions in three parts. First, we consider the theoretical issues about politicians' choices between policy principle and political expediency and the relationship of such choices to centrist policy making. We outline some expectations and recognize some important ambiguities in the theoretical considerations. Second, we present evidence from a set of twenty-four case analyses of what we call autonomy issues—issues that pose clear conflicts between substantive and political considerations—from the Clinton presidency, drawn from a larger study of presidential and congressional policy making from the Kennedy to the Obama administrations. As we point out in detail below, our selection of issues and our approach in analyzing them have distinct advantages for our purposes here.

Our findings disagree with ideological critics of triangulation and with some prominent academic works that we will discuss. We argue that presidents act from political expediency quite often, in a wide range of circumstances, and especially when they encounter political adversity. But we also argue that centrist positioning—the key element of triangulation—is neither a cause nor an indicator of politically expedient decision making. In the circumstances that induce them, triangulation and centrist positioning can play a constructive role in principled presidential leadership.

Policy versus Political Goals

The central theoretical issue in this chapter is whether and when presidents pander, to use the vernacular of recent political science literature.[3] We regret the use of that term because its strong moralistic connotations may bias readers to discount the prevalence of politically motivated decisions. We will use the term pander at times because of its convenience and familiarity, but the reader should try to ignore the moralizing connotations. In a representative democracy, one expects elected officials to defer to the demands of voters and interest groups—sometimes even when the officials do not themselves approve of the resulting policies.

The issue is whether presidents make policy decisions largely on the basis of expected electoral or other political effects—in the language of David Mayhew's account of legislators, act in terms of the "electoral connection"[4]—or whether they make such decisions on the basis of their own autonomous judgments about the merits of policies. Realistically, the issue is how much presidents use each kind of decision making and under what circumstances they do so. We will use various conventional, roughly synonymous terms and related concepts for each type of decision making—referring to behavior as, on the hand, electorally or politically motivated, concerned with approval or support, or demand-driven, or, on the other hand, substantively oriented, principled, responsible, or autonomous. The reader should keep in mind that nothing guarantees that principled decisions, in our terms, are necessarily correct or right in some absolute sense. In some cases, what we call *principled* decisions are the ones favored by independent experts or by a large majority of nonpartisan observers. In others cases, such decisions are preferred on the basis of the actor's ideological beliefs—and thus would be opposed, on equally principled grounds, by adherents of alternative ideological views.

This distinction figures prominently in ordinary citizens' political discourse. Does the president do what he believes is best for the country or what's best for his own political interests? But it is strangely neglected in political science. Some theorizing is based explicitly on one or another assumption—that politicians seek reelection exclusively;[5] that they pursue a combination of goals, such as re-election, good policy, and influence;[6] or (for some specialized analytic contexts) that they pursue policy goals exclusively.[7] But although scholars have been interested in deriving predictions from basic assumptions about motivation, they have rarely sought to assess the relative merits of the competing assumptions.[8]

Another neglected issue is whether autonomous, substantively oriented policy decisions by presidents or legislators actually serve the public's interests or whether these politicians perform best from the public's standpoint when they respond—without competing impulses—to the public's wishes.[9] To the extent that electoral interests are shaped by demands from narrow groups seeking special-interest benefits, the advantages of policymakers' autonomy seem relatively clear. When the electoral interests are shaped by public opinion, however, some will question whether policymakers do indeed know better. We do not attempt to answer this question. We suppose, however, that when policymakers feel sufficiently motivated to take political risks for the sake of some policy, they will have reasonably strong grounds for believing that the public will actually benefit from their doing so.

Theories of Presidential Decision Making

In the literature on the presidency, two prominent theoretical and empirical works have directly addressed the roles of autonomy and electoral or political-support motivation. Both use the term pandering and both discount the phenomenon it identifies, but on different grounds and to different degrees.

In a work that focuses largely on an in-depth case study of the Clinton administration's health care reform proposal, Lawrence R. Jacobs and Robert Y. Shapiro argue, as the title of their book bluntly states, that "politicians don't pander."[10] Their argument turns on a claim about sweeping changes in the nature of politicians' incentives in the American political system. They suggest that as a result of "elite-driven" ideological polarization, politicians—that is, the president, the congressional parties, and individual members of Congress—no longer have incentives to respond to median public opinion. Rather, they act on their own ideologically based policy opinions. In this account, politicians use polls not to find out what a majority of the public wants for the purpose of enabling them to provide it but only to test arguments, appeals, and specific language that would cause the public to endorse what the politicians want to do for their own reasons. Jacobs and Shapiro support this account in large part by accepting the accounts of White House officials in interviews.

In an earlier article, Quirk has argued that Jacobs and Shapiro define pandering or (equivalently) responding to the public too narrowly as responding to the center of overall national public opinion, as measured in polls.[11] They thus overlook the significance of interest groups, party constituencies, party activists, and state or district constituencies in shaping electoral incentives for politicians. Taking these forces into account, Quirk argues that politicians' deviations from the median of national opinion often reflect not autonomous action but rather their response to "ideologically mobilized mass constituencies."[12] To be sure, Jacobs and Shapiro are not mainly attempting to explain variations in presidential motivation in policy making. Taken literally, however, they predict consistent, largely ideological, autonomous policy making, with little or no electorally motivated policy making.

In the second work, Brandice Canes-Wrone acknowledges that electorally motivated presidential policy making occurs—particularly in the form of deference to public opinion—and she has useful suggestions for explaining variation in that influence.[13] But her account also treats presidential "pandering" as unusual, in sharp contrast to theories of policy making shaped mainly by electoral goals. Canes-Wrone presumes that presidents have both substantive policy goals and strong concerns about reelection. In principle, she would expect election-oriented pandering if the electoral rewards were substantial and the policy costs were not excessive. However, she identifies two conditions for sufficient electoral rewards that, taken together, are highly restrictive. First, the president must have a moderate level of public approval—that is, not too high (so they have some need to pander in order to achieve the electoral goal) and not too low (so the electoral goal is not out of reach, even with pandering). Second, the policy decision must occur late enough in the term that the adverse societal consequences that the president expects will not be noticed until after the next election. In short, pandering will occur only with moderately popular presidents in periods near elections. Canes-Wrone presents an analysis of the effects of public opinion on presidential budget proposals that provides support for these expectations.

In our view, both of Canes-Wrone's required conditions are problematic. First, we doubt that either high or low popularity will dissuade presidents from using policy to seek electoral goals. Presidents appear to keep the hope of electoral success alive even in dire circumstances and appear not to take success for granted even in highly favorable ones. These dispositions comport with the actual uncertainty of presidential politics.[14] So we would expect only relatively subtle differences between those presidents who are moderately popular and those who are either more popular or less popular in their inclination to make policy decisions on electoral grounds.

Second, we doubt that the prospect that the effects of a policy will produce a loss of voter support at the time of the next election will prevent pandering on many issues at any point in a president's term. For electorally motivated policy making to be a potential option, there must be a strong constituency demand for a certain policy, which means that electoral rewards will attend the policy decision. For actual adverse consequences to cancel out those rewards, they must either be clearly associated with the decision—making after-the-fact criticism of the decision costly to the president—or of sufficient magnitude to impose electoral costs through voters' response to prevailing conditions, such as the state of the economy.[15] Such rapid and substantial adverse effects of inadvisable policies can occur in the case of severe mistakes in economic management or national security policy, but they are rare. When constituency demands promote policies that the president considers harmful, it is mainly the president's own concern for good policy—not fear of electoral punishment for bad consequences—that may prevent his or her adopting them.

Expectations

To establish some expectations about the conditions for electoral distortion of presidential policy decisions, we begin with the assumption that presidents make trade-offs between substantive goals and electoral goals. Presidents typically respond to both kinds of goals and sometimes must deal with conflicts between them. How they do so is the result of five kinds of factors: individual attributes (personality, background); general political circumstances (the electoral cycle, approval ratings, the stages of the president's term); issue characteristics (expected policy consequences, constituency mobilization); agendas (including other issues being decided); and interactions with Congress (especially the congressional majority).

First, we expect presidents to have strong motivations for both substantive policy achievement and political success. They will have policies and societal outcomes that they care about and they will have learned to deal with political demands. Thus they will strike some balance between considerations of electoral gain and those of policy substance (their own policy beliefs, their legacy, their sense of responsibility for the country's well-being, and so on.) Although some individuals may focus entirely on one sort of goal (for example, winning reelection), most are uncomfortable acting in a purely instrumental way.[16] Thus in making a trade-off, for example, the president will tolerate a small expected loss with respect to one goal (either political support or good policy) in exchange for a large gain with respect to the other.

Second, we expect individual differences in the weights presidents attach to competing goals and perhaps in other aspects of trade-offs. These differences relate to personality, career experience, and perhaps cultural background. Because so few people have been president, there is no point in trying to develop and test systematic predictions. But we would expect, for example, that a career of publicly promoting certain political values would normally result in a genuine emotional investment in those values. Similarly, high-level executive officials (such as military officers) will have strong commitments to national security interests, and accomplishment as a policy thinker will lead to strong concerns about the relevant policies. As M. Stephen Weatherford has argued, President Richard Nixon's long-standing interest in foreign affairs and lack of comparable interest in domestic and economic policy promoted a willingness to manipulate economic policy for electoral ends.[17]

Third, general political circumstances, including stages of the presidential term, should have several effects. At the beginning of their first terms, presidents—having just achieved the singular accomplishment of winning the presidency—will have elevated confidence in their capabilities and prospects for political and policy success. This confidence will encourage an idealistic focus on substantive policy goals—indeed, on ambitious ones. According to research based on oral histories of the Jimmy Carter administration, in the first meeting of his cabinet and staff, Carter admonished them not to argue for decisions on the basis of political considerations. He only wanted to hear about what was best for the country.[18] His presidency got off to a rocky beginning, partly because that attitude overlooked the realities of maintaining support in Congress.

We expect presidents to become more instrumental about policy—more prone to electoral calculations—as a result of various developments. These include a loss of popular support; a major political defeat; the approach of an election, especially if the president is campaigning for a second term; and losses in congressional elections. We agree with Canes-Wrone that presidents will be more prone to pandering when an approaching election is expected to be close. But we expect any election to heighten political concerns (psychologically, all elections feel close), and we expect political losses or failures to have the same effect—regardless of whether they increase or decrease the perceived closeness of the election. Put differently, we think that presidents almost never take election outcomes for granted.

Fourth, we suggest that individual differences and general political circumstances are less important than particular issues and their immediate political contexts. A president will more likely cater to a constituency if it is highly concerned and likely to be mobilized, or if the policy it demands appears to have relatively modest substantive costs. He will act on the basis of policy objectives if they appear to be substantively important. President Carter pushed hard for the highly unpopular Panama Canal Treaty, which ceded control of the canal territory to Panama, because the issue had acquired major symbolic importance in Latin America and the Third World. Presidential responses on an issue may change. For example, if a scandal, disaster, or other event raises the public salience of an issue, the president will more likely respond to public opinion on the issue. A rise in gasoline prices, for example, will greatly increase the disposition to impose economically inefficient price controls. The president also will anticipate responses based on latent opinions or sentiments. Thus, although the income tax deduction for mortgage interest is never a focus of public attention, no president has challenged it as part of a tax reform effort, knowing that a tax measure that benefits most homeowners would become highly salient in the event of a challenge.

Beyond specific policy issues, even parts of policies or programs may elicit differing presidential responses. To take one striking example, presidents sometimes will undertake a major military intervention despite public opposition, and yet will defer to public resistance on critical aspects of the intervention—such as by stipulating that American troops not perform in combat roles ("no American boots on the ground") or that they end their engagement by a date certain. The multiple features of a large public program may reflect a complex mix of political and substantive goal seeking by presidents and other policy makers.

Fifth, the strength of incentives for demand-driven policy decisions depends heavily on partisan constituencies. Most issues do not feature demands from the whole public or from a wide range of interest groups. Instead, such demands come from one or more partisan constituencies—for example, a business group or upper-income taxpayers on the Republican side or labor unions or beneficiaries of entitlement programs on the Democratic side. It is not difficult for presidents to reject substantively adverse demands from constituencies of the opposing party: satisfying them likely would not win much support from them and often will offend the president's own party constituencies. But presidents have more trouble resisting policy-adverse demands that arise from their own party. Indeed, they may find it hard even to recognize the substantive problems with those demands. Since the 1980s, many Republicans, for example, have largely accepted the proposition that large tax cuts are always desirable, regardless of fiscal circumstances.[19] Partisan ideological blinders can eliminate perceived conflicts between political and substantive considerations.

Sixth, we expect agenda effects. Whether a president chooses autonomous or demand-driven policies will depend on the status of an issue on the agenda—for example, whether Congress is already debating a proposal—and on the other issues that are on the agenda at the same time. Presidents can more easily refrain from initiating a measure that would confer new benefits on a powerful constituency than they can block such a measure once Congress has initiated it. In addition, whether a president chooses demand-driven or autonomous policy making will depend on the other issues on the agenda—for example, on how many politically costly, autonomous measures are already on the president's plate or how many issues are currently occupying public attention. The implication of the fourth, fifth, and sixth expectations taken together is that political motivations are not confined to certain general political circumstances or to the phases of the electoral cycle. We expect *some* pandering *all* of the time.

Seventh, and finally, whether a president chooses demand-driven or autonomous policy making will depend on their interactions with Congress and, in particular, on whether control of the presidency and Congress is unified or divided. That said, divided government is partly a wild card in this context.[20] It encourages the president and a Congress controlled by the opposition party to focus on electoral goals in the positions they take, since control of the entire government may be at stake in the next election. A possible result is a bidding war in which each institution, led by a different party, tries to out-pander the other.

Yet divided government also can facilitate bipartisan agreement to share responsibility for a politically painful yet substantively worthy policy change. Some major accomplishments of deficit reduction have taken that form—such as the 1990 budget agreement between the George H. W. Bush administration and the Democratic Congress. Although major feats of bipartisan cooperation in divided government are rare, lesser ones are quite common.[21]

Another consideration complicates the expectation that divided government will produce competitive pandering. As we have noted, Democrats and Republicans cater to different constituencies. What happens with such positions, then, when the presidency and Congress are controlled by different parties and must cooperate to achieve policy change? Divided government could produce bipartisan pandering, or demand-driven policies favoring both parties' constituencies. In contrast, it could block both kinds of deference to constituencies and produce generally autonomous policy that is biased toward the status quo. We see no clear way of knowing what to expect. But we speculate that the tendencies of divided government with respect to demand-driven policy will depend on the individual dispositions of the president, congressional leaders, and other Congress members. The case of President Clinton and Speaker Newt Gingrich might differ considerably from that of President Barack Obama and the Tea Party–encumbered John Boehner.

Centrist Policy, Triangulation, and Autonomous Policy Making

We turn finally to the question of how presidential centrist policy or triangulation relates to the distinction between demand-driven and autonomous policy making, or between so-called pandering and principled decisions. If the president pursues a strategy of triangulation—alternating between pushing for hard-line partisan policies and splitting the difference with partisan opponents—can we infer that his or her record amounts to a profile in convenience? In fact, triangulation and centrist presidential leadership can take distinct forms.

The central issue is why, for example, a Democratic president would endorse policies that are also attractive to congressional Republicans. For critics—especially from the president's party—the obvious explanation is the president's lack of ideological commitment. But we can expect three other major conditions for this behavior, implying different degrees of political expediency in presidential policy making. First, with a Democratic president, for example, a policy status quo may be extremely conservative relative to current preferences, such that even conservative Republicans support change toward more liberal policies. That situation might occur, for example, because a recession, an environmental scandal, or some other crisis sharply increases support for government action. The president may then compromise with the Republicans to facilitate the policy change, much as in Republican George W. Bush's big-spending response to the 2008 financial crisis. This scenario suggests not pandering but a principled response that is conditioned by strategic constraints.

Second, Republican initiatives may have such intense or broad-based support within the party's constituency—say, for a tax cut or a tough crime policy—that even a Democratic president will encounter heavy pressure to adopt them. Some Democratic constituencies may support such a policy or members of Republican constituencies may be ready to mobilize in retaliation if the president rejects it. Depending on the substantive policy considerations, the resulting deference to overwhelming demand from a constituency may or may not signify pandering.

Third, however, a Democratic president may recognize that a policy that Republicans initiate or that is attractive to them offers general substantive benefits—for example, a tax reform that increases economic productivity—and thus adopt it, even if Democratic constituencies are ambivalent or opposed. Such policy making would reflect autonomy, not pandering, and might even represent a highly principled or courageous decision.

In a word, presidential triangulation can amount to either sinking beneath ideological principle or rising above it. When such issues arise, the personal dispositions of presidents and congressional leaders—in particular, how they define their fundamental ambitions—will shape the choices they make.

Thus far we have offered theoretical analysis, identifying a number of expectations about presidential decision making and identifying some issues where we do not have firm expectations. We now look at the evidence of President Clinton's domestic policy making.

Policy Making on Autonomy Issues in the Clinton Presidency

We draw on a set of cases that we developed for a larger study in progress that examines presidents from John F. Kennedy to Barack Obama. That set of cases deals with analytic issues that are somewhat broader than those we address in this chapter. In this chapter, we use the cases that present reasonably identifiable choices between constituency- or demand-driven policy making (or pandering), on the one hand, and principled or autonomous policy making on the other hand. We call the issues in such cases autonomy issues.

Concepts and Methods

The larger study compares the performance of presidents with that of Congress with respect to four kinds of challenges that confront policy making in democratic political systems. Three of these challenges—the ones we deal with in this chapter—concern potentially distorting pressures from constituencies and thus the temptation to engage in demand-driven policy making. These challenges are:

1) to overcome pressures from organized interest groups seeking expansion or maintenance of special-interest benefits in order to serve diffuse or general interests. We call these interest-group cases and distinguish between special-interest and general-interest policies.

2) to overcome pressures from an uninformed, misinformed, emotional, or stereotyping mass public in order to serve a more informed or sophisticated view of the public's interests. Public opinion is of course never fully informed or highly sophisticated about public policy. We look at particular issues for which mass opinion is by most accounts subject to severe bias. We call these biased-opinion cases and distinguish between bias-driven and bias-correcting policies.

3) to overcome resistance from constituencies (often combining mass, interest-group, and elite elements) that do not update beliefs effectively in order to act on new, complex, or sophisticated policy information. We call these information cases and distinguish between evidence-deficient or non-analytic and evidence-based or analysis-supported policies.[22]

When policy makers face any of these challenges, they can act in either of two ways. On the one hand, they can act on the basis of informed assessments and widely recognized policy objectives. We call such policies policy-goal oriented—that is, driven by broadly based policy goals. For short, we call them responsible or principled policies. It is important to clarify that we make no implication that such policies are correct or desirable from some objective standpoint. Informed assessments can be wrong. But these responsible or principled policies are directed by credible beliefs about widely shared, defensible values. On the other hand, policymakers can act in ways that satisfy demands from powerful public or interest-group constituencies. We call such policies demand-driven, electorally oriented, or constituency-driven policies—that is, driven by the immediate preferences or demands of the most powerful relevant constituencies. In other words, pandering.[23]

An advantageous feature of our selection of policy issues is that it was designed for the purposes of the larger study and should not have any systematic bias with respect to the Clinton presidency. In the larger study, we looked for long-term policy issues that recur fairly frequently from one presidency to another, that would each fit one of the challenge types relatively cleanly (instead of reflecting a combination of two or more of the challenges); and that, collectively (not in each case), would avoid conferring any marked advantage in expected performance to presidents or congressional majorities of either political party. Our assessment of potential cases was guided by the existing literature on the nature of policy problems and the political forces that shape and may distort policy making. None of our selections of issues derive from our own thinking; they are not the policies we happen to favor and they do not derive from our own interpretations of policy making. Our distinctions have no consistent relation to ideological direction. Nor do we rely on categorizing broad classes of policies as demand driven or principled—for example, assuming that expansion of environmental regulation is always principled, that expansion of entitlement programs is always demand driven, and the like. Rather, in coding the direction of specific policies, we rely on the specific issues and the nonpartisan commentary and policy literature on each issue.

This process yielded twelve long-term policy issues that include cases in the Clinton administration. The interest-group cases include those related to tax reform, pollution control, agriculture subsidies, management of public lands, and support for competitive deregulation. The biased, demand-driven cases include those related to energy pricing and conservation, drug abuse and violent crime, entitlement programs, and regulation of health and safety. The cases related to assessment of information include those about economic stabilization, compensatory education, and employment programs. For any issue, a relevant case occurs only when the stipulated conflict arises. For example, an economic stabilization case occurs in the information category only when a significant proposal calls for stimulus spending under conditions when most economic analysis does not support it. A pro-competitive deregulation case occurs in the interest-group category only when economic analysis calls for deregulation but there is powerful interest-group opposition.

Within each policy area, we identified all relevant legislative proposals mentioned in academic histories or studies of policy making. We included any proposals that were prominently proposed by either branch of Congress or were actively considered in that body, including those that ultimately failed to be enacted. Any bill that met the threshold of attention and support was included whether it became law, was vetoed, failed in legislative floor votes, or died in committee.

This process of policy identification resulted in a data set of twenty-four legislative measures during the Clinton presidency. We do not claim that our cases are representative of the universe of domestic policy issues in the Clinton presidency. Rather, they are a diverse set of cases that should be free of selection bias associated with the Clinton presidency and that test the relevant performance tendencies in distinctive ways.

TABLE 2.1 Selection of issues and measures

ISSUE	TYPES OF MEASURES INCLUDED	POLICY ANALYSIS	POLITICAL ANALYSIS
Management of public lands	Interest-group politics: Proposals to encourage multiple use of public lands were coded general interest; proposals to preserve low-cost access for industries were coded special interest.	Long-standing low fees and prices encouraged overuse, leading to environmental damage and loss of government revenue.	Regulated industries (mining, grazing, timber, and water) advocate special-interest policies.
Tax reform	Interest-group politics: Efforts at tax reform by reducing the extent of tax expenditures were coded general interest; proposals for new or expanded tax expenditures (without widely credited benefits to the general public) were coded special interest.	Economists do not see most tax expenditures as being in the general interest.	Well-organized beneficiaries of tax expenditures advocate special-interest policies.
Pollution control	Interest-group politics: Proposals to regulate new forms of pollution were coded general interest; proposals to make major exceptions or allowances that benefited well-organized groups were coded special interest.	Federal action is required due to the interstate nature of many pollution problems, which prevents effective state and local action.	Regulated industries, mainly manufacturing and power, advocate special-interest policies, frequently in alliance with ideological conservatives
Agricultural commodity subsidies	Interest-group politics: Proposals to expand price supports were coded special interest; proposals to reduce price support benefits were coded general interest.	Agricultural policy analysts see price supports as inefficient.	Well-organized beneficiaries advocate special-interest policies. Farmers are a publicly sympathetic constituency, further complicating general-interest policy making in this area.
Pro-competitive deregulation	Interest-group politics: Proposals to deregulate protected industries were coded general interest; proposals to defend the regulatory regimes were coded special interest.	Policies that suppress competition have the effects of reducing services and raising prices for consumers.	Regulated industries and related labor organizations that benefit from the protection of anti-competitive policies advocate special-interest measures.

(Continued)

TABLE 2.1 (Continued)

ISSUE	TYPES OF MEASURES INCLUDED	POLICY ANALYSIS	POLITICAL ANALYSIS
Energy pricing and conservation	Biased-opinion policies: Proposals that efficiently reflected energy costs were coded bias correcting; those that insulated the public from those costs were coded bias driven.	Analysts recommend economically efficient energy conservation policies that reflect the true cost of the resource and incorporate social costs such as pollution.	Effective policy making is challenged by mass public resistance to personal conservation and dislike of higher prices.
Drug abuse and violent crime	Biased-opinion policies: Policies that shifted the balance of criminal justice efforts away from a punitive direction were coded bias correcting; those retaining punitive approaches were coded bias driven.	Criminologists urge more emphasis on prevention; drug policy experts urge more emphasis on education and treatment.	Effective policy making is challenged by public preference for strong responses, probably most pronounced among conservatives.
Entitlement spending	Biased-opinion policies: Proposals to reform entitlement programs by addressing long-term budget issues were coded bias correcting; those that would expand program benefits were coded bias driven.	Analysts concerned with the long-term federal budget recommend a variety of ways of reducing the flow of benefits.	Effective policy making is challenged by the wide popularity of program benefits. Entitlement programs for the elderly have particularly large, well-organized, and sympathetic clienteles.
Health and safety regulation	Biased-opinion policies: Proposals to reform regulations to take account of costs and benefits were coded bias correcting; those that would expand regulation without addressing risk assessment were coded bias driven.	Analysts recommend more systematic risk assessment, including accounting for cost-benefit ratios	Effective policy making is challenged by public concerns about regulated dangers and mis-estimation of health risks. These are overlaid with ideological attitudes toward regulation, with liberals tending to support regulation and conservatives tending to oppose it regardless of risk assessment.

	Evidence based policies	Shifting views	Public officials
Economic stabilization	Evidence based policies: Policy responses that incorporated the current macroeconomic consensus were coded evidence based; those that reflected ideological views or an outdated consensus were coded evidence deficient.	Shifting views among economists about macro-economy, especially after the collapse of the Keynesian paradigm	Public officials are often slow to react to new economic information because of the mass public's preference for stimulative action during recessions and because of ideological preferences for public works programs (liberals) and supply-side economics (conservatives).
Compensatory education	Evidence based policies: Proposals that accounted for new research evaluations were coded evidence based; those that reflected outdated information were coded evidence deficient.	Shifting evaluations of Head Start and Chapter I programs	Public officials are often slow to react to new research about the effectiveness of compensatory programs because of the mass public's support for those programs.
Employment programs	Evidence based policies: Policy responses that incorporated the current economic consensus were coded evidence based; those that reflected ideological views or an outdated consensus were coded evidence deficient.	Shifting views among economists about causes of structural unemployment	Public officials are often slow to react to new research on employment programs because unemployed workers who want job training are a sympathetic constituency, probably most so among liberals.

Using a wide range of sources, we classified each proposal according to its overall tendency within the specific policy dimension—for example, to reduce or eliminate existing special-interest benefits or to defend those benefits or create new ones. We identified the positions Clinton and the most relevant congressional actors (for example, a House or Senate majority that passes a bill) took. Finally, we looked at the change in the president's position during the time the policy was considered. Our identification of Clinton's initial position is based on policy statements when possible, as is our identification of his final position. When initial policy positions were not available, we used a default assumption that he started from a mainstream Democratic Party position, so that a subsequent less liberal stance represents a change.

Scholars of the Clinton administration define triangulation as (1) moving to the center when Republican positions are popular; (2) resisting the GOP's unpopular initiatives; and (3) promoting Democratic policies that are popular with the public. This pattern appears in a number of policy issues.[24] In analyzing particular cases, we focus on whether Clinton's position moved closer to that of Republicans—a triangulating concession, in our terms. We also determine whether such triangulating concessions improved or worsened the measure's performance on the particular policy challenge and note whether it enabled a measure to pass.

Cases and Findings

We now review the evidence of our cases in three periods, each with distinct political characteristics, commenting on their bearing on our expectations as we proceed. As noted above, each legislative proposal in our data was considered significant enough to be discussed in a secondary work about the policy area and each one dealt with a policy issue that, on the basis of relevant scholarship, we identify as presenting a relatively clear conflict between a responsible or principled position and some form of demand-driven, politically expedient, or pandering position. Thus, the proposals were either principled or demand driven, they were initiated by the president or Congress, and they were either successful or blocked.

A New President and Unified Control

When Clinton assumed office in 1993, he was the first Democratic president in twelve years. Both houses of Congress were under Democratic control, as they had been for most of the preceding six decades. But with the Democrats three votes short of a filibuster-proof, 60-vote supermajority in the Senate, the Republicans still had considerable leverage. Democratic congressional leaders were eager to promote the success of a Democratic president.

In his first Congress, in 1993–1994, President Clinton initiated most of the measures in our survey, six of eight. As we would expect of a new president, nearly all of his proposals, five of six, were coded as principled. In promoting these measures, Clinton made triangulation-style concessions (taking an ideologically more moderate position) to the Republicans on three of these five. In each of the three cases, the result was a gain for principled, goal-oriented policy.

Clinton's 1993 deficit reduction plan included a modest-sized, principled, bipartisan approach to Medicare costs. Centrist Democratic members of Congress, led by Senators David Boren of Oklahoma and John Breaux of Louisiana, had sought a more fundamental overhaul, which Republicans also favored, but Clinton rejected such an ambitious approach—an element of constituency deference within the context of a large, complex measure—because of concerns about public reaction. The deficit reduction act as passed by Congress included small, triangulated steps toward cost reduction: cuts in hospital reimbursement rates, cuts in physician fees, and cuts in salaries of residents and interns at teaching hospitals. The act also addressed the shaky financial future of the Social Security program by raising the cap on individual earnings subject to the payroll tax.[25]

In February 1993, President Clinton proposed a liberal, principled, broad-based energy tax, which he defended on both environmental and economic grounds. The "Btu tax" would have affected all energy consumption, including an increase in pump prices for gasoline of 7.5 cents per gallon. It met with strong resistance in both congressional parties. Republicans opposed it unanimously, some Democrats objected to the effect it would have on the oil industry, and other Democrats were nervous about the public's reaction to a tax increase targeted at their lifestyles. Economic advisor Alice Rivlin suggested later it may have been too technically based to have any political appeal: "It sounds sort of weird. Everybody knew what a gasoline tax was, but what's a British Thermal Unit, for heaven's sakes?"

Following what Senate Democratic leader George Mitchell called "an extremely long struggle to get enough Democrats to agree to any tax increase," enough senators were found to support a smaller increase that applied only to gasoline. Clinton agreed to limit the tax to 4.3 cents per gallon, which was probably too small to affect consumer behavior. The triangulated measure barely passed Congress.[26]

Clinton succeeded in nudging crime policy away from the traditional, predominantly punitive approach that most experts criticized and toward the bias-correcting prevention provisions of the 1994 Violent Crime Control and

Law Enforcement Act. At the same time, in deference to mass public demands, many of the bill's provisions emphasized longer or more severe punishment. It funded prison construction and police hiring, made federal grants conditional on states' enacting tougher policies, made about fifty federal crimes subject to the death penalty, provided for life imprisonment for a third violent felony conviction (a Republican proposal dubbed "three strikes and you're out"), and extended provisions for trying juveniles as adults. Polling advisor Stanley Greenberg claimed that "we didn't do any polling on which elements of the Crime Bill would be the most popular. Only after they had developed an approach on dealing with crime did we then poll the elements," but the mass appeal of get-tough crime policies would have been obvious even in the absence of hard polling numbers. Liberal policy advisor Peter Edelman described Clinton's team as politically on the defensive when it came to crime: "Essentially they were passive. . . . Basically they were like a little boat in the ocean being pushed around by the waves." Liberal House Democrats' amendments to restrict the scope of the death penalty provisions were defeated.

Clinton's proposal also contained principled elements aimed at crime prevention. It targeted about a quarter of its funding toward prevention programs, such as inner-city midnight basketball leagues, and increased the budget for drug treatment programs. The prevention programs made the bill controversial in Congress. House Republicans defeated the rule for one conference agreement in August 1994. But a second conference report cleared both houses, and Clinton signed it. The move away from a punitive approach was real, although modest: about $7 billion out of a total authorization of $30 billion went for crime prevention. However, Clinton's proposed increases for drug treatment programs were slashed from $355 million to $57 million.[27]

Clinton did not triangulate on his other two principled proposals, but there were arguably no opportunities to do so. Both bills died in Congress. He introduced an expert-informed, nonideological compensatory education proposal in 1994. In response to criticism from education experts that the existing aid program failed to target areas of greatest need, Clinton proposed refocusing money on the poorest districts. The proposal was defeated in the House because too many districts would have lost funding under the new formula. Although a subcommittee of the House Education and Labor Committee was controlled by Democrats, it rejected the measure; only members from poor districts supported it.[28]

On drug policy, Clinton proposed a bias-correcting principled change—cutting the government's interdiction budget by 7 percent. His Office of Drug Control Policy's report called interdiction "an expensive high technology endeavor . . . [whose] effectiveness has been undercut by increased drug production and the continued high profitability of the trade."[29] Edelman credited the administration with "actually reaching the best ratio of treatment and prevention to law enforcement that we'd had as a country since we started the so-called drug war. We got the numbers closer to 50/50 than they'd ever been." But the proposed cut got no support from either congressional party and appropriations reflected no change. On compensatory education and drug control, Clinton had no apparent chance for genuine accomplishment and settled for principled position taking.

The only early Clinton initiative we coded as constituency driven or pandering was the emergency supplemental appropriations bill of 1993, known as the stimulus bill. Clinton did not make triangulating concessions on the bill, and conservatives in the Senate blocked it. The Clinton administration and congressional Democrats proposed liberal spending measures to stimulate the economy, despite contrary economic advice and signs of recovery from the 1990–1991 recession. Leon Panetta, then director of the Office of Management and Budget, later characterized the administration's thinking: "Politically, . . . you [may] need to do it, but substantively it's not going to make that much difference in turning around the economy. It will take effect too late and it's going to cost a lot of money."

The Clinton stimulus package initially called for $30 billion for job creation and highway-related infrastructure. The House cut the amount nearly in half to allay the concerns of conservative Democrats—essentially triangulating on the president's behalf—and then passed it on a vote that followed party lines. Republicans successfully filibustered it in the Senate. Democrats had hoped that public enthusiasm for the demand-driven measure would shift the ground in the Senate, but the public proved ambivalent about further stimulus.[30]

Two congressional initiatives are among our 1993–1994 cases—one principled, one demand driven, but neither successful. Despite Clinton's attempt to use triangulating concessions to increase the chances for success of a principled (general-interest) mining reform bill, it was blocked in the Senate. Democrats on the House Committee on Natural Resources produced a liberal general-interest measure that would have increased royalties on minerals extracted from public lands to 12.5 percent. Clinton included the measure in the 1993 deficit reduction package. Although the House approved the provision, western senators, led by Montana Democrat Max Baucus, persuaded Clinton to drop it in the Senate—a triangulating move toward the center. House Democrats tried again, passing a strong mining reform bill that included an 8 percent royalty and environmental regulations on a vote that mostly followed party lines. The Senate, which was more responsive to mining interests in small, mostly western states, then approved a weak, industry-backed bill that Committee on Energy and Natural Resources chair J. Bennett Johnston (D-La.) called a "ticket to conference,"[31] implying that he hoped to strengthen it there. But the mining industry refused to make significant concessions during the conference committee negotiations and Johnston's efforts to fashion a compromise collapsed.[32] Congressional allies of the mining industry from both parties consistently thwarted Clinton's responsible (general-interest) mining-reform efforts for the remainder of his administration.

The second 1993–1994 congressional initiative was demand driven. Clinton took no public position on a 1994 special-interest tax measure that died in the Senate Finance Committee. The finance subcommittee on taxation held hearings on two measures to provide tax relief to the oil and gas industry, sponsored by David Boren (D-Okla.) and John Breaux (D-La.), respectively. At a friendly meeting, President Clinton gave members from oil and gas states the impression that he would consider including the tax relief in an omnibus tax bill or even the health care reform bill, but no such agreement was ever reached and the measures died.[33] Clinton may have taken advantage of internal divisions in Congress over a special-interest measure to avoid overtly offending a powerful group and its Senate patrons.

During 1993–1994, then, Clinton triangulated on four of six principled bills and three of those passed. He did not triangulate on four bills—two principled, two not—and none of them passed. In these cases, at least, presidential triangulation generally served principled policy making.

The "Gingrich Congress"

Circumstances in Congress changed dramatically after historic gains in the 1994 midterm elections swept Republicans to majority status in both chambers. Led by the energetic, exceptionally ambitious new speaker of the House, Newt Gingrich of Georgia, Republicans seized the policy initiative and sought to enact the measures contained in their campaign platform, which they called the Contract with America. Much like a newly elected activist president,[34] Gingrich overestimated his public mandate and the Republicans were quickly accused of overreaching. Although the majority-dominated House of Representatives passed almost the entire Contract with America, only five of its twenty-one bills eventually became law. The Republicans' momentum ended in a budget standoff with Clinton in which they were surprised to find public opinion siding strongly with the president.[35]

The Republican Congress initiated six of the seven measures in our survey during this period. Four of the six were principled, driven by substantive policy goals rather than driven by constituency demands. Clinton made triangulating concessions on two bipartisan measures both of which were enacted and produced policy gains: a fundamental reform of agricultural commodity support programs and a measure requiring cost-benefit analysis for health and safety regulations.

The Gingrich-led Republican Congress in 1995 initiated a dramatic bipartisan general-interest measure that called for the complete abolition of farm subsidies, which supporters generally regarded as a wasteful and inefficient legacy of the 1930s Depression. Clinton initially resisted but eventually joined the reform effort. He vetoed the first version of agricultural reform; Clinton's agriculture secretary said it would be "just plain stupid . . . to unilaterally disarm"[36] while European countries were still subsidizing their crops. But with planting season imminent, Clinton felt he could no longer block the reform and signed a new version of the bill in April 1996.[37] His switch to a principled position illustrates the effect of congressional agenda setting on the president's choices. In the absence of the congressional initiative, Clinton certainly would have let sleeping special-interest agricultural policy dogs lie.

In a similar process, Congress achieved policy-oriented reforms of two regulatory statutes in 1996. Challenging mass-opinion bias toward rigid regulation to protect public health and safety, Senators John Chafee (R-R.I.) and Max Baucus (D-Mont.) won an amendment to the Safe Drinking Water Act requiring the Environmental Protection Agency to use cost-benefit analysis when formulating rules. That same year, congressional Republicans won unanimous passage of a bill to modify the standards for approving agricultural pesticides. The Delaney Clause, part of the Food Additives Amendment of 1958, barred processed food from containing any measurable amount of any chemical found to cause cancer in any animal in any concentration; the new law required "a reasonable certainty" that pesticide residues in raw or processed food would cause no harm.[38] Clinton, who made no counterproposals, signed both bills into law, having again been led to accept principled reform by the agenda setting of the Republican Congress.

Clinton did not make ideological concessions on the Gingrich Congress's two identifiably conservative principled measures in our study, both of which were blocked: a regulatory reform bill killed by a Democratic-led Senate filibuster and changes to Medicare that Clinton vetoed. On Medicare, his position clearly reflected the hard-line partisan posture that a broad triangulating strategy calls for on issues where the president's party has a popular advantage. Concerning regulatory reform, House Republicans introduced a collection of conservative measures in 1995 that carried out one of the planks in the Contract with America. The proposals included bias-correcting requirements for risk-assessment and cost-benefit analysis. Clinton announced his opposition to the comprehensive reform bill, stating that he preferred a statute-by-statute approach. The House ignored him and quickly passed the comprehensive reforms, but the Senate was unable to break a Democratic filibuster.[39] Although Republican members of Congress continued to introduce comprehensive reform bills in subsequent years, the party eventually deemphasized that approach in favor of the incremental bills Clinton supported. A *New York Times* columnist suggested that the Republicans had "lost . . . enthusiasm for regulatory reform" because the 1995–1996 government shutdown had created a public perception that the party wanted to disable the government.[40]

In 1995, Clinton blocked an expert-driven, conservative Medicare policy. Gingrich and the House Republicans sought to address rapid growth in Medicare expenditures by encouraging recipients to switch to managed care programs. The bill also would have slowed Medicare spending increases by $270 billion over seven years.[41] Clinton vetoed the congressional plan and presented a smaller-scale alternative that bought some time for the Medicare trust fund but did not address the long-term issue. Republicans agreed to Clinton's approach, reportedly fearing a drubbing in the 1996 elections if they pushed the structural changes.[42] Notably, it was the hard-line side of triangulating—firm defense of Democratic constituency demands—that scotched the principled reform.

Clinton did not make triangulating concessions on the two Republican congressional measures that were largely driven by constituency demands, one calling for substantial environmental deregulation and the other calling for punitive anti-crime measures.

In the first, Clinton vetoed a Republican-sponsored special-interest effort to limit drastically the regulatory authority of the Environmental Protection Agency. The bill would have weakened regulation in seventeen specific areas, including industrial and refinery emissions, pollutants in drinking water, and sewage overflows. Leon Panetta and Alice Rivlin, speaking for the president, issued veto threats on several occasions between July and November 1995. The bill was narrowed considerably in the Senate, retaining only one provision related to regulation of pollution in drinking water. House conferees did not push to restore the stricken provisions, and Clinton vetoed what remained of the bill on December 18.[43]

In the second case, Clinton, with the help of Senate Democrats, blocked a series of conservative crime bills in which congressional Republicans catered to bias-driven mass opinion with a series of punitive measures. One bill sought to move nearly all funding for crime-prevention programs into law enforcement or prison construction. In that case, Democrats were able to prevent committee action in the Senate.[44] The House passed another bill to decrease funding for crime-prevention programs, but a Democratic filibuster blocked it in the Senate. When Republicans added the provision to an appropriations bill, Clinton vetoed it.[45] In these cases, the differences in party constituencies helped defeat partisan pandering by the congressional majority.

The Gingrich-dominated 1995–1996 Congress featured few initiatives by the president. The only Clinton initiative in our set of cases from this period was a demand-driven increase in spending for job-training programs. Despite his constructive, triangulating appeal to the Republican desire to consolidate job-training programs, the bill died in both houses. Clinton and most congressional Democrats ignored or discounted extensive research that demonstrated the ineffectiveness of traditional, large-scale training programs. Meanwhile, Republicans on the House Economic and Educational Opportunities Committee followed expert advice and consolidated the job-training programs they proposed, reducing the number from 100 to four in the committee bill. They also sought to devolve the programs to the states, which was more politically contentious. Clinton cautiously supported the Republican consolidation effort in 1995 while continuing to argue for more funding. Both houses passed jobs program bills with bipartisan support. But when the conference committee made its report six months later, congressional Democrats rejected Republican positions on funding levels and oversight, and the measure died without a final vote on either floor. [16]

Overall, Clinton made triangulating concessions on three measures in the 104th Congress: two principled congressional initiatives passed and one demand-driven presidential initiative did not. He did not make concessions on four congressional bills—two principled, two not—and none of them passed. In general, the triangulating concessions had constructive effects in promoting principled policy change. Indeed, further opportunities for triangulating policy achievement were left on the table.

Clinton's Second Term

The 1996 elections returned Clinton to the White House and Republican majorities to both the House and Senate, with a small loss of seats in the House and a small gain in the Senate. The 105th and 106th Congresses featured less dramatic domestic policy making than during Clinton's first term; both Democrats and Republicans promoted more subdued policy ambitions. Both branches were also distracted from domestic issues by U.S. military involvement in the former Yugoslavia and, throughout 1998 and early 1999, by investigation of Clinton's Monica Lewinsky scandal, the latter of which culminated in impeachment proceedings.

The Republican Congress initiated seven of eight measures in our survey during Clinton's second term. A majority of them, four of seven, were demand driven. Clinton did not make triangulating concessions on any of the four. Three of these congressional initiatives catered to Republican constituencies: repeal of regulations on mining on public lands, an income tax cut, and increased penalties for juvenile criminal offenders. With Clinton opposed, none of them passed.

Clinton refused to support a Republican special-interest bill that would have benefited mining companies, resulting in the defeat of that constituency-driven measure. In 1999, during Senate action on Interior Department appropriations, Senator Larry Craig (R-Idaho) won an amendment that would have rolled back regulations on mining sites. Although the Senate passed the appropriations bill with Craig's amendment, Clinton's veto threat meant that the conference committee removed it.[47]

Clinton resisted congressional Republicans' constituency-oriented, economically dubious supply-side tax cut. A 1999 House Republican tax bill would have deeply cut personal income taxes and capital gains taxes and phased out estate taxes altogether. The projected revenue loss would have been $792 billion over ten years. Insisting on more restraint, moderate Republicans succeeded in making the cuts in the final version contingent on a shrinking national debt. Nevertheless, Clinton vetoed the modified bill.[48]

Clinton also helped block the passage of a 1999 bill generated by congressional conservatives that would have increased penalties for juvenile offenders. Republicans on the House Judiciary Subcommittee on Crime offered the provision. Congressional Democrats were divided; some supported the constituency-driven effort and others objected to its punitive approach. Although Clinton did not endorse the juvenile punishment provisions, he did propose including liberal gun safety requirements in the bill. But negotiations with congressional Republicans stalled. Despite resumed efforts after a 1999 mass school shooting in Colorado, the bill failed in conference committee in 2000.[49] In short, Clinton's opposition helped block Republican constituency-oriented measures on all three of these issues.

The fourth congressional demand-driven initiative was bipartisan—an agriculture bill that began the unraveling of the 1996 reform. Clinton supported and worked to expand a 1998 effort to undo the drastic reductions in agriculture commodity support that had been enacted only two years earlier. A sharp drop in crop prices created an opportunity for farm lobbyists to challenge the phasing out of price supports, bolstered by a generally sympathetic public. Far from reluctant, Clinton advocated a higher level of emergency farm aid than congressional Republicans did, and in October 1998 he even vetoed the first agricultural appropriations bill as too stingy. Congress tried again by adding $2.7 billion in aid and tax breaks, which roughly split the difference between the two sides, and Clinton signed the new bill.[50] Clinton had reluctantly joined the Republican Congress in a principled reform of agriculture in 1996 and rushed to the vanguard of the bipartisan movement to undo that reform in 1998.

Three congressional initiatives in this period were principled. Clinton made major triangulating concessions on two of them: cuts in Medicare spending, which passed, and the deregulation of electric utilities, which did not.

Clinton and congressional Republicans agreed to make small cost cuts in the financially troubled Medicare program. Surrendering ideological ground at a budget summit after the 1996 elections, Clinton accepted a mishmash of Medicare spending cuts while continuing to avoid dealing with the program's long-term financing problems.[51] In the end, progress on entitlement financing reflected economic fortune more than political fortitude. When Social Security revenue grew more quickly than expected, Clinton and the Republicans canceled their earlier decisions to cap the growth of Medicare and reduce cost-of-living adjustments for retirees.[52]

President Clinton agreed in 2000 to a nonideological, general-interest congressional approach to deregulating markets in electricity, setting aside some liberal concerns about consumer protection. The gesture went for naught, however, because Congress could not settle on specific provisions. The natural gas industry and independent power producers supported the deregulation of electric utilities, but the utilities strongly opposed it.[53] In 1999, Representative Joe L. Barton (R-Tex.), chair of the House Energy and Power Subcommittee, sponsored a bill to break up local electric power monopolies by allowing consumers to buy their power from any utility. His subcommittee approved the measure in the fall. Clinton joined in, calling for the opening up of electricity markets.

Despite broad political support for that objective, however, the bill was blocked in both chambers in the summer of 2000, when deregulation advocates disagreed among themselves about several issues. Clinton and many congressional Democrats wanted provisions to ensure equitable access to power transmission lines; without them, charged Massachusetts Democrat Edward J. Markey, the bill would give industry "a green light to engage in a wide array of unfair, predatory and manipulative practices."[54] Clinton also wanted the bill to promote the growth of renewable energy sources. Meanwhile, the House Commerce Committee had difficulty resolving both the roles of the state and federal governments in implementing the law and policy toward power firms that had suffered financial losses on new generating plants.[55] Although electricity deregulation offered an opportunity for bipartisan policy achievement, it was too complex to be handled in the time available before the 2000 elections.

The third of the policy-oriented congressional initiatives in Clinton's second term was the Ocean Shipping Reform Act of 1998, a nonideological general-interest law that sought to deregulate shipping rates. Clinton supported the four-year effort in Congress that resulted in its passage. The measure originated with House Republicans on the Transportation and Infrastructure Committee. Democratic support was intermittent because of labor union opposition, and coastal senators blocked consideration in that chamber in the 104th Congress.[56] In 1997, however, Senator Kay Bailey Hutchison (R-Tex.) found a formula satisfactory to all sides. By making shippers' rates publicly accessible, her proposal allayed fears that large companies could underbid their smaller competitors. The bill passed both houses by voice vote, and Clinton signed it into law in October 1998.[57] On a general-interest reform that was bipartisan even in Congress, Clinton had only to join with the supportive Democrats to help bring about successful action.

Clinton was the initiator of only one bill in our study during his second term, an indication of the Republican Congress's control of the agenda. It was a principled measure on dairy pricing. There was no occasion for ideological concessions. In any case, the bill died in the House Agriculture Committee.

Clinton had attempted a nonideological general-interest reform on dairy price supports in 1999, but it was blocked by the House Agriculture Committee. Clinton's bill would have enacted a smaller, more streamlined system of supports, which the Department of Agriculture sought. But dairy state members of both parties opposed the effort and pushed through appropriations language defending the existing price support system. Rep. John Boehner (R-Ohio), who unsuccessfully sought to abolish all dairy price supports by 2001, grumbled afterward, "It's a wonder any gallon of milk gets from the cow to the marketplace."[58] Clinton signed the unreformed appropriations package on November 29.

Of the eight measures that fit our study criteria from Clinton's second term, the president had both the occasion and the disposition to make ideological concessions to the Republican Congress on only two. Both bills were substantive goal-driven, principled initiatives by the Republican Congress—one of which (Medicare cuts) passed, a significant achievement, while the other (electricity deregulation) died in the Senate, notwithstanding Clinton's flexibility. He did not make ideological concessions on five other congressional bills, all but one of which were driven by Republican constituency demands. Without requiring triangulating concessions, Congress passed one major principled measure, the Ocean Shipping Reform Act, and one massively costly constituency-driven bill, the restoration of farm price supports. So in this period, triangulating concessions sometimes facilitated policy achievement, but they were not always required for it.

Conclusion: Two Cheers for Triangulation

Our analysis of case-study evidence provides support for some of our theoretical expectations and sheds light on questions we could not answer, one way or the other, on theoretical grounds. The twenty-four cases cited in this chapter are certainly not representative of the universe of domestic policy issues that the president and Congress dealt with during the Clinton administration. Rather, they are distinctively revealing—cases in which the relevant actors (the president and either Congress or a part of Congress) addressed issues that presented

conflicts that were more than normally clear between respectable policy considerations and predominant constituency demands and thus made either principled or demand-driven responses. The cases also enabled us to take note of
what happened when President Clinton offered triangulating concessions—that
is, ideological concessions to the Republicans. The results are revealing, both
about President Clinton's motivations and, more generally, about the nature and
consequences of presidential compromise and moderation. The findings do not
support left-wing Democrats' jaundiced view of triangulation. They also provide a relatively benign view of divided party control of government, even when
marked by considerable ideological polarization of the parties.

Party control of Congress had a dramatic effect on whose bills—the president's or Congress's—became significant enough to warrant comment by scholars and thus be included in our study. In Clinton's first Congress (1993–1994),
almost all of the bills were presidential initiatives; in all Congresses after the 1994
midterm elections, congressional initiatives predominated and presidential ones
nearly disappeared.

Our set of twenty-four cases from Clinton's eight years in office do not permit
a fine-grained analysis of the effects of time or general political circumstances
on Clinton's choices between principled and demand-driven policy making.
We do find evidence of some "pandering" (or decisions based on electoral considerations) all of the time. Clinton was led by concern about support from
the general public or a particular constituency on one or more issues in every
period: 1993–1994, 1995–1996, and 1997–2001. This finding comports with
our suggestion that the crucial political conditions that elicit demand-driven
or principled responses are tied to particular issues, constituencies, and issue
contexts. The principled reform that the Gingrich Congress led on agriculture
price supports in 1996 did not withstand the development of a farm crisis two
years later.

The cases also support our expectation that a new president will start out
ambitious and principle driven, then become more attuned to electoral goals and
constituency demands as he or she encounters the inevitable political defeats.
Clinton's initiatives and positions were nearly all principled in his first two years,
which ended with his embarrassing defeat on health care reform and crushing
party losses in the 1994 midterm elections. His choices were more mixed thereafter. A comparable pattern emerges for the Republican Congress.

We find clear support for our view that demand-driven decisions are generally
tied to partisan constituencies. Clinton deferred to the interests or preferences
of low-income people, consumer and environmental activists, and entitlement
recipients; Republicans deferred to the interests or preferences of upper-income
people and business. Some constituency leanings were less clear: both Clinton

and the Republicans were initially opposed to inefficient farm subsidies that benefited farmers but later supported them. In general, however, each party's willingness to ignore pressures from the other party's constituencies was more pure and consistent than we anticipated.

Indeed, the partisan divide in targeted constituencies had strong implications for the effects of divided government and policy moderation. Neither the Democrats (including Clinton) nor the Republicans abandoned the positions of their own partisan constituencies in response to powerful demands of other-party constituencies. Under divided government, congressional Republicans proposed bold measures that appealed to their constituencies, such as upper-income tax cuts and relief from environmental regulation. In a nightmare scenario, the Democrats, seeking to contest such constituencies or reduce the Republican advantages with them, would have gone along with the measures, allowing them to be enacted into law. Instead, Clinton and the Democrats blocked them. In turn, Republicans blocked proposals by the Democrats that were directed toward their constituencies. The overall result was notable: In Clinton's entire two-term presidency, taking our twenty-four bills dealing with twelve ongoing issues together, only a single predominantly demand-driven measure was enacted. That measure was the 1998 reversal of the dramatic and unexpected law that enacted a phased abolition of agricultural price supports in 1996—a policy that merely returned policy to the pre-1996 status quo. In contrast, policy improvements—that is to say, changes that moved toward principled policy—occurred in a variety of areas: control of entitlements, deregulation of competitive industries, expansion of crime prevention, and others. Bipartisan pandering bidding wars did not occur in these areas.

It is unclear how far we can generalize this favorable assessment of the effects of divided government and partisan compromise on the tendency for the president and Congress to produce principled policies. The Clinton experience may contrast with the experience of President George W. Bush, during whose administration tax cuts and program expansion combined to produce fiscally disastrous long-term policy outcomes.[59] And the performance of divided government during the Obama administration was deeply problematic, to the extent that international leaders increasingly discounted American economic leadership.[60] The obvious starting point for explaining differences in the performance of divided government at different times is the degree of ideological polarization between the parties.[61] We suspect, however, that the inclinations of leaders—the degree to which they have goals for policy achievement, beyond winning elections—are also crucial.

Clinton's strategy of triangulation was a constructive approach to presidential leadership, at least in the circumstances he faced. The president's concessions on ideological issues were central to the possibilities for significant policy change. And because of the dispositions of the period's main political leaders—in particular, President Clinton and Speaker Gingrich—and the preferences and commitments of the two parties, significant policy change usually served a constructive purpose.

Part II
DOMESTIC AND
ECONOMIC POLICY

COMPROMISE AND CONFRONTATION

Clinton's Evolving Relationship with Congress

Sean M. Theriault, Patrick T. Hickey, and Megan Moeller

In the days after the November 2014 midterm elections, some argued that the Clinton presidency furnished the best playbook for Barack Obama in confronting Republican majorities in the House of Representatives and Senate. According to the pundits, Obama needed to bargain, compromise, and problem solve with House Speaker John Boehner and Senate Majority Leader Mitch McConnell in the same way that Clinton had worked with Speaker Newt Gingrich and Majority Leaders Bob Dole and Trent Lott. Just as Clinton and Republicans in Congress had ended welfare as we knew it, balanced the budget, and provided for the largest peacetime economic growth in our country's history, so could Obama and the Republicans reform the immigration system, rewrite the tax code, and spur economic development.

Consistent, in part, with the punditry after the 2014 elections, we think the Clinton-Congress relationship can usefully be analyzed to offer insight into Obama's quandary. In contrast to the punditry, though, we do not think that the lesson to be drawn is that Clinton was able to overcome an opposition Congress to achieve major legislative successes. (After all, the House of Representatives impeached him.) Rather, we think the relationship between the president and Congress fundamentally changed during the Clinton years. Presidents had always found their relationships with an opposition-dominated Congress to be cantankerous, but we uncover a worsening inflection point in Clinton's second term. Over the intervening twenty years, the names have changed, but the relationship has increasingly deteriorated.

In this chapter, we take a closer look at President Clinton's record with Congress. We argue that the relationship between the president and Congress, especially the Senate, underwent a transformational change in the late 1990s. We pin this change on a group of senators who brought Newt Gingrich–style politics to the Senate. This brand of politics was particularly damaging because of the Senate's unique features, which give incredible power to each individual senator. We make this argument in a series of steps. First, we outline the tools that all presidents have at their disposal to get a recalcitrant Congress—or even a compliant one—to enact their legislative program. Second, we compare the legislative record of the Clinton Congresses with the records of other modern American presidents. Third, we examine more closely the relationship between Clinton and his Senate adversaries. Fourth, we conclude by arguing that the trends that started under Clinton continue almost with reckless abandon today.

The Tools of the President

The modern American president's role in the legislative process is aptly summarized as "the legislator in chief." This role results from what the Constitution prescribes and the development of both formal and informal presidential powers over the course of American history. At the ultimate step in the legislative process, the president can either sign a bill into law or make its enactment much more difficult with a veto. Furthermore, the constitutional mandate to update Congress "from time to time" and recommend "necessary and expedient" measures (Article II, section 3) gives the president significant power in setting the legislative agenda. The president can also call Congress back in to session at will (Article II, section 3).

Beyond the dictates of the Constitution, the president also exercises the formal powers of submitting a budget and reporting on the state of the economy. Presidents can also achieve their preferred policy through the extra-legislative means of executive orders and can curb the implementation of certain provisions of new laws through signing statements. Although presidents cannot unilaterally declare war, their request for such a declaration from Congress is a necessary step.

Presidents augment these formal powers with informal powers. For example, the bond between the president and the American people can impart power if the people support the president's actions and ideas. Thomas Jefferson, Andrew Jackson, Theodore Roosevelt, Woodrow Wilson, Franklin Roosevelt, and Ronald Reagan are just a few of the presidents who used the people's support to enact major political changes. The development and exercise of these powers over the last 225 years has strengthened the standing of presidents vis-à-vis Congress.

Today, the American public expects the president to set a legislative agenda and to work with Congress to enact it into law.

The president has a number of resources to draw upon to fulfill this awesome responsibility. First, the president's strongest resource is the size and unity of his or her party in Congress. Political scientists consistently find a strong relationship between the size of the president's party in the government and the president's legislative success.[1] Presidential popularity is a second potential resource for presidents who are working to enact their agenda into law. The president's national popularity helps determine the ambitiousness of the executive's agenda[2] and appears to be at least marginally related to his or her ability to enact that agenda.[3] The president's popularity in members' constituencies also influences the voting behavior of individual members of Congress.[4]

Personal relationships with congressional leaders of the opposition party can also help presidents win the votes they need to enact their agenda into law. Lyndon Johnson's regular drinks with Republican Senate minority leader Everett Dirksen and Ronald Reagan's weekly meetings with Democratic speaker of the House Tip O'Neill are two commonly cited examples of presidents who forged personal relationships that helped them achieve their political goals. Presidents continue to cultivate personal relationships today despite the polarized climate in Washington. For example, President Obama famously golfed with Republican speaker John Boehner, invited Republicans such as Aaron Schock and Scott Rigell to join him on Air Force One, and hosted a number of congressional Republicans at his first White House Super Bowl party in February 2009.

Public appeals are a familiar part of the president's informal powers. Political scientists debate how effective it is for presidents to use public appeals to sway public opinion and pressure Congress. Samuel Kernell notes the historical rise of public appeals and argues that presidents are forced to "go public" in today's political environment.[5] George Edwards suggests that such appeals fall "on deaf ears," finding that presidents are almost always unable to move public opinion with their appeals.[6] Brandice Canes-Wrone takes a middle position and finds that presidential appeals to the public can be successful if they are used on appropriate issues at appropriate times.[7] Otherwise, she argues, they will fail.

Finally, the president's ability to direct some discretionary federal funds through control of the executive branch is another potential source of presidential power in dealings with Congress. Presidents have used patronage to extract concessions from members of Congress and other political actors for most of American history. Although political reforms have curtailed this power resource over time, presidents still use patronage. Christopher Berry, Barry Burden, and William Howell find that congressional districts receive more federal money when they are represented by members of the president's party.[8] In addition, presidents can also use fund-raisers and campaign appearances as opportunities to influence the behavior of members.

The president's ability to accomplish his or her task as legislator in chief and pass policy through Congress depends on how well he or she strategically uses these resources given the political environment at the time. Before turning to an analysis of how Clinton used these resources, we first put his presidency into its historical context.

Clinton's Relationship with Congress and the American People

Various measures have been developed to assess the relationship between Congress and the president. In this section, we discuss several of these measures and compare Clinton's record with those of other modern American presidents.

On January 20, 1993, when Clinton first took the oath of office, the Democrats enjoyed an 83-seat majority in the House and a 14-seat majority in the Senate. Although the 1992 elections brought about a Democratic president and Democratic majorities in both chambers of Congress for the first time since 1976, the Democrats on Capitol Hill never felt that they owed their victories to Clinton—after all, he was merely a small-state southern governor with little Capitol Hill experience who had secured only 43 percent of the popular vote.[9] One of Clinton's main legislative liaisons, John Hilley, notes that President pro tempore of the Senate Robert Byrd said that as a newcomer to Washington, Clinton would have to learn what the Senate's prerogatives were and answer to Byrd himself. Additionally, Clinton's policy priorities differed from those of some long-standing Senate Democrats, which meant that the president had a lot of trouble getting the full Democratic caucus in the Senate on board with some of his early policies. Former Senate majority leader George Mitchell points to opposition from two senators representing states Clinton lost as a key factor in the defeat of the president's April 1993 economic stimulus bill. Mitchell recounts that "Senator [David] Boren and Senator [John] Breaux launched a public initiative" to kill the bill.

Clinton's problems with the Democrats during these first two years were minor compared to the problems he had with the Republicans. Lawrence Stein, a former legislative liaison for the White House, recalls that "the Republicans did a great job, from day one, of coming out and trying to contend that he really was an accidental president." John Hilley recalls that Clinton and the Democrats probably underestimated the strength and resilience of the Republican opposition. "Some of the Republican leadership openly said that part of their job was to make sure he was a one-term President," adds Mitchell. Republican Senator Alan

Simpson confirms that many congressional Republicans believed it was their duty to embarrass Clinton and cause him as many political problems as possible. Simpson recounts that "there were guys in our caucus who were always just out to screw Bill" because they "wanted to be back in the majority." In part, this sentiment was a function of Republicans' desire to win the majority in both the House and Senate and, in part, it reflected the negative rhetoric about Clinton that took root in Congress during the campaign.

After two years, the Republican strategy worked, and the Democratic majorities in both the House and Senate crumbled. During the last three Congresses of the Clinton presidency, the Republicans had majorities in the House (15, 22, and 12 seats, respectively) and Senate (6, 10, and 10 seats, respectively). Faced with an opposition Congress for three-quarters of his presidency, Clinton relied upon two skills he had been developing since his early days in Arkansas: an acute policy-focused mind and a gregarious personality. Clinton learned the politics of legislating in Congress with impressive speed, according to Simpson and South Dakota Democratic senator Tom Daschle. Most notable was Clinton's interest in, and knowledge of, domestic policy issues. Mitchell reports that "Clinton knew the details as well or better than any committee chairman on most issues . . . [and] he was obviously the most active, engaged, best prepared in terms of specific knowledge of the issues of any President with whom" Mitchell had dealt. As the Senate Majority Leader, Mitchell found Clinton's acumen and expertise very helpful in persuading members of Congress to adopt the president's position.

Second, Clinton used personal relationships to win political battles when other tools did not do the job. He had close friends who were in the Senate at the time, such as his home-state senators, Dale Bumpers and David Pryor. Lloyd Bentsen of Texas, Clinton's secretary of the treasury, had just concluded a 22-year Senate career following three terms in the House. Clinton's vice president, Al Gore, had been a two-term senator from Tennessee. Clinton quickly learned to leverage these friendships, using the savvy and experience of Bumpers, Pryor, Bentsen, and other leaders of his party to optimize his effectiveness on the Hill. Hilley believes that "one of the great strengths of his administration was maintaining great relationships with the Democrats."

The president's successful courtship of Marjorie Margolies-Mezvinsky's critical vote in support of his first budget proposal demonstrates that presidents can use personal relationships to win critical votes needed to pass bills through Congress. Representative Margolies-Mezvinsky knew that supporting the president's budget would be unpopular in her district. She says that early in the day that the budget vote came to the floor she told the administration, "I know this is important, but you're nuts to come to me." She also confirms that President Clinton personally called her on the phone in the House cloakroom and asked what it would take for her to vote for the budget. Margolies-Mezvinsky mentions that the president expressed deep knowledge of her district during the call. Despite knowing it had the potential to end her political career, she voted for the bill after her phone call with President Clinton because she believed it was the right thing to do.

The 1994 Republican victories contained a silver lining for Clinton: they forged a bond between the Democrats on Capitol Hill and the Democrat in the White House. As Daschle notes, Clinton continued to grow "progressively more sophisticated . . . at building relationships, especially with Democrats in Congress." The president also did political favors for other congressional Democrats. His campaign visits for them and their increased support for his agenda after their victories demonstrate how a mix of personal relationships and patronage politics can influence congressional voting behavior.

Richard Conley finds that ideological cohesion within the Democratic Party in Congress helped Clinton sustain his vetoes and stifle much of the Republican agenda listed in the GOP's Contract with America.[10] Congressional Republicans used their power to set agendas to introduce bills on controversial issues intended to split the Democratic Party, but that tactic did not work in the 104th Congress.[11] Even while struggling for relevance in the wake of the Republican tsunami, the Clinton White House was surprisingly successful.

Clinton's success was most vividly realized in his 1996 election. Although in the days after the 1994 election, few thought Clinton would see a second term, he used his personal popularity to undermine the Republicans' power. A number of studies find that citizens approved of President Clinton because they found him to be highly competent in the political world even though they had less favorable views of his personal character.[12] These high evaluations of President Clinton's competence may have been because the Clinton administration used polling to gauge public opinion more often than other presidents.[13] The administration's novel use of polling methods may even have helped save Clinton from impeachment during his second term. Clinton attempted to shirk the Monica Lewinsky scandal for the first months after it broke, but internal polls suggested that the American people respected the president's leadership ability despite their doubts about his personal conduct. After seven months of stalling, the president responded to the Lewinsky scandal by admitting personal wrongdoing and insisting that he did not break any laws when asked highly personal questions. Diane Heith finds that this response was formulated in response to the administration's use of extensive polling.[14] The combination of the president's response and his popularity in their districts led some House Republicans to vote against the proposed impeachment Article IV, which accused the president of abusing his power and misleading a congressional committee.[15]

President Clinton's popularity and use of frequent polling may help explain why his personal approval remained so high even as his legislative successes faltered. Communicating with the public was a priority of the Clinton campaign and presidency. In fact, candidate Clinton was the first presidential candidate with a campaign website.[16] Scholars suggest that public communication was one of President Clinton's biggest strengths.[17] His ability to speak optimistically about the challenges facing the nation was part of this strength. Clinton focused on the economy more than the average president when he spoke to the public, and he spoke optimistically about challenging economic issues such as inflation, unemployment, and the deficit.[18]

The president's popularity and public appeals helped create a more favorable political environment on Capitol Hill even in the context of divided government. Canes-Wrone uses Clinton's public appeals to the nation during the 1995 budget impasse as an archetypal example of a president successfully utilizing the strategy of going public to win a political battle and gain an advantageous position for future political battles.[19] After losing the political debate over the federal budget and the government shutdown, congressional Republicans became more likely to work with the president. Winning this battle even helped President Clinton expand the gender gap in the 1996 elections.[20]

In the sections that follow, we use data to evaluate Clinton's relationship with Congress. The record suggests that the Republicans, especially in the Senate, fundamentally changed how they interacted with him starting in 1996, when Clinton easily secured reelection. The Republican strategy of confronting the president on some issues and compromising on others during the 104th Congress helped Clinton secure reelection. Further compromises, GOP leaders reasoned, would only help him enhance his legacy.

Presidential Support Scores

Since 1953, *Congressional Quarterly* (*CQ*) has assessed the president's record in Congress by determining his "success" on votes for which "the president or authorized spokespeople" provided a "clear statement" of the president's view.[21] These scores yield two different metrics. First, at the aggregate level, *CQ* determines the percentage of votes on which the president "wins." Clinton's win rate, which incorporates both chambers and each year of his presidency, was 58 percent (see figure 3.1). It was highest, at 86 percent, during his first two years, when the Democrats controlled both chambers. Once the Republicans became a congressional majority, it dropped to an average of 48 percent. His overall win rate ranks him near the bottom of the modern presidents. The only president who fared worse was George H. W. Bush, who faced an opposition Congress during

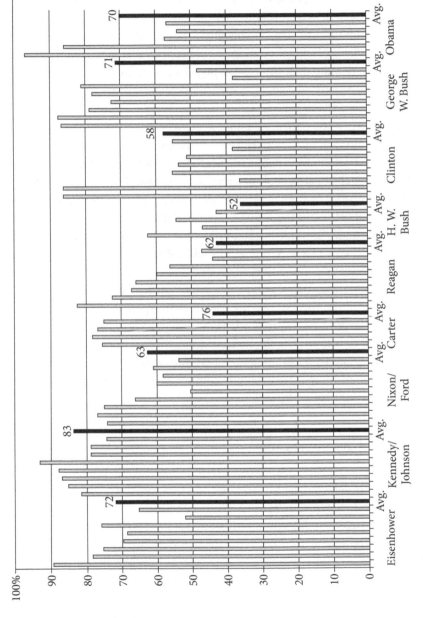

FIGURE 3.1 Presidential yearly "win rates" in Congress, 1953–2013

Source: Congressional Quarterly Almanac.

his entire presidency. Reagan, whose party controlled the Senate for six years, did marginally better than Clinton, at 62 percent.

Second, *CQ* determines the proportion of support that the president receives from each representative and senator. Not surprisingly, Clinton fared best among his fellow partisans. Democrats in the House voted in line with Clinton's announced position 74 percent of the time, which was 11 points lower than the Senate Democrats (see figure 3.2 for the yearly data). House Republicans supported Clinton about one-third of the time, whereas Senate Republicans supported him on two out of every five votes. Because the Senate votes include presidential nominations, which attract bipartisan support more frequently than legislative proposals, senators are usually a bit more supportive than House members, even those who are members of the opposite party.

Clinton's support among both his own party and the opposition party ranked in the middle of the modern presidents. What the Clinton numbers show, perhaps most vividly, is the trend over time of fellow party members being more supportive and opposite party members being less supportive.[22] As an example, the difference between the political parties in the House during the Clinton years was 42 percentage points, which is two and a half times more than it was during the Eisenhower years (17 points) and more than two-thirds higher than it was during the Carter years (25 points). Since the Clinton years, the difference in how the parties have voted on presidential support votes has gotten even bigger.

State of the Union Initiatives

Although *CQ*'s presidential support scores provide a first glance at how a president's position resonates in Congress, they do not provide a comprehensive understanding of how Congress handles the president's priorities. Not every vote the president takes a position on is necessarily important to the president or the nation. Furthermore, the mark of a president's legacy is in policies, not votes. To rectify these deficiencies, political scientists Donna Hoffman and Alison Howard[23] have collected a massive data set to assess presidents' success in Congress by examining the fate of the initiatives they outlined in their annual State of the Union Addresses.[24] They have categorized the issue content of each request and placed its outcome into one of three categories: "Fully Successful," "Partially Successful," and "Not Successful."

In evaluating president's relative success, Hoffman and Howard present data on both counts and percentages. In both, Clinton is in the middle of the pack of the modern presidents (see figure 3.3). Again, success rates are heavily influenced by which party has the congressional majority. Under unified governments,

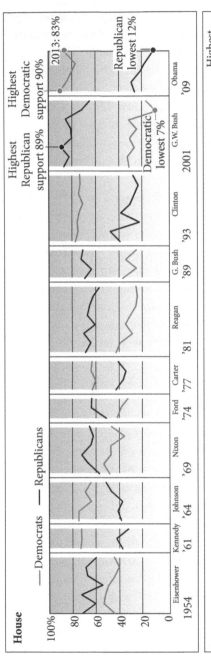

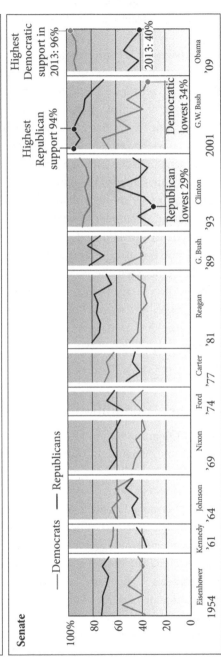

FIGURE 3.2 Presidential support scores by chamber and party, 1953–2013

Source: Congressional Quarterly Almanac.

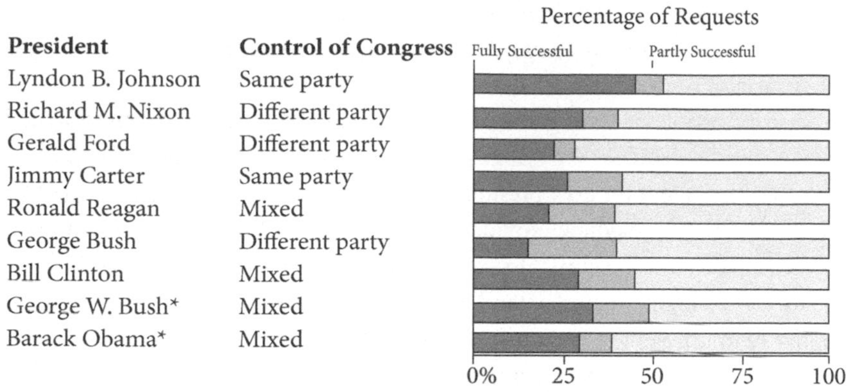

Percentage of Requests

President	Control of Congress	Fully Successful	Partly Successful
Lyndon B. Johnson	Same party		
Richard M. Nixon	Different party		
Gerald Ford	Different party		
Jimmy Carter	Same party		
Ronald Reagan	Mixed		
George Bush	Different party		
Bill Clinton	Mixed		
George W. Bush*	Mixed		
Barack Obama*	Mixed		

0%   25   50   75   100

FIGURE 3.3 Success of presidential initiatives based on State of the Union Requests

Source: Mark Landler, "Obama Pledges Push to Lift Economy for Middle Class," *New York Times*, February 12, 2013, http://www.nytimes.com/2013/02/13/us/politics/obama-delivers-state-of-the-union-address.html, accessed February 23, 2015.

Note: Just over half of the requests President Obama made have been enacted, but his success rate has declined since the Republicans took control of the House in 2011.

Clinton (52.1 percent "full" or "partial" success) finished behind Johnson (57.5) and ahead of Carter (50.0). In eras of divided government, he (41.6) finished behind G. W. Bush (48.9) and Reagan (44.9—only House opposed) and ahead of G. H. W. Bush (38.8), Nixon (37.7), Reagan (33.2—both chambers opposed), and Ford (28.5).[25]

Major Legislation

Although helpful in assessing the broad contours of a president's relationship with Congress, both *CQ*'s presidential support scores and Hoffman and Howard's assessment of presidential initiatives suffer from two problems. First, both pieces of data are generated dynamically. That is, the relationship presidents have with Congress in part determines the publicly stated positions they take and the "wants" they outline in the State of the Union Address. Clinton clearly took public positions and made presidential initiatives that took into account the Congress he faced. What he asked of the 103rd Congress, when Democrats controlled both chambers, was much different than what he asked of the 104th Congress, when Republicans controlled both chambers. Furthermore, in times of divided government the opposition party often intentionally places items on the congressional agenda in order to force presidents to take controversial positions.

So long as a president takes into consideration the Congress he or she faces, these measures will always skew away from both a high proportion of success and a low proportion of success.

A second problem in using the CQ scores to evaluate congressional-presidential relationships is that they only examine how a president's initiatives fare in Congress; they are silent on how presidents react to congressional initiatives. Political scientist David Mayhew provides data that better encapsulates—or, at least, provides additional insight into—the relationship between Congress and the president.[26] In trying to understand if divided government is inherently less productive than unified government, Mayhew catalogs all of the major congressional enactments that have occurred since 1947. He bases his list on two different sources. His first source is the yearly accounts of what Congress did and did not accomplish that run in *CQ Weekly Report*, the *New York Times*, the *Washington Post*, and other national papers of record. The second source is sixty-eight major books written by historians covering forty-three different policy areas. In the end, Mayhew finds that divided governments are nearly as productive as unified governments.

Beyond determining the relative productivity of divided versus unified government, we can also use these data to assess the relationship between Congress and the president. The timing of enactments allows an assessment of the record within each individual Congress. Before placing Clinton in context, it is important to recognize two shortcomings of these data for this purpose. First, how well a Congress and a president get along is not the only factor that determines whether major legislation will be enacted. Events, circumstances, and crises that are beyond either branch's control can either inflate or deflate the number of enactments. For example, the terrorist attacks on September 11, 2001, spurred ten of the seventeen major enactments of the 107th Congress (2001–2002). Second, deciding which legislation is "major" is somewhat subjective. In reviewing each Congress, Mayhew is explicit about what barely made the cut and what barely missed the cut. The transparency with which he makes his decisions increases the data's credibility.

As with the data presented above, the relationship between Congress and the president during the Clinton years falls in the middle of the range of modern presidents. Clinton and his four Congresses were responsible for thirty-nine major enactments, which is two more than during the Reagan years, but fourteen fewer than during the George W. Bush years (see table 3.1 for all the data since 1954).

Aggregating congresses across presidential administrations obscures an interesting result from the Clinton years. Clinton's first Congress passed eleven major pieces of legislation and his second passed fourteen. Interestingly, the divided 104th Congress passed more major enactments than the Democratic

TABLE 3.1 Major enactments, 80th to 112th Congresses (1947–2012)

ADMINISTRATION	BY CONGRESS		BY TERM	TOTAL
Truman*	80th	10	10*	
	81st	12		
	82nd	6	18	28*
Eisenhower	83rd	9		
	84th	7	16	
	85th	12		
	86th	5	17	33
Kennedy	87th	15		
	88th	14	29	
Johnson	89th	22		
	90th	16	38	67
Nixon	91st	22		
	92nd	16	38	
	93rd	22		
Ford	94th	14	36	74
Carter	95th	12		
	96th	10	22	22
Reagan	97th	9		
	98th	7	16	
	99th	9		
	100th	12	21	37
G. H. W. Bush	101st	9		
	102nd	8	17	17
Clinton	103rd	11		
	104th	14	25	
	105th	8		
	106th	6	14	39
G. W. Bush	107th	17		
	108th	10	27	
	109th	14		
	110th	13	27	54
Obama	111th	16		
	112th	7	23	23

* Truman ascended to the presidency upon Franklin Roosevelt's death. Because of this, the categorization by term for his administration is irregular.

unified 103rd Congress. The success that the congressional Republicans and Clinton achieved did not last. In his second term, Congress enacted only eight (105th Congress) and six (106th Congress) major laws. Although second-term presidents may be disadvantaged because they are lame ducks almost upon their reelection, no other president since Truman experienced such a decline from his first term to the second. Eisenhower had one more enactment in his second term than in his first; Reagan had four more. George W. Bush had exactly twenty-seven major enactments in both of his terms. Clinton went from twenty-five to fourteen.

The Site of Failure

In the debate over productivity during divided government, political scientist George Edwards and his co-authors developed a list of major legislative failures.[27] By replicating Mayhew's methodology, they made their lists compatible with his. Only thirty-three major failures occurred during Clinton's first term: they are almost equally divided between the Democratic Congress in 1993–1994 and the Republican Congress in 1995–1996. In his second term, the number of failures jumped to fifty-two. As with the change in major enactments, no other modern president experienced nearly as large an increase in major failures. In fact, Reagan and George W. Bush both had fewer failures in their second term than they did in their first (Reagan had thirteen fewer and Bush had twenty-five fewer).

The relationship that dominated Washington during the Clinton years was that between Clinton and Gingrich. From opposite sides of the escalating partisan war, both men had politics pumping through their veins. Clinton and Gingrich's highly public conflicts might lead some observers to conclude that the House was Clinton's major obstacle with Congress, but the data suggest otherwise. During the Clinton years, the House—the chamber that eventually impeached him—was not the graveyard of major bills. In fact, the House passed 62 percent of the major legislation that ultimately failed. The Senate was the graveyard. The Senate's final passage rate (37 percent) was little more than half that of the House. That the Senate, with its filibuster rule that allows forty-one senators to block measures, would prove to be the harder chamber to satisfy may not be surprising except when the data from all the other presidents are examined. From Eisenhower to George H. W. Bush, the House passed 206 of the 599 major bills that ultimately failed in the Senate (34.4 percent). The Senate passed 204 that ultimately failed in the House (34.1 percent). In no previous modern presidency was the Senate record as bleak in comparison to the House as it was during Clinton's presidency. The trend of the Senate as a legislative graveyard has continued for Clinton's successors.

Confirmation Votes

The different institutional roles of the House and Senate offer one additional piece of evidence to examine. Only the Senate considers presidential nominations. As with legislation, the Clinton years saw the biggest change in how the Senate dealt with presidential nominations.[28] The confirmation process before the Clinton presidency looked entirely different than it did in the presidential administrations starting with Clinton.

First, nominations became subject to much more scrutiny than before. Although every one of Reagan's nominations to the appellate courts was confirmed in his first two years in office, only 85 percent of Clinton's nominees were.[29] George W. Bush, who faced an opposition Senate for most of his first two years, had only a 41 percent success rate (see figure 3.4). Obama, with 62 percent, fared worse than Clinton, even with a Democratic majority and a filibuster-proof majority for most of the 111th Congress.

Second, Clinton's nominations took longer to get a vote on the Senate floor than those of his predecessors (see figure 3.5). Reagan's judicial appointments

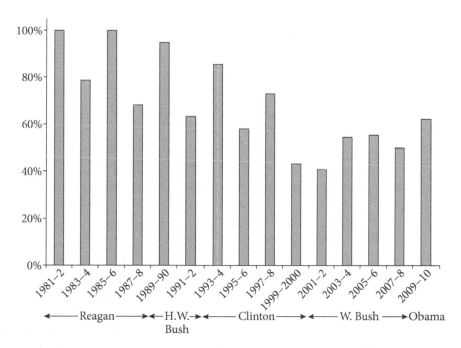

FIGURE 3.4   Success rate of appellate judicial nominations, Reagan to Obama administrations (1981–2010)

Source: Sean M. Theriault, *The Gingrich Senators: The Roots of Partisan Warfare in Congress* (New York: Oxford University Press, 2013).

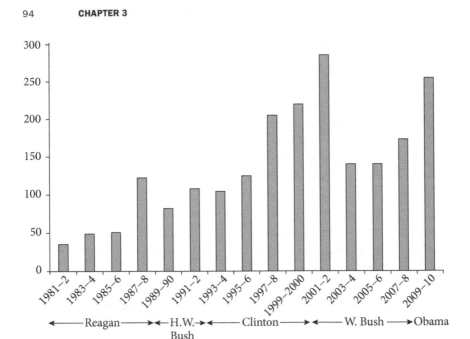

FIGURE 3.5   Average number of days from nomination to vote on appellate judicial nominations, Reagan to Obama administrations (1981–2010)
Source: Theriault, *The Gingrich Senators.*

took, on average, more than two months to be voted on by the Senate. Clinton's took more than twice that long. The data on nominations to the cabinet and independent agencies display the same trend.[30]

These data show that more nominees faced additional levels of scrutiny before being ultimately rejected by the Senate and at greater rates than ever before. Some congresses experienced larger fluctuations than other congresses. To see if any of these increases introduced a new normal in the battle between senators and presidents over confirmation, we conducted an exhaustive statistical analysis to see if there are any inflection points in the data. In other words, did any congresses show a particularly large increase in rejection rates or in the length of Senate consideration from previous congresses, and if so, did a new pattern form at this heightened level of conflict? The analysis reveals that the trend in the number of votes jumped up in the 105th Congress (1997–1998), the failure rate for cabinet and judicial appointments jumped up in Clinton's second term (1997–2000), the failure rate for appellate judges jumped up in the 106th Congress (1999–2000), the length of time for cabinet and judicial appointments jumped up in Clinton's second term (1997–2000), and the length of time for appellate nominees jumped up in the 105th Congress (1997–1998). Clearly a major and lasting change in the Senate's relationship with the president materialized during Clinton's second term.

Clinton and his staff were acutely aware of this trend as it played out. Lawrence Stein recalls that judicial nominations were "one of the constant, continuing irritations" of his tenure in the White House Office of Legislative Affairs during Clinton's second term. Stein says that Clinton's chief of staff during much of this period, John Podesta, reportedly "felt very strongly . . . that [Republicans made] an effort to keep [Clinton] from having the number of judicial appointees that he ought to have." Both the president and Stein agreed with Podesta. Stein remembers, "It got really difficult. . . . Judges became a very significant thing for Clinton, and he was very worried" about the failure rate of his nominations. Clinton thought that "it was important to go to some extra effort to get as many of his judges through" as possible, and the Office of Legislative Affairs devoted a lot of time and effort to confirmation negotiations. Although some of Clinton's nominees were relatively liberal, "he went to great lengths to pick reasonably moderate judges" whom he believed might be more acceptable to Senate Republicans. Stein concedes that he expected that the Republicans might hold up nominations "a little, as you get to the end of a Presidency," but instead, "in our particular case, [Senate Republicans] had been very slow on judges, . . . as slow as they could reputably be." Charles Brain, Clinton's final director of legislative affairs, indicates that by the last few years of the administration, Senate Republicans openly acknowledged their new strategy of obstructing nominees. He recalls that on "numerous instances we were told [by Senate Republicans], 'No you're just not going to get it. This [nominee] could be a good guy, or woman, we're not going to process that. Because we're going to wait. We're going to see what happens after the [2000] election. If we win, we're going to get our guy.'" Although delaying—and hence, killing—nominee had been a long-standing practice when a president faced an opposition Senate, the record from Clinton's second term suggests that this practice had never been as comprehensive or pervasive.

A Closer Examination of Clinton's Relationship with Members of Congress

Congressional Republicans and Clinton achieved far fewer major enactments in his second term than they did in his first term. The Senate was primarily responsible for this decline. The Senate also changed the rules of the game concerning presidential nominations. In this section we examine more closely the evolving role of the Senate during Clinton's presidency.

The Gingrich Senators

Sean Theriault has documented the transformation that Newt Gingrich led, first in the House Republican conference and second, more surprisingly, in the Senate Republican conference.[31] The reason for the latter is that numerous House members who began their congressional service in the Gingrich-transformed Republican conference were elected to the Senate and went on to transform the Senate Republican conference in Gingrich's likeness. By definition, these "Gingrich Senators" share three characteristics: they are Republicans, they served in the House before taking up their Senate seats, and they were elected to Congress after 1978, which was the year of Gingrich's first election to the House.

Forty-eight senators fulfill all three characteristics, including six who were elected in 2014 (see table 3.2 for a list of them). Through the 112th Congress (2011–2012), they were 78 percent more conservative than the other Republicans

TABLE 3.2 The 42 Gingrich Senators

		SENATE		HOUSE OF REPRESENTATIVES	
NAME	STATE	TENURE	IDEOLOGY[1]	TENURE	IDEOLOGY[1]
Allard	Colorado	105–110	0.613	102–104	0.597
Allen	Virginia	107–109	0.407	102	0.474
Blunt	Missouri	112–present	*	105–111	0.602
Boozman	Arkansas	112–present	*	107–111	0.521
Brown	Colorado	102–104	0.543	97–101	0.456
Brownback	Kansas	105–111	0.459	104	0.546
Bunning	Kentucky	106–111	0.630	100–105	0.505
Burr	North Carolina	109–present	0.579	104–108	0.445
Chambliss	Georgia	108–present	0.518	104–107	0.427
Coats	Indiana	101–105, 112–present	0.407	97–100	0.297
Coburn	Oklahoma	109–present	0.907	104–106	0.815
Craig	Idaho	102–110	0.512	97–101	0.487
Crapo	Idaho	106–present	0.493	103–105	0.523
DeMint	South Carolina	109–112	0.831	106–108	0.704
DeWine	Ohio	104–109	0.192	98–101	0.343
Ensign	Nevada	107–112	0.554	104–105	0.635
Flake	Arizona	113–present	*	109–112	*
Graham	South Carolina	108–present	0.473	104–107	0.477
Gramm[2]	Texas	99–107	0.561	98	0.548
Grams	Minnesota	104–106	0.526	103	0.530
Gregg	New Hampshire	103–111	0.429	97–100	0.412
Heller	Nevada	112–present	*	110–112	0.646
Hutchinson	Arkansas	105–107	0.457	103–104	0.412

NAME	STATE	SENATE		HOUSE OF REPRESENTATIVES	
		TENURE	IDEOLOGY[1]	TENURE	IDEOLOGY[1]
Inhofe	Oklahoma	104–present	0.689	100–103	0.475
Isakson	Georgia	109–present	0.504	106–108	0.500
Kirk	Illinois	111–present	0.333	107–111	0.453
Kyl	Arizona	104–112	0.616	100–103	0.527
Mack	Florida	101–106	0.407	98–100	0.520
McCain	Arizona	100–present	0.371	98–99	0.302
Moran	Kansas	112–present	*	105–111	0.494
Portman	Ohio	112–present	*	103–109	0.447
Roberts	Kansas	105–present	0.399	97–104	0.407
Santorum	Pennsylvania	104–109	0.373	102–103	0.294
Scott	South Carolina	113–present	*	112	*
Smith	New Hampshire	102–107	0.747	99–101	0.545
Sununu	New Hampshire	108–110	0.423	105–107	0.634
Talent	Missouri	108–109	0.305	103–106	0.455
Thomas	Wyoming	104–110	0.525	101–103	0.396
Thune	South Dakota	109–present	0.509	105–107	0.358
Toomey	Pennsylvania	112–present	*	106–108	0.795
Vitter	Louisiana	109–present	0.623	106–108	0.550
Wicker	Mississippi	110–present	0.444	104–110	0.487

* Ideology scores are not computed until the senator completes at least one congress.
1 Ideology is measured by the average DW-NOMINATE scores.
2 Gramm was first elected as a Democrat to the 96th Congress. In January 1983, he resigned his seat, switched
   parties, and won reelection as a Republican. The data analysis includes only his service as a Republican.

with whom they served (see figure 3.6). Although their numbers and behavior were not especially distinctive at the time of Clinton's inauguration, the Gingrich Senators became much more prominent over the course of his administration. On the day Clinton first took the oath of office, only eight of them were serving: Hank Brown, Dan Coats, Larry Craig, Phil Gramm, Judd Gregg, Connie Mack, John McCain, and Robert Smith. Although these eight were more conservative, on average, than the other Republicans with whom they served, their behavior had not yet distinguished them from their fellow Republicans.

During the Clinton years, twelve additional Gingrich senators were elected. Brown and Coates retired, though the latter reappeared in the Senate twelve years after he first retired. Senators Wayne Allard, Sam Brownback, Jim Bunning, Mike Crapo, Mike DeWine, Rod Grams, Tim Hutchinson, Jim Inhofe, Jon Kyl, Rick Santorum, Pat Roberts, and Craig Thomas all joined the Senate during the Clinton presidency. By the time Clinton left office, this group, in terms of both numbers and actions, was distinct not only from the Democrats with whom they served but also from the other Republicans. Based upon all Senate roll-call votes, the Gingrich Senators contributed 27.5 percent of the total Republican

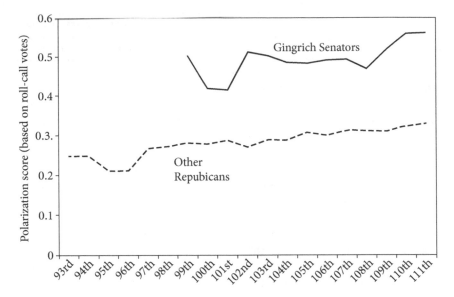

FIGURE 3.6   Polarization of Gingrich Senators and the other Republican senators, 93rd to 111th Congresses (1973–2010)
Source: Theriault, *The Gingrich Senators.*

Party polarization in the Senate in the 103rd Congress. By the time Clinton left the White house, their contribution increased to 42.2 percent.[32] Their increasing contribution to polarization occurred even though they continued to constitute less than one-third of the Republican conference.

The big difference in the Senate in Clinton's second term was that there were more Gingrich Senators and they became more effective at using the tools of the Senate to bring the legislative process to a halt. Examining the Senate Republicans' behavior in Clinton's second term demonstrates how successful they were in implementing Gingrich's strategies in the upper chamber. Their politics of stalemate and obstruction were more successful in the Senate because of rules that permit individual legislators to have much greater power than in the larger lower chamber.

Presidential Support Scores

Having isolated the Clinton years as the ones when the most change in the relationship between presidents and senators took place, in this section we focus more explicitly on individual senators' presidential support scores during the Clinton presidency. These scores have more validity when making comparisons within a congress in which the agenda is held constant across all senators than across congresses when the agenda changes. In other words, comparisons of senators within the same congress are not subject to the same criticisms as comparisons of senators' scores across time.

In Clinton's first congress, Senator Jesse Helms (R-N.C.) was the least supportive senator. On Clinton's publicly announced positions, Helms supported the president on 14.5 percent of the votes. Smith (R-N.H.), a Gingrich Senator, was only slightly more supportive at 15 percent. Of the ten biggest Clinton opponents in his first congress, the Gingrich Senators held four spots. By his last congress, they accounted for eight of the top ten least supportive of Clinton's positions (see table 3.3). In this last congress, Smith and Helms switched order in maintaining the biggest opposition to the president.

TABLE 3.3 Senators with the lowest presidential support scores, 103rd to 106th Congresses

CLINTON I			CLINTON II		
103rd Congress (1993–1994)			*105th Congress (1997–1998)*		
1	Helms	14.5	1	**Inhofe**	**31.0**
2	**Smith**	**15.0**	2	Faircloth	31.5
3	Faircloth	17.5	3	Helms	34.5
4	Nickles	21.0	4	**Smith**	**35.0**
5	**Brown**	**21.0**	5	Ashcroft	37.5
6	**Craig**	**22.0**	6	**Allard**	**38.0**
7	Kempthorne	23.0	7	Nickles	40.5
8	**Gramm**	**26.5**	8	Enzi	41.0
9	F. Murkowski	28.0	9	**Craig**	**41.5**
10	Lott	29.0	10	**Hutchinson**	**41.5**
104th Congress (1995–1996)			*106th Congress (1999–2010)*		
1	Faircloth	20.5	1	**Smith**	**22.0**
2	**Gramm**	**20.5**	2	Helms	24.5
3	**Kyl**	**21.5**	3	**Inhofe**	**26.5**
4	Helms	22.5	4	**Bunning**	**28.5**
5	**Smith**	**23.5**	5	**Allard**	**29.0**
6	**Inhofe**	**25.5**	6	Enzi	29.5
7	**Thomas**	**25.5**	7	**Hutchinson**	**31.0**
8	**Coats**	**26.0**	8	**Gramm**	**32.0**
9	**Craig**	**26.0**	9	Sessions	33.0
10t	Kempthorne	26.5	10	**Roberts**	**33.5**
10t	Ashcroft	26.5			

Source: Theriault, *The Gingrich Senators.*

Note: Data for Gingrich Senators is in bold.

The trend visible in the top ten withstands greater statistical sophistication. In each congress, the Gingrich Senators had lower support scores and in each, the difference between the Gingrich Senators and the other Republicans is statistically significant. Over the four congresses, the Gingrich Senators' scores were, on average, 9 percentage points lower than those of the other Republicans. Because of their growing numbers, the Gingrich Senators cast an increasing proportion of "no" votes during the Clinton presidency. In the first congress of Clinton's administration, the Gingrich Senators were only responsible for 21 percent of the votes against Clinton. By the last congress, they were responsible for 37 percent, even though their proportion of the Republican conference only grew from 19 to 33 percent.

Confirmation Votes

President Clinton's nominees for U.S. surgeon general proved to be some of the most controversial of his entire presidency. Shortly after his inauguration, Clinton nominated Joycelyn Elders, who had previously been his state health director in Arkansas. Her road to confirmation was torturous. The daughter of an Arkansas sharecropper who used the GI Bill to attend medical school after serving in the army, Elders faced questions on ethical grounds extending from her time on the board of directors of the National Bank of Arkansas and for her controversial public stands on abortion and teenage sex, which led some of her opponents to call her the "Condom Queen."

After a lengthy review, the Senate Labor and Human Resources Committee decided, in July 1993, to recommend Elders's confirmation to the full Senate on a 13 to 4 vote. Leading the charge against her nomination were Coats and Gregg, the only two Gingrich Senators serving on the committee. Coats worried that her views and style would be "polarizing and divisive," while Gregg based his opposition to her tenure on the bank's board.[33]

Although the committee spent seven months thoroughly investigating her past, Elders had to wait until after the summer recess for her nomination to get an airing on the Senate floor. After a contentious floor battle, the Senate voted to confirm Elders, 65–34. Again, the Gingrich Senators led the opposition. Although thirteen of thirty-five other Republicans voted to confirm Elders, only one of eight Gingrich Senators (Brown) did so.[34]

Coats's admonition proved prophetic. In December 1994, in the wake of the massive Republican victories the previous month, Clinton fired Elders for making controversial comments at a United Nations conference on AIDS about preventing the spread of HIV by promoting masturbation. Clinton's nominee to replace Elders, Henry Foster, was defeated on the Senate floor in June 1995, when the Democrats could not muster enough votes to invoke cloture on his nomination. All fourteen Gingrich Senators who served in the 104th Congress (1995–1996) voted against cloture twice; twenty-nine of the forty other Republicans voted with them.[35] When David Satcher was finally confirmed on February 10, 1998, he enjoyed the support of nineteen Republicans, only two of whom were Gingrich Senators.[36]

To cast an additional spotlight on these years, we computed senators' opposition scores to the president's nominees during Clinton's two terms. In his first term, three of the eight Gingrich Senators were among the top ten most opposed (see table 3.4). In his second term, when the Gingrich Senators' numbers increased to eighteen, they claimed seven of the top ten spots.

Between Clinton's first two years in office and his last two, a variety of measures indicate that the Senate entered a new era in dealing with presidential nominations. The new era is characterized by more roll-call votes, longer delays in the process, and a higher failure rate. The data over the four congresses in which Clinton was president shows that the Gingrich Senators were the most supportive of subjecting presidential nominations to more scrutiny. This trend persisted into the Obama administration as an increasingly larger share of the Republican conference adopted the politics of obstruction.

The Gingrich Senators, by and large, were not part of Clinton's charm offensive. Simpson notes that Clinton grew to know and like some Republican senators, such as himself, Lincoln Chafee, and David Durenberger. In fact, Mitchell recalls that Clinton "went out of his way to be accommodating to Republicans." Even when Republicans would directly and bluntly criticize him to his face at

TABLE 3.4   Senators with the lowest support for Clinton's nominees

CLINTON I (1993–97)			CLINTON II (1997–2001)		
1	Helms	5.9%	1	R. Smith	38.3%
2	R. Smith	11.8%	2	Faircloth	38.9%
3	Abraham	16.7%	3	Allard	44.7%
4	Kyl	16.7%	4	Inhofe	46.7%
5	Thomas	16.7%	5	Helms	48.9%
T6	Kempthorne	20.6%	T6	Enzi	50.1%
T6	Nickles	20.6%	T6	Gramm	50.1%
T6	Craig	20.6%	8	Bunning	51.9%
9	Faircloth	21.2%	T9	Craig	55.3%
T10	Dole	23.5%	T9	Brownback	55.3%
T10	Lott	23.5%			

Source: Theriault, *The Gingrich Senators*.

Note: Data for Gingrich Senators are in bold.

leadership meetings, Clinton always he remained courteous and attentive, and "he never engaged in any confrontational way." Clinton knew they were playing a political game and doing what was required for them to win.

Clinton, Congress, and a Changing Senate

The relationship between Congress and the president underwent major and lasting changes in the 1990s, especially in the Senate. President Clinton's time in office encapsulated a number of larger trends in the relationship between Congress and the president. Clinton was most effective passing legislation during his first term, a period characterized by both unified and divided government. This success was not easily accomplished at first, when the Democratic Party was divided in Congress and Clinton's legislative operation was not working inefficiently. The Clinton White House quickly learned Neustadt's lesson that "presidential power is the power to persuade" and by 1994 had figured out how to persuade Congress to work with the president.[37] The onset of divided government after the 1994 Republican revolution changed the congressional agenda and put the brakes on some Clinton agenda items. Even so, the White House was still able to work with the 104th Congress thanks to improved efficiency in the White House Office of Legislative Affairs and Clinton's interpersonal skills with both members of Congress and the American public.

By Clinton's second term, his legislative team was working at a high level. John Hilley says of the team, "We were organized. We knew our message, we knew our policy, and we knew what we were doing." Despite its increased efficiency, this team ran into a brick wall during Clinton's second term. An important, lasting change took place in the Senate during this term. An influx of "Gingrich Senators" moved from the House to the Senate and used the rules of the Senate to bring the legislative process to a halt. Members took the polarizing, scorched-earth tactics they had learned while serving with Newt Gingrich in the House to the Senate. The combination of Gingrich Senators, Senate norms, and the Senate's institutional design led to increased gridlock and polarization.

Senator Simpson notes that the House passed a number of bills that died in the Senate. He concludes that the House is "always destined to be pissed off at the Senate" even when the same party controls both. The reason is the design of the American system and the peculiar way the Senate developed. Gingrich Senators exploited this design to derail Clinton's agenda and diminish his effectiveness with Congress despite a highly effective White House Office of Legislative Affairs and Clinton's own immense talent. A willful minority of senators can stall the entire legislative process. The willful minority was too small during Clinton's first two years, but by the time he handed the White House keys over to

George W. Bush in 2001, their numbers had grown and their tactics had become more lethal. They were able to severely derail his legislative accomplishments. The Gingrich Senators, of course, are not the only set of senators who have used this strategy. Democratic senators during the George W. Bush presidency, the Gingrich Senators, and the Tea Party senators have all learned the lessons well. What hampered Clinton in the 1990s still affects Obama today.

ROOT CANAL POLITICS

Economic Policy Making in
the New Administration

Brendan J. Doherty

Bill Clinton became president in January 1993 after a campaign in which he promised to restore strength to the faltering economy. Faced with a budget situation that was far more dire than had been anticipated, Clinton and his team had to make difficult decisions about which of his campaign commitments to pursue. The ways in which they reconciled their policy priorities with economic reality set the stage for a contentious legislative battle over his budget plan, the success of which was by no means guaranteed. These economic policy decisions played an important and intensely debated role in the dramatic economic expansion of the late 1990s. Clinton's friends and foes can argue about the wisdom of his policies, but few will dispute the fierceness of the fights over them and their important consequences for the lives of ordinary Americans.

Commitments and Constraints

Considering both Clinton's policy commitments and the economic and political constraints he faced is essential to understanding how economic policies were forged at the beginning of Clinton's first term. In the fall of 1991, Governor Clinton laid out his economic policy agenda in one of a series of speeches at his alma mater, Georgetown University. Mickey Kantor, who was chair of Clinton's 1992 campaign and later served as United States trade representative and secretary of commerce, argued that the Georgetown speeches were critical. "If you look back at . . . the speeches at Georgetown that fall, I believe you will agree with me that in the history of modern politics, in terms of winning presidential candidates, he was more consistent with what he had laid out and throughout his presidency than almost anyone. . . . It made a difference in the campaign. . . . Everyone who came in understood what he wanted to do and where he wanted to go."[1] Clinton had given a great deal of thought during his time as governor of Arkansas to the economic policies he hoped to implement on a national stage.

What were Clinton's commitments in the campaign? He promised to enact a series of measures designed to provide relief to what he called the forgotten middle class, including a tax cut for the middle class and investments in education, job training, and other programs that he argued would spur economic growth. Additionally, and perhaps most importantly for the political battles that lay ahead, he pledged to cut the federal budget deficit in half in four years.

The economic constraints Clinton faced were substantial. On January 6, 1993, just two weeks before he was inaugurated, Richard Darman, the outgoing director of President George H. W. Bush's Office of Management and Budget, announced that the budget deficit was considerably larger than had been previously estimated and was projected to keep rising. The revised budget deficit for fiscal year 1994, which would run from October 1, 1993 until September 30, 1994, was $282.4 billion, almost $20 billion higher than Darman had publicly forecast in the summer of 1992. The deficit was expected to rise to almost $320 billion by 1998.[2] Clinton has often said that he brought arithmetic back to the budgeting process.[3] The arithmetic of higher deficits meant that the president-elect could not keep all the promises he had made in the campaign.

The main political constraint Clinton faced in 1993 was less evident at first glance. His victory in the 1992 election placed Democrats in control of the presidency and both houses of Congress for the first time in twelve years. Democrats enjoyed strong majorities in both chambers: they held 258 of the 435 seats in the House and 57 of the 100 seats in the Senate.[4] While this might seem to have presented a golden opportunity for productive policy making, Democrats on Capitol Hill were not in the habit of taking the lead from a president of their own party. Republicans had held the White House since 1981 and for twenty of the previous twenty-four years. At the start of 1993, more than two-thirds of the Democrats in the House and more than half of the Democrats in the Senate had never served with a Democratic president.[5] Democrats had held majority control in the House for the previous thirty-eight years and in the Senate for thirty-two of those years. They were, in the words of Alan Blinder, chair of Clinton's Council of Economic Advisers, "an unruly majority. The saying then was, when Democrats form a firing squad they stand in a circle."

Another factor that hampered Clinton's ability to get Congress to enact his agenda was the independent candidacy in the 1992 election of Ross Perot, who received almost 19 percent of the national popular vote. Although Clinton out-polled President George H. W. Bush by more than five million votes, Perot's share kept Clinton far short of a majority.[6] While Clinton had to compete in a three-way race, most members of Congress ran in a two-way race. As Clinton's legislative affairs director Charles Brain explained, "There were only a handful of members of Congress who were elected who hadn't taken their districts by a big-ger percentage than Clinton did. Nobody felt particularly indebted to Bill Clinton for getting there." Senator Tom Daschle of South Dakota said that when it came to the president's agenda, "Congress is likely to listen, but not necessarily comply."

Republicans in Congress were not eager to help the newly elected Democratic president enact his legislative priorities. They were not impressed that Clinton had won 370 out of 538 Electoral College votes (68.8 percent) or that he had handily defeated a sitting president.[7] Instead, on the morning after the election, Bob Dole, the Republican leader in the Senate, declared, "Fifty-seven percent of the Americans who voted in the presidential election voted against Bill Clinton, and I intend to represent that majority on the floor of the U.S. Senate. If Bill Clinton has a mandate, then so do I."[8] Additionally, the 1990 budget deal that Bush had struck with congressional Democrats, thereby breaking his famous, "Read my lips, no new taxes" pledge, had made Republicans even more opposed to raising taxes. Deputy Treasury Secretary Roger Altman believed that "most Republicans had the view that they would rather die than vote for a tax increase." These political and economic constraints set the stage for contentious and con-sequential economic policy making during the Clinton presidency.

Competing Priorities and Economic Reality

Bill Clinton made the economy the central focus of his presidential campaign. Roger Altman, who would become deputy secretary of the treasury, recounted, "This had been the thrust of the campaign, so expectations were very high that Clinton would come forward with a real economic program, a comprehensive program, and from the moment that all these folks were chosen the question was, what is that program going to be? Clinton had talked of course during the campaign about cutting the deficit in half during his first four years. He talked about a middle-class tax cut and, of course getting the economy moving. So it was job one."

Soon after his election, the president-elect started to fill the team that would help him make the critical policy and political decisions that loomed. In early December 1992, he made a group announcement in Little Rock of his choices to fill key economic posts. Lloyd Bentsen, chair of the Senate Finance Committee, would be secretary of the treasury, and Roger Altman, an investment banker who had served in the Treasury Department during the Carter administration, would be his deputy. Leon Panetta, chair of the House Budget Committee, would serve as director of the Office of Management and Budget (OMB), and Alice Rivlin, who ran the Congressional Budget Office, would be his deputy. Robert Rubin, a senior executive at Goldman Sachs, would chair the newly established National Economic Council (NEC).[9]

Altman explained the logic behind Clinton's selection of Bentsen. "I think Clinton recognized that, by virtue of his being an outsider in Washington—he never served in Washington—he needed a link to the Congress, a really superb link, of the type that Bentsen afforded, especially since Clinton's first priorities were economics. The Senate Finance Committee was going to be, more than any other single place, where the action was. So he chose someone who not only had a great reputation and tremendous stature, but who could particularly help him with Congress, and it was a shrewd choice." Panetta provided a similar connection to the House of Representatives, Rubin offered a link to economic interests on Wall Street, and Rivlin and Altman brought relevant experience in congressional budgeting and the workings of the Treasury Department, respectively, to the team.

The goal behind the creation of the NEC was to fix what Rubin called "a process problem," and it was explicitly modeled after the National Security Council (NSC). Rubin explained, "President Clinton thought Bush 1 had had his national security issues very effectively coordinated. They managed to get everybody to the same table and could share their views. . . . But he felt that, with respect to economic issues, they hadn't done that, which they clearly hadn't. But also, as you look back, he thought there was a problem in the sense that every administration had struggled with this idea of how to get all these different agencies that are involved in so many of these issues together." Clinton's answer was the NEC, which he charged with coordinating economic policy discussions in much the same way that the NSC coordinates national security policy discussions. Rivlin said that Rubin's role was to serve as "the honest broker. His job was to get everybody saying what they thought was the right thing to do in front of the President, so the President could decide." Clinton's two successors continued this institutional innovation.

The principal early challenge facing Clinton and his team was which of his campaign promises to focus on given the new economic reality of larger budget deficits. His personnel choices would play a significant role in his economic decision making. Altman argued that "by choosing Panetta, and Bentsen, and Rubin, he chose economic conservatives. Panetta had made a very distinguished career as House Budget Chairman out of pushing for lower deficits and a more transparent budget process. Rubin was well known as an economic conservative, and Bentsen, of course, had a very long legislative record, which was in the same direction. Lloyd Bentsen was a classic Texas conservative Democrat. So, looking back on it, the nature and the history of those three men had a lot to do with the eventual outcome. Also, strong figures, not weak figures."

A divide soon emerged between the members of the economic team, who favored deficit reduction, and other aides who had been more involved with the campaign and wanted the president to invest in programs that they thought would spur economic growth. Alice Rivlin, who preferred deficit reduction, recalled, "You also had the political folks who had been running this campaign and talking about all the things that the new president was going to do: a middle-class tax cut, a big investment in infrastructure, national health insurance. . . . The political folks were saying, 'Hey, wait a minute. We've got to deliver on these promises that we made in the campaign, and if you're doing all this deficit reduction, you can't do that.' So that was really the fight."

Speechwriter David Kusnet summed up the surprise that many aides felt at the emergence of deficit reduction as the top policy priority: "Deficit reduction as an end in itself, or as a touchstone of economic policy, had not been, as I understood it, central to the Clinton campaign. The title of our campaign document was 'Putting People First.' It wasn't 'Getting America's Fiscal House in Order.'" Campaign pollster Stan Greenberg said, "The biggest issue that we pressed [in setting economic policy priorities] was not losing track of the investment agenda." He was convinced that these were the policies that Clinton really cared about. Recalling his efforts to build support for the investment agenda among fellow Democrats, Greenberg said that he made the case that these programs were in Clinton's "gut, and that if you go back through his entire history, this is what it is rooted in. This is how he wants to govern."

Clinton was aware of the divisions within his team. He asked Greenberg to make a presentation at a staff retreat at Camp David soon after the inauguration. According to Greenberg, Clinton said, "Remind these people what we ran on. I have all these people who came in here, particularly the economic team, who were not part of the campaign. They don't know our mandate. Make sure they understand what we ran on."

Rivlin was surprised by the animosity she felt from aides who had been involved in the campaign. She recalled a meeting to discuss a budget document she had helped to prepare during Clinton's first month in office. "I looked around the room, and I thought, 'These people look really angry. What's going on here? What have I done? Why are they so mad?' And I thought, 'Well, I guess they're mad because they've been the spokespeople, they've been running this campaign, and this is the first time they're not.' It was extremely hostile. They all just dumped all over this document. They didn't like it. What they really didn't like was the policy. They didn't like the deficit reduction, and they didn't like the fact that their programs that they'd been out there campaigning for weren't in it."

Alan Blinder, who served on Clinton's Council of Economic Advisers, described senior economic policy aide Gene Sperling as the "bridge. He would be with the politicals, and then he'd come back to us and say, 'They're griping about this. You can't do this.' And we'd say, 'You have to do this.' And he'd go back to the politicals." Panetta also cited Sperling's central role. "I learned early on that the most important thing was to bring Sperling in. At OMB I basically took Gene and sat him down at the table. I said, 'This is what we're going to present, now you tell me where the campaign minefields are.' . . . I knew that in a room if he suddenly said, 'Oh, Mr. President, you didn't . . .' it would blow up everything. So I learned very early that it was better to know Gene's thoughts, what he said or didn't say." Panetta recalled that Gene Sperling and George Stephanopoulos "were the keepers of the conscience, the campaign conscience." Sperling echoed this assertion, declaring, "I was his campaign conscience."[10] The task of squaring campaign commitments with economic reality was not an easy one.

Deficit Reduction and the 1993 Budget

Roger Altman credited Alan Blinder with making the case for deficit reduction that eventually carried the day. At a meeting in Little Rock during the transition period, Blinder argued that "the most stimulative thing we could do for this economy is to induce a monetary response." In Blinder's view, deficit reduction would lead the bond market to reduce interest rates, which in turn would stimulate economic growth. Altman compared the effect of interest rate reduction to that of increased government spending. "Well, if you think about spending initiatives that you could take today that are politically imaginable, they amount to a hill of beans in a [multi-trillion dollar] economy. . . . But it's just a reality that in an economy of that size, spending changes aren't going to have much effect on the economy; monetary changes can. So that was the revelation, so to speak."

Clinton aides who favored the investment agenda did not readily accept that argument. Panetta recalled a conversation during the transition with Robert Reich, whom Clinton appointed as secretary of labor, in which Panetta contended that "you've got to confront, first thing that's out of the box is the budget, that's the thing you have to focus on. That will define you as an administration and it will tell the country whether you're serious about dealing with it. . . . Even a Bob Reich knew that for him to get there, he had to walk through the deficit fire."

Greenberg later lamented that Clinton "committed to parameters on the budget, coming out of the early January meetings, which basically precluded the investment agenda. It was no longer possible." Clinton campaign aide James Carville famously remarked, "I used to think if there was reincarnation, I wanted to come back as the President or the Pope or a .400 baseball hitter. But now I want to come back as the bond market. You can intimidate everyone."[11]

Clinton's decision to focus on deficit reduction promised potential rewards down the road but also carried substantial risk. Reducing deficits entails cutting spending or raising taxes or both. As Alan Blinder put it, "This was root canal politics—whose ox are you going to gore?" Rubin made clear to the president that the path on which they were embarking was uncertain: "Look, there's no guarantee this is going to work." Blinder recalled warning Clinton that the possibility of failure was real, explaining that "if things go wrong, what you'll probably have is a recession about the size of the one that George Bush experienced." Clinton was "aware that there were hazards here, that if we didn't get the bond market rally, if we didn't get cooperation from the Fed [Federal Reserve Board] . . . there was a hazard that you raise taxes and cut spending and the economy is not that strong anyway, and you wind up with a recession." In short, Blinder said, "Here's this guy from Arkansas, untested and a Democrat to boot. He was going to have to rely on the kindness of strangers in the bond market for his political salvation."

Roger Altman emphasized that even if the hoped-for benefits materialized, it would take time to do so. "Everyone understood there was a lag factor. Remember, you're playing for four years, you're not playing for one year. I mean one of the oldest rules of presidential management is, take your pain up front." As Panetta put it, "there was a lot of pain on the table." Blinder gives Clinton a great deal of credit for embracing the pain:

> He knew he was taking a big risk here. I think it is to his tremendous credit that he sized this up and decided to take the risk because he thought it was good policy. You know, a lot of bad things have been said about Bill Clinton over the years, but I really believe he decided to take this calculated risk because he thought it was good for the country. And, incidentally, if it proved to be good for the country, that would help him get reelected in '96. But that's the way you want a President to think. You do something that's good, four years later the good chickens come home to roost and you get reelected, and you don't worry so much about four weeks later.

Blinder also noted that "the strength of the Perot vote and the attribution of that strength to angst about the budget deficit had a very big effect on Clinton,

I think. And it was certainly consonant with what he was hearing from his economic team. I do think Bill Clinton is a very good politician, a very keen observer of popular sentiment. And after all, there was a vote and this guy Perot got, what was it, 19 percent of the vote. This guy, who was a little bit wacky, got 19 percent of the vote. A politician as astute as Bill Clinton is not going to fail to notice that."

The Fight in Congress for the 1993 Budget

Clinton's deficit reduction goal was ambitious, and the plan he put forward included both spending cuts and tax increases. The 1993 budget bill evolved over the course of the year. It began as a White House proposal and then proceeded through both houses of Congress to a conference committee that had to reconcile the differences between the measures each chamber had passed, then back to each house for a final vote on the conference report. Along the way, certain measures were added and others were dropped. The most important revenue provisions in the final bill that was considered by the House and Senate in early August 1993 were increases in both income taxes and Medicare taxes for higher income earners, a tax on some Social Security benefits, an increase in the federal gasoline tax, a rise in corporate income taxes, and an expansion of the earned income tax credit, which provides tax benefits for lower-income earners. The White House estimated that in five years the plan would yield $241 billion in new tax revenue and $255 billion in cuts to government spending and in the reduced interest payments that would result from deficit reduction.[12]

The reception Clinton's economic plan received on Capitol Hill was not overwhelmingly positive, to say the least. The White House had hoped to win at least some Republican votes, but that did not happen. Blinder recalled, "I think it was a surprise to us how obstinate and absolutely partisan, right to the last man or woman, the Republicans were. . . . We knew . . . we weren't going to get all the Democratic votes. We'd probably need some Republican votes on almost anything." But as Republican senator Alan Simpson explained, his colleagues faced pressure not to help Clinton, because if the president failed, that would help Republicans regain a majority in the Senate. "They were in a caucus where ten other guys would get up and say, 'You son-of-a-bitch, you stick with us this time or, by God, we'll be in the minority forever! Unless you get off your ass and just give us this one vote.' Now [Senate Republican Leader Bob] Dole would never do it that way, but the hard-liners, they'd say, 'Don't you want to be chairman again? You love wandering in the swamp around here?'"

Leon Panetta recalled Republican senator Pete Domenici saying, "There is the sense that obviously Clinton is going to have to raise taxes and he'll become vulnerable by virtue of that. And there is a basic decision that this is one he's going to have to pretty much carry on his own." Republican senator Chuck Grassley vividly described the bill as "five pounds of manure pounded into a four-pound sack. The point is, if you vote for this package, you're voting for deep doo-doo."[13]

As Blinder anticipated, not all Democrats were on board with Clinton's plan. Senator Daschle recalled that the White House had "a little bit of a sense of arrogance: 'Well, this is what we want.' It wasn't easy to accommodate that with members who had similarly strong views about policies and the direction they thought we should take, many of whom had been around a long time." Long-serving Democratic members of the House and Senate were not used to working with a president of their own party and did not uniformly line up to support his ambitious and controversial combination of spending cuts and tax increases.

The stakes for the Clinton administration were high. Sperling recalled, "That economic plan was everything for us. If that failed, we really worried about the domestic legacy of the president." The administration launched an all-out effort to promote the president's plan. According to Sperling, "It was an eight-month blur. That is all you did every day of your life, to try to pass that deficit reduction act."[14] Roger Altman concurred. "That entire team was out there promoting the President's economic package, both crisscrossing the country for that purpose, speaking, visiting Congressional districts and so forth, testifying on it of course, visiting one-on-one with members of Congress. It was quite a full-bore effort. Very, very intensive, one of the most intensive things I've ever been involved in."

To coordinate their efforts, the White House set up a war room modeled after the communications unit during the 1992 campaign. Altman described it as "very effective because it was a group of roughly 20–25 people, working literally 19–20 hours a day with only one mission, and that mission was to get this bill passed. So, when it came to answering Congressman Smith's questions, or Senator Jones' questions, we were able to get those answers up there within two hours because we had all the people right in the room."

The outcome was far from certain. Altman recalled Clinton worrying that the bill would fail. "The President said to me at one moment when we were alone, and with great heat, he said to me, 'Roger, you see, there's no constituency at all for Wall Street economics,' which is how he viewed his plan, that he'd sold himself to Wall Street and you see there's no constituency for that because we're about to lose. I didn't say anything to that. But you can imagine the irony of that comment because the Republicans to a man were opposing it because it is tax and spend economics, and the President is saying it's going to go down because it is Wall Street economics. Somebody was wrong."

To sell the bill, Clinton tried to focus public attention on the economic benefits of deficit reduction in a way that was readily understandable. Alan Blinder remembered giving "one of these didactic briefings in the White House," in which he discussed the complicated economic ramifications of the plan. "Clinton corrected me and said, 'No, no, no, this is about jobs. You must always say this is about jobs.' Politically he was right, because people weren't ready to hear the other rationale. But I think one legacy of the Clinton administration is a greater understanding of what this budget control is all about. It's not because of our Puritan forebears, and it's not because of Polonius saying, 'Neither a borrower nor a lender be.' It's about investment and growth and real wages and productivity."

The Battle in the House

Making the case for the bill in Congress required different pitches to different members. According to Panetta, "You'll have a group of members who substantively want to know why this is the right thing to do. They'll have questions about the tax package, the cuts, and you walk through that with them. I think they're being intellectually honest about their substantive concerns. . . . Then there's another group of members who basically wheel and deal, who will say, 'What can you give me? You want my vote? I need a road, I need a highway, I need a bridge, I need whatever it is.'"

One member who fell into the latter category made an impression on Panetta because of the unusual way in which she framed her request:

> And there was a member from Detroit whom I could not understand. She was a black representative from Detroit who clearly has got to be a good vote for the president. . . . And she's being resistant. Ultimately it's like, "Why? What's going on?" I remember, I had the leadership talk to her, I had Bill Richardson who was working on the whips' group and working it out. I talked to her, I had others talk to her, and finally she called and said she wanted to meet with me. I figured, okay, here it comes. She basically said Jesus had talked to her the night before. I said, "That's very special." What did Jesus have to say? And she said, "Jesus said that I really ought to support the President on this, it is very important to the president and it's the right thing to do. I ought to do this if I can get this casino approved in Detroit."[15]

The final votes on the 1993 budget bill occurred in the first week of August when both chambers voted on a conference report that reconciled differences between the bills each house had passed. The House voted first and, Altman recalled, "We didn't think we had the votes, or at least we thought the odds were too high that we would lose. The most frantic imaginable effort was going on during the five or six hours preceding that vote. Whatever was going on on the deck of the *Titanic* was comparable, but it was absolutely frantic and incredibly dramatic and tense."

Clinton spent the day of the vote working the phones. Altman said, "He knew that if we lost this vote it was a severe blow. So he was frantically calling members of Congress as various requests came in for him to do so. The number of possible votes at that stage had dwindled down to a tiny number, votes that were undecided." The case he made to member after member was that "the country needs it, the Democratic Party needs it, I need it. We can't afford to lose it." White House aide Charles Brain echoed the president's arguments. "If congressional Democrats hadn't delivered for him, they would have stuck a knife down his back, put it in his heart. Can't do that." Representative Marjorie Margolies-Mezvinsky, who dramatically cast the deciding vote on the bill, explained that if the bill had failed, "for 44 months it would have been a lame-duck presidency—or an *extremely* challenging one. . . . It was a presidency that needed momentum, and this was the linchpin of the presidency." She recalled that even Republicans acknowledged that "the thing had to pass. . . . [House Republican leader Robert] Michel stood up on the floor that day and said, 'We know that this has to pass.'"

But to those in the White House, the outcome was by no means predetermined. Altman said, "When the voting began, we did not know if we were going to win. We just didn't know, and that's pretty amazing, the biggest piece of legislation, the voting has actually begun." Clinton's staff and cabinet put substantial pressure on wavering Democrats. Margolies-Mezvinsky initially resisted supporting the bill. She recalled, "Earlier in the night they all came to me and I said, 'I know how important this is but you're nuts to come to me.' It was that kind of conversation. Then I stood outside. I said to [two staffers], 'I think we've got to vote for it,' and both of them said, 'You're crazy. They can find somebody else.' I said, 'I hope they can, but I'm getting the feeling that it might be awfully close.'"

One of the people the White House tried to bring on board to cast the decisive vote was Arkansas Democrat Ray Thornton. As Charles Brain recalled, "One of the reasons Marjorie Margolies-Mezvinsky had to vote for the budget bill is that Ray Thornton from Arkansas didn't. Should you expect some loyalty, you'd expect it out of the Arkansas delegation and didn't get it there." Clinton echoed these sentiments in his memoir, writing:

> Thornton had an easy vote. He represented central Arkansas, where there were far more people who would get a tax cut than a tax increase. He was popular and could not have been blown out of his seat with a stick of dynamite. He was my congressman, and my presidency was on the line.

And he had lots of cover: both Arkansas senators, David Pryor and Dale Bumpers, were strong supporters of the plan. But in the end, Thornton said no. He had never voted for a gas tax before and he wouldn't start now, not to get the deficit down, not to revive the economy, not to save my presidency or the career of Marjorie Margolies-Mezvinsky.[16]

Thornton's refusal put the focus on Margolies-Mezvinsky. Altman said, "I recall speaking about 20 minutes before the vote to Marjorie Margolies-Mezvinsky, with whom I had developed a friendship, and it became evident to me that she was very reluctant but willing to vote for the bill. I put the President on the phone with her and of course, she cast the decisive vote."

For Margolies-Mezvinsky, casting the crucial 218th vote was traumatic. Looking back, she reflected, "I think what nature does is it protects you from remembering very bad accidents, and voting at 218. It was just like a very bad, head-on collision for me. It was so dramatic, it was so awful. They had to find an office for me. It was so unpleasant. It was absolutely one of the most unpleasant days of my life." Altman recounted sitting with Secretary Bentsen, "watching [the vote] on television, mostly in silence. Then Marjorie made her famous walk to the well, with the Republicans serenading her, 'Bye, Bye Marjorie,' but if there's a more dramatic moment that one can have in government service, at least if you're working in some sort of economic capacity, I can't think of it." Margolies-Mezvinsky later wrote, "I still remember how, after I voted, [Republican representative] Bob Walker jumped up and down on the House floor, yelling 'Bye-bye, Marjorie!' I thought, first, that he was probably right. Then, that I would expect better behavior from my kids, much less a member of Congress. And then, that he was a remarkable jumper."[17]

The Republicans taunted Margolies-Mezvinsky because they knew her vote would place her in electoral peril. She represented one of the few districts in the country where more people would face an income tax increase than would benefit from a tax cut as a result of Clinton's economic plan. As she recalled with a bit of exaggeration, "1.2 percent of the population faced tax increases and they all lived in my district. Nobody else in any other district in the entire United States was going to be hit by these tax increases, according to the polls in my district." The White House was aware of how tough the vote would be for her. She recalled, "Clinton knew. I'll never forget what he said. 'This is the 14th wealthiest district in the country.' I didn't even know that. I knew we were wealthy; it was a very fancy district." She explained that she was also a victim of bad timing. "What happened, interestingly, was in '82 there had been a ratcheting of the tax code that came online in '92, which reduced refunds in some manner. So what happened is it appeared as if people were being taxed, getting less back in returns, when in fact they weren't. The feeling in a very wealthy district was that immediately—there was no way that that happened that quickly. People were walking up to me and saying, 'I didn't get anywhere near what I should be getting back because of your vote.' It had nothing to do with that."

Regardless of why her constituents' taxes were going up, Margolies-Mezvinsky faced anger at home because she had won her seat in 1992 by attacking her opponent for having raised taxes. Although many accounts of the 1993 budget battle allege that Margolies-Mezvinsky had pledged not to raise taxes, she disagreed in her oral history interview. "I never said that I wouldn't raise taxes. But when the vote came, the 30-second commercial against me was, 'She broke her promise. She's a liar. . . .' I just never promised. It wasn't a thing I did." Her account is corroborated by a local news story that ran near the close of her successful congressional campaign in 1992 that was headlined, "No Promises on Taxation from Fox, Mezvinsky, Miller." Although she was described as opposing, "an across-the-board hike," she declared at the time, "I'm not going to make a promise I can't keep. Look what happened with 'read my lips.'"[18]

Although Margolies-Mezvinsky did not break an explicit campaign pledge, she paid the price in 1994 for casting the decisive vote in the House. As Altman said, her vote "turned out to be the equivalent of walking the plank" because she was defeated in her bid for a second term. Seventeen years later, she wrote an op-ed in the *Washington Post* during the congressional debate over President Barack Obama's health care bill. "I hear that when freshmen enter Congress they are told, 'We don't want to Margolies-Mezvinsky you.'" A generation after her famous vote, she had become an object lesson in the perils of voting for a bill that is critical to a president of one's own party but severely unpopular at home. She explained that she was proud of the vote that had cost her a seat in Congress. Her advice to wavering House members in 2010 was summed up in the headline of her op-ed: "Democrats: Vote Your Conscience on Health Care."[19]

The Struggle in the Senate

With the battle won in the House, Clinton's focus turned to the Senate, which voted the very next day on his budget plan. According to Altman, "We only had 49 votes that we knew about and Senator Bob Kerrey was the undecided vote, the only one left. Fifty [senators] had announced their opposition, 49 Democrats had announced their support, and Bob Kerrey was strolling around, going to the movies, which is what he was doing." Senator Daschle, who had been working to build support for the bill, was asked to win over Kerrey. He recalled, "I did have other assignments [senators to persuade], but the other assignments were a piece of cake compared to Bob." Altman said, "I knew Bob Kerrey quite well by that time and Bob was very unpredictable. You couldn't say to yourself, 'Well in the end he'll be fine.' You couldn't do that."

Kerrey did not make up his mind until just hours before the vote. Altman recalled, "During the day two or three people from the administration spoke to Kerrey—Mack McLarty and Leon Panetta spoke to Kerrey. Then the President spoke to Kerrey. They had a very unsuccessful discussion, which resulted in name calling and cursing. But then Senator [Daniel Patrick] Moynihan spoke to Kerrey late in the day and I thought that was, if not decisive, very influential. He and Kerrey had a very close relationship. Then about an hour before the vote, that's it, we knew that Kerrey would vote for us and then of course [Vice President Al] Gore could break the tie."

Kerrey announced his decision on the Senate floor in what the *Los Angeles Times* described as "a dramatic speech . . . that ended days of Hamlet-like public agonizing." Altman recalled the speech as "excoriating Clinton." Kerrey urged, "Get back on the high road, Mr. President, where you are at your best." While Kerrey's sharp criticism made it clear that he was deeply disappointed with Clinton's leadership, he declared that this would not prevent him from supporting the bill. "I could not, and should not, cast a vote that brings down your presidency." Democratic senators reacted jubilantly, as did Clinton's aides at the White House. Kerrey's vote made it a 50–50 tie, and Gore cast the tie-breaking vote.[20]

The Legacy of the 1993 Budget Bill

The early economic policy decisions and the battle for the 1993 budget set the stage for economic policy making for the rest of the Clinton administration. The bill had a number of important consequences, both political and economic. The electoral cost for the Democrats was one that few of them could have imagined at the time of the vote. In 1994, the Republicans took control of both chambers of Congress for the first time in forty years. Daschle explained that because of their large majority in the Senate when Clinton took office, "the thought of being in the minority in just two years just didn't occur to most Senators."

Lawrence Stein, who served as a congressional liaison for Clinton, explained, "One could argue that '94 happened for a lot of different reasons, but certainly a component was the votes Democrats cast, alone, on Clinton's first budget. . . . When [Tennessee senator Jim] Sasser was beaten, that was the core of the ads run against him by Bill Frist," his Republican opponent. Stein attributed the tough choices that Clinton and his party had to make on the budget to the deficits they inherited. "One can look at '94 and say that's pretty much the consequence of Democrats having assumed responsibility for what Reagan was doing in the

'80s. I think there's much truth in that. The converse is that Clinton's historical credit will probably come largely from having corrected the imbalances Reagan created. But at the congressional level, we massively suffered for that—multiple lost races."

The new Republican majorities in Congress engaged in high-profile standoffs with Clinton, most notably the partial government shutdowns that resulted from disputes over bills to fund the government in late 1995 and early 1996. Many congressional Republicans were convinced that Clinton would sign bills he disliked rather than veto them and thereby shut down the government. But Clinton vetoed the bills, and James Dyer, the Republican staff director of the House Appropriations Committee, called the GOP brinksmanship on the spending bills "one of the worst political strategies in the history of mankind, which was that they were going to start shutting down agencies, and they were going to start targeting certain people and certain institutions. It didn't work. . . . All of a sudden we had taken a fairly bipartisan process and had made it very partisan. That was not about to work."

Alice Rivlin claimed that the shutdowns showed the American people "that the government does do some useful things. The Republican leaders in Congress were totally out of touch. They were so caught up in their anti-government rhetoric that they did not understand that the public outcry was going to be enormous as soon as people realized they couldn't go to the national park, and they couldn't get their student loan, and they couldn't do any of these normal things that citizens expect from government."

Politically, many Clinton aides believed that the shutdown battles helped define Clinton as a strong leader and thereby paved the way for his reelection in 1996. Leon Panetta declared:

> I am absolutely convinced that what the shutdown did was give Bill Clinton the opportunity to identify who he was with the public in contrast to what Gingrich and the Republicans wanted to do. And it in essence did what he could not do the first two years, which is to say to the American people, "This is what Bill Clinton is about, this is what I believe in. This is what I'm trying to do." What the shutdown did is it created that contrast, it created that political leverage that helped the public identify who Bill Clinton was. That happening was, to a large extent, one of the deciding moments in terms of the President's ability to get reelected in '96.

Democrats were not the only ones of that opinion. Republican congressional aide Dyer said, "The first two years [of the Republican congressional majorities in 1995 and 1996], I think the Republicans overreacted a little bit to what they could achieve, and I think that helped reelect the President."

The legacy of the shutdown fights carried over into Clinton's second term, when in 1997 he struck a balanced budget deal with the Republican Congress. White House chief of staff Erskine Bowles explained, "The most important thing in my opinion that came out of the shutdown is that the Congress saw that this president had a backbone, that if you challenged him, he would stand up. You couldn't push him. He wouldn't cave. He would stand on his own principles, and not only did we survive the shutdown, but I think he came away with a great victory. It made all the things we did afterwards so much easier."[21]

The bitter partisan fight over the 1993 budget led to a split among Democrats about whether to strike a deal with the Republicans in 1997 to balance the budget. According to Lawrence Stein, "Daschle's point of view was, 'Look, we did the heavy lifting in '93 because you couldn't have gotten there without raising taxes, something our side believed. Therefore, we ought to do the rest of the job. . . . We took the tough votes. There's no sense in not completing this, and we can take credit for it.'" Stein recounted that the Democratic leader in the House, Representative Dick Gephardt of Missouri, saw the matter quite differently. He contended that Democrats had taken "the tough votes in '93. We're not going to let [Republicans] get credit for completing the job." Those advocating a deal with the Republicans prevailed over Gephardt and his allies, and Clinton and the GOP forged a bill in 1997 that was designed to bring the budget into balance.

The full economic consequences of the 1993 budget bill took longer to be felt than did its political effects. Roger Altman recounted that the bill would lead to economic pain in the short term, while its potential benefits would take more time to materialize. Indeed, one observer noted that the plan's tax increases would be enacted immediately, with some of them retroactive to the start of 1993, while the American people would not reap any economic benefits that might result from deficit reduction for years.[22]

But over time, Clinton's team began to see actual reductions of the deficit. Thomas "Mack" McLarty III, who served first as White House chief of staff and then as counselor to the president, described the consequences: "As we really started to get some traction that the economy was getting better, to our relief, we saw that it was actually going to pay down a bit of the deficit. . . . I remember Lloyd [Bentsen] called me and said, 'Mack, we're going to borrow less money this month. We're not going to have to issue bonds, because we're paying down debt.'" And as that happened, the White House tried to sell the public on the benefits of the plan. "We put a full-court press on: This is not a tax increase, it's a comprehensive economic plan. And here's why it's good for you. . . . Once people started to feel it in their own lives—their mortgages went down, their consumer credit went down, jobs were better, unemployment went down, crime started going down—people said, 'Wait a minute, things are getting better. This young President, I believe, has made a sound decision here, and things are moving forward.'"

During Clinton's second term, the economy grew faster than most had anticipated, and, due in part to a surging stock market, the government began to run annual surpluses instead of deficits. The Clinton administration web site—the first presidential site—attributed economic growth to the president's policies: "After eight years, the results of President Clinton's economic leadership are clear. Record budget deficits have become record surpluses, 22 million new jobs have been created, unemployment and core inflation are at their lowest levels in more than 30 years, and America is in the midst of the longest economic expansion in our history."[23] Of course, congressional Republicans who forged compromise budget deals with the president during his later years in office believe that they deserve substantial credit for these economic accomplishments as well.

How much credit should Clinton and his team receive for the economic growth that took place on his watch? One perspective was offered by Clinton economic advisor Alice Rivlin, whom other Clinton aides described as being relatively apolitical:

> I think there were multiple causes for the boom of the '90s. . . . But I think policy helped. . . . We finally got the budget deficit coming down and very low interest rates, or interest rates coming down, and by the end of the decade, very low. The effort to get the budget deficit down—the main thing was getting it coming down rather than going up. At the beginning of the decade, all the forecasts had it going up, and more and more upward pressure on interest rates would have occurred if the turn hadn't come. Whether it was important to get it to balance, who knows? But that the direction was down, and that it was taking pressure off the bond markets and releasing more capital for investment, is certainly significant. . . . I think that if we hadn't taken the steps to move the deficit down, you might not have gotten the growth in the '90s that you got. Policy can mess things up, badly.

Robert Rubin sounded a similar note. He acknowledged that Clinton's policies didn't cause the boom in the technology industry in the late 1990s but argued that "what he did in '93, and then continued doing through his whole time, was probably indispensable to having the productivity gains you had. It created this environment in which there was a greatly increased willingness to invest. That fortunately coincided with these immense technologies available. Some people say that productivity gains are what the economy was about in the '90s. In one sense that's true, but they didn't just happen. What he did was play an absolutely critical role. I'd call it an indispensable role." Clinton's aides tend to downplay the role that the balanced budget negotiations with Republicans in Congress played in both deficit reduction and the growth of the economy. To be sure, Clinton's initial budget passed without a single Republican vote. But the president and the GOP Congress did work together during Clinton's second term to bring down the deficit even further.

Deficit reduction that helped to spur economic growth isn't the only part of Clinton's economic legacy his aides and allies tout. Several cited with pride the 1993 expansion of the earned income tax credit. According to Alan Blinder, "The earned income tax credit [EITC] is the biggest antipoverty program in America now, thanks to what we did in 1993. It wasn't that big before. But we got a huge liberalization of the EITC." Al From, who chaired the centrist Democratic Leadership Council (DLC) that helped launch Clinton's rise to national office, sounded a similar note. "The earned income tax credit was part of the budget plan, which was a big DLC initiative, the biggest antipoverty program ever."

Economic advisor Gene Sperling calculated the effect of the EITC in 2014, more than twenty years after it was expanded in 1993:

> When people ask, does what you do in government matter, or can you do more outside of government? Look at that one decision. A refundable tax credit at that time that he increased was $7 billion, $8 billion a year. Over time, it became $10 billion a year. That tax cut alone over 20 years now has given over a quarter trillion dollars to low income families. You can put Warren Buffett and Bill Gates' wealth together, and you couldn't do that much.

One Clinton aide who attributed at least part of the economic boom of the 1990s to Clinton's policies expressed frustration that the Republicans who opposed the 1993 deal did not pay a political price. Roger Altman said, "The [1993 budget] vote itself and the fact that not a single Republican voted for this, which even by its critics is seen now as having been at least a contributor to the economic prosperity and fiscal balance that later resulted. . . . One of the many stunning things about it is the fact that none of those Republicans paid a price of any kind for that. . . . [Republican senator] Phil Gramm, I'll never forget, predicted that it would usher in a new depression—I mean depression, not recession. He voted against it, we had a boom, he never paid a dime's worth of price for that."

Although Republicans did not pay a political price for opposing the 1993 bill, Clinton's aides have tried to shape the perception that their boss deserves a great deal of the credit for the growth that followed. Said Altman, "Clinton went for it, Clinton listened, Clinton deserves tremendous credit. He saw the opportunity, he seized it, went against the grain and, let's face it, presided over a period of unprecedented prosperity and balanced the budget for the first time in approximately 50 years." Leon Panetta concurred. "I think the centerpiece is what he did on the economy and on the economic plan, because I think that really did take leadership to do that and he was willing to do it, knowing all of the risks involved. I think it led, in part, to a nine-year period of the strongest economy in the history of this country." Alan Blinder assessed Clinton's legacy by saying, "I have no doubt in my mind that in the fullness of time, history is going to associate Clinton with . . . budget discipline, turning deficits into surpluses, presiding over the greatest prosperity probably we ever had in this country—partly his doing and partly by luck."

In enacting his economic policies, Clinton also changed the direction and reputation of his party. Domestic policy aide William Galston said, "I think that the most important thing the President did was demonstrate there was indeed a serious governing agenda—that was neither the traditional Democratic agenda, nor movement Republican conservatism—which had an integrity of its own, and which could work. Exhibit A is obviously his management of the economy during that period." Altman agreed, asserting that Clinton "may turn out to have transformed the Democratic Party. Certainly, when he captained it, it was a different party than it had been for the previous 50 years. He moved it to the center, made it the party of fiscal responsibility—whoever would have believed that?— and enabled the party to shed much of its old baggage." But Clinton's transformation of Democrats into the party of deficit reduction was not a permanent one. The next Democratic president, Barack Obama, would assume the presidency amid the worst economic recession since the Great Depression and would focus more on stimulating an economic recovery through government spending and other measures than on reducing the deficit.

Presidents are often judged in the eyes of history by the positive and negative developments that occurred on their watch, whether or not they can appropriately claim responsibility or blame. Clinton's critics will likely continue to contend that the economic expansion of the 1990s occurred in spite of and not because of his policies. But at least one Clinton skeptic has come around. Mack McLarty recalled a conversation with Bob Kerrey after Clinton had left office in which Kerrey declared, "Thank goodness you all persuaded me to vote [for] that economic plan. It would have been a disaster had I not done it."

THE BROKEN PLACES

The Clinton Impeachment and American Politics

Andrew Rudalevige

"As required by Section 595(c) of Title 28 of the United States Code, the Office of the Independent Counsel hereby submits substantial and credible information that President William Jefferson Clinton committed acts that may constitute grounds for an impeachment."[1] So began what became known as the Starr Report, which was delivered to the House of Representatives on September 9, 1998, accompanied by thirty-six boxes of evidentiary material.

Two days later, the House voted overwhelmingly to make the 450-page report public, even though most members had not read or even seen it.

Two hours later, the text was posted to the then-novel World Wide Web.

And approximately two minutes after that, the nation suspended its afternoon business as it discovered that the blandness of the first sentence was no guide to the overall contents. The narrative rendering of Bill Clinton's strange relationship with his former intern Monica Lewinsky went viral (to use a term that had not yet been coined), its explicit exposition of their sexual encounters "simultaneously captivating and repulsing the American public."[2]

The Starr Report sprang most directly from the January 1998 revelation to the Office of the Independent Counsel (OIC), led by Judge Kenneth Starr, of recorded conversations with Lewinsky. But its seeds were sown as far back as the Clinton investments in the 1970s that led to the Whitewater investigation and, more recently, the March 1991 conference in Little Rock that brought then-governor Clinton together with Arkansas state employee Paula Corbin Jones.

In the years that followed, the political and legal aftermath of these events flowed through seemingly separate channels that wound up converging in unlikely ways, shaped by the president's enemies and by his own actions. Their confluence finally surged to public notice with another revelation on the Internet, this one in the wee hours of January 18, 1998, when the Drudge Report proclaimed "Blockbuster Report: 23-Year Old, Former White House Intern, Sex Relationship with President"[3]—less than a day after Clinton testified in a different case that he never had "sexual relations" with Lewinsky and just two days after the FBI and OIC had interrogated her for hours in a Pentagon City hotel room. Early on January 21, the *Washington Post*, the *Los Angeles Times*, and ABC News gave Matt Drudge's "blockbuster" headline serious substantive form. And nearly immediately Clinton's presidency was existentially threatened. "I think everyone knew at that point that this was extraordinary," White House aide Lawrence Stein later recalled. It was, he agreed, "resignation material."[4]

The morning the Starr Report became public, Bill Clinton was at a White House prayer breakfast. There, he made a moving—and what many thought his first sincere—public apology for his actions in the Lewinsky matter. "I don't think there is a fancy way to say that I have sinned," the president said. "Legal language must not obscure the fact that I have done wrong." He said he hoped his behavior might teach a useful lesson. "The children of this country can learn in a profound way that integrity is important and selfishness is wrong, but God can change us and make us strong at the broken places."[5]

Here Clinton may have been alluding to the passage from Isaiah he used as a theme in his second inaugural address in January 1997. Translated in the King James Version as "thou shalt be called the repairer of the breach," in the more colloquial New Century Bible the prophet refers to "repairing the broken places."[6] Or perhaps the reference was to Ernest Hemingway's *A Farewell to Arms*: "The world breaks every one and afterward many are strong at the broken places."[7]

If Hemingway was Clinton's inspiration, he left out the next sentence: "But those that will not break it kills." After all, Hemingway got it wrong: by the time the Senate voted not to remove him from office in early 1999, Clinton's presidency had come close to breaking, but neither it nor his political career was ever again close to death. As White House counsel Bernard Nussbaum later noted, "[Clinton] survives much better than anybody could survive, survives and triumphs." Or as the president himself once told Speaker of the House Newt Gingrich: "I'm the big rubber clown doll you had as a kid, and every time you hit it, it bounces back. That's me—the harder you hit me, the faster I come back up."[8]

Yet the American political system did not bounce back fast from the impeachment process, and surely was not stronger at its broken places. Contemporary polarized dysfunction mirrors the snarling politics that took root in the 1990s. Far from repairing the breach, Clinton and his enemies made it deeper.

Crosscurrents

The impeachment story's byzantine plot and colorful cast of characters has nourished an enormous literature on the topic.[9] But it begins simply enough: with a river. Add to that the young attorney general of Arkansas, Bill Clinton, and his wife, Hillary Rodham, casting about for investments and readily persuaded by local entrepreneurs James and Susan McDougal to become co-owners of a proposed vacation resort. Looking down on the White River from the Ozark bluffs one sun-splashed day in 1978, Susan McDougal gave the project its name: White Water Estates.

"Whitewater" would become famous, but not for its natural beauty. As early as 1979, the planned development—hampered by a remote location and sky-high interest rates—was in the red. That fact would be hidden for some time by the relentless optimism and fiscal chicanery of Jim McDougal, channeled through his bank, Madison Guaranty Savings and Loan.

Meanwhile, Hillary Rodham became a power in the local legal world and Bill Clinton moved up the political ladder. As Arkansas governor from 1979 to 1992 (with a two-year interregnum during which Hillary embraced his surname), he earned a national reputation for his innovative policy ideas, chairing the National Governors Association and becoming the leading figure in the Democratic Leadership Council.

Governor Clinton also earned a less welcome local reputation for womanizing.[10] Indeed, concerns that this might doom a national campaign apparently helped dissuade Clinton from running for president in 1988.[11] His White House political director, Joan Baggett, later noted that "there is no one who could have ever worked in or around a Clinton Administration who had any illusions that there weren't issues there." But one such "issue" seemed to be a mere footnote, arising from a chance meeting at a Little Rock policy conference at the Excelsior Hotel. A low-level state employee named Paula Corbin caught Clinton's eye and accepted an invitation to join him in a room upstairs. What happened then is disputed. Nothing, he said; a crude sexual advance, she said.

All of these plot lines—Clinton's talent for politics and policy, his personal finances, and his alleged dalliances—converged when he sought the presidency in 1992. Suddenly small-state gossip had big-time resonance.

Sex was first. As the 1992 New Hampshire primary approached, an Arkansas woman named Gennifer Flowers told a tabloid she had had a twelve-year affair with Clinton. To calm the resultant media firestorm both Clintons decided to appear on national television. There, Bill Clinton said that Flowers's story was not true and Hillary Clinton defended her husband and their marriage. Clinton later parsed his claims when he admitted a past affair with Flowers but stressed that it did not last twelve years.[12]

Then came money. In March 1992, the first national story on Whitewater appeared, raising vague questions about whether the Clintons had benefited somehow from bank fraud.[13] By then, McDougal's Madison savings and loan had joined many of its peers in expanding far beyond its capacity or capital; it went bankrupt in 1989, at a cost to the public of nearly $50 million. The Whitewater project itself had gone under in 1988, but not until late 1992 did the Clintons transfer their interest in it to McDougal. Meanwhile Hillary Clinton, whose Rose Law Firm had done legal work for Madison in the 1980s, sought thousands in Whitewater-related expenses from him. This enraged McDougal, who was already bankrupt and suffering from mental illness. He was indicted and later convicted for various financial frauds; along the way he sought revenge on the Clintons, talking to anyone who would listen about what he saw as their double-dealing.[14] Clinton's many local foes were delighted to help publicize these charges. "Everyone was saying things, and there are so many nutcases in Arkansas," Clinton aide Susan Thomases later sighed. But they found an eager audience in the Washington press corps' sense of its responsibility to introduce this little-known southern governor to the presidential electorate.

Throughout all this, Clinton's transcendent political skill was on display. As his polls sank in the wake of the Flowers allegations (and, especially, revelations of his 1960s maneuverings to avoid the Vietnam draft), Clinton redoubled his efforts in New Hampshire, telling voters that "the character issue is: who really cares about you?" He would stand by them, he pledged, "'til the last dog dies."[15] On February 18, Clinton placed a strong second in the primary: voters had made him the "Comeback Kid," and not for the last time. On November 3, he was elected the forty-second president of the United States.

Inside the White House "–Gates"

Whitewater did not vanish when Clinton entered the White House. "Right out of the box," as Senate majority leader Tom Daschle (D-S.D.) recalled, Republicans in Congress pressed the Resolution Trust Corporation (which was in charge of winding down the S&L crisis) to dig deeper into Madison's books. Deputy Treasury Secretary Roger Altman recalls that throughout 1993, Sen. Al D'Amato (R-N.Y.) "went to the Senate floor [with] a gigantic calendar. . . . Each day he'd give a speech and mark off a day, counting down the days to the expiration of the statute of limitations and saying these people at the RTC damn well better be sure that justice is served, the Clintons aren't off the hook." Editorial boards (and the House Banking Committee) took up the cry: had "taxpayers' money [been used] to cut the loss in Whitewater, or to fuel Bill's political ambitions?"[16] "It was juicy," Thomases admitted. "Everyone always assumed there was some dark underbelly. You know, this was Arkansas . . . there must be *something*."

It didn't help that Clinton's transition to the presidency was, as Daschle noted, "rocky." . . . "Things weren't going well" on the Hill, from nomination hiccups to battles with the military brass. Whitewater merged in the public mind with other contentious events the president's opponents saw as scandals, although Nussbaum later derided, "All these so called scandals! . . . It was all political nonsense to try to undermine this President." Still, the May 1993 dismissal of career officials in the White House travel office for accounting improprieties was dubbed "Travelgate" when press reports suggested that those officials had been mistreated and that friends and relatives of the first family might benefit from taking over the office's work. Soon "Filegate" would join the pile, when hundreds of raw FBI files on George H. W. Bush administration personnel were unearthed in the White House. (These proved to have been mistakenly sent by the FBI in response to a different request.)[17] Even Clinton's May 1993 haircut on Air Force One, originally—and inaccurately—reported as having caused flight delays, spawned leading questions: "Is there any concern," one reporter asked, "[that] it adds up to the picture of a man who is to some degree heedless of the consequences of his personal behavior on others?"[18]

Farce turned tragic in July 1993, when White House deputy counsel Vince Foster committed suicide. Foster had been a law partner of Hillary Clinton in Little Rock and was close to the first family. His suicide note bemoaned the constant press attacks on the White House—"here ruining people is considered sport"—but conspiracy theories erupted immediately.[19] Had Foster been murdered?—by the Clintons?—to cover up their crimes, or perhaps a love triangle? Self-anointed experts rushed to welcoming cameras: suddenly any issue Foster had touched, from Whitewater to Travelgate, was newsworthy again. It didn't help that some materials from his office had been removed and others were turned over only belatedly to investigators.[20] (Most famously, 115 pages of billing records from the Rose Law Firm were rediscovered in a White House office in early 1996, more than a year after they had been subpoenaed by congressional investigators.)[21] "All of a sudden," Nussbaum noted, "people started connecting things that were not connectable: Vince, Whitewater, Clinton having affairs."[22]

Rounding out an awful first year in office was "Troopergate."[23] Back in Arkansas, troopers from Clinton's gubernatorial security detail had been trying to sell a story about their boss's extramarital adventures. These eventually hit the newsstands in *The American Spectator*. Of their array of sordid alleged escapades, one soon took hold. Most names in the article were redacted, but one was mistakenly left in, and that name was Paula. According to the story, after a meeting in a hotel room with the governor, "Paula told [the trooper] she was available to be Clinton's regular girlfriend if he so desired."[24]

In short, as Representative James Rogan (R-Calif.) later put it, from the vantage point of his opponents, Clinton's "White House had more 'gates' than a lab researcher's mouse maze."[25]

Taking Counsel

As 1994 began, two legal trains started moving toward the White House, albeit at different speeds on different tracks.

The first sprang from Paula Corbin Jones's decision to sue Clinton for sexual harassment, spurred on by the *Spectator* article and by her new husband, Steve Jones.[26] Her suit charged that Clinton had made "abhorrent" sexual advances to her at the Excelsior and that her rejection of them led to punishment by her supervisors in state government. Jones wanted not only money but also an explicit apology from the president. Clinton refused to provide either.[27] His lawyers held that neither advances nor punishment had occurred.

Jones went through a sequence of lawyers, each more politically conservative, connected, and motivated than the last, with both sides spurning settlement possibilities even as each dropped strong hints of blackmail.[28] In any event, it was far from clear that a president could be subjected to a civil suit while still in office. That question had to be settled by the Supreme Court, which in May 1997 held that Jones's case could proceed. Justice John Paul Stevens wrote that the separation of powers did not rule out judicial examination of a president's unofficial actions: such "distractions" might be "vexing" but surely rare. Turning to "the case at hand," Stevens produced perhaps the least accurate prediction in twentieth-century jurisprudence: "It appears to us highly unlikely to occupy any substantial amount of petitioner's time."[29]

The other important legal development in 1994 was Clinton's decision to request the appointment of a special prosecutor in the Whitewater controversy. The president was under strong pressure to do so not just from the press and congressional Republicans but also from senior figures in his own party and within his staff. Appointing a special prosecutor even before the independent counsel act passed after Watergate, which had lapsed, was reauthorized would prove the president had nothing to hide, they claimed; it would eliminate the distractions undermining the administration's substantive agenda, notably health care reform. As one of Clinton's legislative liaisons recalled, Whitewater was "just chopping at our credibility and having a very powerful effect on the President, a negative effect on his ability to do anything."[30]

White House counsel Nussbaum was one of the few to oppose Clinton's deci-sion. A special prosecutor, he said, was "a roving spotlight," "a weapon . . . to try to get the President, to try to get the Presidency . . . an institution designed to trap him." But Clinton felt trapped already. "I'm being killed!" he yelled over the phone from Prague. "I'm going to press conferences here in Europe and White-water is all they want to know about. I can't take it."[31] Thus on January 20, 1994, Attorney General Janet Reno announced that she had appointed well-respected former U.S. attorney Robert Fiske as special prosecutor. Fiske was tasked with examining whether the Clintons had benefited directly from Jim McDougal's dubious fiscal dealings; the charges that both McDougals, among others, were involved in bank and tax fraud; and, for good measure, the ongoing rumors sur-rounding Vince Foster's death.

Fiske quickly set up an office in Little Rock and hired a staff. By the end of June, he had confirmed Foster's suicide. He also sought to discourage the House Banking Committee from continuing its Whitewater hearings, worried that they would contaminate his criminal probe. These actions outraged Republicans, who just five months earlier had fervently praised his appointment. Senator Lauch Faircloth (R-N.C.) decried the Foster report on the Senate floor as a "cover-up," and told Reno that Fiske was "unfit for the job."[32]

Meanwhile Congress passed and Clinton signed the Independent Counsel Re-authorization Act, which gave a panel of three senior judges authority over the appointment and jurisdiction of each independent counsel.[33] When Reno asked the panel to reappoint Fiske, most assumed the matter was a formality. But its chair, Judge David Sentelle, argued that Fiske was "compromised" by his earlier appointment and that it was important to appoint someone "not affiliated with the incumbent administration." The panel replaced Fiske with former federal circuit court judge and Bush solicitor general Kenneth W. Starr. Although Starr had a stellar reputation, angry Democrats pointed to his lack of prosecutorial experience—and to a lunch meeting between Sentelle and Senate Republicans several days before the appointment—as proof of partisan perfidy. Clinton him-self later charged that the change was made because Fiske "was actually going to do his job": Starr was the Republican right's "errand boy."[34]

Starr, of course, did not view himself that way and at the outset sought to keep Fiske's staff on board. He even hired a hero of the Watergate investigation, Sam Dash, as his ethics advisor. The early phase of his investigation was generally well reviewed. But Starr was a part-time independent counsel, living in Washington while continuing to take cases in private practice. Meanwhile more was added to OIC's plate: Travelgate, Filegate, yet another probe into the Foster suicide. All of this prolonged his investigations.

After Midterm

In November 1994 another storm buffeted the White House—this one emanating from the midterm ballot box. Republicans gained fifty-four seats in the House and eight in the Senate, taking control of both chambers for the first time in four decades. Of this electoral earthquake's many aftershocks, two are notable here.

First, majority status gave Republicans the levers of congressional oversight. White House deputy chief of staff Roy Neel admits they "used those tools very effectively," although, he argued, "eighty percent of the resources and the time devoted to those hearings . . . were pure political vendettas." In the Senate, a new committee was created to investigate Whitewater "and related matters." The new committee shed little new light; the White House, scorning Chairman D'Amato's search for a Watergate-esque "smoking gun," said he had barely unearthed a "squirt gun."[35] But its hearings kept past controversies in the news and Clinton staffers in the witness chair.

Second, newly fierce budget battles between Congress and the White House shut down the government twice, for a total of nearly thirty days in late 1995 and early 1996. "Non-essential" federal employees were barred from working, shrinking the White House staff from 400 to about 90.[36]

The slack was taken up by unpaid interns. One of them was a 22-year-old from Beverly Hills, just out of college. Her name was Monica Lewinsky. Her yearbook had named her "most likely to have her name in lights."[37]

Monica and "The Big Creep"

Lewinsky began her internship in July 1995, answering correspondence for White House chief of staff Leon Panetta. She later moved to a paid job in legislative affairs, and while her boss didn't know her name ("Monica worked for me, although I never recall actually meeting her," John Hilley later said), she had already made an impression on the president. Flirtatious conversations in Panetta's office quickly escalated into a sexual affair that began on the second day of the first government shutdown in mid-November.

Panetta recalled later that "the President always had an eye for attractive women. But nothing had developed out of that." Clinton himself had told his personal lawyer, "As for women, I'm retired. *I'm retired.*"[38] Much of the shock at the affair, at least in Clinton's inner circle, was over his willingness to take such risks—to let something develop, especially with someone so predictably indiscreet—after attaining the pinnacle of political power. Indeed, Panetta observed that "I've never seen someone who was so immersed in the job of being

President of the United States. . . . We all knew the background . . . but I was always convinced that he cared too much for the Presidency to do that."

Clinton testified in the Jones case that "I had a high level of paranoia. There are no curtains on the Oval Office, there are no curtains on my private office. . . . I have done everything I could to avoid the kind of questions you are asking me here today."[39] Even so, there were safeguards in place: one of Panetta's deputies, Evelyn Lieberman, kept a watchful eye on the Oval's orbit. Hilley notes that "in '96, the decision had already been made to get [Lewinsky] out. . . . Lieberman said, 'She's wandering around the West Wing, and we can't have junior staffers—'—I took it quite literally: . . . She's walking around the White House. At that time, I had no idea what it was." Panetta too was told that Lewinsky was "spending too much time around the West Wing" and that "the appearance it was creating" was a problem.[40] And so in April 1996, Lewinsky was transferred to a job in the Pentagon.

But not in time. The shutdowns had led to what Betty Currie, President Clinton's personal secretary, would call a "compromised protection system": otherwise "she wouldn't have been in that position, that's what I would say." While in that position, though, Lewinsky and Clinton managed to engage in a half-dozen encounters, consisting mostly of oral sex, before her transfer.[41] The relationship continued intermittently by phone and then again in person in early 1997 until Clinton broke it off in May. At one February tryst, Lewinsky wore a blue Gap dress that would later become infamous for its semen stain.[42] Throughout, she sought to return to work in the White House. Clinton's skeptical staff successfully prevented that. But as a consolation, the president asked UN Ambassador Bill Richardson and later Democratic powerbroker Vernon Jordan to help Lewinsky find new opportunities in New York.

Connecting the Threads

Three dangling threads would twine together to make impeachment inevitable.

First, Lewinsky's affair with the president was not as secret as Clinton believed. She had told not only her mother and numerous friends (the Starr Report listed nine) but also another exile from the White House staff, a co-worker at the Defense Department named Linda Tripp. Tripp was *Zelig*: she worked with Vince Foster; she testified in the Travel Office case; she encountered a woman named Kathleen Willey who was exiting a 1993 appointment with the president during which, Willey later charged, an unwanted sexual advance occurred;[43] and now she befriended Lewinsky in the basement of the Pentagon. Not coincidentally, Tripp was set on profiting from the growth industry in anti-Clinton books and had made contact with a literary agent who catered to that market, Lucianne

Goldberg.[44] At Goldberg's suggestion, Tripp began to tape her phone calls with Lewinsky. Much of the twenty hours recorded, her agent complained, was merely "slumber party central"—gossip about work and clothes. But one thing became clear: Tripp's young friend was having an affair with the president of the United States.

Second, with the Jones case again moving forward, the legal process of discovery began. A White House deposition of the president was scheduled for January 1998. Jones's attorneys were naturally interested in establishing a pattern of lechery by Clinton, with the side benefit of placing humiliating evidence about him on the public record.[45] To this end, they were delighted to hear about Kathleen Willey's charges—which Tripp had apparently passed on, pretending to be Willey on the phone—and even more so to be connected to Tripp herself in November 1997.[46] Numerous women in Arkansas and elsewhere were subpoenaed. Thanks to Tripp, one of them was Monica Lewinsky.

Soon this development would connect the third strand: the independent counsel's investigation. Lewinsky, when subpoenaed, asked Vernon Jordan for advice. He put her in touch with an attorney who suggested—since (as she told him) she had never had an affair with Clinton—that she submit a sworn affidavit to that effect, hoping it would quash the subpoena.

In her conversations with Lewinsky, Tripp had taken to calling Clinton the "Big Creep." But in another sense, the phrase could apply to the mission of Starr's OIC. Although by December 1997, Starr had concluded that there were insufficient grounds for a Whitewater-related impeachment referral to Congress, his mandate had expanded into various investigations unrelated to Whitewater and he was increasingly exploring Clinton's "bimbo eruptions."[47] A tip from the Jones legal team—then a call from Tripp herself—seemed to promise another angle of attack. The president had had a sexual relationship with an intern, Tripp said; he had told the intern to lie about that in her Jones case testimony; the intern had, in turn, tried to get Tripp to lie; and the president had even helped get the intern a job to reward her for lying.

If all this seemed tangential to Whitewater, it was, but the last allegation was the entry point for OIC jurisdiction, for which Starr lobbied hard: "jobs for silence" allegations had arisen in Whitewater as well.[48] With Clinton's deposition in the Jones case coming up in a few days and Lewinsky's false affidavit denying any affair already in the works,[49] the OIC felt it had to move fast to "flip" Lewinsky against the president. Accordingly, on January 16, 1998, investigators converged on Lewinsky at a meeting Tripp had arranged at a mall food court. An episodic interrogation that stretched out over nearly twelve hours followed. As it proceeded, OIC lawyers threatened Lewinsky with twenty-five or more years in jail, even as they strongly discouraged her from contacting her attorney. The whole episode attracted much opprobrium and was criticized in a later Department of Justice report as a violation of departmental guidelines.[50]

The next day, Clinton was finally deposed in the Jones case. The president was asked a series of questions about various women linked to a convoluted definition of "sexual relations." To Clinton's nervous surprise, the most detailed questions involved Lewinsky: time spent alone, gifts given and received. Finally: "Did you ever have sexual relations with Monica Lewinsky, as that term is defined in Deposition Exhibit 1?" Clinton replied, "I have never had sexual relations with Monica Lewinsky."[51]

"We Just Have to Win"

Four days later, the Lewinsky affair hit the headlines.[52]

Deputy press secretary Joe Lockhart remembered the scene inside the White House by noting that it "is a vibrant place that's very hard to rattle. Well, this day, the place was rattled. You could just tell that everybody was—saying 'in a state of shock' would be overdoing it—in a state of high anxiety, because no one knew anything about this. It was very explosive, and nobody had heard from the President. . . . There was some presumption that maybe this was bullshit. But there was also a sense that if there was something to it, we had big trouble on our hands."

Clinton's immediate reaction was to deny everything. He broadened his brief as he went through the day, from denying an "improper relationship" in the present tense to a wider disavowal of past "sexual relations" to saying "I know what you mean, and the answer is no."[53] A few days later, Clinton paused before leaving an unrelated public event. "I want you to listen to me," he said, jaw clenched, finger wagging. "I did not have sexual relations with that woman. Miss Lewinsky. I never told anyone to lie, not a single time—never. These allegations are false!"[54] But during this time, Clinton had reconnected with longtime political advisor Dick Morris and been a bit more candid. "I didn't do what they said I did, but I did do something," he said. Morris offered to take some soundings and reported back with poll results: voters cared little about sexual misadventures but they did care about lying, especially under oath. "Well," Clinton responded, "we just have to win, then."[55]

The finger-wagging denial was one effort toward that end; another came the next morning when Hillary Clinton appeared on the *Today* show. She warned the television audience against accepting "rumor and innuendo," stressing that the president had "unequivocally" denied "these allegations." Years of investigations had yielded no wrongdoing, despite a "politically motivated prosecutor who is allied with the right-wing opponents of my husband." In fact, she went on, "this is the great story here: . . . this vast right-wing conspiracy that has been conspiring against my husband since the day he announced for president."[56]

The phrase "vast right-wing conspiracy" was one of the scandal's enduring gifts, although it was more evocative than strictly accurate. A "fairly small (but very intense) right-wing collaboration" would have been closer to the truth. Clinton's detractors had indeed found each other over time, working to link Whitewater to Jones to Lewinsky—first in the press and then in the OIC and soon enough through Congress. At the same time, even as Clinton—both Clintons— "marinated in his sense of victimhood,"[57] it is worth recalling that the president's own behavior was the root of the problem. "Finally," Clinton would concede in his memoir, "after years of dry holes, I had given them something to work with."[58]

In any case, the purpose of Clinton's denials was not so much to deny as to delay. Clinton sought to duck under the looming wave of speculation that he might resign, driven by news reports leaked by Goldberg (via Drudge, including hints of a soiled Gap dress), Jones's lawyers, and the OIC.[59] Senator Chuck Robb recalls that "when the thing broke the next day, you had to believe him, because if not there is just no way I thought he could survive."

Thus, as Clinton himself told a friend, "that lie saved me."[60] Since proving the allegations was not easy—the dress, for instance, would not move from rumor to evidence for seven months—the public had time to reflect on Clinton's character and performance in office. On those attributes they came to divergent conclusions that probably saved his presidency. As Clinton confidant Mickey Kantor noted, "From the very first moment two things were clear in the polls. One, they did not believe him when he said he did not have sex with that woman, Ms. Lewinsky; and two, they did not want him removed from office and they supported him as President." On the evening of January 27, the same day as his wife's *Today* show defense, Clinton put forth his own case, delivering a bravura State of the Union address interrupted by applause more than 100 times. He never mentioned Lewinsky, instead focusing on an expansive domestic agenda centered on using the looming budget surpluses achieved by bipartisan effort to "save Social Security first." Clinton's job approval ratings soared to 67 percent, the highest of his presidency—and those ratings, as distinct from the public's assessment of his personal qualities, remained strong during the entire crisis.

Summertime Blues

On April 1, 1998, Arkansas federal district court judge Susan Webber Wright dismissed the Jones case, citing Jones's failure to show the "tangible job detriment" required by federal law for a harassment case to succeed.[61] The conventional wisdom suddenly shifted in Clinton's favor—after all, any allegations of perjury were linked to a case now deemed to have insufficient merit even to go to trial. The OIC was also under fire for leaking sealed grand jury proceedings to the media.[62] And it had finally abandoned its long effort to bring a Whitewater-related criminal case against the first lady.

But the OIC case against the president continued to build. Most crucially, Starr finally managed to negotiate an immunity deal with Lewinsky. The agreement required her to turn over physical evidence (notably, the dress) to the OIC and to testify before the grand jury. After Clinton refused many times to testify voluntarily, he was subpoenaed and asked to submit to a blood test.[63] His testimony was scheduled for August 17.

One OIC attorney later said that in arranging Clinton's grand jury testimony, his team "had gotten the ever-living shit beat out of us."[64] The president's team negotiated hard over the parameters, limiting the session to four hours (not the two days the OIC wanted) at the White House (not at a courthouse.) On the day itself, Clinton's personal lawyer, David Kendall, surprised Starr with news that the president would open with a prepared statement. In it Clinton admitted that his conduct was "wrong" and included "inappropriate intimate contact" but that it "did not constitute 'sexual relations' as I understood that term to be defined."[65] The OIC team tried gamely to show the implausibility of Clinton's reading of that definition;[66] the president's parsing in response would become an enduring punchline. When asked to square his claim that he had never been alone with Lewinsky, he argued "it depends on how you define *alone*." Most famously, when asked about his attorney's claim in January that "there is absolutely no sex of any kind," Clinton answered that "it depends on what the meaning of the word *is*, is."[67]

It was, Starr's deputy would say, like "trying to nail Jell-O to the wall"—and yet the day was no unalloyed triumph for Clinton. Starr would later say that by refusing to come clean the president had "crossed the Rubicon."[68] If so, that night Clinton taunted the opposing legions, with predictable results. In a short televised address, the president admitted to "a relationship with Miss Lewinsky that was not appropriate. In fact, it was wrong."[69] But, he said, though he regretted that he had "misled people, including even my wife," he had never asked anyone "to take any...unlawful action."[70] The questions were "being asked in a politically-inspired lawsuit that has since been dismissed." And, pivoting quickly from apology to justification to attack, he denounced the OIC investigation, which "has gone on too long, cost too much, and hurt too many innocent people." After all, he said, "even presidents have private lives."

Clinton closed by asking Americans "to turn away from the spectacle of the past seven months." But the tone of the speech guaranteed that the spectacle would continue. Beltway reaction was uniformly critical, even angry.[71] Those within the White House—except for the president himself, who remained glumly self-righteous about his approach—were not much happier. Betty Currie recalls, "A bunch of people in the office were watching it. I heard someone say, 'He didn't say anything.' They were not pleased with it at all." Legislative liaison Lawrence Stein was nervous about congressional reaction: "When he made the speech and didn't hit a home run as he had in the State of the Union (and I think he'd acknowledge that himself)—yes, I was worried. We were all worried."

Matters were, if anything, worse upstairs in the White House solarium, even before Clinton's address. Various drafts urged various levels of contrition. The lawyers wanted Clinton to attack, which chief of staff Erskine Bowles argued was "stupid and wrong." Bowles spoke for Clinton's political advisors, who wanted the speech to feature unalloyed apologetic accountability. As for going on the offense, "That's why God invented James Carville." But as the room grew increasingly chaotic, Hillary Clinton interjected a combination of disdain and angry enablement. "It's your speech," she said to her husband, who had told her the truth about Lewinsky only two days before. "You should say what you want to say."

The first lady paused, then twisted the knife: "You're the President of the United States—I guess."[72]

White House Workings

As the solarium snapshot suggests, 1998 offers a rare look at the organization of a uniquely pressured presidency. As with many crisis situations, the attacks on Clinton tended to work toward a rally-round-the-flag sense of unity, fostering within the White House an aggrieved sense of persecution by a common partisan enemy. But the pressures nonetheless affected White House staff behavior in ways that undercut efficient communication and perhaps effectiveness. In Joan Baggett's remembrance, Whitewater and the rest "certainly affected the type of notes you kept, records you kept. . . . Whether you believed in right-wing conspiracies or not, you had to understand that we were more prone to investigations on pretty much anything that occurred." Health and Human Services Secretary Donna Shalala recalled "we didn't keep any" written records "in the Clinton White House." Even so, the time spent dealing with regular requests for files and testimony meant that staffers had additional burdens. As Betty Currie would later say, "I've got two jobs now. I've got this subpoena job and I've got my regular job." Even the organization chart changed: new staff in the White House counsel's office were hired as lawyers but reported to political staff and the first lady. "That was a big source of friction," recalls then-counsel Abner Mikva.[73]

The Lewinsky revelations fractured the White House along various fault lines—not least between the president and the First Lady.[74] Chief of staff Bowles was known to be particularly upset at both the actions and the deceptions, but many staff were bitter about having been lied to and angry that the president had jeopardized their shared mission.[75] Shalala, who lambasted Clinton at a Cabinet meeting after his August 17 speech, recalls, "We sort of hugged at the end of the thing, but I was just pissed off. . . . When they told me, I just *couldn't believe* it, couldn't believe it. Then I was furious. We were on a roll. We had a lot we wanted to get done." Clinton's "body man," Kris Engskov, says that over the summer of 1998 "people were just whipped. They were just tired. . . . I vacillated between that and then just anger at the President for doing something so stupid. What do you do? You try to move beyond these things."

Amazingly, no one resigned from the administration, realizing the dangerous symbolism that such an action would represent. In this, unity returned. "If two or three senior people, particularly if there's a woman in there, had gone to the North Lawn and resigned," one advisor said, "I think it could in fact have brought down his presidency."[76] Shalala, who could have been that woman, noted that despite conversations with her peers about "whether we should resign over this, I think we actually all decided the same thing. That we should not turn this into a constitutional crisis. We should just get our work done and keep the government together." Some staffers even delayed planned departures. Joe Lockhart recalled that his predecessor, Mike McCurry, "stayed probably nine months to a year longer than he wanted to because of all the Lewinsky stuff. . . . It says a lot about how much we knew about the other side and how ruthless they were and how hard we were going to fight against allowing them to get their way."

Nonetheless, journalist Peter Baker found that "whatever esprit de corps had once existed in the White House . . . degenerated into political cannibalism."[77] The staff splintered along both functional and factional lines. Gaps arose between the legal team, the political advisors, and those still seeking to do substantive work. As Lockhart notes, each had a different mission: "Ours was to preserve the President's political standing. Theirs was to keep the President from going to jail. There were times when those two things didn't go together."[78] Even within the groups of presidential lawyers—who hid information from and even lied to the political advisors—there was what one called an "insane asylum of alliances" based on personal, professional, and organizational lines.[79]

"Scandal management" was parceled out to a relatively small group—Bowles, notably, refused to have anything to do with it. Communications strategy (including a near-daily conference call to give talking points to administration allies) and its tactical codification were closely guarded. Intergovernmental affairs staffer Marcia Hale recalls that morning senior staff meetings sometimes made coded references to the other side of the scandal firewall; "it would be, 'Okay, we're going to have this meeting here, or . . . So-and-so is doing this.' There would be separate meetings. You would get enough so that you knew what was going on, but if you weren't directly involved in the preparation of testimony or anything like that, you really didn't go [into it.] Maybe that's one reason why I was happy doing my Governors and mayors. There was no scandal involved in any of that." Joe Lockhart notes that "when we fast-forward to Lewinsky, this was eight to ten people out of the entire White House, and no one else was welcome in the meetings. You just were not part of this, and you were not allowed to weigh in. We did it, and for better or worse, on a regular basis, it was a small group of people." Everyone else kept their head down and sought refuge in ignorance or black humor.[80] "We had to run the country," Currie said. "I kept thinking, 'We're going to beat this so just keep on working.'"

The White House line throughout was that Clinton could "compartmentalize" the scandal. That is, he put the distraction into a separate box and got on with the job; "I just decided," he said, "that the only way that the whole thing could go bad was if I was unable to function as the president."[81] Susan Thomases said, "He has the ability to keep multiple things in his brain at the same time in ways that you and I can't. . . . He can keep many things afloat and juggling. He's a great juggler." One evening, for instance, the president went from a meeting with his lawyers to a State of the Union prep session to a film screening with his wife and some friends. "A person who hasn't read the papers—a visitor from Mars, say—would never, ever guess there's anything extraordinary going on in his life," one aide told a reporter.[82]

Still, although the White House itself was compartmentalized, most observers suggest that the scandal affected both the president and his ability to guide policy making. Clinton was frequently distracted, "so preoccupied that he appeared lost during meetings," wrote one reporter.[83] A second chronicled "another presidential advisor [with] a different take on Clinton's apparently effortless swings from meeting to movie. 'Pure bunk,' he was quoted as saying more than two years later. He and other colleagues said that 'during the [Lewinsky] scandal Clinton often seemed utterly lost to the world, overcome by a combination of rage toward his opponents and recrimination toward his own weak self.'"[84] Mickey Kantor later put it even more bluntly:

> The whole thing created chaos and took away from the ability of the U.S. government to function. The ability of the presidency and the White House to function. It is not even arguable. . . . It had a huge effect, not just on his presidency in terms of how people viewed the presidency, but on his ability to get things done. Just out of the sheer expenditure of

time, not to mention the loss of prestige. . . . It cannot even be argued. I don't know how anybody can keep a straight face and argue otherwise. I watched it happen and it was devastating to see that.

But the policy process did not grind to a halt, partly as a result of the division Kantor hints at between the White House and the wider executive branch. As Shalala put it, "It's almost as if the government adjusted to his limping."[85] Domestic policy staffer Chris Jennings noted that "you did your work, but you no longer could get the exposure for it that [the White House] normally could. . . . So we did the implementation issues." This meant "a lot more second term executive actions. . . . We did them, first, to get things done. The President hated nothing happening on the Hill . . . so anything we could do to expedite his agenda through executive action was desirable. Second, the communications people loved it because it showed him being strong and acting and doing something. That was particularly important in '97 and '98, because the press and the Congress were focusing on Monica."

Often these actions and "implementation issues" worked through the Cabinet departments. Frequently shut out of the policy-making process during the first term, the Cabinet may in fact have discreetly celebrated the White House's preoccupation with the scandal. Shalala recalls that "people asked me during Monica Lewinsky whether it was awful and we couldn't get anything done. I said, 'No, we got more done,' because the White House people were totally focused on that . . . [while] Cabinet members worked together." Indeed, she went on, "If you look [at the] second term . . . it was quieter because the White House was distracted by Lewinsky. It was quieter—and far more effective. . . . It was a much more exciting time from the point of view of getting things done, making a difference, a measurable difference." This is a useful reminder that the executive branch, and presidential policy making, extends beyond the gates of the White House.

Impeachment

Republicans in Congress eagerly awaited (while Democrats dreaded) the OIC report, which they assumed would substantiate a range of charges reaching far beyond Whitewater and Lewinsky.[86] Indeed, as early as March 1998, according to Representative Rogan's diary, House Judiciary chair Henry Hyde (R-Ill.) told the committee's Republican members that he was receiving information from Starr's office. Hyde added: "if we have to do an impeachment inquiry—oh, hell: it's not *if*—it's *when*."[87] With this in mind, in the spring Hyde began to hire a prosecutorial staff, led by Chicago lawyer David Schippers. Schippers was a Democrat, as he liked to point out, but hardly a Clintonite. He felt that the president had "soiled not just himself, but the Constitution, the public trust, and the Presidency itself."[88] In this he was in tune with his elected bosses. In April 1998, Speaker Gingrich told the House Republican conference that "my personal belief is that the President of the United States is engaged in a vast criminal conspiracy." Hyde added that calling Clinton a "scumbag" (as Representative Dan Burton [R-Ind.] had recently done) might in fact be "mild"—but that "the Judiciary Committee must appear judicious."[89] In meetings with Democratic leader Richard Gephardt (D-Mo.), Hyde gave assurances that he aimed for statesmanship: "It is a recipe for failure if it is partisan."[90]

But judiciousness proved hard to come by. Republicans were hardly disinterested empiricists searching for unbiased evidence. Democrats, for their part, were happy to play along. The minority counsel to the Judiciary Committee, Julian Epstein, told Democratic members they should welcome a partisan lynch mob: "We want [people] to look back at this as the way *not* to conduct impeachments."[91] According to Lawrence Stein, "We had a public strategy of attempting over and over again to show that this was a partisan witch hunt, that the charges against [the president] certainly didn't rise to the level of impeachable offenses, that Starr was hugely, hugely partisan, that he had abused his office, and that the counsel for the committee was a rabid dog."

Republicans made this strategy more workable by deciding to use the Starr Report as the basis for the impeachment inquiry, without conducting an independent investigation by the House Judiciary Committee. Starr made it more effective still by providing a report that was only about Lewinsky and that could be pilloried as, in Stein's phrase, "antiseptic pornography." That is, instead of a broad road map that simply provided information about potential offenses, Starr felt that his mandate under the new independent counsel act was to release a detailed case against the president. In a separate section of his report he presented eleven "grounds for impeachment."[92] Further, the report explicitly and repetitiously chronicled each of the president's encounters with Lewinsky—from furtive gropings to the president's use of a cigar as an instrument of sexual stimulation. The tone aimed at clinical neutrality but mainly achieved, as columnist Joel Achenbach wrote in a mock literary review, a "postmodern . . . rejection of 'readability'. . . . The material, for all its sexual exertions, is not at all titillating."[93]

Worse, perhaps, the "repulsive" lead characters were eclipsed by the "almost crazed zeal" of the narrator: Achenbach noted that "perverse readers may actually begin to root for the despicable President."[94] Democrats sought to capitalize on this, arguing that Starr's report proved that the charges against Clinton were "just about sex." Lying about an extramarital affair was hardly admirable, of course, but it was not illegal and hardly rare. Republicans countered that nothing less than the rule of law was at stake: the president had lied under oath and sought to obstruct the judicial process. Sotto voce—sometimes—they also suggested that Clinton was a sexual predator, emphasizing Willey's claims and other disturbing but unsubstantiated charges in the raw files the OIC had provided for the House's private perusal.

As Rogan put it, "a melee became inevitable, barring some creative intervention."[95] But creativity was limited to GOP efforts to forestall limits on the scope of the inquiry or to censure the president rather than impeach him.[96] The Judiciary Committee's recommendation that it be authorized to formally begin an impeachment inquiry broke firmly along party lines. The full House vote, on October 8, was 258–176, with less than 15 percent of the Democratic caucus breaking ranks. Recalling the bipartisan nature of the Watergate investigation, Hyde groused: "I thought there might be some courageous Democrats who would emulate the Republican record and I was wrong."[97]

Midterm Interlude

One reason for the lack of bipartisanship was that public opinion was not moving in the direction Clinton's accusers expected. The president's Gallup poll job approval numbers never dipped below 60 percent in 1998. Two-thirds of respondents consistently said that Clinton should not be impeached.[98] Rogan, baffled, wrote in his diary that "the more Clinton covers himself in sludge, the higher his poll numbers climb."[99]

Republicans were nonetheless confident of gaining as many as forty seats in November's midterm elections—so confident that Speaker Gingrich encouraged his caucus to quickly pass the fiscal 2000 budget, the better to hit the campaign trail early. This meant giving Clinton key substantive concessions. Stein recalls that "we cleaned their clock, we got everything we wanted. . . . They were counting on impeachment to be their political weapon. They were, therefore, giving in on the policy side." But this only showed that Clinton could still deliver as president despite the shadow of impeachment.

Worse yet for Republicans, internal tracking polls suggested that Democratic candidates were running well. Clinton "didn't turn out to be an albatross for anyone," Charles Brain, Clinton's House liaison, observed. "Didn't bring anybody down, nobody lost their seat as a result of what he had done." Quite the opposite, in fact: Republicans lost five seats in the House and only broke even in the Senate—just the second time since Reconstruction that the president's party had gained strength in a midterm election.[100]

"Polls Be Damned"

The electorate's sharp rebuke forced Gingrich to resign as speaker, and the media (and the White House) quickly jumped to the conclusion that impeachment was dead. Even the new speaker in waiting, Bob Livingston (R-La.), conceded that "the American people have certainly indicated in the polls that they don't see . . . an impeachable or dismissible offense."[101]

But Livingston was not yet speaker, creating a leadership vacuum of sorts, and the GOP majority on the House Judiciary Committee decided to press forward with impeachment in the lame-duck session. "I don't recall any discussion of them not proceeding," Brain said later.

If anything, attitudes on both sides of the aisle hardened. Democrats felt increasingly confident as they realized the president's strength with the public. Further, on November 13, Clinton belatedly settled the Jones case, squelching any appeals of its dismissal. A case that didn't exist could surely not spawn perjury.[102] But Republicans represented districts that were far more supportive of impeachment than national polls indicated. And their spines stiffened with moral certitude as they considered Clinton's unfitness for office, especially after the president's attorneys stonewalled a series of eighty-one written questions from the Judiciary Committee. Rogan noted "a sudden readiness among my colleagues to disregard public opinion and administer some street justice to the neighborhood bully. . . . Polls be damned—no man is above the law."[103]

Two committee hearings illuminated the distance between the two parties' positions. One dealt with Democrats' efforts to force Republicans to define what "high crimes and misdemeanors"—the Constitutional standard for an impeachable offense—actually means. Alexander Hamilton, in Federalist #65, wrote that such crimes "may with peculiar propriety be denominated *political*, as they relate chiefly to injuries done immediately to the society itself": in other words, offenses against the state rather than those of a personal, tawdry nature. Given the limited number of impeachments in U.S. history (just seventeen, nearly all of them of judges, and only seven of which resulted in an official's removal from office), the question was necessarily speculative, even in practice. Then-Representative Gerald Ford's 1970 declaration was technically correct: "An impeachable offense is whatever a majority of the House of Representatives considers it to be at a given moment in history."[104]

Still, a number of constitutional scholars and former members of Congress testified that Clinton's conduct did not meet the constitutional standard. For example, Princeton historian Sean Wilentz claimed that impeachment "would do . . . much greater damage [to the rule of law] than the crimes of which [he] has been accused." Former representative Wayne Owens argued that the charges were "improper and serious, but by nature personal misconduct and therefore not impeachable."[105] Republicans in turn argued that undermining a court proceeding, whether by perjury or witness tampering, obstructed justice and that this was most certainly a public crime, consistent with what Hamilton called "the abuse or violation of some public trust." They held that Democrats had themselves defined impeachable offenses broadly in the past, citing a memo written by a 26-year-old Watergate staff attorney named Hillary Rodham.

Other legal definitions also received attention. Few outside the White House truly doubted Richard Posner's conclusion that "several of the false statements in Clinton's deposition were clearly perjurious," notably his claim to have forgotten he was ever alone with Lewinsky and his parsing of the definition of "sexual relations" to apply to her ministrations to him, but not his to her.[106] But Democratic witnesses doubted that a criminal perjury charge against Clinton would have been brought by any practicing prosecutor. Former U.S. Attorney Thomas Sullivan claimed the case "would be declined out of hand." Obstruction of justice, likewise, foundered on the fact that no person involved in the case (Lewinsky, Jordan, Currie, etc.) had testified that the president had asked them to lie or evade. "Prosecution should never be brought where probable cause does not exist," concluded Ronald Noble, former chief of staff in the Justice Department's criminal division.[107]

Republican committee members argued generally, however, as Rep. Bob Inglis (R-S.C.) put it, that "the score is now zero to four": four panels of witnesses discussing "legal opinions. Not a single person has presented a fact."[108] They recalled the testimony of two witnesses who had been convicted of lying under oath—about sex, to boot. Representative Bill McCollum (R-Fla.) railed about the "double standard we might be creating. . . . Is this fair?"[109]

The battle of partisan talking points culminated in Starr's long day of testimony before the committee on November 19. Even before his opening statement, Democrats denounced the independent counsel as a "federally paid sex policeman," and they soon forced him to concede that none of the other cases the OIC had investigated had borne fruit. Clinton's lawyer David Kendall harangued Starr for illegally leaking grand jury material and for mistreating Lewinsky during her original questioning. Starr's appearance actually prompted his ethics advisor Sam Dash to resign in protest, saying that the OIC should perform no advocacy role in an impeachment proceeding.

Republicans, in contrast, praised "the integrity, the honesty, and the decency" of Starr's investigation and his investigators. At the close of the day-long session, committee counsel Schippers told Starr that "I want to say I'm proud to be in the same room with you and your staff." As he did so, Republicans in the hearing room—including most of the committee members and even Hyde—rose to give Starr a standing ovation. Democrats sat, sullenly, as the applause dispelled whatever bipartisan smokescreen may have remained.[110]

Day of Judgment

On December 12, 1998, the House Judiciary Committee voted to recommend four articles of impeachment. The first accused the president of perjury in his grand jury testimony; the second, of perjury in his Jones deposition; the third, of obstruction of justice via false statements, the coaching of witnesses, and the offer of a job to Lewinsky in return for her silence; and the fourth, of an abuse of power grounded in Clinton's refusal to cooperate with the impeachment proceedings.

All but one article was passed along the strictest of party lines: all twenty-one Republicans voted in favor and all sixteen Democrats voted against.[111] That pattern continued in the full House in a proceeding that veered between churchyard solemnity and circus-tent chaos. The surreal tone was set first when Clinton ordered air strikes against Iraq on the day debate was to begin. Politics did not stop at the water's (or desert's) edge: Secretary of Defense William Cohen, a Republican and former senator, was dispatched to Capitol Hill to calm suspicions that the president had invented the Iraq crisis to derail the impeachment vote. Speaker-designate Livingston agreed to put off that vote by one day, but no more; too many in his caucus felt, with Majority Leader Dick Armey (R-Tex.), that Clinton, "after months of lies," had given the world "reason to doubt that he has sent Americans into battle for the right reasons."[112]

Thus, on December 18, the full House gathered to consider the articles of impeachment. Over twelve hours and more than 260 speakers, arguments broke largely along the lines rehearsed in committee.[113] Democrats attacked the "Republican coup d'état," calling the proceedings a "constitutional assassination." "To force an impeachment vote," Representative David Bonior (D-Mich.) argued, "is to completely ignore the will of the American people."

Republicans, by contrast, argued (in Hyde's words) that the charges were not grounded in "lying about sex" but in "lying under oath" and that this was "a public act, not a private act . . . a question of the willful, premeditated, deliberate corruption of the nation's system of justice." Hyde accused the Democrats of admitting Clinton's acts but following a "so what?" line of argument—namely, that no one should care. To do so, he argued, was to undermine the rule of law embodied in the spirit of the Ten Commandments, the Magna Carta, and even the Battle of Bunker Hill. "Catch the falling flag," he implored his colleagues, "as we keep our appointment with history."

Early the next morning, the first lady made an unexpected appearance at a meeting of the House Democratic caucus. "It was like a pre-game pep rally. Forget the weightiness of constitutional role here," Brain recalled. Hillary Clinton knew that she alone could give House Democrats moral absolution for their votes; she did so, thanking them for supporting "the commander in chief, the President, the man I love." White House staffers looked on gratefully. "She was absolutely great, they loved her," Lawrence Stein recalled. "It was extemporaneous. It was beautifully done."[114]

Then, as debate opened, Livingston took to the floor. He called on Clinton to resign, to "heal the wounds you have created." Democrats on the floor shouted back, "*you* resign!"—and to their shock, he did. Conceding his own extramarital affairs, Livingston said "I must set the example that I hope President Clinton will follow." Hyde, whose own past affair had also been uncovered during the impeachment investigation, told the Judiciary Committee Republicans, "If you're not convinced by now that these people in the White House are evil, then I don't know how else to convince you."[115]

Finally the roll was called. A motion to substitute censure for impeachment was defeated. Articles II and IV were also defeated—the first narrowly, the latter by a wide margin.

But Articles I and III were adopted.[116] Only five Democrats voted for, and five Republicans against, Article I. For the first time since 1868, the president of the United States had been impeached.

To the Senate

Immediately after the vote, a procession of the most vocal House Democrats arrived at the White House for an impromptu rally with and for the president. The first lady had been so persuasive, Stein recalled, "that Charlie Rangel insisted—I resisted this, but we ultimately capitulated—that we get buses and bus people down to the White House after the vote, as support for the President." Brain recalls Hillary Clinton telling Rangel, "'That would be great, come on down.' . . . I didn't realize until afterwards that there was going to be news coverage and helicopters filming the buses going down, how big a deal it was." As a spectacle it was, indeed, in somewhat dubious taste.[117]

Still, the rally's very tackiness managed to suggest that this was just another political fight, rather than a moral crusade over falling flags. And it sent a message of solidarity to potentially wavering Democrats in the Senate, the next venue for the impeachment debate.[118] Additional good news on this front soon arrived: Clinton's public approval rating in a December poll taken immediately after impeachment vote was 73 percent, the highest of his presidency. Indeed, on January 2, 1999, Gallup reported that Clinton was the most admired man in America, beating out Pope John Paul II.

"Senate on Trial"

On January 8, the 100 members of the Senate—fifty-five Republicans and forty-five Democrats—gathered together to decide how to conduct the impeachment trial. They had little historical precedent to guide them. Further, as the 81-year-old Robert Byrd (D-W. Va.) warned, his colleagues needed to protect their chamber from the "political quicksand" and "salacious muck" the House process had stirred up. Senator Mitch McConnell (R-Ky.) added that the president was only nominally the defendant. Instead, "the Senate is on trial because we're sure of the outcome."[119] That is, since the Constitution requires a two-thirds vote in the Senate to remove an impeached official, Clinton could only be convicted if twelve Democrats deserted him.

Nonetheless, most accounts of the Senate trial suggest that Clinton was hardly invulnerable. One presidential aide said later that the only thing obvious at the time was "how inevitable nothing was."[120] Thus, Byrd's words came as some relief. The elderly West Virginian was a major worry for the White House. Himself a Senate institution, Byrd took the chamber's prerogatives very seriously. Stein later reflected, "I think Byrd could have burned down the house. Listen, Tom Daschle saved this Presidency, and that's the truth . . . He knew from day one what could do it, and that is Byrd going down to the floor and delivering a thing that he does extraordinarily well, and that he is looked to for—an institutional speech. If he had validated this process, it would have meant a lot."[121]

But the Senate was determined to win its own trial by staying out of the quicksand. As Stein put it, along with Daschle and Byrd, "[Majority Leader Trent] Lott . . . watched what happened in the House and absolutely refused to let that happen in the Senate." The result of a rare joint party caucus was an agreement over procedure brokered by conservative Texas Republican Phil Gramm and liberal Massachusetts Democrat Ted Kennedy. Back on the Senate floor, the resolution passed by a 100–0 vote.

Only two groups were unhappy with this development: the House of Representatives and the White House. The thirteen House managers assigned to serve as prosecutors for the trial were angry that the Senate planned to limit the duration and scope of the case they could present. David Schippers later complained of "our own guys, selling us down the river!"—"it was a flat-out rigged ball game."[122] Among other issues, the managers objected to the Senate's desire to have the Starr report serve as the entire trial record and thereby prevent witnesses from being called. Lott had originally hoped, in fact, to wrap up the trial within six days.[123] James Rogan, now one of the managers, wrote in his diary that he wanted to "demand that the Senate let us try our case properly, or else tell them to take their bipartisan screw job and shove it where the senatorial sun doesn't shine."[124]

White House deputy chief of staff John Podesta, for his part, railed against the senators "preening their little unity dance."[125] The president's men did not want the Senate to give the impeachment credence by appearing to take it seriously. Ideally they wanted the charges to simply be dismissed. They wanted the trial to be about Ken Starr. They certainly did not want a parade of witnesses dredging up thirty years of Arkansas history and gossip, clothed in the gravitas of the Senate chamber.

But the Senate didn't want that either. As Stein remembers, "This was where the House managers lost significant credibility with Republicans. . . . They were insisting on a long trial, a lot of witnesses. Keep in mind, the Republicans had just lost ground in the elections. And among political people, there is only one clear registration of reality: at the ballot box. . . . I think that people like [Ted] Stevens [R-Alaska], people like [Pete] Domenici [R-N.M.], people like [Arlen] Specter [R-Pa.], [Fred] Thompson [R-Tenn.], thought, 'We're dealing with something a little extraordinary here, and we don't like it.'" Sen. Pat Leahy (D-Vt.) said of the House managers that "they flunked the exam in their body. They hope to do a makeup exam in the Senate, and that's not going to happen."[126]

In the midst of this came another State of the Union address—thus marking the Lewinsky scandal's first birthday. As he had done one year before, Clinton delivered a lengthy tour of the policy universe. He made no mention of the ongoing Senate trial except to express the hope that a future president would look back and conclude "that we put aside our divisions and found a new hour of healing and hopefulness." But he did take a moment to praise the first lady "for all she's done," even mouthing "I love you" as the cameras zoomed in.[127]

The president's appearance was bookended by trial proceedings that added little that was new to the record, although often with some eloquence. White House Counsel Charles Ruff sought to cast the managers' case as "a witch's brew of charges." It was a "nice try—no facts." Just-retired senator Dale Bumpers, Clinton's fellow Arkansan, gave a folksy but telling address; Clinton had behaved badly, he conceded, but had been punished for that. The rule of law, Bumpers stressed, meant respecting the results of presidential elections and the will of the people: there was "a total lack of proportionality, a total lack of balance in this thing."[128] The three witnesses who testified before the Senate—Lewinsky, Jordan, and White House staffer Sidney Blumenthal—added little to the prosecution's case.[129]

However, the House managers scored points too, especially when they had the chance to interact more directly with the president's legal team during questions. "A president should not be impeached . . . for a mistake of judgment," Representative Charles Canady (R-Fla.) said. But "he should be impeached and removed if he engages in a conscious and deliberate and settled choice to do wrong, . . . to violate the laws of this land." Hyde told the Senate that the managers were not partisans, but profiles in courage. He urged those in the chamber to "take [your] place in history on the side of honor and, oh yes: let right be done."

A tough question from Senator Byrd—quoting the Hamiltonian invocation of the "public trust"—gave the managers brief hope that he might defect from the Democratic bloc and set off the chain reaction the White House feared. But shortly thereafter Byrd moved that the case be dismissed entirely. This was "not because I believe the President did not do wrong." But there was no chance he would be removed; and the trial would "only . . . deepen the divisive, bitter, and polarizing effect that this sorry affair has visited upon our nation."[130] In the end, Byrd had decided the trial was a bigger threat to the Senate than Clinton was to the nation.

Byrd's motion failed, but his (and McConnell's) earlier prediction turned out to be right. Party divisions—although papered over at the outset—did not change much during the course of the proceedings. Democrats stuck by Clinton, even as they decried his behavior. Some Republicans also felt that Clinton's behavior was, as Senator Susan Collins (R-Me.) wrote in her diary, "so tawdry, so dispiriting"—but not impeachable.[131]

Various efforts to censure the president, or to adopt some sort of "fact-finding" resolution that would condemn Clinton without removing him from office, faltered. Republicans felt that these were transparent gestures to give Democrats cover they didn't deserve, while Democrats—or at least Clinton—feared that such a course would both undermine the vindication of an acquittal and give a future prosecutor a list of Senate-endorsed charges to use in criminal court.[132] Instead, those who wanted to criticize the president took to the floor during the Senate's final deliberations. Although the sessions were closed to the public, senators were later allowed to insert their remarks in the *Congressional Record*. Those remarks were not kind. "The difference between Nixon and Clinton," said Senator Gramm, "is that Nixon had shame."[133]

But those speeches were not votes. When the senators emerged into public session on February 12, 1999, they voted to acquit Clinton on both articles. On the first, perjury, the Senate split 50–50, with five Republicans voting against removing the president from office. An additional five Republicans did not support the second count of obstruction of justice, giving the article only forty-five votes. Publicly, the White House response to acquittal was muted. "Our one instruction to ourselves," Lawrence Stein said, "was: 'Do not show any sign of satisfaction.'"[134]

The Clinton Impeachment and American Politics

Clinton's long personal nightmare was over—mostly. Judge Wright declared him in contempt of court for his behavior during the Jones deposition. Robert Ray, the independent counsel who succeeded Starr in October 1999, seriously considered bringing criminal charges against a post-presidential Clinton.[135] Instead, ending the OIC's seven-year-long investigation, Ray closed the books—but only in exchange for a fine, a five-year suspension of Clinton's law license, and, most painfully, Clinton's public admission that he had lied under oath.

It is hard to conclude that President Clinton's behavior did not warrant sanction. But it is even harder to conclude that impeachment was the proper vehicle for imposing it. Charles Ruff was not wrong when in his closing argument he accused the president's enemies of "wanting to win too much."[136]

Yet they would have said the same of Clinton. Few observers find much heroism on display in this saga. Jeffrey Toobin, for instance, said the participants' common trait was "the narrow pursuit of self-interest. . . . , the assiduous pursuit of immediate gratification—political, financial, sexual."[137]

It is not that such a dynamic would have surprised the framers of the Constitution. Hamilton predicted in Federalist #65 that impeachment would often "connect itself with the pre-existing factions, and will enlist all their animosities, partialities, influence, and interest on one side or on the other." The framers expected self-interested actors to hold office in the government they created; they knew, as James Madison had put it in Federalist #10, that "enlightened statesmen will not always be at the helm."

But they trusted that the institutions they had designed would counteract the "defect of better motives."[138] The system, in short, was supposed to channel self-interest toward the public interest. Yet this did not happen here. "Whatever else the Clinton impeachment stood for," political scientist Paul Quirk observed, "it was symptomatic of a chronic and frequently debilitating condition of the political system."[139] With the elected branches gridlocked, the judiciary and legal system became a prime instrument of partisan warfare.[140] At the same time, the media failed to act as an evenhanded watchdog. Instead, scandal was a blessing for the new commentariat that flourished with the rise of cable television and, soon, the Internet.[141] More generally, the "intense, bitter, divisive, dogmatic politics" of the impeachment arose from a developing combination of structural electoral changes and shifts in media, money, and patterns of participation in voting and governance that largely benefited ideological activists.[142] Research shows that far from bravely defying the polls, most members of Congress who supported impeachment voted in accordance with their homogenous constituencies.[143] "Senior members of the Republican Party are terrified of their own base," Clinton told historian Taylor Branch during the Senate trial.[144] But if these developments were not Clinton's doing, as a willing and very skilled participant in the "war room" politics he helped perfect, he certainly exploited them.

The parties were polarized not just over policy preferences but over their opponents' very legitimacy. One side's "vast criminal conspiracy" ran up against the other's "vast right-wing conspiracy" in self-reinforcing self-righteousness. Certainly the Clintons attracted astonishing opprobrium; Roy Neel notes that "Clinton was everything that the social conservatives hated, in a visceral, personal kind of way."[145] As House manager James Rogan wrote, "Clinton lies, cheats, and destroys people's lives. He gets away with it time after time. I don't understand what is wrong with America."[146] But such feelings were returned with interest: Maxine Waters (D-Calif.), for instance, denounced the "extremist radical anarchy [couched] in pious language" that she said showed "the Republicans are the vehicles being used by the right-wing Christian Coalition extremists to direct and control our culture."[147]

Along the way, both sides claimed to be defending the Constitution. Hyde told the House managers that their "devotion to duty and the Constitution has set an example that is a victory for humanity."[148] But Bill Clinton, toward the end of his presidency, said "I think we saved the Constitution of the United States. I'm not ashamed of the fact that they impeached me. . . . As a matter of law, the Constitution, and history, it was wrong."[149] That opinion is reflected in the Clinton Library and Museum's dismissive treatment of the subject. A single panel complains of Starr's tactics, claims that the Jones case had "no legal or factual merit," and states that "the impeachment battle was not about the Constitution or the rule of law, but was instead a quest for power that the President's opponents could not win at the ballot box."[150]

Yet the Constitution calls for compromise, something the moral valence of partisan certainty made virtually impossible. Interestingly, Clinton had originally tried "to try to center the Democratic Party in the mainstream of American politics, to lessen the influence of the liberal wing and try to resituate it," as John Hilley put it. But

> he was simply short-circuited from that. Once the Republicans got him on the scandals, I saw him having necessarily to fall back and depend on the liberal wing. In other words, these were the . . . ones who would rush to the floor and defend the President to their dying breath against the Republicans. And so, the whole move to the middle—which he'd been doing so successfully in '96 and '97—once impeachment came, the energy was gone, his attention was diverted, and the caucus he had to depend upon for survival was the left-leaning one.

Impeachment, then, pushed Clinton left and the Republicans right. It stranded the strategy of triangulation that had brought centrist success—including welfare reform and a budget surplus—to American politics in the post-shutdown, pre-impeachment period.

The opportunity costs for both sides, in policy terms, were immense. Clinton's successors pledged to be uniters, not dividers—they pledged allegiance to the United States, not red or blue states—but they became, in quick succession, the most polarizing presidents in the history of modern public opinion. Outrage remained the dominant trope of American political discourse. Senator Susan Collins, who voted against removing Clinton from office in 1999, was still speaking by 2015 about the curse of "hyperpolarization," in which "ideology and partisanship dictate far too much of our conduct" as "one insult generates another, ad infinitum and ad nauseum."[151]

Clinton's own "broken places" would knit strong. After leaving office he again became the most popular politician in America. But the impeachment saga was a cause as well as an effect of "hyperpolarization." The system, too, was broken; and those wounds have proven slow to heal.

CLINTON AND WELFARE REFORM

An Oral History

Michael Nelson

A frequent assertion about the presidency of Bill Clinton, one that has congealed into conventional wisdom, is that he signed landmark welfare reform legislation—formally the Personal Responsibility and Work Opportunity Reconciliation Act of 1996—for short-term and crassly political reasons.[1] As the accepted narrative goes, electoral consigliere Dick Morris "told him flatly that a welfare veto would cost him the election" because it "would transform a fifteen-point win into a three-point loss" to Republican presidential nominee Robert J. Dole in the November election.[2]

Buttressing this interpretation is testimony from several Clinton administration officials who wanted the president to forgo political expediency, steel himself in the service of principle, and veto the bill. "Morris was fulminating about the importance of taking welfare off the table before the fall campaign, so Dole couldn't beat B[ill] over the head with it," wrote Secretary of Labor Robert Reich, a participant in the July 31, 1996, Cabinet Room meeting at which Clinton heard final arguments about whether to sign. "Dick Morris isn't in the room but he might as well be. I can hear his staccato-nasal voice: 'The *suburban swing!* The *suburban swing!*'"[3] According to White House chief of staff Leon Panetta, Morris "continued to push Clinton to take away issues that Republicans once owned in order to secure his hold on the center. In 1996, that meant welfare reform."[4] In political aide George Stephanopoulos's view, Clinton's "heart urged a veto, while his head calculated the risk. They were reconciled by his will—a will to win that was barely distinguishable from the conviction that what was best for the poor was for him to be president."[5] Peter Edelman and Mary Jo Bane, each an assistant secretary in Clinton's Department of Health and Human Services, resigned from the administration in disagreement with the president's decision. "By signing the bill," Edelman later argued, Clinton "helped (as he saw it) to ensure his own reelection but also helped the Republicans retain control of Congress."[6]

Oral history interviews of administration alumni organized by the University of Virginia's Miller Center as part of the William J. Clinton Presidential History Project offer a different, more nuanced perspective on Clinton and welfare reform.[7] Oral history, like all historical methods, is an imperfect instrument. Memories are fallible, incomplete, and subject to conscious self-aggrandizement and unconscious bias. But as historian Philip Zelikow has argued from long experience serving in and studying government, "In weighing the value of oral histories, consider that there are only two kinds of primary sources about the past. There are the material remnants of what happened—documents, coins, statues. Then there are the preserved recollections of the human observers."[8]

Two advantages that are lacking in "material" sources attend oral history. One is that in contrast to a written document, scholars can ask questions of interviewees, probing deeply for elaboration, clarification, and context and seeking comment on apparent contradictions with the written record or the accounts of others. (In contrast to journalistic treatments of events that are based on unattributed quotations, oral history interviewers place respondents on the record.) Andrew Card, a high-ranking official in several Republican administrations, says that in his experience, oral history sometimes is more accurate than the history recorded in documents. From personal observation, Card offers the example of a foreign leader who, asked by an American president to do something that might cause domestic political difficulties, told the president no for the record while emphatically nodding yes.

The other advantage of oral history is that fewer written records concerning sensitive or important matters are being created, the result of reasonable fears of congressional or judicial subpoenas. "You'll find a lot of memos, but I didn't keep notes," says Donna Shalala, Clinton's secretary of health and human services in her oral history interview. According to national security advisor Anthony Lake, "More and more officials are loath to put anything in writing." Consequently, argues political scientist Russell L. Riley, "The White House operates largely as an oral culture" in which "much of the most important business occurs only in spoken, not written, words."[9] For example, according to the archivist at the Clinton Presidential Library, no formal record of the crucial July 31, 1996, meeting on welfare reform exists, but participants' spoken memories are extensive.

In this chapter, I offer a narrative account of welfare reform comprised mostly of the words of relevant policy-making participants.[10] I draw chiefly on Miller Center oral history interviews but also include other spoken words and written memoirs (the other form of "preserved recollections," according to Zelikow), along with occasional connecting material. Two conclusions emerge from this account that complicate the conventional wisdom. First, Clinton's concern about welfare policy, far from being an artifact of his 1996 reelection campaign, had deep roots in his life and career. Second, although politics mixed with policy in his approach to the subject, Clinton's most meaningful political considerations were long term, not immediate. Specifically, he wanted to restore the Democratic Party's competitiveness in presidential elections by removing the long-damaging issue of welfare from the national political agenda.

The welfare system that Bill Clinton worked to reform originated in the Social Security Act of 1935. Called Aid to Dependent Children (later Aid to Families with Dependent Children, or AFDC), it was designed to help widows with children. By the late 1960s, however, the program's typical client was an unmarried mother with little education and little ability to secure employment that would pay enough to make up for the loss of Medicaid and other benefits that accompanied AFDC. According to the leading scholar of welfare policy, David T. Ellwood, the average person on welfare at any given time had been receiving benefits for the previous ten years.[11] Something approaching a permanent welfare class had developed, which fostered resentment among many taxpayers directed at both welfare recipients and the Democratic Party. As more and more middle- and working-class women with children entered the work force, a program that paid other women to stay home with theirs for an extended period of time became harder to defend. Republican president Richard Nixon and Democratic president Jimmy Carter made serious but unsuccessful efforts to persuade Congress to reform the welfare system.

Arkansas

As a boy growing up in Arkansas who saw his widowed mother rise before dawn to go to work, Clinton was aware of the dignity of labor. As governor of the state, he became convinced that the welfare system was broken in ways that served everyone poorly.

Bill Clinton:

I had spent enough time talking to welfare recipients and caseworkers in Arkansas to know that the vast majority of them wanted to work and support their families. But they faced formidable barriers, beyond the obvious ones of low skills, lack of work experience, and inability to pay for child care. Many of the people I met had no cars or access to public transportation. If they took a low-wage job, they would lose food stamps and medical coverage under Medicaid. Finally, many of them just didn't believe they could make it in the world of work and had no idea where to begin.[12]

Bruce Reed (Deputy Domestic Policy Advisor in the Clinton White House):

What too many didn't realize and too few social scientists had come around to studying was just the deep frustration of people trapped in welfare themselves—that the fault was with the system, not with the people in it. If you're a senator or an HHS [Health and Human Services] Secretary, it's just a lot harder to actually talk to a real person. But if you're a governor in a state, and someone with Clinton's personality—he loved to drive to the Delta, go to the small towns, go to places where they'd never seen a governor before—I think he was able to get a different perspective than a lot of people for whom it was just politics. . . . As he would later say, he probably spent more time in welfare offices than anyone else who'd ever sought the presidency, so he was able to speak about the issue in a way that shared the frustrations of welfare recipients and voters alike.

After his election as governor in 1978, Clinton participated in a Carter administration demonstration project aimed at encouraging people to move from welfare to work by providing support to help them make the transition. Later in the decade, as leader of the National Governors Association, Clinton worked with Congress and the Reagan administration in writing the Family Support Act of 1988, which made modest changes in the system.

Bill Clinton:

At one of our governors' meetings in Washington, along with my welfare reform co-chair, Governor Mike Castle of Delaware, I organized a meeting for other governors on welfare reform. I brought two women from Arkansas who had left welfare for work to testify. One . . . was in her mid to late thirties. Her name was Lillie Hardin, and she had recently found work as a cook. I asked her if she thought able-bodied people on welfare should be forced to take jobs if they were available. "I sure do," she answered. "Otherwise we'll just lay around watching the soaps all day." Then I asked Lillie what was the best thing about being off welfare. Without hesitation she replied," When my boy goes to school and they ask him, 'What does your mama do for a living?' he can give an answer." It was the best argument I've ever heard for welfare reform. After the hearing, the governors treated her like a rock star.[13]

Bill Clinton:

I'm not that mad, but it still burns me when people say, "Well, Clinton caved to the people on welfare reform, to the Republicans so, you know—because he wanted to get re-elected." That's just false. Jimmy Carter gave six states a chance to experiment in moving people from welfare to work. I lobbied for my state to be one of them and we were. When Ronald Reagan was president, I was the Democratic governor charged with representing our side in negotiating welfare reform.[14]

Bruce Reed:

[Hillary Rodham Clinton] was always, because she'd been chair of the Children's Defense Fund, presumed to be a defender of existing programs. Quite the opposite was true. They had been partners and had come up with the agenda in Arkansas, so she'd seen it work there. . . . [Responsibility] was the most important word in his lexicon. She was also a big believer that where we'd gone astray in our social policies was where we had forgotten to ask something in return.

Running for President, 1992

As was the case throughout his governorship, Clinton developed his views on major issues in consultation with Hillary Rodham Clinton when preparing to run for president in 1992. He also drew on the experience of fellow governors through the National Governors Association and on the emerging centrist ideas of the Democratic Leadership Council, both of which he led.

Hillary Rodham Clinton:

By 1991, when Bill launched his campaign for president, it was clear that the reforms [passed by Congress in 1988] weren't producing much change because the [George H. W. Bush] Administration didn't fund the new programs or aggressively implement them in the states. Bill promised to "end welfare as we know it" and to make the program pro-work and pro-family.[15]

Bruce Reed:

In the key paragraph of [Clinton's October 3, 1991, speech declaring his candidacy for president], he announced his intention. He said that, "Government has a responsibility to provide more opportunity, and people have a responsibility to make the most of it." It was the first time he'd ever said it quite that way. Those were his words. I've always thought that his biggest intellectual, philosophical contribution to the Democratic Party was to restore the link between those two concepts. Almost everything that he did that mattered combined more opportunity and more responsibility. . . .

When the campaign started, we decided that our competitive advantage was that Bill Clinton had more ideas on more subjects and a clearer world view than anyone else, so we set up three speeches for him to give at Georgetown. The first one was the New Covenant speech, where he laid out his social vision and laid out the new bargain of opportunity and responsibility.

Bill Clinton:

To turn America around, we need a new approach founded on our most sacred principles as a nation, with a vision for the future. We need a New Covenant, a solemn agreement between the people and their government, to provide opportunity for everybody, inspire responsibility throughout our society, and restore a sense of community to this great nation. . . .

The New Covenant must be pro-work. That means people who work shouldn't be poor. In a Clinton Administration, we'll do everything we can to break the cycle of dependency and help the poor climb out of poverty. First, we need to make work pay by expanding the Earned Income Tax Credit for the working poor. . . .

The New Covenant can break the cycle of welfare. Welfare should be a second chance, not a way of life. In a Clinton Administration, we're going to put an end to welfare as we know it. I want to erase the stigma of welfare for good by restoring a simple, dignified principle: no one who can work can stay on welfare forever.

We'll still help people who can't help themselves, and those who need education and training and child care. But if people can work, they'll have to do so. We'll give them all the help they need for up to two years. But after that, if they're able to work, they'll have to take a job in the private sector, or start earning their way through community service. That way, we'll restore the covenant that welfare was first meant to be: to give temporary help to people who've fallen on hard times.[16]

Bruce Reed:

The speech did take the political world by storm. Michael Barone wrote that it was the best political speech of the cycle. It set the tone for the rest of the ideas offensive that he went on to do that fall, and it ended up becoming the issue that defined him as a different kind of Democrat. . . . Welfare was the best example of what Clinton would prove to be a master of, of taking an issue that Republicans had demagogued for years and turning it into an affirmative, political, and substantive agenda for Democrats.

Fits and Starts, 1993–1996

Clinton was elected president in 1992 by an electoral vote majority of 370 to 168. The Democratic Party retained control of both houses of Congress. Congressional Democrats were much less interested in changing the welfare system than Clinton or congressional Republicans.

Bill Clinton:

[In the 1993 budget negotiations] I insisted that we include in the budget the full $26.8 billion cost of my campaign proposal to more than double the tax cut for millions of working families with incomes of $30,000 or less, called the Earned Income Tax Credit (EITC), and for the first time offer a more modest EITC to more than 4 million working poor Americans without dependents. This proposal would ensure that . . . working families with incomes of $30,000 or less would still receive a meaningful tax cut. On the campaign trail, I had said at virtually every stop, "No one with children who works full-time should live in poverty." In 1993, there were a lot of people in that situation. After we doubled the EITC, more than four million of them moved out of poverty into the middle class during my presidency.[17]

Bruce Reed:

[In addition to the EITC increase, welfare reform] was such a central issue to the campaign that I didn't worry about Clinton losing interest in it. I knew that it was a defining issue for him personally and he cared an awful lot about it. I was more worried about what we were going to do about the fact that the only allies we had were the American people and everybody trapped in the welfare system.

Our real problem was that it quickly became apparent to us that nobody in Congress—nobody on the Democratic side, none of the Democratic leaders— wanted us to do a welfare bill. [Speaker of the House Thomas] Foley and [House Majority Leader Richard] Gephardt in particular pleaded with Clinton not to send one. Bob Matsui, who was the head of the subcommittee that would write the welfare bill in the House, told us we were crazy to try to send up a bill, that it would divide the party.

This was an issue where we knew it was going to be a fight and we knew we'd have to work in a bipartisan manner to get it done because we couldn't get there with just Democrats. We also knew that this issue had been the Waterloo of many previous administrations. Welfare reform had been talked about for years, but it had been a disaster for Nixon and for Carter. Reagan had gotten a welfare bill, but it was not very effectual.

Mickey Kantor (U.S. Trade Representative, Secretary of Commerce):

[During the postelection transition, Clinton] committed to Tom Foley, George Mitchell and Dick Gephardt, at a dinner in Little Rock, that he would not go for welfare reform because they didn't want him to do so.

William Galston (Deputy Domestic Policy Advisor in the Clinton White House):

There were substantial forces—not only in the permanent bureaucracy but also among the president's own political appointees—who never agreed with him about welfare reform. He really needed to step in early and say, "This is going to happen, and it's not going to be an incremental change in the system. Yes, I want to see options, but the options have to be within a particular range, and there are some things that are not open to discussion. I went around the country for a year telling people we were going to end welfare as we know it. I meant it, and I mean it. Let's do it." . . . The draft legislation wasn't really finished until the summer of 1994, which was much too late. As a result, he totally lost control of the legislative process and was back on his heels on a signature issue.

Bruce Reed:

I think we were handicapped by the fact that on welfare reform, as on health care, we had a lot of details to fill in. Time-limited welfare was a brand-new concept that we put on the political scene. It hadn't been on Washington's radar screen. Nobody had a bill to put on the table. . . . Now there was enough resistance in the bureaucracy that it took forever to reach agreement on the most obvious of questions. There were plenty of people at HHS and elsewhere who didn't want to do the whole thing. . . . We sent a bill to Congress on the morning of June 21, [1994,] thirty minutes before the start of summer.

There were other dynamics going on. I think that it's entirely possible that [Secretary of the Treasury] Lloyd Bentsen didn't want to do welfare reform because he knew Pat Moynihan[, Bentsen's successor as Senate Finance Committee chair] wanted to.

In the November 1994 midterm election, the Republicans won control of both the House and Senate for the first time in forty years. During the campaign, Republican House candidates united behind the Contract with America, a list of promises compiled by GOP leader Newt Gingrich that included welfare reform. In January 1995, Gingrich was elected Speaker of the House.

Bruce Reed:

The White House woke up and realized that the President's interests and congressional Democrats' interests weren't the same. So the day after the election he stopped taking orders from Democrats in Congress. Now they weren't in position to give orders anyway. . . .

Welfare reform was something the Republicans wanted to do. So we had one area in common, one item that was at the top of their agenda and at the top of our agenda. . . .

When the Republicans got around to debating this issue in the House, the first bill they put forward in committee was a block grant to the states with minimal work requirements because the conservative governors wanted control of this problem and they didn't want Washington telling them what to do. Gingrich said, "Fine." We immediately attacked the Republicans for being weak on work and for not having stiff work requirements, and that threw them for a loop. They didn't know what to do because no Democrat had ever accused a Republican of being weak on work before.

Finally in September [1995] we had the Senate debate. We beat back, we stripped out, most of the conservative mandates. We beat them on unwed mothers and on mandatory no additional benefits for additional children and a host of other conservative amendments. We added more money for child care. We got all the things that we had hoped for, and then some. . . .

The Senate debate was winding to a close in late September, the end of the week, but the vote wasn't going to be until the following Tuesday, so we decided to do a radio address endorsing the Senate bill. Despite some consternation at HHS, the president did that. Then the Senate passed it by 87 to 12, overwhelmingly bipartisan, but it wasn't a perfect bill, so we endorsed the Senate bill but said we'd like to see further improvements in conference. So we had a terrible House bill, we had a Senate bill that was good, and we were hoping to get a compromise that was better than the Senate bill, which didn't make much sense to people. We weren't quite sure how we were going to do it, but we thought that we would be in a much stronger position to advocate for the changes we wanted if we were actually for something.

So things were going swimmingly. We were on track to get a bipartisan bill, and then the budget showdown [between the Republican Congress and President Clinton] heated up and subsumed the entire welfare reform debate. Congress decided to have a [budget] reconciliation debate that encompassed the entire federal budget and folded everything else in there. So we were no longer in a position where we were able to have a bipartisan debate, build a bipartisan coalition, because both sides retreated to their respective camps on the budget battle. They passed a budget bill that we opposed that was unacceptable on a thousand different fronts.

Congress voted to include the Republican welfare reform bill in the budget reconciliation act for Fiscal Year 1996.

Peter Edelman (Assistant Secretary of Health and Human Services for Planning and Evaluation):

Wendell [Primus, the deputy assistant secretary for human services policy at HHS] worked up a memorandum that says enacting the Republican version with ending the entitlement and having the fixed time limits [for welfare] is going to drive a million kids into poverty. [Secretary] Donna [Shalala] is taking that and personally handing it to Clinton in the White House and saying, "This is what is going to happen if you come out"—as he had not yet—"if you come out and say that you'll take a bill that ends the entitlement and creates an arbitrary time limit, this will be the result. Don't send that signal to Congress that you're willing to sign a bill that does it." Last ditch effort. [Clinton] sends that message. In mid-September 1995, he informally sends word to Congress that he would sign a bill with those features.

My wife writes him an open letter in the *Washington Post*, an op-ed in the *Washington Post* that says, "Mr. President, please don't sign a bill that does those two things," and she quotes the Old Testament, the New Testament, Reinhold Niebuhr, Rabbi [Abraham] Heschel, Martin Luther King, Moses, and Jesus. It was an amazing thing to do—an open letter to the President saying, "Don't sign a bill like that."

Marian Wright Edelman (President of the Children's Defense Fund):

An open letter to the president:

It would be a great moral and practical wrong for you to sign any welfare "reform" bill that will push millions of already poor children and families deeper into poverty, as both the Senate and House welfare bills will do. It would be wrong to destroy the sixty-year-old guaranteed safety net for children, women and poor families as both the Senate and House welfare bills will do.

Both the Senate and House welfare bills are morally and practically indefensible. . . . They are Trojan Horses for massive budget cuts and for imposing an ideological agenda that says that government assistance for the poor and children should be dismantled and cut while government assistance for wealthy individuals and corporations should be maintained and even increased. Do you think the Old Testament prophets Isaiah, Micah and Amos—or Jesus Christ—would support such policies?[18]

Bruce Reed:

We shut down the government. The President vetoed the reconciliation bill. Then Leon Panetta was on one of the Sunday shows, was asked about welfare, and said that the welfare bill was so bad that the president would have vetoed it on its own, which we never debated, but the Republicans thought, "What a great idea." So they passed the welfare bill again, separately, the same portion of the reconciliation bill that we just vetoed, and just for fun sent it down to the President and made him veto it again. . . .

We knew that most of the Republicans, especially [Senate Majority Leader Robert] Dole, who at this point was in the heat of the Republican presidential primaries, didn't want the president to sign welfare reform. They wanted it as an issue for the '96 campaign.

Bill Clinton:

I vetoed their first two bills because they also wanted to block grant Medicaid and food stamps and I wouldn't let them do that because I believed, rightly as it turned out, that there would be forces at some point in the future that would be prepared to deny low-income people in the aftermath of a severe recession, nutritional, and medical assistance. So that's what all those vetoes were about.[19]

Peter Edelman:

Then you get in June [1996], the 104 freshmen and sophomore [Republican House] members write this letter to Gingrich in which they say, "You've got to decouple the Medicaid and the welfare because we've got to send him a bill that he can sign. We can't get reelected if we don't show that we've done something." They really hadn't done very much. Gingrich agrees to that and they decouple it.

Bruce Reed:

Eventually in June of '96, House Republicans panicked, and the class that had been elected in the '94 elections realized that they were in danger of facing the electorate without having enacted a single item from the Contract [with America] into law, and that they couldn't afford to go 0 for the 104th Congress, so a group of House Republicans wrote Gingrich a letter saying, "We want welfare reform to become law. Please drop the Medicaid poison pill. Let's send President Clinton a welfare bill and force the question." That broke the log jam. The House passed the bill in July, the Senate did as well.

Bill Clinton:

By the time the [final] welfare reform bill passed, we had already given 43 or 44 states waivers to implement welfare-to-work plans. In other words, most of what was in the law was already given to most of the states and most of the people on welfare before the law ever passed. But I did want a law and we needed one.[20]

Consultation and Decision, 1996

By the end of July, Congress was on the verge of passing a third version of welfare reform legislation. Compared with the first two versions, the bill included more financial support for welfare recipients making the transition to work. Although it preserved the two-year limit for staying on welfare (five years over a lifetime,) it did not convert Medicaid and food stamps to block grants. The bill also included controversial provisions denying welfare even to legal immigrants. On July 31, Clinton met in the Cabinet Room with Vice President Al Gore, a majority of the cabinet, and some key White House staff.

Bill Clinton:

We had a meeting and I said, "Look, if anybody ever comes in here and tells me what you think I want to hear, I might as well get rid of all of you and just run this place with a computer. That's a recipe for disaster. No one will ever be dismissed, demoted, sidelined, or silenced for disagreeing with me. Now, when we make a decision, we all need to saddle up and implement it. If you can't do that in good conscience, it's okay. You should resign, but if you do resign, I will not condemn you or let anybody back-stab you. I will applaud you because you might be right, and I might be wrong. But we all—once a decision is made, if you can't implement it in good conscience, you should go." And we had, I don't know, two or three people resign over the welfare reform bill, and I lauded them.[21]

Bruce Reed:

It was probably the most remarkable meeting I took part in during the Clinton years because everybody recognized what a hard decision it was for the president and how momentous a decision it would be, so no one wanted to overstate their case, which was unusual. We had a remarkably civilized, respectful debate on an issue where everybody felt very strongly but no one wanted to put their thumb on the scale.

[The meeting included] just key White House staff and most of the domestic Cabinet: Shalala, [Secretary of the Treasury Robert] Rubin, [Housing and Urban Development Secretary Henry] Cisneros, [Secretary of Commerce Mickey] Kantor, [Secretary of Labor Robert] Reich—Panetta was chief of staff by then—[White House staff members] Don Baer, Rahm Emanuel, Stephanopoulos, [Harold] Ickes, Ken Apfel, who was the PAD [Program Associate Director] at OMB [Office of Management and Budget] for these issues, the vice president, and a couple of others.

The meeting started off with Ken Apfel laying out what the [congressional] conference committee had agreed to and the plusses, and on the list of improvements we wanted, what ones we had gotten and what ones we hadn't, then Shalala made the case against the bill, and then the president opened it up for advisors to speak their minds. We went around the table. Most of the cabinet was against it, with the exception of Mickey Kantor.

Donna Shalala (Secretary of Health and Human Services):

Everybody thinks that the department was opposed to welfare reform. We weren't at all. We just thought that the bill was a mess, with a lot of immigration stuff we didn't want. Clinton finally decided that politically he couldn't veto it again, even though all of us had recommended he veto it. Because we were improving it every time he was vetoing it. The Republicans were giving in after each veto. . . . But Clinton always cut his deals a little earlier than I would have cut the deals and it was his right.

John Hilley and Lawrence Stein (White House legislative affairs directors):

Hilley: [If Clinton had vetoed this version of the bill] the Republicans would have been happy about it.
Stein: They'd have been delighted.

Robert Rubin (Secretary of the Treasury):

We all went there and it was a remarkable process. We sat around that table, the Cabinet table, and people expressed their views openly and vigorously. All of us recognized that both substantively and politically it was a very difficult decision. It's a matter of public record, it got out, that I was against the welfare reform program. I felt too many people could fall between the cracks— I still feel that, by the way—but everybody was sensitive to how difficult this was. Nobody sat there and said you have to do this. . . .

I don't know whether he had the meeting because he felt that was how to get a bit of buy-in, or whether he made up his mind beforehand. My guess is he probably pretty much knew what he wanted to do, but if he'd heard something at the meeting that was different from what he had thought of—that he was running it by a meeting to see—two things, one, running it by a meeting to see if something else emerged that he hadn't thought about, and secondly, to have a process that people would buy into.

John Hilley:

Clinton had a habit. Whoever he asks the most questions of and sounds the most sympathetic to, that's who he's going to go against. It's all in fairness to the other side. But it was pretty wired up in advance that he needed to sign this.

Bill Clinton:

Most advocates for the poor and for legal immigration, and several people in my cabinet, still opposed the bill and wanted me to veto it because it ended the federal guarantee of a fixed monthly benefit to welfare recipients, had a five-year lifetime limit on welfare benefits, cut overall spending on the food stamp program, and denied food stamps and medical care to low-income legal immigrants. I agreed with the last two objections; the hit on legal immigrants was particularly harsh and, I thought, unjustifiable.[22]

Bruce Reed:

We probably spent half an hour listening to people's arguments against it, and then the president turned to me and said, "So Bruce, what's the case for the bill?" I told him that the welfare reform elements of the bill were better than we could have hoped for, that it had more money for work, more money for childcare, and we'd gotten every improvement we'd asked for, so that as a welfare reform bill it was a real achievement. He agreed that it was a good welfare bill wrapped in a "sack of shit," I think was his phrase.

I said that the child support enforcement provisions alone were worth enacting the bill and that the dire consequences the opponents of the bill predicted really wouldn't happen because the cuts in benefits for legal immigrants were too onerous and would never stand up over time. Congress would have to come back and fix them. Most important, we'd made a promise to the American people that we were going to end welfare as we know it and we'd be hard-pressed to go to them and explain why this bill didn't do that. We shouldn't assume that we'd ever get another chance, that the history of the issue was that it wouldn't come our way again and that we owed it to the country to keep our promise.

The president agreed that this might be his only chance. He said he didn't think a Democratic Congress would have given him a welfare bill he could sign. Harold Ickes had argued against the bill, so I told him the story of how [Franklin D.] Roosevelt had faced this same dilemma when he created the WPA [Works Progress Administration], that [Harry] Hopkins had wanted to make sure that the dole was based on work and that another Harold Ickes had argued the opposite. Of course he wanted to know how that turned out, so I told him that Hopkins had won. The discussion continued from there for a while longer. A few other people chimed in on my side after that—Don Baer, John Hilley, who was the legislative affairs director. Rahm said, "Do what you think is right." There's no question that Rahm was for it, but it was probably the best evidence that nobody was putting their thumb on the scale when Rahm, who never restrained himself, held himself back. The vice president turned to me a couple of times and whispered a couple of times—I was sitting next to him—asking me questions, and during the course of the meeting asked a number of helpful, leading questions that made me think he was in favor of the bill.

I didn't know where the president was coming out, I didn't know for sure where the vice president was coming out, and they gave no indication whatsoever at the meeting. I think the president didn't want to decide at that meeting. The meeting broke up finally. . . .

He went into the Oval Office and then Panetta came to get me because the President had another question about a memo Shalala had given him. I went into the Oval Office to talk to him, to rebut yet another criticism, and we ended up having the meeting all over again with the president, vice president, Panetta, John Hilley, and me.

The president's sitting at his desk. We're standing around him. He was asking questions, but in essence, Panetta made the case against the bill, I made the case for it. The president agonized, the president desperately tried to get the vice president to help break the tie, and the vice president tried mightily to avoid making the decision, to avoid tipping the balance, but eventually said he thought that the cuts in benefits to immigrants would have a harsh impact on them and that the president had a responsibility to look out for groups of people who couldn't speak up for themselves. But on balance, the welfare system was so broken and had to be fixed, and this was our chance to do it, and the benefit of the welfare reform outweighed the cuts in immigrant benefits we didn't like. The president agonized some more. . . . The president was happy with the welfare reform provisions but agonizing over whether the benefit of welfare reform was worth the pain of the immigrant cuts.

We spent about half an hour in there with him. Finally he looked up from his desk and said, "Let's do it, I'll sign it," and told me to write the statement. We went down to Don Baer's office, and fortunately we'd written a signing statement instead of a veto statement, so we made a few changes to incorporate what he had said in the Cabinet Room. The president changed into a suit, reviewed the statement, went to the press room, and announced that he would sign the bill.

Henry Cisneros (Secretary of Housing and Urban Development):

[After the meeting,] we went back to the department. About 1 o'clock I got a call. The president needs you at 2 o'clock in the White House pressroom for his announcement on welfare reform. So here was a wall in the pressroom and there were Panetta, myself, Shalala, those of us who had advised the opposite position, but we were expected to be there and endorse his decision, which was to sign.

So we were against the wall there, and in the New York Times photograph the next day it was the most hangdog-looking group you've ever seen. We literally should have been more careful, should have had better poker faces, but we all looked like pictures of defeat. . . .

In retrospect he did the right thing. Time limits came, provisions were made, people are working. I think it was the right call.

Bill Clinton:

Good afternoon. When I ran for president four years ago, I pledged to end welfare as we know it. I have worked very hard for four years to do just that. Today the Congress will vote on legislation that gives us a chance to live up to that promise: to transform a broken system that traps too many people in a cycle of dependence to one that emphasizes work and independence, to give people on welfare a chance to draw a paycheck, not a welfare check. It gives us a better chance to give those on welfare what we want for all families in America, the opportunity to succeed at home and at work. For those reasons

I will sign it into law. The legislation is, however, far from perfect. There are parts of it that are wrong, and I will address those parts in a moment. But on balance, this bill is a real step forward for our country, our values, and for people who are on welfare.

For fifteen years, I have worked on this problem, as governor and as a president. I've spent time in welfare offices. I have talked to mothers on welfare who desperately want the chance to work and support their families independently. A long time ago I concluded that the current welfare system undermines the basic values of work, responsibility, and family, trapping generation after generation in dependency and hurting the very people it was designed to help.

Today we have an historic opportunity to make welfare what it was meant to be, a second chance, not a way of life. And even though the bill has serious flaws that are unrelated to welfare reform, I believe we have a duty to seize the opportunity it gives us to end welfare as we know it.

Over the past three-and-a-half years, I have done everything in my power as President to promote work and responsibility, working with 41 States to give them 69 welfare reform experiments. . . . I have also worked with members of both parties in Congress to achieve a national welfare reform bill that will make work and responsibility the law of the land. I made my principles for real welfare reform very clear from the beginning. First and foremost, it should be about moving people from welfare to work. It should impose time limits on welfare. It should give people the child care and the health care they need to move from welfare to work without hurting their children. It should crack down on child support enforcement, and it should protect our children.

This legislation meets these principles. It gives us a chance we haven't had before to break the cycle of dependency that has existed for millions and millions of our fellow citizens, exiling them from the world of work that gives structure, meaning, and dignity to most of our lives. . . .

The bipartisan legislation before the Congress today is significantly better than the bills I vetoed. Many of the worst elements I objected to are out of it, and many of the improvements I asked for are included. . . .

However, I want to be very clear. Some parts of this bill still go too far, and I am determined to see that those areas are corrected. . . . I am deeply disappointed that the congressional leadership insisted on attaching to this extraordinarily important bill a provision that will hurt legal immigrants in America, people who work hard for their families, pay taxes, serve in our military.[23]

Bruce Reed:

He said that he'd never been so proud of his administration as he was of the way they conducted themselves in that meeting. He felt the same way, that it was an honest debate where people were respectful of each other's differences. We waited for him in the anteroom next to the press room and he came out and he said, "Sometimes you never know how right something is until you do it." As he was answering questions, he got more and more convinced that he was doing the right thing.

Congress quickly passed the Personal Responsibility and Work Opportunity Reconciliation Act by 328–101 in the House and 78–21 in the Senate. President Clinton signed it into law on August 22. The new, time-limited Temporary Assistance for Needy Families program replaced AFDC as the nation's basic welfare program.

Bruce Reed:

The down side, the price we paid for having Morris as our resident madman was that his presence made everything the president did look expedient, even when it wasn't. So we weren't sorry to see him go because, from my standpoint, the shame of it was that Clinton had laid out this clear philosophy in '92. He'd been punished in '93 and '94 because his administration had seemed to wander from it, and then when he returned to it in '95 and '96, he was criticized for being expedient in doing so, even though he was the one who came up with the philosophy in the first place. Morris was a lightning rod for that criticism from within the Democratic Party that this was all politics, no principle.

William Galston:

My deepest regret . . . is that it created the impression that the reform strategy of New Democrats was essentially a political tactic and not a governing agenda. We had worked for years creating a governing agenda (that I still believe in) to rebut that charge. It was a charge made by the opponents of the New Democratic movement from day one: This is a political tactic, it's unprincipled. Then here comes this politically androgynous advisor [Morris]. It was our worst nightmare, because it was impossible to dispel the impression that the president had embraced this way of thinking as a tactic, and that's all it was.

Aftermath

Clinton's decision to sign the welfare reform bill, which was supported by First Lady Hillary Rodham Clinton, outraged some of their closest friends and supporters, including Marian Wright Edelman, with whom Mrs. Clinton had worked closely at the Children's Defense Fund. Edelman's husband Peter and his fellow assistant secretary at Health and Human Services, Mary Jo Bane, resigned from the administration a few weeks later.

Bruce Reed:

[Clinton] called me a few days later to say, "We did the right thing," and to tell me the conversation he had with Mayor [Richard] Daley [of Chicago], who said that welfare recipients had come up to him on the street and told him the president had done the right thing.

The president signed the bill in the Rose Garden, and we brought [Lillie Hardin,] the woman from Little Rock who had given him that great answer fifteen years earlier. She had four kids; by now two of them were college graduates. He never agonized over that. In fact one of the reporters who came to the signing remarked about how much at peace he was with the decision. We spent the second term carrying out the law and making sure that some of the rough edges got fixed. It happily turned out to be the right thing.

We came up with an ambitious agenda of what to do next on welfare. The President was adamant on that score, as he said when he signed the bill, that those of us who were for it had an obligation to make sure that it worked. So he challenged the business community that had been complaining of welfare recipients for so long to start hiring them. We set up a nonprofit to encourage that, and we proposed a big initiative to provide even more money for hiring people off of welfare. Over time, to our pleasant surprise, just as we had predicted, the cuts in benefits for legal immigrants turned out to be a political disaster for the Republicans, and [in 1996] Clinton got 73 percent of the Hispanic vote. Republicans quickly realized that they had to reverse course, and so the following year we were able to undo about half of the cuts.

Eli Segal:

It's December of '96 and . . . [w]hen I went to the Cabinet Room, it was Bill Clinton at his mesmerizing best. He had, sitting in the room, five or six cabinet secretaries and five or six CEOs of the largest companies in America: United Airlines, Sprint, Monsanto, UPS, and two others. He goes around the room and he asks each one of the companies what they are doing on welfare reform, what they are doing about hiring. He makes this incredible plea that he and our government did their part, whether you like the legislation or not. We signed the legislation that time-limited welfare so no one could stay on the rolls for more than five years, day in and day out. Our government had done its part, the private sector had to do its part, and he really laid down the gauntlet.

The meeting comes to an end and . . . he says to me, "You know, Eli, you are really good at organizing things like this. Can you help me get the business community behind this?" . . . [That's] the origins of Welfare to Work. The bottom line, the Welfare to Work Partnership was a huge, huge success. We went from nothing to over a thousand companies that didn't simply pledge to hire people but in fact hired 1,100,000 people in the course of a year, all of which is documented—who they hired, what kinds of quality jobs they had. What happened is—it's the reason I became such an advocate of welfare reform—it became clear that rather than the welfare queen, the stereotype that we had all grown up with, the people who hated the welfare rolls the most were those who were on the rolls. It wasn't nice people like Bill Clinton or Newt Gingrich, it was the people who suffered every day.

Peter Edelman:

Fortunately for everybody concerned, the economy took a huge forward leap shortly thereafter, so the employment prospects for welfare recipients improved measurably, very substantially. Nobody knew it was going to be that way, they couldn't know that. The result is that the predictions I made in the *Atlantic Monthly* article in significant respect didn't come to pass.[24] Studies show that 60 percent of former welfare recipients have a job on any given day, and of course there was this huge decrease in the welfare rolls from 14.3 million at the top two years prior to the legislation, but that was the peak, 14.3— down to about 5 million. Some of that is due to the policy, but most of it is due to the availability of jobs. Some of that is also due to the Earned Income Tax Credit, which was an incentive for people to take a low-wage job.

But there's no question that the combination of facing a lifetime time limit and in particular sanctioning policies of state and local welfare offices for failure to cooperate and so-called diversion policies, not letting people on, all played a role in pushing people toward a labor market in which there were jobs available fortunately. The result of that is that a significant number of people found work, and the studies show that about half of those people got out of poverty, half didn't. That's not the worst problem, because it's relatively easy to fix. You can add to people's income if they're working. But on any given day, 40 percent of the former recipients have no job and no cash assistance. In the course of a year some of those will have a job, some of those have gotten married or moved in with family and are in some way stable. So it is not that all of that 40 percent, which is about 1.2 million women plus their children, about 2.4 million children, are worse off, but a substantial number of them are worse off.

Bill Clinton:

The two things that I worry about were, one, that I didn't get, were the five-year lifetime limit on welfare, I thought should be suspended in the event of a recession that lasted more than six or nine months, just for that period. And we may still see some blow-back on that in the next year or two, even as the economy picks up. And the other thing was they wanted to get rid of benefits to all legal immigrants, but I got back most of them before I left office.[25]

Roger Altman (Deputy Secretary of the Treasury):

I support what the president did and I think he deserves a lot of credit for it. It's not clear to me, however, that history will accord him that credit. There are too many people in his own administration . . . who think that all he finally did was succumb to the Republican position. . . . So if you survey the fifty most senior people who ever served in the Clinton administration, about twenty-five of them will say welfare reform was a great triumph for the president, about twenty-five will say he just caved.

In the 1960s and 1980s, welfare rolls had continued to climb even when the economy grew rapidly. During the economic boom of the mid- to late 1990s, however, that trend was reversed. Welfare rolls dropped more than 50 percent from 1996 to 2001, when Clinton left office. With more people working and wages supplemented by the earned income tax credit, child poverty decreased 25 percent in that same period.

Reflecting on these changes eight years after they were enacted, Clinton said:

Policy-making and policy-implementing are really important. Whether people agree with what we did or not, what you decide to do and whether you can do it and how you do it is really, really important. It matters to people. It matters to the country. It matters to the world. It matters to people in their daily lives, and the details matter.

And one of the most touching things that has happened to me since I left office is I was invited to the Kennedy School where one of [the people who served in my administration] hosted me and he said, "You know, this is my first chance to publicly say this, but he was right and I was wrong, welfare reform, on balance, did for more good than harm."[26]

Conclusion

Not all agree with Clinton on the merits of welfare reform as public policy. The 1996 law has been criticized as racist because a disproportionate number of welfare recipients are African Americans and sexist because nearly all are women.[27] The law clearly fared less well in moving people from welfare to work during the economic hard times of the late 2000s than during the first half decade of its implementation.[28] It changed welfare from an entitlement to a discretionary block grant program and, in conjunction with increases in the earned income tax credit for the working poor, "altered the terms on which social assistance is provided in fundamental ways that are highly consequential for the lives of many on social benefits."[29] But as the oral history interviews indicate, Clinton's decision to sign the act was the culmination of his long experience with the issue, his deep reflection on it, and his close consideration of his advisors' differing perspectives.

Policy considerations aside, the long-term political consequences of welfare reform have been profound. These consequences fulfilled Clinton's hopes to restore his party's competitiveness in presidential elections by removing what had been a powerful Republican issue from the national political agenda. Democrats, who had lost five of the last six presidential elections (all but one by a landslide) prior to Clinton's embrace of welfare reform in the 1992 campaign, won four of the next six, starting with his own victories. Welfare reform was not the only cause of this change in partisan balance, but it was an important one.

Since then, no Democratic nominee for president has proposed undoing the 1996 act, nor have congressional Democrats made any serious effort to roll back the reform. Equally important has been the act's effect on the Republican Party. Even as the GOP moved rightward on most other issues, candidates who once ran against "welfare queens" stopped raising the issue, which used to be one of their bedrock political appeals. Indeed, because Clinton and the 104th Congress removed welfare bashing from the Republican playbook by enacting welfare reform, the one successful Republican presidential candidate in the last quarter-century, George W. Bush, was able to win his party's nomination four years later as a new-style "compassionate conservative."

HILLARY RODHAM CLINTON
Recasting the Role of First Lady

Barbara A. Perry

"Don't do it, Hillary! Don't let them talk you into it! Don't do it!" Hearing Jacqueline Kennedy Onassis's distinctive voice shouting at her, Hillary Clinton thought, "Now there is the voice of reason and experience." She was "sure that there were countless times when Jackie said, 'No, I just won't do that.'" So Mrs. Clinton responded to the former first lady, "You know, you're right!"[1]

The exchange between two presidential spouses was not over a matter of state. Rather, it occurred in 1993 on a casual summer boat cruise off Martha's Vineyard. At the urging of her husband and daughter, Clinton had climbed to a platform, forty feet above the water, on a yacht piloted by Maurice Templesman, Jackie Onassis's longtime companion in the later years of her life. While others exhorted Hillary to plunge into the water below, Jackie could see that the new first lady was tentative and urged her to follow her own instincts. Hillary accepted Jackie's advice and climbed down from the platform.

The amusing anecdote, which Clinton included in her post–White House memoir, reveals a basic truth about its chronicler. She was only forty-seven years old and had been first lady for just six months when her family sailed with Jackie Onassis. Clinton could be tempted to the heights and readily accepted challenges, but she occasionally second-guessed her decisions. She and health care reform might have been better served had she thought twice about taking on such a complex policy issue, one that was filled with political pitfalls. "I think she's much more politically astute now [2003] than she was in early 1993. I think she learned. She's really smart. She learns, and she knows she made mistakes. She's said it herself," remarked economist Alan Blinder, who served in Bill Clinton's 1992 campaign and subsequently in his administration.[2]

A product in many ways of the 1960s women's movement, Clinton broke new ground as a presidential spouse. Aside from Eleanor Roosevelt, a sui generis first lady, modern presidential wives did not advocate signature public policy causes (beautifying America, fighting drug use, promoting the Equal Rights Amendment, championing mental health, spreading literacy, encouraging healthful diets and exercise) until Lady Bird Johnson launched her "Keep America Beautiful" campaign in the mid-1960s. Hillary Clinton, of course, chose health care reform as her primary cause, but she went far beyond her predecessors by leading a task force that developed legislation and then presented it to Congress. This chapter examines the controversy surrounding Clinton's expanded policy functions as first lady and offers conclusions about how Americans view the position in the context of presidential power and women's political participation.[3] So much of what observers knew about Clinton's initial work as first lady arose from her public advocacy of health insurance reform, but her task force labored behind closed doors and much of its work remained hidden.

At the leading edge of the post–World War II baby boom, Hillary Rodham was born on October 27, 1947, to Dorothy and Hugh Rodham. She grew up in Park Ridge, Illinois, a white, middle-class suburb of Chicago. Her father owned a successful fabric business and her mother was a 1950s homemaker straight out of that decade's sitcom genre. Hillary, an excellent student, attended public primary and secondary schools. Mrs. Rodham taught her daughter to eschew peer pressure and be independent. Her father ran a regimented household and, as a Great Depression survivor, imposed strict limits on the family's finances.[4]

Except for lessons in social justice taught by her Methodist youth group minister, which included a field trip to hear Martin Luther King speak at a Chicago event, Hillary fell under the sway of her father's staunch conservatism. High school teachers encouraged her to apply to Smith and Wellesley; she loved the campus lake featured in the latter's literature and chose the famed women's college in the Boston suburbs. In the fall of 1965, middle-class, Midwestern Hillary Rodham arrived at the elite school and immediately felt out of place with her upper-crust classmates. Yet Hillary's Wellesley metamorphosis was political rather than socioeconomic. "By the time I was a college junior," she wrote, "I had gone from being a Goldwater Girl to supporting the anti-war campaign of Eugene McCarthy, a Democratic senator from Minnesota, who was challenging President Johnson in the [1968] presidential primary."[5]

Hillary responded to the changing world on her campus and beyond, from Vietnam War protests to the modern civil rights and feminist movements. By the time she graduated with the class of 1969, Betty Friedan had published *The Feminine Mystique* and helped found the National Organization for Women, the manifesto of which insisted that "a true partnership between the sexes demands a different concept of marriage."[6] During college, Hillary had experienced politics firsthand as a Capitol Hill intern and as an eyewitness to the protests outside the 1968 Democratic Convention in Chicago. She decided to embrace civic activism as a career and determined that law school would offer the best preparation. She chose Yale, after a Harvard law professor told her that "we don't need any more women at Harvard." As president of Wellesley's student government, she was asked to speak at her 1969 commencement ceremony—the first student in the college's history to do so. Her speech reflected baby boomers' angst about coming of age in a tumultuous world. Defending both political protest and "respect between people," she received a standing ovation from her classmates and attracted national media attention, including a feature story in *Life* magazine.[7]

Matriculating at Yale Law School in the fall of 1969, Hillary Rodham was one of only twenty-seven women among the 235-student entering class. As a result of her Wellesley graduation address, the League of Women Voters invited her to speak to its fiftieth anniversary banquet in May 1970. She argued at the Washington event that the Nixon administration's extension of the Vietnam War to Cambodia was illegal and unconstitutional. A growing interest in child advocacy convinced her to specialize at Yale in how law related to minors. During her second year at Yale, Bill Clinton arrived on campus, fresh from his Rhodes Scholarship at Oxford. According to Clinton lore, when Hillary noticed the tall Arkansan eying her one evening in the library, she walked up to him and introduced himself. As Bill Clinton relates the tale, he was so stunned by her extroversion that his characteristic loquaciousness failed him and he could barely sputter out his name.[8] By the next academic year, they were living together in New Haven as they completed law school. When he proposed marriage in 1973, Hillary demurred, unsure of the direction she wanted her life to take. She served on the House Judiciary Committee staff, investigating the impeachment of President Nixon.

Senior committee staffer Bernard Nussbaum, a future Clinton White House counsel, recalled a memorable conversation with young Hillary:

> One night, I dropped her off last [after work]. . . . I liked Hillary very much. She was very smart and very tough, and I got along with her very well. As I dropped her off, she says to me, "You've got to come and meet my boyfriend tomorrow. He's coming in." . . . She says, "His name is Bill Clinton. I went to Yale with him, and he's from Arkansas. I'd like you to meet him. He's a lawyer, graduated from Yale." I said, "Oh, great. What

firm is he going to be with?" She said, "Actually, Bernie, he's going to run for office." I said, "Hillary, how old is he?" She says, "He's 28," or something like that. I said, "What's he running for, the state legislature?" "No, he's running for Congress this year." "He's running for Congress? He's 28 years old." She said, "Yes, he's running for Congress in Arkansas this year." I said, "Hillary, he should go to work first. He should get a job and get some experience." She said, "No, no, he's going to run for Congress and he's going to win. You'll see, Bernie. He's going to win, and then he's going to go on to be a U.S. Senator or Governor from Arkansas." I said, "What?" . . . And then, the *coup de grace.* "Bernie, he's going to be president of the United States." . . .

At this point—this is a true story—from all the pressures, I crack up. I start screaming at her. "Hillary, that's the most idiotic—" What difference does it make if somebody tells you her boyfriend is going to be president of the United States? Why should you get mad at her? I got mad. I start screaming, "I'm working with a bunch of idiots! They think their boyfriend is going to president of the United States! These crazy people! What are you saying?" It was really these other pressures, obviously, that were affecting me. Normally, I would laugh if somebody said their boyfriend was going to be president of the United States. I was furious at her for telling me this, which is crazy.

But you don't know Hillary. Hillary is a tough lady at 26 years old. I don't know if I should use the actual words, but I remember the actual words. She looks at me and says, "You don't know a goddamn thing you're talking about. You're a *blank.* You're a *blank.*" She used a strong curse word that she uses—. . . God, she started *bawling* me out. I mean, she worked for me on the staff but she was reacting to this. She walks out and slams the door on me and she storms into the building.

The next morning, I was sort of sheepish about this. I walk in to see her and I apologize for screaming at her. And she apologizes for screaming back at me in a much more effective way than I screamed at her. She introduced me. Her boyfriend came in. He was a very nice guy. He was a handsome guy from Arkansas. I asked him. He said yes, he's going to run for office. I wasn't going to get into more fights with Hillary. And ultimately he does run.

Despite Nussbaum's reaction to what he thought were Bill Clinton's absurd ambitions, Hillary decided to follow her heart and move to Arkansas to help Clinton campaign for Congress. His 1974 run for a House seat ended in defeat, but the next year Bill and Hillary married in their modest Fayetteville home.

The bride chose not to take her husband's surname. "Because I knew I had my own professional interests and did not want to create any confusion or conflict of interest with my husband's public career, it made perfect sense to me to continue using my own name," she wrote.[9] She and her husband were both teaching at the University of Arkansas Law School, and Rodham was trying cases, writing, and speaking as Hillary Rodham. She reasoned that the practice of a wife keeping her maiden name was becoming more common, but she failed to recognize that it was not yet accepted practice in conservative Arkansas.[10]

A year after their marriage, Bill Clinton ran again for office, this time winning the 1976 election for state attorney general. Unopposed in the general election, he had had time to work for Jimmy Carter's presidential campaign, as did Rodham. Carter's staff asked her to serve as the campaign's field coordinator in Indiana, while her husband led the effort in his home state. Rodham, often the only woman in the Indiana strategy sessions, sometimes had to go head to head with hostile older men. Although Carter lost Indiana to incumbent president Gerald Ford, she enjoyed working on the successful national campaign that put Carter in the White House.[11]

After Clinton became Arkansas's chief legal officer, Rodham wanted to avoid any conflict of interest that might result from her work in the public sector. She joined the prestigious Rose Law Firm in Little Rock, where she served in the litigation section and worked pro bono on child advocacy cases. She also helped found the Arkansas Advocates for Children and Families, which successfully promoted changes to the state's child welfare system. Within three years, Rodham had earned a partnership in the Rose firm, by which time she had also become the first lady of Arkansas, after her husband's gubernatorial victory in 1978. In addition to hosting social events at the governor's mansion, she served as chair of the state's Rural Health Advisory Committee, appointed to that position by her husband, and helped him establish health clinics in underserved areas of the state. In early 1980, she and Bill Clinton welcomed daughter Chelsea to their family.[12]

When her husband lost his bid for reelection as governor in the fall of that year, despite Rodham's attempts to save the floundering campaign in its last weeks, friends and advisors urged her to take Bill's surname to placate traditional Arkansans. She decided to do so if it would help her husband regain the governorship. As Nussbaum observed, "So when she sort of changed herself, I don't think she was grooming herself. I think she was reacting to a reality that would require a change to happen in order to foster his career. And it's not surprising that she did it, just like he's shaping his life now [in 2002] to foster her career. And he says it overtly. It's not covert."

Mrs. Clinton took a leave of absence from Rose to head her husband's campaign, along with two other aides. Perhaps hoping to present a traditional family image, she, baby Chelsea, and Bill traveled as a trio on the campaign trail. The strategy may have worked. In 1982, Arkansas voters returned Clinton to the governor's office, where he served for the next decade.

Governor Clinton thought that his wife should continue to serve in child advocacy roles, so he appointed her chair, over her objections, of the Education Standards Committee, entailing another leave from the Rose firm. Mrs. Clinton's reservations were valid; the committee's suggested reforms, after seventy-five meetings, included tax increases and student/teacher testing, all contentious propositions. Her advocacy of the changes included an address before the Arkansas General Assembly, after which one of its members exclaimed, "Well, fellas, it looks like we might have elected the wrong Clinton!"[13]

During her years as Arkansas' first lady, Clinton performed three important roles for her husband; she was his "protector, financial guarantor, and public relations trouble-shooter," according to biographer David Maraniss.[14] As Alice Rivlin, President Clinton's director of the Office of Management and Budget, observed, "The thing he lacks is discipline, both in his personal life and his intellectual or decision-making life, unless he's rescued by somebody. I think for a good part of his career, he was probably rescued by Hillary by her being a more decisive, more disciplined kind of person who kept things moving."

These skills did not transfer effectively to the national political stage after Governor Clinton announced his candidacy for the presidency on October 3, 1991. Hillary Clinton was paying more attention to her own image by updating her hairstyle, makeup, and wardrobe, but she could not protect her husband or herself from the public relations fiascos triggered by press reports of his Vietnam-era draft dodging, past marijuana use, and chronic womanizing. The latter was no secret to Washington insiders. Rivlin thought Bill Clinton was presidential material from the first time she met him, but her friend, Donna Shalala, future secretary of health and human services, believed that the charming, talented, brilliant Arkansas governor would "never" capture the Oval Office because he had a "woman problem."

In fact, the Clinton campaign had to convene strategy meetings on how to address his reputed serial infidelity. As Clinton pollster Stanley Greenberg remembered, "We had one meeting that was solely on this subject at which Hillary was present. It was an uncomfortable meeting, I can assure you, raising the issue." He recalled Hillary's wishful thinking, as she commented, "Obviously, if I could say no to this question [about Bill's extramarital affairs], we would say no, and therefore there is an issue."

Clinton assembled her own campaign staff, a break from tradition, which had previously dictated that candidates' wives accept the supervision of their husband's "handlers." When Governor Clinton made an offhand comment in New

Hampshire that voters could "buy one, get one free" because his wife would play as active a role in his White House as she had in his gubernatorial administration, especially on children's issues, the negative response was swift. "Widely reported in the press, it took on a life of its own, disseminated everywhere as evidence of my alleged secret aspirations to become 'co-president' with my husband," Hillary Clinton recalled years later.[15]

To make matters worse, what had been private discussions of Bill Clinton's liaisons became public with specific allegations of his indiscretions. In the midst of the New Hampshire primary battle, an Arkansas lounge singer, Gennifer Flowers, claimed that she had engaged in a twelve-year affair with Bill Clinton. The Clintons and their staffs swung into crisis mode and tried to dilute the Flowers story by appearing on *60 Minutes* for a lengthy interview on Super Bowl Sunday of 1992. They refused to answer direct questions about adultery or divorce, but Governor Clinton admitted that he had "caused pain" in his marriage. Upset that the interviewer described her marriage as "an arrangement," Hillary Clinton angrily responded, "You know, I'm not sitting here, some little woman standing by my man like Tammy Wynette. I'm sitting here because I love him and I respect him and I honor what he's been through and what we've been through together. And, you know, if that's not enough for people, then heck, don't vote for him."[16] Clinton's frustration, indeed anger, appeared frequently, even in public. "She may have been critical from time to time with temper tantrums and things like that," said Nussbaum. "But she was very strong, and he needed her desperately. He would not have been president, I don't think, without her." Indeed, Clinton campaign advisor James Carville had insisted that the Clintons appear together on *60 Minutes*: "Because in the end, if the wife is with [her husband] . . . , people overwhelmingly . . . say, 'Look, that's his wife, they're fine.' . . . Clearly had he gone on [national television] without her it would have been a big gap. . . . Then my advice would have been if she wouldn't go, don't go."[17]

Years later, Nussbaum summarized his views about the never-ending speculation on the Clintons' relationship: "They have a close bond to each other. They need each other on various levels. Psychologically, politically—they just rely on each other. They can fill needs of each other on very fundamental levels. They've helped each other over the years. Obviously, they've fought with each other, and from time to time they've had a difficult marriage, I presume. Some of it I've seen, but not a lot. They have a *marriage*. Any marriage is hard. Maybe theirs is harder in some respects. I don't know for sure. But I do have a sense of their tie to each other, and it's very close."

Two months after the *60 Minutes* interview, Hillary Clinton again responded sharply to the press, this time to a question about a possible conflict of interest in her Arkansas law firm's state litigation while her husband was governor. "You know, I suppose I could have stayed at home and baked cookies and had teas, but what I decided to do was fulfill my profession, which I entered before my husband was in public life," she said. "And I've worked very, very hard to be as careful as possible, and that's all I can tell you."[18]

Susan Thomases, a longtime friend and advisor to both Clintons, recalled how Bill's presidential campaign had trouble determining the most effective role for Hillary. "They could not simply put her on the sidelines; they had to fully integrate her into the campaign and accept the fact that she had to be a major decision-maker in the campaign. They couldn't just treat her as 'campaign wife.' They had to include her and understand the relationship between the Clintons, and that she was going to be included in all decision-making." Yet some staffers worried that featuring husband and wife together did not create a whole greater than the sum of its parts. According to Thomases, they feared that Hillary Clinton conveyed such a powerful image of herself that it detracted from her husband.

Liberal women appreciated Clinton's candor and proudly sported campaign buttons emblazoned, "I'm for Hillary's Husband!" Yet Republicans labeled her a "radical feminist" who would be "the ideological leader of a Clinton-Clinton Administration that would push a radical-feminist agenda."[19] There is no doubt that Clinton was a modern feminist. After she left the White House, Clinton interpreted the criticism she received during the 1992 campaign as reflecting "the extent to which our society was still adjusting to the changing roles of women. . . . I embodied [social change]. I had my own opinions, interests, and professions. For better or worse, I was outspoken. I represented a fundamental change in the way women functioned in our society. And if my husband won, I would be filling a position in which the duties were not spelled out, but the performance was judged by everybody. I soon realized how many people had a fixed notion of the proper role of a president's wife."[20] Clinton was right. Americans still cared about, and often criticized, her choices of clothing, hairstyle, and accessories.

Clinton's role in the 1992 presidential campaign was akin to that of a "co-campaign manager," as *Time* magazine described it just prior to Election Day.[21] She had reorganized Bill Clinton's staff the preceding June when he was running third behind Republican president George H. W. Bush and independent candidate Ross Perot. And she provided focus for the campaign when it threatened to succumb to centrifugal forces. Her friend, Hollywood producer Linda Bloodworth-Thomason, described Clinton's contribution: "She's very savvy about people. She's very savvy about what makes [Bill] look good. And she's very savvy about the people who make him look good."[22]

Bill Clinton's victory in the election was the result of his charting a "third way" between traditional liberalism and conservatism, as represented by the Democratic Leadership Council's centrist creed. Hillary Clinton approved and told the DLC's founder, Al From, that her husband would be a "New Democrat" candidate. She was not above micromanaging, even vetoing numerous choices for a campaign theme song. Bruce Lindsey groused to From that every suggested tune received a thumbs down from the candidate's wife, until the ultimate choice, Fleetwood Mac's anthem "Don't Stop (Thinking about Tomorrow)" was suggested. The song captured the moment for baby boomers who now were poised to become the ruling class they had disdained in their 1960s protests.

On inauguration day, January 20, 1993, the *Washington Post*'s feature on the new first lady noted that "Hillary Clinton has been credited with being Bill Clinton's number one advisor in his governorship and during the presidential campaign." Betsey Wright, long-time strategist for Bill Clinton, explained it more colorfully: "Arkansas knew this ballsy woman for a long time. [Her vital campaign role] was not a shock to anybody."[23]

First Lady Hillary Clinton established her unprecedented role in the White House from the day her husband took the presidential oath. As *USA Today* declared, "[She] moves into the White House with a staff that packs more clout, and will make more money, than any [previous staffers who] . . . serve[d] her predecessors."[24] Moreover, Clinton became the first presidential spouse to have an office for herself and her chief of staff, Maggie Williams, in the West Wing, in addition to the customary suite in the East Wing. Clinton created her own team in the White House that came to be called Hillaryland, and "they were a little island unto themselves," as the president's secretary Betty Currie put it. Clinton's relation with her staff was remarkable, according to Deputy Treasury Secretary Roger Altman. "She inspired, continues to inspire, fierce loyalty and he [Bill Clinton] doesn't [with his staff]. It's quite a difference, and I ascribe it to the fact that she does not look at the world as . . . solely and only politically. She wears her heart on her sleeve much more than he does. Less and less now [in 2003] that she's her own public figure [as senator], but that's her nature."

Maggie Williams received the title of assistant to the president (the first in her position not to be designated "deputy assistant") and attended the daily meetings of the president's senior staff.[25] The president had already announced that he intended his wife to be a key advisor, and he had even charged her with selecting his nominee for attorney general during the transition. Both wanted a woman in that important cabinet position, but they suffered through two abortive selections before settling on Janet Reno for the top spot at the Justice Department. "It was not, 'Hillary wanted a woman,'" Bernie Nussbaum recalled. "Hillary and Bill Clinton are one mind on a lot of these things. They wanted women in high positions, and the attorney general slot seemed like a good one for a woman to be appointed to."

Clinton settled into her West Wing office, down the hall from the president's policy staff, and she had a domestic policy advisor and presidential speech writer assigned to her. Her offices for visitors, correspondence, and social secretary remained in the East Wing, while the Office of the First Lady took up residence in the Old Executive Office Building, across from the White House. Clinton's 20-member staff included a deputy chief of staff, press secretary, scheduler, travel director, and daily briefing book compiler. Her press secretary received the title of deputy assistant to the president, and the social secretary and scheduler were designated special assistants to him.[26]

Clinton took on one of the traditional roles of first ladies, refurbishing the White House, which Jacqueline Kennedy had accomplished with flourish and acclaim thirty years earlier. The Blue Room, the East Room, the Cross Hall, the Grand Staircase, and the Entrance Hall were given makeovers by the Committee for the Preservation of the White House, which Clinton served as honorary chair and active member. The committee approved her initiative to exhibit American twentieth-century sculpture in the Jacqueline Kennedy Garden outside the East Wing. She also presided over full funding of the $25 million White House Endowment Fund that helped pay for restoration projects in the Executive Mansion.[27]

Clinton worked diligently on White House entertainment, as she explained, "to dispel the notion, percolating in the media, that I had little interest in the customary function of the first lady's office, which included overseeing White House social events."[28] Yet as members of a more informal generation and people who had a more informal lifestyle, the Clintons never rivaled the Kennedys' or Reagans' elaborate model for state entertainment.[29]

Just six days after her husband's inauguration, Clinton made a pilgrimage to see the paradigmatic White House hostess, Jacqueline Kennedy Onassis, at her Fifth Avenue apartment in Manhattan. President Kennedy's widow wanted to speak to the new first lady about childrearing in the White House fishbowl. She offered this advice: "You've got to protect Chelsea at all costs. Surround her with friends and family, but don't spoil her. Don't let her think she's someone special or entitled. Keep the press away from her if you can, and don't let anyone use her."[30] Although Kennedy had fended off intrusion from television and print media,[31] she had not had to contend with the insatiable publicity appetite created by 24/7 cable news and the tabloidization of the mainstream press that her successor confronted three decades later.

The former first lady also cautioned Clinton, "You have to be you. [Otherwise], you'll end up wearing someone else's idea of who you are and how you should look. Concentrate instead on what's important to you."[32] Clinton was not uninterested in the traditional concerns of her new position, but when she focused on the customary first lady domains of entertainment, food, décor, and fashion, she incurred the wrath of some liberal supporters. "In my own mind," she later recalled, "I was traditional in some ways and not in others. I cared about the food I served our guests [replacing French cuisine with American], and I also wanted to improve the delivery of health care. To me, there was nothing incongruous about my intentions and activities. I was navigating uncharted terrain.... We were living in an era in which some people still felt deep ambivalence about women in positions of public leadership and power. In this era of changing gender roles, I was America's Exhibit A."[33]

Clinton became Exhibit A for the prosecution when many Americans decided she had taken on too much power in the health care initiative. Less than a week after his inauguration, President Clinton had named his wife to chair a task force, consisting of cabinet secretaries and White House officials, for developing a comprehensive health care plan. In addition, Clinton became "involved in most major decisions made by her husband—and some minor ones as well.... No one doubted that Mrs. Clinton was in on anything she wanted to be in on, and some made their arguments to the president through her."[34]

Yet Clinton's primary focus in her husband's first presidential year was health care. Having resigned from her partnership at the Rose Law Firm, she had time to head the task force, which was charged with constructing a policy to provide health insurance for more than 40 million Americans who lacked it, offer more and less costly options for those who did have it, and rein in exploding health care costs through a unified government policy. Senior advisor to the president Ira Magaziner, a longtime friend of the first lady, would run the task force on a daily basis.

Chris Jennings, deputy assistant to the president for health policy, explained in a 2003 interview that the first couple knowingly assumed a risk in assigning Clinton such a powerful role. Jennings said, "I don't think they had time to fully calculate how risky it really was, though. They were basically transferring a successful experience of using her and her abilities to navigate difficult policy issues and present something to him and help him promote it. That approach had already proven to be successful in Arkansas on education, so that wasn't so unusual. But I think they had little idea the degree to which it would be different in Washington and on the national stage." In short, the Clintons suffered from the first-year naïveté that frequently stymies new presidential administrations, especially those led by former governors with a dearth of Washington experience and knowhow.

From the beginning, the health care policy process was unwieldy. The task force's "working group" consisted of nearly 600 health care experts from throughout the government and nation, who were organized into 34 subgroups. Some attendees noticed that, when the president was present at the task force meetings, he deferred to his wife, who knew more about the topic.[35] The task force and its subgroups closed their meetings to the public and press, prompting a conservative interest group to file suit, claiming that the first lady was not a government employee and therefore, under federal law, had to open her advisory panel meetings to the public. A federal appeals court decided that the first lady was a "de facto official or employee" of the federal government and the meetings could remain closed.[36] Nevertheless, opening the process voluntarily might have forestalled problems that ultimately derailed health care reforms.

The task force completed its work in May 1993, having produced thirty large binders of findings and recommendations. In the fall of that year, the president presented his proposed 1,342-page American Health Security Act to Congress and the American people. Hillary Rodham Clinton signed her name to the foreword for the nearly 300-page tome entitled *The President's Health Security Plan*, which contained a description of the legislation and the White House Domestic Policy Council's report on it.[37]

On September 28, 1993, Clinton appeared before the House of Representatives Ways and Means Committee to present testimony and answer questions on the health care bill. First Ladies Eleanor Roosevelt and Rosalynn Carter had testified before congressional committees but not as the lead witness on behalf of a major public policy initiative. Years later, Clinton recalled how nervous she had been, but she delivered a masterful performance for more than two hours, without using notes or consulting with the staffers who accompanied her.

Charles Robb, Lyndon B. Johnson's son-in-law and a senator from Virginia during the Clinton era, admitted that he had overlooked Hillary Clinton's talents until she made her debut on Capitol Hill as first lady. "When she came over to give her first brief to a number of senators on health care, it was a tour de force," he recalled. He asked himself at the time, "How did you get so attracted to this Bill Clinton guy that you missed Hillary Rodham Clinton?" Even Republicans praised her (at least some years later): "Hillary never turns her head when she's talking to someone," explained former Wyoming Senator Alan Simpson. "She is absolutely riveted. She doesn't look around, like, 'Oh, hi there, Tilly. How are you?' or divert her attention from the person she's talking to. That's a gift."

In the course of three days, Clinton testified before a trio of House committees and two Senate panels. But the legislation unleashed a wave of opposition in Congress, among interest groups, and in Republican circles throughout the land. After a bruising 20-month battle over health care reform, both Clintons "conceded defeat. We knew we had alienated a wide assortment of health-care industry experts and professionals, as well as some of our own legislative allies," she later admitted. "I knew I had contributed to our failure, both because of my own missteps and because I underestimated the resistance I would meet as a first lady with a policy mission," she concluded.[38]

Clinton correctly summarized the reasons for health care reform's collapse, but she might have focused on exactly which "missteps" led to legislative defeat. The co-presidency that her husband had touted in the campaign, and that opponents decried, seemed to be a reality to both the nation and the administration as the first lady led the charge for health care reform. She and the president worked as a team; they were completely loyal to each other's policy initiatives. However, voters who had cast ballots for Bill Clinton had not elected his wife to office. She was completely unaccountable to the electorate.

If administration officials disagreed with the first lady, they could expect backlash from the president. Mickey Kantor, Bill Clinton's 1992 campaign chair and later secretary of commerce, remarked, "He really reacts violently when people criticize Hillary. I mean he really gets angry—you can just see it. He literally gets red in the face." Kantor observed that the president himself was in a quandary; if he disagreed with his wife on policy, he couldn't very well fire her. In fact, if the president ever had a different viewpoint from his wife on any important subject, his second White House counsel, former federal judge Abner Mikva, could not recall a single example of the first lady's position not prevailing.

Bold cabinet secretaries who took their complaints directly to the president's wife provoked a prickly response. According to Health and Human Services Assistant Secretary Peter Edelman, Hillary told Health and Human Services Secretary Donna Shalala, who predicted a disastrous end for the health policy initiative, that Shalala was simply envious of the first lady's role in leading the charge to reshape health care. An atmosphere of intimidation settled over the White House, as Chief of Staff Leon Panetta remembered. White House economists who tried to steer the policy in a different direction, recalled Alice Rivlin, met with formidable opposition that left them feeling like the "enemy" in their own administration. In a fair policy fight, Alan Blinder thought that the president's advisors could have won the day over the first lady. Ignoring revisions suggested within the administration, however, the Clintons won the battle but lost the war. Down to defeat went the centerpiece of the president's 1992 election campaign.

In the aftermath of the defeat of health care reform, Clinton made a concerted effort to soften her image, including sitting for a typically nonconfrontational *Parade Magazine* interview and cover story in the winter of 1995. The article, which referred to the first lady as the president's "closest advisor," enthused, "Mrs. Clinton—for all the harsh portrayals putting right up there with the Dragon Lady—presented an image that was simultaneously pixieish and utterly feminine."[39] Leaving the hard-hitting debate over health care behind, Clinton returned to another of her past policy interests, one that she chose because she thought Americans would view it as a more traditional concern: advocacy on behalf of children. In 1996, she published a best-selling, prize-winning book, *It Takes a Village: And Other Lessons Children Teach Us.*[40] She also wrote, spoke, and traveled on behalf of women's issues, including breast cancer, domestic violence, family planning, female suffrage, microfinance, and equal rights.

In 1995, the first lady delivered a speech in Beijing on these subjects to the United Nations' Fourth World Conference on Women. Secretary of State Madeleine Albright, whose appointment Clinton had recommended to her husband, described the dramatic reaction to her remarks: "She really blew them away up there [on the stage in China]. Her statement was stunning." The first lady's conflation of human rights and women's rights has survived as part of her legacy.

Throughout her eight-year tenure in the White House, Clinton traveled the globe, with and without her husband, from Mongolia to Latin America to Africa to Europe to Central Asia to the Middle East. The State Department even requested that she serve as an emissary to Bosnia-Herzegovina to bolster the 1995 Dayton Peace Accords in that war-torn region. Although in 2008 she exaggerated the danger of her 1996 visit to Bosnia, inaccurately describing "sniper fire" at the airport, her symbolic influence at the time should not be diminished.[41] As Albright explained, "Sometimes I went to a country with her, and we would meet with women's groups or human rights' groups. But she was a presence in terms of, not in doing negotiations or anything like that, but she was a very good ambassador. She would travel a lot. Sometimes Chelsea would go with her. She had her agenda in terms of women's issues and health issues, and generally she was a presence."

At home, Clinton's influence over foreign policy making may have been confined to pillow talk. As Deputy National Security Advisor Sandy Berger summarized, "She did not participate in the foreign policy decision-making formally, although I suspect in the evening, the president had such great respect for her views and her judgment—I often thought in the morning I heard some echoes of Hillary in something he said. So I suspect they talked about these things privately."

Yet Berger gives her credit for the goals Clinton accomplished in globe-trotting. Like Eleanor Roosevelt, she served as an additional set of eyes and ears for her husband abroad. In fact, Clinton often preceded the president's visits to foreign countries, and this practice had salutary effects on people abroad. "By the time [he and the president] got there," Berger observed, "they'd already fallen in love with Hillary Clinton, so they were predisposed to like the president. I think the traveling expanded her view of what's important and how to look at the world, not just from an American perspective but from a global perspective. It certainly foreshadowed a number of our trips."

Clinton became an early supporter of the microcredit movement that Bangladesh's Grameen Bank, led by Muhammad Yunus, established. Small loans, frequently less than $100, went to women in developing countries to start cottage industries, such as making pottery, furniture, clothing, or building materials. Studies revealed that women used the loans much more responsibly than their husbands and reinvested the proceeds in their small businesses. In addition to promoting microcredit through her trips to villages in Africa and South Asia, Clinton spotlighted the deplorable treatment of Afghan women under the Taliban regime. Berger noted that the first lady organized a White House conference on the abuse females faced in Afghanistan. "There were many issues like that, development-oriented issues she brought to public life," Berger observed.

Despite the health care reform defeat, Clinton continued to play a public political role, shoring up her husband's electoral base among liberal women, blacks, and the elderly, whose support the president would need to win reelection in 1996.[42] His first term's scandals were but a prelude to the impeachment crisis that threatened to truncate his second term, which he had won over Republican senator Robert Dole of Kansas. Investigations into personnel changes in the White House Travel Office; the suicide of Clinton's former Rose Law Firm partner and friend, Deputy White House Counsel Vince Foster; the Clintons' Whitewater real estate ventures in Arkansas; Hillary Clinton's speculative investment in cattle futures; and Paula Jones's sexual harassment lawsuit against Bill Clinton, based on his alleged actions toward her while governor, kept the first-term Clinton White House in turmoil.

The first lady had to face a grand jury to testify about the Rose Law Firm's role in Whitewater transactions. She resisted releasing documents on the Arkansas real estate deals and "just let everybody have it," Leon Panetta recalled, when advisors suggested that she should do so. Some of the president's aides thought the scandalmongering might diminish with the appointment of an independent counsel. Bowing to this argument, the Clintons agreed, but the muckraking and lawsuits did not subside.

All of the first-term investigations paled by comparison, however, to the firestorm prompted by the 1998 accusations that President Clinton had had an affair with a White House intern, Monica Lewinsky, and then asked her to lie about it to Paula Jones's lawyers. The first lady immediately went on the defensive to save her husband's presidency by deflecting the accusations. In a television interview on NBC's *Today*, she famously labeled the charges against her husband "a vast right-wing conspiracy."[43] When he finally admitted to her his culpability in the Lewinsky affair, Clinton, by her own account, sobbed over the betrayal and "wanted to wring [his] neck."[44] Or as friend Susan Thomases put it, "She would have hit him with a frying pan if one had been handed to her." Instead, she subjected him to the silent treatment for days following his admission.

Matters were no better for the president in the West Wing. At a Cabinet meeting, Health and Human Services Secretary Shalala gave him a verbal shellacking. "No one at the White House seemed mad at me [for chastising the president]," she said. "Hillary certainly wasn't." Shalala later elaborated on her personal outrage at the president: "It was that it was an intern. I just couldn't tolerate that." Yet Susan Thomases speculated, "I don't think [Hillary] ever in her mind imagined leaving him or divorcing him."

As she had so often in their relationship, Hillary focused her anger on saving her philandering husband from himself. She went to Capitol Hill to tell congressional Democrats that the Republicans were engaging in a "coup" by impeaching her husband. President Clinton's director for legislative affairs Lawrence Stein described her performance before the Democratic caucus as "absolutely great. They loved her." The overzealous investigation of Bill Clinton's transgressions by Special Prosecutor Kenneth Starr and House Republicans undercut their case against him. The Clintons' approval ratings actually rose as Congress acted on impeachment.[45] Ultimately, the Senate acquitted President Clinton.

In the final two years of her husband's presidency, Clinton continued to appeal to the Democratic base. As she inched closer to declaring her candidacy for a Senate seat from New York, she maintained an active presence at traditional first lady events, including state dinners; cultural, charitable, and social outings; teas; lunches; and award ceremonies. She also traveled abroad and attended conferences on the women's and children's issues she planned to make centerpieces of her Senate campaign.[46] In 2000, she once more broke new ground by becoming the first incumbent first lady to run for elective office.

President Clinton joined the effort with gusto, even satirizing his role as the secondary mate in this historic political duo. At the 2000 White House Correspondents' Association dinner, he starred in a video spoof that showed him doing the laundry and mowing the White House lawn. As Hillary Clinton departs the Executive Mansion in a limo, her husband runs after her with a brown bag, shouting, "You forgot your lunch!" before turning around forlornly and trudging back to his househusband duties. Clinton was elected and took her Senate seat in January 2001, just prior to her husband's last days in the Oval Office.

Clinton took lessons from her experiences as first lady into her subsequent positions as senator, candidate for the Democratic presidential nomination in 2008, and secretary of state in the Obama administration. Although many first ladies were delighted to fade into the background and regain their privacy after their husbands' presidential terms ended, Clinton followed her own desire to fashion a political career independent from, but inextricably linked to, that of her husband. When comedian David Letterman asked Bill Clinton in 2015 if he would move back to 1600 Pennsylvania Avenue should Hillary Clinton win the 2016 presidential election, the former president chuckled, "If she asks me!"[47]

What legacy did Hillary Clinton leave for future first ladies? The women's movement, intrusive media, and blowback against her all complicated the position for her successors. First ladies' historian Nancy Beck Young argues that the American public's expectations for presidential wives are often a generation behind what it accepts as appropriate roles for women in general.[48] Laura Bush, whose style, political partnership with her husband, and initial policy concern (literacy) were much more traditional than Clinton's, scored considerably higher in opinion polls than Hillary Clinton did. Only after George W. Bush was safely ensconced in his second term did he propose a more substantive policy function for his wife, namely, leading an anti-gang initiative.[49]

The "unHillary" model seemed to shape Michelle Obama's first ladyship, too, even though she had professional credentials and an independent career that equal Hillary Clinton's. Nevertheless, Obama's focus on raising two young daughters, on military families, and on children's nutritional and lifestyle choices clearly squared with traditional first lady roles.

In 1962, poet Robert Frost observed, "There have been some great wives in the White House—Abigail Adams and Dolley Madison—so great that you can't think of their husbands, presidents, without thinking of *them*."[50] It remains unclear how history will rank Hillary Rodham Clinton as first lady, but it is undoubtedly true that her husband's presidency will never be thought of without thinking of *her*.

Part III
FOREIGN POLICY

THE RELUCTANT GRAND STRATEGIST AT WAR

Diplomacy and Force in Bosnia and Kosovo

Spencer D. Bakich

The end of the cold war signaled no "holiday from history" for the United States.[1] The period from the fall of the Berlin Wall to the terrorist attacks on 9/11 was of tremendous historical importance, particularly in Europe, where core issues pertaining to U.S.-Russian relations and the continent's security architecture came to a head. For President Bill Clinton, the collapse of the Soviet Union offered Washington and Moscow a unique opportunity to forge a relationship based on cooperation, if not genuine friendship.[2] At the same time, continued progress toward democracy in Eastern Europe was not guaranteed. Instability and threats (real or perceived) could undermine the democratic developments made since the demise of the Soviet satellite system. To protect Europe's fledgling democracies, Clinton championed the eastward expansion of the North Atlantic Treaty Organization (NATO).[3] Under the best of conditions, realizing these potentially mutually exclusive objectives would be difficult. The mid-1990s proved to be anything but ideal, however, as the wars of Yugoslav secession threatened to undermine both NATO as an organization and democratization as a process.[4]

Despite significant strategic challenges and the at-times yawning gap separating the objectives of the states in the region, NATO proved itself a viable security alliance in the wars of Bosnia (1995) and Kosovo (1999), while Russia and the West forged ways of cooperating to resolve the conflicts short of dramatic escalation. In other words, America's strategies in the Bosnia and Kosovo wars succeeded.[5] In both cases, strategic success—the realization of America's political objectives through the skillful combination of diplomacy and force—was produced by a decision making process that was open, inclusive, and flexible. Clearly, the outcome of any particular conflict is not reducible to a single cause. Nevertheless, a common feature in both of America's Balkan wars was the deftness of the Clinton administration's foreign policy process. At the same time, Clinton administration officials exhibited a grand strategic nonchalance regarding the likely consequences of America's successful use of power in the Balkans. In the end, Moscow viewed Washington's successes as defeats, and this sowed the seeds of future challenges for Europe and the United States.

Bosnia: Learning How to Lead

Along with crises in Somalia and Haiti, the war in Bosnia rounded out the agenda bequeathed to the Clinton administration by its predecessor. For two and a half years, from 1993 to mid-1995, the United States engaged the Bosnian crisis in fits and starts, oscillating between diplomatic ventures designed to end the conflict by renegotiating political boundaries and provincial relationships and half-hearted attempts to contain the hostilities by insisting that "ancient hatreds" were problems for Europeans to resolve.[6] Throughout this period, many of President Clinton's top advisors—primarily Special Assistant to the President for National Security Affairs Anthony Lake and Ambassador to the United Nations Madeleine Albright—endeavored to find a way to end the conflict on strategic terms favorable to the United States.[7] Their failure to do so was caused by a number of factors, two of which stand out as particularly salient: Lake's and Albright's inability to leverage the logic of democratic enlargement entailed in President Clinton's grand strategy and the administration's process of strategic decision making, which continually generated lowest-common-denominator solutions.

By early spring 1994, Clinton and his top advisors were committed to three primary goals in Bosnia: stopping the wanton bloodshed and ethnic cleansing perpetrated by the combatants, primarily by the Bosnian Serbs; doing so in a way that kept American ground forces out of the war;[8] and preserving the unity of NATO.[9] Also by this time, Clinton and his national security team had settled on an overriding grand strategic objective, the enlargement of the number of democratic states abroad. Because the strategic contours of the new post–Cold War era were far from firm, Washington focused on Europe, specifically seeking the expansion of NATO to states previously allied with the former Soviet Union and supporting the process of democratic consolidation in Russia under President Boris Yeltsin.[10] All of these objectives were on the table, but in the administration's second year they remained disconnected from each other, and at a growing cost. As long as the conflict in the Balkans continued to fester, NATO's value as a security organization would erode. Further, as the credibility of American leadership in European security affairs diminished, Washington's ability to facilitate the spread of democracy to the states of Eastern Europe lessened as well.

In setting the broad contours of statecraft, President Clinton was at best a reluctant grand strategist.[11] Part of the reason for this was the way Clinton approached politics generally, through an inductive process of fashioning narrow solutions to discrete problems.[12] For the president, the purpose of grand strategy was to provide a thematic representation of foreign policy—a conceptual framework that would allow others to understand what America was doing in the world. Yet Clinton was skeptical that American grand strategy had ever driven policy in a meaningful sense. He believed that "strategic coherence 'was largely imposed after the fact,' and that successful leaders like [Harry S.] Truman and [Franklin D.] Roosevelt had 'just made it up as they went along.'"[13] Moreover, Clinton was deeply concerned that grand strategy would serve as a Procrustean bed for foreign policy. "The Cold War was helpful as an organizing principle," the president noted, "but it had its dangers because every welt on your skin became a cancer."[14] Indeed, Lake describes Clinton as offering only lukewarm support for the idea of democratic enlargement, never evincing a "passion" for that goal early in his presidency. The national security advisor found himself frequently reminding the president and his speech writers to include a call for democracy promotion in presidential addresses.[15]

Yet on the twin issues of NATO expansion and security engagement with Russia, President Clinton was fully committed. To address the apparent contradiction in these objectives, the administration launched a program designed to reconcile them, the Partnership for Peace (PFP). Clinton and his top advisors viewed NATO expansion as the cornerstone of a new security architecture for post–Cold War Europe. Engagement with Russia was one of the most important issues for the president, who recognized that the United States had the opportunity to forge a new relationship with a former foe. The PFP initiative linked the two objectives by establishing a track for NATO membership for former communist states in Eastern Europe with Russia's buy-in.[16] In May 1995, when Russia joined the PFP, officials in Washington could reasonably believe that they were well on their way toward the creation of a "peaceful, undivided, and democratic Europe."[17] The problem was that the perennial fighting in Bosnia threatened every aspect of this agenda.

The war in Bosnia began soon after Bosnia and Herzegovina declared independence from Yugoslavia in February 1992, an act that followed the 1991 secessions of Croatia and Slovenia. Although the distribution of ethnicities within Yugoslavia was by no means orderly, the extent to which Muslims, Croats, and Serbs comingled in Bosnia was particularly problematic. Every region within the territory was ethnically mixed and no one group claimed an overall majority.

The Bosnian Serbs, who accounted for 31 percent of the population, feared permanent political exclusion—at best—by the larger combination of Muslims and Croats (who accounted for 44 and 17 percent, respectively). Following Serbian president Slobodan Milosevic's strategy of exploiting nationalist myths of ethnic superiority and persecution for the purpose of political coalition building, the Bosnian Serbs mobilized their own political and military resources with the objective of achieving Serbian control of Bosnia. Fearing for their safety, Bosnian Muslims and Croats followed suit, though to a lesser degree. This process culminated in the generation of an ethno-nationalist security dilemma among the groups. As the result of the extreme pressure of mutually perceived insecurity, war among them erupted with horrific consequences.[18]

By 1995, the realities on the ground seemed intractable to outside parties. Years of combat produced nothing but bloodshed, and the United Nations Protection Force (UNPROFOR) proved incapable of providing security for Bosnia's citizens. Many in the American national security bureaucracy were adamant that the United States avoid taking the lead in imposing peace on the warring factions.[19] To the extent that the goals of maintaining NATO unity and keeping U.S. ground forces out of the conflict outweighed the goal of stanching the bloodshed, the United States could content itself with a strategy of simply containing the violence. Beyond the immediate crisis, however, the festering war challenged America's broader foreign policy initiatives for Europe. As James Steinberg, the State Department's director of policy planning, recounts,

> Having articulated the grand strategy, I think that it was hard to explain in the context of that grand strategy why we would be either opposed or reluctant to move forward [on NATO expansion] when this seemed to be the obvious outgrowth of the overall approach. The ground shifted to some extent in the sense that the continued instability in the Balkans helped convince [Secretary of State Warren] Christopher and others that we could not allow that to spread. Overall, a number of the countries—Hungary, Austria, Romania, Bulgaria, and others—border along Yugoslavia and the other states, so there was a sense that probably the adverse events in the Balkans were a further argument for going forward, as was the instability in Russia. Although that could have been our rationale, the people who wanted to go slowly said, "Precisely because things are not consolidating well in Russia, we should not put more stress on the system."

In sum, NATO expansion and security cooperation with Russia were held hostage by the war in Bosnia because President Clinton was not strongly committed to the grand strategy of democratic enlargement.

The second, and related, factor that prevented forceful American leadership in the Balkans was the process by which foreign policy decisions were made.[20] Having served in the Carter administration as the director of policy planning in the State Department, Lake had borne witness to the dysfunctional process that resulted from the persistent clashes between National Security Advisor Zbigniew Brzezinski and Secretary of State Cyrus Vance. As Lake saw it, Brzezinski's penchant for vocal policy advocacy impeded the flow of information and advice to the president and truncated information flows throughout the working levels of the national security bureaucracy.[21] Determined to avoid this fate in the Clinton administration, Lake adopted the role of "honest broker," an aspect of the job he had advocated in a book co-authored with I. M. Destler and Leslie Gelb.[22] As the central coordinator of the policy process, Lake maintained an open structure devoid of the problems that were manifest in the previous Democratic administration.[23] In short, Lake and the president designed a system of decision making that was transparent and inclusive and that could have been effective.[24]

The problem was that while Lake was acting as the exemplary honest broker, neither the president nor his secretaries of state and defense were driving the system in a direction that could deliver strategic success.[25] In conceiving of his role solely as a facilitator of information exchanges among the president and his cabinet advisors, Lake denied the president his own advice. This is significant because Lake's central position in the interagency process afforded him the ability to channel the president's ideas about how the United States should engage with the world.[26] Thus, the administration's process of strategic decision making ensured that the United States would continue to muddle through in the Balkans.

The costs of this approach increased dramatically in the early spring of 1995 with the reinvigoration of the Bosnian Serbs' campaign of ethnic cleansing in the key strategic areas of Bihac in the west and Srebrenica, Zepa, and Gorazde in the east. A similar campaign in the vital northern Bosnian port town of Brcko had occurred the previous summer.[27] Each of these areas remained under the control of the Bosnian Federation, thereby posing a threat to the integrity of the encompassing Serb-controlled territory. The challenge for the Serbs was that the UN deemed each as a "safe area" that was protected by predominantly European UNPROFOR peacekeeping troops. To succeed in their campaign, the Bosnian Serbs needed to have UNPROFOR evacuate (if not withdraw completely) from these areas. Bosnian Serb forces thereby began taking UN peacekeeping troops hostage, a development that posed a significant threat to the UN's mission.[28]

The taking of UNPROFOR hostages produced a number of different reactions from parties with political stakes in the Balkans. In Washington, a concerted effort began in May 1995 to impress upon the European allies the benefits of airstrikes against Bosnian Serb positions. The reaction in Europe was decisively against this course of action, however, due to European allies' unwillingness to jeopardize their own lightly supplied and armed peacekeeping troops, which operated under highly restricted rules of engagement. Aerial punishment, the Europeans reasoned, would cause the Bosnian Serbs to ramp up their hostage taking as a means of coercing NATO to cease the campaign. In Paris, French president Jacques Chirac insisted that a rapid reaction force be formed to assist UNPROFOR troops either in a force protection capacity or as a way of redeploying them to areas in Bosnia where they would be freed from the Serb threat. Of course, should the latter course of action be necessary, the Bosnian Serbs would find reaching their goals in the UN-declared safe areas all the more feasible.[29]

Finally, planning began at NATO headquarters in Brussels on a mission designed to facilitate the evacuation—if necessary—of the UN peacekeeping force. Operations Plan (OPLAN) 40104 entailed the deployment of a sizable contingent of American troops (upward of 20,000), something that no American official desired but that Clinton felt obliged to agree to as a member of the alliance. OPLAN 40104 posed a fundamental challenge to U.S. policy because it was very likely that American troops would be deployed to Bosnia in the service of a mission that would accomplish nothing positive in strategic terms.[30] In order to avoid this fate, the administration began thinking of ways that UNPROFOR's mandate could be terminated as a prelude to a more robust and positive approach to resolving the conflict that would keep American forces out of ground combat.[31] With the United States pressing for air strikes, Chirac quickly and publicly losing patience with the status quo, and NATO planning for UNPROFOR's withdrawal under fire, a window opened for a change in American policy.[32] The question was whether (and if so, how) the United States would climb through it.

Facing the prospect that 1995 would produce the same outcomes as years past, along with the admonition of Colin Powell, former national security advisor to Ronald Reagan, to become "more aggressive and more assertive" in his post, Lake decided to modify his role.[33] In addition to continuing to run an open system of decision-making, Lake decided to serve as an internal advocate for policy.[34] The way he did so was important: Lake would conceptually knit together the agreed-upon grand strategic principle of democratic enlargement through the vehicle of NATO expansion in order to craft an approach that sought to terminate the war in Bosnia. Reflecting on his new style, Lake noted, "It was a case of honest broker in the sense that everybody's views were there but I certainly was pushing as hard as I could and in every way I could."[35] The result was a novel approach to the Bosnia crisis, the "endgame strategy" that Lake drove with the president's imprimatur and the full institutional support of all the relevant national security organizations and their principals.[36]

Scholarship on America's intervention in the Bosnian war highlights a number of important proximate causes of the change in U.S. policy in the summer of 1995. Among the most important were: the political downfall of UNPROFOR, which resulted in preparations for a U.S./NATO troop deployment; pressure from Congress to unilaterally lift the arms embargo on the Bosnians;[37] the brutal Serb massacre in Srebrenica in July; and the Croatian military offensive in the Krajina region, which significantly altered the balance of power on the ground in favor of the Bosnian Federation.[38] More broadly, the crisis was a perpetual threat to America's goals for NATO and European security.[39] All of these factors were significant, but they did not—either individually or in combination—point to any particular strategic course of action. Rather, the only way that American strategy in Bosnia could effectively change was to adjust the way strategic decision making was conducted. In light of the renewed Serb offensives in the spring of 1995, Lake believed that the Balkan "cancer" was metastasizing.[40] To address this problem, he did not simply seek to hive off the crisis in Bosnia, resolve it, and then return to the administration's preferred agenda. Rather, Lake decided to capitalize on that agenda, and the progress made toward fulfilling it, in order to craft a coherent logic for achieving Washington's larger strategic objectives.

On June 24, Lake convened a brainstorming meeting with Deputy National Security Advisor Sandy Berger and NSC staffers Sandy Vershbow, Nelson Drew, and Peter Bass.[41] Instead of attempting to forge a new path forward from their current position, Lake suggested that the group leap ahead to the desired end state and then work backward, thinking through the steps that would be needed to reach that point.[42] In late June, Lake's group had a significant advantage over the other participants in the interagency process: they were working on a solution in a novel way with the explicit approval of the president.[43]

In addition to his own proposal, Lake requested position papers from the members of the National Security Council's Principals Committee about where U.S. policy could and should be in six months.[44] Most in line with Lake's preferences was Albright's paper, which posted a vigorous defense of resolving the crisis forcefully. Not only was there a moral imperative to do so, she argued, but dire threats to America's credibility would arise if it failed to lead. Albright did not, however, detail a viable strategy that connected resources and methods to any particular political end state.

Since the early spring, Deputy Secretary of State Strobe Talbott had been holding a series of unofficial meetings at his home concerning Bosnia. These gatherings regularly included State Department officials Tom Donilon, James Steinberg, and Peter Tarnoff and CIA director John Deutch; Vice President Al Gore's national security advisor, Leon Fuerth; and Lake's deputy, Sandy Berger. On June 20, the group considered three courses of action for the coming months: 1) a U.S.-led application of "all necessary means" to coerce the Serbs into ceasing their campaign of violence; 2) a continuation of the muddling-through policy;

and 3) a plan for accelerated withdrawal from the crisis. The participants quickly rejected the first course and settled on the second. Tellingly, Deutch stated that the United States could not "flap around as a government without an end point."[45] Yet the absence of an agreed-upon end state made the second option attractive because it had the benefit of being the least risky. By the end of June, the State Department had settled on a policy designed to avoid the participation of U.S. ground forces in the war at all costs. Christopher recommended that Washington find a way to keep UNPROFOR active by means of a regional settlement plan in exchange for relief of sanctions against the Serbs.[46]

Lake's progress was soon spurred by two events. On July 5, the Bosnian Serbs committed a series of atrocities in the UN-designated "safe area" of Srebrenica. By mid-July, the Serbs had slaughtered roughly 7,000 Muslim boys and men, an act the president said "made a mockery of the UN and, by extension, of the commitments of NATO and the United States."[47] The Srebrenica massacre had three significant effects on American policy. First, although it did not convince President Clinton to consider decisive action, it fueled his determination to re-solve the crisis through American leadership. Second, because this Serb action was widely seen in Europe as the worst event on the continent since World War II, European leaders became far more willing to seek a solution that did not involve UNPROFOR. Among allied leaders, Chirac leaned furthest forward by arguing for a major NATO intervention to retake the safe area—a proposal that, although unrealistic, put the French president in the rhetorical lead in the West-ern Alliance. Third, the fall of Srebrenica forced the hand of Secretary of Defense William Perry.[48] Widely respected by both officers and civilians in the Pentagon, Perry led a department that up to that point had strongly opposed an active American role in Bosnia. Perry advised that an ultimatum be presented to the Serbs: "Don't even think about going into Gorazde or any other safe areas. If you do, you will be met by a massive air campaign."[49] With that endorsement, Lake had backing from the president, the secretary of defense, and the UN ambassador for a decisive response.

Shortly after the fall of Srebrenica, the balance of military power in the Bal-kans shifted substantially in favor of the Bosnian Federation. From July 22 to August 6, Croatian military forces initiated a massive offensive intended to retake the Krajina region of that country. Even though in years past the United States had strongly opposed the retaking of that area by the Croats, Washington had not objected to (but rather facilitated) the rebuilding of the Croatian army.[50] Sensing an opportunity to change the dynamics on the battlefield favorably, Washington tacitly approved the Croatian offensive. The result was that the Croats cleared the region of its Serb population and put Serb forces on the defensive for the first time. President Clinton admitted that he was "rooting for the Croatians," knowing full well that the effectiveness of a NATO military engagement would be substantially bolstered by Serb losses.[51]

On August 5, Lake submitted four proposals to Clinton for how the United States should move forward in the Balkans. To the State and Defense Departments, the situation in Bosnia was bleak, yet the stakes were not so high as to warrant a major and risky policy of intervention. Both departments' proposals urged that the United States help the Bosnians consolidate the territory in their possession, but they were not willing to help them recover parts that had been lost to the Serbs. Most important, the United States should avoid taking steps that would lead to a long and costly military engagement. In contrast, for the National Security Council and Albright, the stakes in Bosnia were worth running risks. To Albright, the combined policies of the United States and its allies had seriously eroded the credibility of NATO and the UN. "Worse," she later wrote, "our continued reluctance to lead an effort to resolve a military crisis in the heart of Europe has placed at risk our leadership of the post-Cold War world."[52] To the National Security Council, it was imperative that Washington decisively back the Bosnians as a way to force the Serbs to the bargaining table. Lake and his colleagues proposed a coercive diplomatic strategy that would seek a single Bosnian state comprised of a 51–49 territorial split between the Bosnian Federation and Serbs. Should that proposal meet with resistance, then the United States would seek UNPROFOR's withdrawal, lift the arms embargo, and use air power to help the Federation take the remaining territory it would acquire in the final settlement. This last task had become feasible with the arrangement worked out by July 26 that ended the UN Secretary-General's control over the timing and targeting of Western air power.[53]

Two days later, the president met with the National Security Council's Principals Committee to hear the various proposals. Before the meeting started, Christopher told the president that although laudable, Lake's proposed strategy promised more militarily than the United States could deliver. Aware of Christopher's position, Lake focused the president's attention on the stakes involved and the risks he believed the United States should be willing to run. The principals all had the opportunity to make their case to the president. In the end, Clinton agreed that Lake would travel to the major European capitals to inform leaders of Washington's intentions, a presentation that would be "part invitation, part ultimatum."[54] From there, the various warring factions in Bosnia would be given specifically tailored ultimatums, each of which pointed in the direction of a comprehensive negotiated settlement. Should force be necessary—as all thought was likely—it would be employed by NATO's air power to secure the territorial arrangement laid out in the endgame strategy. Finally it was decided that Assistant Secretary of State for Europe Richard Holbrooke would lead the team that would conduct extensive shuttle diplomacy between the Bosnian Federation and Serbia.

From August to October 1995, the United States led an international campaign of coercive diplomacy aimed at securing a durable peace in Bosnia. Critical to success in coercive diplomacy is the tight integration between military force and diplomatic negotiations—that is, the marrying of threats and inducements designed to bring about a favorable outcome short of all-out war. In Bosnia, the diplomatic track began with substantial American momentum that was attributable to the Croatian army's successes on the ground, the recently secured threat of NATO bombing, and the consent of European capitals to press ahead with the new approach. Notwithstanding these sources of leverage, Holbrooke and his team faced considerable challenges, not the least of which was the dizzying array of parties involved in the conflict. Among his most significant early accomplishments was the reduction in the number of participants to two: the Bosnian Federation (Croatians and Muslims) and Milosevic, who would represent the Bosnian Serbs.[55] The military front opened on August 30 after the Bosnian Serbs bombed a crowded market in Sarajevo, an act that challenged Western credibility by defying the warning against any further attacks on "safe areas." Operation Deliberate Force, which lasted until September 20, buttressed the diplomatic effort by degrading Bosnian Serb military capabilities and denying them the ability to withstand Croatian and Federation ground advances. Roughly three weeks of bombing and extensive diplomatic pressures proved decisive, inducing all parties to agree to meet at Wright-Patterson Air Force Base in Dayton, Ohio, to conclude a peace agreement. On December 14, 1995, the conferees met in Paris to sign the treaty that had been painstakingly crafted in Dayton. Of significance in the final accords was the codified territorial division between the Serbs and the Federation: roughly the same 51–49 split that was the goal of Lake's endgame strategy.

Kosovo: Integrating Force and Diplomacy

Although the 1995 agreements at Dayton gave the West some expectation that stability in the Balkans was at hand, the accords proved catastrophic for Kosovo's Albanian population. The way the Bosnian Federation achieved its national aspirations made a mockery of the policy of passive resistance against Serbia that the leader of the Democratic League of Kosovo, Ibrahim Rugova, advocated. For the more militant Kosovars, including the Kosovo Liberation Army (KLA), Dayton showed that Western assistance would be forthcoming only in response to violent instability.[56] Seeking just such an outcome in the summer of 1998, the KLA insurgency took steps to provoke a brutal Serbian military response. By October, Serb forces had turned more than 250,000 Kosovars into refugees, 50,000 of whom were threatened by the approaching Balkan winter.[57]

In January 1999, Serbian security forces massacred forty-five civilians in the town of Racak,[58] galvanizing the international community into diplomatic action.

In February, delegations from Kosovo and Serbia met at Rambouillet, France, to consider a political solution to the conflict, drawn together by the Contact Group, which included the United States, Britain, France, Germany, Italy, and Russia. The terms of the Contact Group's offer were for Kosovo to gain a substantial degree of self-governance within Serbia and to have the three-year interim agreement enforced by NATO peacekeepers.[59] Fearing Western abandonment, the Kosovo delegation agreed to these terms. Unable to abide a foreign force operating on Serbian territory, Milosevic rejected them at the Paris Conference in mid-March. Believing that Moscow would shield Serbia from any Western military response, Milosevic's intransigence was NATO's casus belli.[60] From March 24 to June 2 NATO waged a bombing campaign against Serb forces in Kosovo and in Serbia itself, the outcome of which was capitulation by Belgrade.

The Kosovo War was a strategic success for the United States and for NATO. In general terms, Milosevic's decision to quit the war was straightforward. According to John Norris, "The Yugoslav president calculated that the cost of continuing the war outweighed its benefits. Milosevic had determined that a peace deal was the best way to ensure his continued hold on the presidency,"[61] an outcome that Milosevic feared would be threatened by the anticipated escalation in NATO bombing and the certainty of Russia's withdrawal of diplomatic and material support.[62] Yet the process by which that cost-benefit calculation occurred was far from simple. It included the physical destruction caused by the bombing campaign against Serb forces and civil infrastructure, the looming threat of a NATO ground invasion, the continued unity of the Western alliance, and ultimately the decision by Russia to sell out Milosevic by supporting NATO's war aims. Although never in complete control of events, Washington played a pivotal role in orchestrating each of the pressure points that compelled Milosevic to end the war. The ability to manage the competing military and diplomatic components of what turned out to be the first war ever won by air power alone,[63] through an alliance that had never before gone to war, was a significant cause of strategic success in the Kosovo War.

For Washington, the immediate rationale for the Kosovo War was again stopping the Milosevic regime from ridding a portion of Serbia of its non-Serb population. More than that, however, Milosevic's actions ran counter to the vision, held in the American and European capitals alike, of a post–Cold War Europe that was "whole and free."[64] In addition, Serbia's serial aggression occurred despite NATO's involvement in Balkan security affairs. Failure to take decisive action in Kosovo threatened to fatally undermine the credibility of the Western alliance.[65] In many ways, the Kosovo War was not principally about Kosovo but rather about NATO's future.[66] In waging war, unity among NATO's nineteen member states was critical in bringing to bear Western military preponderance and effectively coercing the Serb leadership. Maintaining unity within the alliance was going to be difficult no matter what the situation was. As Sandy Berger, who became national security advisor in March 1997, noted, "NATO had been created in the late 1940s and never really used except in Serbia for a brief period of time. This was the first war that NATO had fought. It was like building this great fire engine and never taking it out of the garage. When we finally took it out of the garage, it was kind of creaky and it didn't make decisions instantly."

Compounding NATO's problems were two challenges the changing strategic environment posed. The first was the real possibility that air power alone would prove insufficient to compel Serbia to withdraw from Kosovo, thereby necessitating a ground invasion, an escalation in the war that would have undermined NATO's unity. Yet as the duration of the bombing campaign extended, the probability of a ground campaign increased. These conflicting pressures—the need to demonstrate resolve through a willingness to open a land campaign and the need to avoid such a campaign to ensure NATO unity—came to a head on the war's last day and were resolved only by Milosevic's capitulation. The second strategic challenge concerned the interplay between force and diplomacy. Securing Milosevic's acceptance of NATO's terms short of a ground war required Russia to play an active role in convincing the Serb president that Moscow would not support him militarily or diplomatically. Achieving Russian cooperation was complicated by the historically close relationship between Russia and Serbia, the disarray in Moscow caused when an ailing Yeltsin confronted a challenge to his leadership and by significant bureaucratic infighting within the Russian national security establishment, and by the likelihood of a dangerous break in relations between Russia and the West should NATO launch a ground campaign.

Time would play against the Western alliance as it attempted to address both strategic challenges. To be in a position to expel Serb forces from Kosovo and to protect the tens of thousands of refugees stranded in the frigid mountains, Washington and NATO had to decide to use land power in the war by early June 1999. NATO was quickly approaching a "winter wall," a barrier that could be avoided only if the strategic dilemmas were resolved by late spring.[67]

As the world's sole superpower and the leader of the Western alliance, only the United States could maintain unity among NATO's nineteen member states, manage the competing pressures of simultaneously avoiding and preparing for a land campaign, and elicit Russian cooperation in ending the war on NATO's terms. In large measure, strategic success was the product of a foreign policy process that tightly integrated the military and diplomatic fronts of the war. To be sure, the two were not always in lock step. Rather, it was the flexibility and willingness to tack between military force and diplomacy as circumstances warranted that characterized the Clinton administration's handling of the war.

NATO commenced its bombing campaign on March 24 with the objective of ensuring the alliance's credibility in the post–Cold War security order in Europe. Yet the key factor in reaching that objective, NATO unity, came under immediate strain. The principal source of tension was the combination of illusions about and aspirations for a short war that captured all of the actors in the initial phase of the conflict: Clinton administration officials, NATO allies, Serbian leaders, and Russian interlocutors. Administration officials, especially Madeleine Albright, who became secretary of state in January 1997, expected Milosevic to accede to the West's demands after an initial demonstration of NATO's air power.[68] This presumption shaped the decision to wage the war from the air, but only partly. An air-only campaign strategy also had an intrinsic allure to an administration intent on limiting domestic political risks. For a president who had spent much of the preceding year mired in a sex scandal, committing American ground forces in a war that had neither immediate nor direct implications for American national security and about which public and congressional opinion was divided was an unappealing prospect.[69] At the same time, a bombing campaign had distinct merits for the administration, not the least of which was that this course of action was believed to maximize NATO's coercive leverage. As Berger explains,

> We decided on an air campaign for a reason. This is important because many people think the only reason we did an air campaign was because we didn't want to have casualties. I believe that from the air we had a thousand to one advantage on Milosevic. Once we got into those mountains of Yugoslavia where the Germans had been savaged—we were on the ground—our advantage was no longer a thousand to one. Maybe it was two to one. It would have been a daunting prospect to go over the Albanian Alps and send a land force into Belgrade.

While the United States anticipated a short war, other NATO members hoped for one. At the outset, France, Germany, Italy, and Greece faced domestic opposition to the use of military force in Kosovo. Among NATO leaders, British prime minister Tony Blair was by far the most resolute. These early strains within the alliance increased as the war dragged on.[70] Because of the fissures within NATO, Milosevic initially expected a short war in which he would prevail. The Serb president sought to exacerbate those strains by ramping up his program of ethnic cleansing in Kosovo, causing a massive humanitarian crisis that he hoped would be blamed on NATO.[71] Militarily, Milosevic believed he had little to fear.[72]

Diplomatically, the Serbian president fully anticipated that he would be shielded from Western pressure by his ally in Moscow.

Whether or not Yeltsin initially thought that the war would be short is unknown, but clearly he wanted it resolved quickly and not on NATO's terms. Yeltsin was under extreme domestic pressure, and open NATO warfare against Serbia made his situation all the more precarious.[73] At the same time, Yeltsin stood to lose influence internationally from a complete break with the United States and Europe.[74] As the bombing continued and as Yeltsin played a diplomatic game designed to resolve both of his problems, the situation grew steadily worse. Ultimately Moscow's perception that the alliance was divided generated a bipolar pattern to Russian foreign policy, an approach that stood to benefit neither Russia nor NATO.[75]

The combination of these competing illusions about and aspirations for a short war created a conflict that was unlikely to be resolved quickly. The test for the Clinton administration came relatively early, roughly three weeks after the start of the bombing. As Milosevic's intransigence (and Russia's support of it) continued and as the flood of refugees became a deluge, Clinton faced a stark choice: minimize domestic political fallout by continuing to muddle through the war at a level of intensity that was incapable of achieving anything approaching success or insist on an outcome that reversed Serbian aggression in a way that was sustainable no matter what the domestic political cost might be.[76] Adopting the latter course, however, posed additional risks. If an intensified bombing campaign failed to bring Milosevic to heel, then the employment of ground forces would be necessary. In addition to the logistical and strategic problems entailed in such a campaign, Russia's reaction was widely expected to be hostile.[77]

The best the United States could hope for, and the approach it sought, was to entice Russia to play an active and supportive role in pressuring Milosevic to agree to NATO's demands. To achieve this outcome, the United States would have to intensify the bombing, move away from the president's declared policy of not putting troops in Kosovo, and begin planning for the possible use of ground forces.[78] Yeltsin's government would also have to be convinced to deliver the message to Milosevic that Russia would abandon Serbia if he did not capitulate. Thus by mid-April, the United States was waging a bombing campaign and three interrelated diplomatic initiatives: against Milosevic, with Russia, and through NATO.

The immediate problem Clinton faced was disunity in Washington regarding the best way forward militarily. Albright and Supreme Allied Commander Europe (SACEUR) General Wesley Clark pressed hard for immediate planning to open a ground front in the war. Not only would a viable ground option increase allied leverage over Milosevic, but for Clark and Albright the stakes in Kosovo were worth ensuring that all options remained open to secure a NATO victory.[79] Opposing them were Secretary of Defense William Cohen and Chairman of the Joint Chiefs of Staff Hugh Shelton, who thought there was not enough time to prepare a ground offensive by the following spring. Cohen in particular was concerned that moving too quickly would magnify the rifts in the alliance.[80] Thus, in the spring of 1999, the prospects for a ground war were dubious. As Shelton later commented, "The Joint Chiefs weren't going to be in favor of a ground plan anyway. We'd already discussed that in the tank. Everybody agreed Clark needed to come up with a plan, but not until we knew for sure the air plan that we'd need to start wasn't going to work. Then we'd have a period during which we'd just continue to bomb the hell out of them while we deployed the ground plan."

Albright also was concerned about the effects of a ground war on NATO's unity. As secretary of state, she knew that although the British favored the option, the Germans and the Italians opposed it and the French were only willing to go along under the unlikely condition of a UN Security Council authorization. In many respects, however, the problem of alliance cohesion was resolved at the ceremony for NATO's fiftieth anniversary in Washington on April 23–25. At that meeting, each member state pledged its support for the war effort, signaling to the Serbs that the alliance was committed for the long haul. This message of unity was not lost on the Russians, who immediately concluded that the opportunity was slipping away to play a meaningful role in Balkan diplomacy. At the conclusion of the summit, Yeltsin telephoned Clinton to suggest that the United States and Russia work together to resolve the crisis in Kosovo. Not long afterward, a trilateral diplomatic effort was launched, headed by Strobe Talbott and Russian presidential envoy to the Balkans Viktor Chernomyrdin, with President Martti Ahtisaari of Finland serving as a neutral third party.[81]

An additional and critical effect of the NATO summit was that it galvanized the administration to integrate the disparate elements of the Kosovo War. As Ivo Daalder and Michael O'Hanlon observe, "Immediately after the NATO summit, the Clinton administration put into place an integrated strategic campaign plan that combined military, economic, diplomatic and other means to achieve core U.S. objectives."[82] National Security Council staff oversight and management of the broader war strategy was critical to the success of this effort for three reasons. First, it brought the Russians along quickly, thereby obviating the need for a ground war. Second, the Pentagon's objections notwithstanding, planning for a ground campaign in 1999 had to commence so that Milosevic would be subjected to maximum coercive leverage. Third, and most important, the diplomatic and military strands of the campaign had to be tightly aligned to prevent one from diluting or undercutting the other.

As Steinberg recounts, the Deputies Committee—the core policy-making body within the National Security Council system—worked well to integrate the various aspects of the broader war strategy.

> We [the Deputies Committee] had a great group of people—Strobe [Talbott], Joe Ralston, John Gordon over at CIA, a combination of John Hamre and Walt Slocombe, depending on the issue, from the Pentagon. They worked together incredibly well and were an incredibly effective team. They represented the interests of their organizations well, but they understood at the end of the day that you had to come around—as we used to say, "check your hat at the door"—to solve the problems. . . . We met together constantly in formal meetings. We had lunch once a week. . . . A lot of the accomplishments, I think, came from this incredibly effective working relationship that we had with each other. Kosovo was the most important example of that, where we hung together and made it work. Ralston in particular . . . was able to mediate between the perspectives of the Pentagon and us, which were often awkward. There was a lot of mistrust at the Pentagon about what the White House was doing. Joe was always the go-to guy to get it done.

Significantly, and much to the Pentagon's dismay, General Clark was directly incorporated into the Deputies Committee's planning effort. Although the president never personally provided Clark with bureaucratic and political cover,[83] the SACEUR's relationship with Berger enabled them to work together closely within the National Security Council system.[84] Additionally, Albright's "conference-call diplomacy" maintained alliance cohesion throughout the war. As she recalled,

> I'd talk only to the British, French, the Italians, and Germans on the phone every single day. . . . Sometimes I would have a conversation with Joschka Fischer first and I'd say, "If I suggest this, this won't work. Why don't you suggest it?" So he'd suggest it. . . . So it was a real partnership and it worked very well. We really all worked together. They even wanted to talk about targeting. I said we can't do targeting on an open line. But we did get the sense they all felt that they were involved in it.

Following the NATO summit in April, then, strategy for the Kosovo War—militarily and diplomatically—was directly managed through Clinton's and Berger's National Security Council system.

On the diplomatic front, the ultimate objective of the Talbott-Chernomyrdin-Ahtisaari forum was to convince Milosevic that he would find no respite from

NATO's escalating military campaign. For that to happen, the United States had to secure Russian support for NATO's war aims. Four points of disagreement with Russia emerged in those discussions. The first concerned what level of Serb security forces would be allowed to remain in Kosovo in order to elicit a halt to the bombing. Chernomyrdin maintained that because Kosovo would remain a Serbian entity, Belgrade had the right to keep a sizable contingent in the province. Talbott insisted that for NATO, "all" meant all Serbian forces must withdraw from Kosovo's territory. The second concerned when the bombing campaign would be called off. Talbott insisted that this should occur only when Milosevic had "unequivocally accepted the conditions and demonstrably begun to withdraw its forces from Kosovo according to a precise and rapid timetable."[85] Chernomyrdin wanted the bombing to cease as soon as Belgrade accepted NATO's terms. The third issue was the composition of the forces to be deployed to Kosovo after the conflict. In order to ensure unity of command, the United States and NATO were determined that NATO be at the core of the post-combat military contingent on the ground. For the Russians, a NATO force was wholly unacceptable, although an international force under UN auspices was palatable. Finally, the makeup of the force came up for debate. Talbott reasoned that so long as unity of command was not jeopardized, forces from any country should be allowed to participate. Seeking to vitiate that principal, Chernomyrdin maintained that Russian troops should be given their own sector, outside of the NATO command structure.[86]

Finding common ground on these issues was going to be difficult on any terms. Over time, however, Talbott and Ahtisaari realized that their task was complicated by disarray in the Russian government. Yeltsin's domestic situation became increasingly precarious when the Russians proved incapable of modulating the intensity of the air campaign against Serbia. Moreover, deep rifts were evident within Chernomyrdin's team.[87] In part, this was a consequence of the ambiguity of the Russian presidential envoy's authority. More palpable was the Russian military establishment's determination to avoid legitimating NATO's actions.[88] Still, Talbott was optimistic that Chernomyrdin would ultimately follow NATO's line and press Milosevic to do the same. "Yeltsin has told him [Chernomyrdin] to do whatever it takes to get this problem solved," Talbott reasoned, "because Yeltsin has absorbed the cold reality of NATO's resolve."[89]

For Washington, the principal challenge was to escalate military pressure on Serbia through intensified air strikes and planning for a ground invasion, but in a way that did not derail Russian cooperation. In walking this line between diplomacy and military action, the United States faced two challenges. The first was the problem of Russian perceptions about NATO's unity. If the Russians thought that the alliance's cohesion was under duress, then Moscow would likely scuttle the trilateral diplomatic effort. Perhaps the best example of this problem came in the wake of NATO's accidental bombing of the Chinese embassy in Belgrade on May 7. Upon hearing of the errant attack, Talbott feared that the Russians "would take heart from the incident and have less incentive to reinforce our hard line with Milosevic."[90] These fears were not misplaced. Russian foreign minister Igor Ivanov hoped that NATO members would split with the United States over the bombing incident. Nevertheless, NATO held together. Even the French, who were "the most openly resentful of American power and resistant to American leadership, remained unshakable on the need to keep bombing."[91]

The second problem was more delicate, entailing the right mix of military pressure to push Belgrade to capitulate while keeping Moscow on board. Days before the April NATO summit, Clinton and Blair agreed to do whatever it took to secure victory in Kosovo. The elements of their approach included intensifying the bombing, ramping up diplomatic efforts against Milosevic, and "updating the ground troops assessment."[92] For Clark, an "assessment" could mean anything "from a one-sentence appraisal to a complete new plan."[93] The SACEUR chose to begin planning in earnest for a ground campaign. One option was to strike hard at Serbia in an effort to take Belgrade. Not only would the terrain be favorable for such an operation, but it had the greatest chance of securing complete victory in the war. The other, to attack Kosovo, was riskier because of the arduous terrain and the likelihood that Serb forces would respond by adopting an insurgency strategy to wear down the invading force. However, military logic alone was of little value in determining which course of action to take. Diplomatic concerns were paramount. In early April, Clark and Talbott discussed taking Belgrade. Upon learning that this approach was under consideration, Talbott "turned pale" and argued that such a course would likely cause governments in Eastern Europe to fall and might even spark a regional conflict.[94]

Clark's preferred option became an attack on Kosovo, a plan that was widely supported by the other member nations' defense chiefs in NATO headquarters. Throughout April and May, Clark and his military planners worked on their Option B(-), which entailed a proposed troop level of 175,000. NATO's endorsement of the strategic concept notwithstanding, in mid-May, Clark found the secretary of defense and the joint chiefs determined to avoid any commitment of U.S. ground forces to the war.[95]

The need to plan for a ground campaign was not lost on Albright, Berger, and the National Security Council staff, however. For the secretary of state, assessment updates were only a start. Rapid force deployments to the region were needed if the alliance was to have any chance of resolving the war favorably by winter.[96] The national security advisor was not nearly as staunch an advocate for the use of ground forces, but Berger's analysis of the alternatives confronting the administration made clear that planning and deployments would have to be done soon. The real challenge in implementing the next phase of Washington's Kosovo strategy was that the Pentagon might "stonewall on the ground force," he recalled.[97] To avoid that outcome, administration officials worked to ensure that the SACEUR had an open line of communication to the White House, though not at the expense of the Pentagon's authority. Facilitating this arrangement were the close professional ties between Clark, Albright, and Berger and Clark's status as both SACEUR and commander in chief of the U.S. European Command, the latter role affording him the ability to speak to the president directly.[98]

On the evening of June 2, as Chernomyrdin and Ahtisaari flew to Belgrade to make a last effort to pressure Milosevic to end the war, Berger drafted a memo to President Clinton laying out the three options facing the United States: 1) arm the KLA to fight on alone, but at the risk of significant regional blowback; 2) maintain the status quo of an air-only campaign that would eventually result in the stranding of hundreds of thousands of refugees scattered in camps and in the mountains in the dead of winter; and 3) open a ground front through Albania and Macedonia with the goal of taking Kosovo from Serbia by force.[99] For Berger, "it was the bleakest memo, because all three of these options were absolutely horrible." The next morning, however, came news that Milosevic had bent under the combined weight of NATO power and Russian pressure. Diplomacy and force together prevailed in securing Serbia's defeat on the terms the United States explicitly sought.

Force, Diplomacy, and the Foreign Policy Process

President Clinton never adopted a radical or innovative grand strategy. His administration did not attempt (or even conceive of) any system-altering approach to foreign policy. Rather, Clinton sought to consolidate the positive developments in Europe made possible by the collapse of the Soviet Union and the region-wide appeal of democracy. Yet to prevent backsliding to authoritarianism, Eastern Europe's nascent democracies needed tangible security guarantees. Toward that end, the Clinton administration supported the eastward expansion of NATO and endeavored to sustain its much-improved relationship with Moscow.[100] Reconciling these goals on their own terms was difficult enough. Warfare in the Balkans further threatened to undermine both agendas by casting doubt on NATO's efficacy and straining relations with Russia.

By any objective measure, the strategic challenges the United States confronted in the mid- to late 1990s were substantial. Nevertheless, the Clinton administration was able to employ American force successfully on two occasions in the Balkans, bolstering NATO's capacities (and membership) while eliciting Russia's active cooperation. Success in realizing these competing objectives was not predetermined either by America's overwhelming military potential or by the perceived benignity of its intentions. On the contrary, U.S. power and motives were causes of concern, certainly for Russia but also for many of America's allies. What made possible the ability to wield power effectively, through the deft balancing of force and diplomacy, was the inclusiveness and flexibility that characterized Clinton's foreign policy process. To be sure, process is never panacea, as the policy stasis prior to Bosnia and the pervasive illusions among American decision makers that a war in Kosovo would be short attest. But America's strategic successes in the Balkan wars owe much to the ways Clinton and his foreign policy team conceived, managed, and implemented foreign policy.[101]

Although they were strategically successful on their own terms, the Balkan wars affected America's relations with both its European allies and Russia in ways that the Clinton administration did not anticipate. The Kosovo war had a transformative effect on the Atlantic alliance. NATO, which Sandy Berger characterized as a creaky fire engine before the conflict, emerged from Kosovo far more capable and focused. NATO survived the rigors of coalition warfare in the service of decidedly liberal objectives and entered the twenty-first century as an alliance that would seek to bring rogue nations inside the bounds of the international community. Moreover, Kosovo underscored that NATO's activities did not require UN authorization or oversight. Despite Russian and Chinese attempts to delegitimize its operations, NATO demonstrated its autonomy in Kosovo, thereby setting the stage for future missions even further afield.[102]

Although liberal principles infused NATO after 1999, realism dominated Moscow's understanding of the international system in the new millennium. The cooperative relationship that the Clinton administration forged with Yeltsin and Chernomyrdin notwithstanding, many in the Russian military establishment viewed the American-led war against Serbia, an informal ally, as a direct challenge to Russia's national security. Acting independently from Moscow, senior Russian military officials took matters into their own hands on June 12, 1999, by temporarily seizing Pristina International Airport in Kosovo. Although Russian forces eventually submitted to NATO's authority (after having to beg for food and water from nearby British troops), the incident was a clear sign that many in Russia saw NATO and the United States as duplicitous and arrogant. As Allen Lynch notes,

> Vectors of force, rather than communities of shared values and interests, increasingly defined Russia's relations with the West in general, with

NATO in particular, and above all with the United States. The experiences of the 1990s decisively altered Russia's initial liberal, internationalist assumptions about the essential harmony of Russian-Western relations.[103]

The individual who fully embodied Russia's political realism was Vladimir Putin, who succeeded Yeltsin as president of Russia in May 2000.

Any assessment of Bill Clinton's foreign policy toward the Balkans must take into account his approach to politics more generally. Reflecting the president's political skills and creativity, he handled the challenges posed by Slobodan Milosevic deftly, successfully, and discreetly. Individual solutions were crafted to deal with what were seen as independent problems. But because the president was a reluctant grand strategist, the downstream consequences of those solutions were largely unaddressed in any systematic fashion. In the end, Balkan stability was purchased at the price of Russian alienation and growing resentment.

PEACEMAKER'S PROGRESS

Bill Clinton, Northern Ireland,
and the Middle East

Robert A. Strong

Scripture tells us that peacemakers are blessed and will be called the children of God. It is good that God is looking out for them, because here on earth peacemakers encounter more than their share of misfortune. Anwar Sadat and Yitzhak Rabin were both assassinated by members of their own faith because of the leadership they provided to peace negotiations in the Middle East. John Hume and David Trimble, the leaders of the largest Catholic and Protestant parties in Northern Ireland, worked hard to produce a peace agreement. That agreement helped more radical parties and leaders secure senior executive positions in the new Northern Irish coalition government. Peacemakers work at some peril.

Even those who aid a peace process take risks. Despite Jimmy Carter's remarkable success in the 1978 Camp David negotiations and the signing of the subsequent peace treaty between Israel and Egypt, he won fewer Jewish votes in 1980 than in 1976. According to Ezer Weizman, the Israeli defense minister at the time of the Camp David Accords, "No American president has ever helped Israel as much as Jimmy Carter," although "I cannot claim that Israel responded with appropriate gratitude."[1]

Peacemakers, and the facilitators who assist them, are often unpopular. They typically ask those involved in long-running conflicts to take chances on future benefits by making immediate sacrifices of arms, principles, or territory. They ask the aggrieved on both sides of a struggle to trust their enemies in circumstances where the normal conditions of trust are nearly nonexistent.

President Bill Clinton devoted surprising amounts of time and attention to efforts to bring about a more peaceful Northern Ireland and Middle East. Strobe

Talbott, Clinton's friend and a member of the administration, observes in his Miller Center oral history interview that the president had "a ferocity of commitment" to "the Ireland negotiations and the Middle East." For Talbott, that commitment came from a lifelong devotion to acts of "reconciliation" that put Clinton at odds with "the adversarial strain in American politics."[2] A fondness for reconciliation made Clinton, by disposition, a bipartisan politician and a peacemaker. But even natural peacemakers encounter obstacles. Clinton certainly did, and his extraordinary exertions in these endeavors had mixed results.

Northern Ireland

Clinton remembers the hotly contested New York primary in 1992 for its complicated ethnic political landscape, which was far more complicated than anything he had seen in Arkansas.[3] In that busy campaign season, Clinton says, "The most important and enduring encounter I had with an ethnic group was with the Irish."[4] In a New York hotel conference room where Jerry Brown and Bill Clinton met separately with a panel of Irish journalists and community leaders, Clinton was asked whether, if elected, he would appoint a peace envoy to Northern Ireland. Like Walter Mondale and Michael Dukakis in earlier presidential campaigns, Clinton said yes—the answer that audience obviously wanted to hear. Then he was asked the harder question. Would he grant a visa so that Gerry Adams could visit the United States? Adams was the leader of Sinn Fein, the political party in Northern Ireland associated with the Irish Republican Army. To the pleasure and surprise of those in the audience, and to the considerable consternation of his own foreign policy advisors, Clinton again answered yes.[5] "I would support a visa for Gerry Adams," Clinton said. "I think it would be totally harmless to our national security interests and it might be enlightening to the political debate in this country about the issues involved."[6]

As the future president correctly noted, permitting Adams to visit was not a major issue for American national security, but it was a more controversial question than he may have realized. At that time, Adams and other Sinn Fein officials were denied permission to come to the United States because they had refused to publicly renounce IRA terrorism and because officials in the American government, working with their British counterparts, were trying to impede efforts by the IRA to raise money in the United States. In Great Britain, Adams was not even allowed to speak on public radio or television and any interviews he gave were subject to censorship. Many British citizens, and certainly the majority of Protestants in Northern Ireland, considered Adams to be a terrorist, not a legitimate political leader. Allowing him to visit the United States would be an enormous insult to the British government. A tired candidate in the midst of a competitive presidential primary made a promise that would strain relations with a major ally if it were ever kept.

The problems in Northern Ireland had ancient origins in the British conquest of the island, in the conflicts between Catholics and Protestants across centuries of European history, and in the long struggle for independence, which was finally granted to the Republic of Ireland in 1921. The compromise that allowed an independent Irish state to be created left six northern counties, where there was a two-thirds Protestant majority, under British rule. Opposition to that compromise in Ireland led to a civil war between those willing to accept partition and those opposed. When the civil war ended, the underlying issues were not resolved.

The most recent round of violence involving these old issues emerged while Bill Clinton was studying at Oxford. In the summer of 1969, Catholic groups, modeling themselves on the American civil rights campaign, protested discrimination in Protestant-dominated Northern Ireland. Riots broke out that the local police could not control. When regular British troops were introduced to restore order, both sides initially welcomed them. But in a very short time the troops became the target for a revived republican campaign against British rule in the north. IRA terrorist attacks, British military responses, and acts of revenge from Protestant paramilitary groups created a cycle of violence that destroyed any semblance of ordinary political life in Northern Ireland. Temporary cease-fire agreements and attempts to negotiate a permanent end to the violence failed in the 1970s and the 1980s, and Northern Ireland joined Cyprus, Kashmir, and the Middle East on the international list of seemingly unsolvable nationalist and sectarian disputes.

In his first year in office, Clinton reneged on his promise to let Gerry Adams visit America. In 1993 the administration twice rejected visa applications from the Sinn Fein leader. Meanwhile, the president toyed with the idea of sending a fact-finding mission to Ireland rather than a special envoy, but when Albert Reynolds, the Irish prime minister, met with Clinton on St. Patrick's Day he asked that the whole envoy idea be shelved. The president was reportedly taken aback by this request, but Reynolds had his reasons.[7] The Irish prime minister, or taoiseach, as the head of government is called in Ireland, was engaged in negotiations with his British counterpart, John Major. Both were looking for some new breakthrough on the problems of Northern Ireland, and Reynolds wanted, for the time being, to avoid any trans-Atlantic controversy about the naming of an American envoy or fact finder.

In the months after St. Patrick's Day, Reynolds and Major worked out an agreement that became known as the Downing Street Declaration. The declaration, which was publicly issued on December 15, 1993, contained concessions from both sides. The British accepted the principle of self-determination and pledged that the political future of Northern Ireland would be decided by its people and not by parliamentary fiat in London. For its part, the Republic of Ireland qualified its long-standing constitutional claims to the northern counties. Reunification remained the ultimate goal for the republic, but now there was a realistic recognition that this would occur only if the people on both sides of the border between north and south wanted it. Of course, establishing what the people of Northern Ireland wanted would require elections, negotiations, and the initiation of a formal peace process. And the precursor to serious peace talks would have to be an end to the violence, assassinations, and terrorist bombings that had become ubiquitous in Northern Ireland and had spilled over into many British communities. The declaration clearly stated that the only parties that could join in subsequent negotiations were the "democratically mandated parties which establish a commitment to exclusively peaceful methods and which have shown that they abide by the democratic process."[8] The IRA would have to disarm or at least begin the process of surrendering its arms before Sinn Fein could participate in peace negotiations.

The progress that Reynolds and Major achieved made some Americans think about the Gerry Adams visa in a new way. Senator Edward Kennedy, who had a long-term interest in Irish issues, had previously urged caution in Clinton's early steps on Northern Ireland. The senator's sister, Jean Kennedy Smith, was Clinton's choice for ambassador to Dublin, and over the holidays at the end of 1993, Senator Kennedy visited with his sister and with a number of Irish political leaders, almost certainly including John Hume. As a result, Kennedy changed his mind about admitting Adams to the United States. After the Downing Street Declaration, Ambassador Smith and her brother the senator became convinced that a visa for Gerry Adams would be a useful American endorsement of an emerging peace process that they hoped Sinn Fein and all the other political parties in Northern Ireland would join. If the United States took Adams and Sinn Fein more seriously, that might help to convince the IRA that negotiations rather than continued violence was the best course of action for advancing their cause.

Early in 1994, a group of Irish Americans, including some of the same people who met Clinton during the 1992 New York primary, organized a one-day conference to which all the elected party leaders in Northern Ireland, unionist and republican, were invited. John Hume, the moderate leader of the largest Catholic party in Northern Ireland and a longtime critic of IRA violence, immediately accepted. Adams again applied for a visa, thereby placing Clinton's campaign promise back on the president's desk. This time the dynamics were different. The British were still opposed to allowing Sinn Fein leaders into the United States.

They were waiting for solid evidence that the IRA and Sinn Fein were fully committed to the negotiations set to follow the Downing Street agreement. The steps they wanted to see more than any others were an IRA cease-fire followed by some disarmament of the terrorist cells that were still active.

The visa issue was vigorously debated within the Clinton administration. Secretary of State Warren Christopher was against it. He knew admitting Adams would sour relations with an important ally at a time when British help was needed with policy initiatives on NATO and Bosnia that were arguably more important than symbolic gestures to the Irish-American community. Attorney General Janet Reno was also against granting the visa. In her view, it was important for the administration to be consistent in its counterterrorism policies.[9] There was ample evidence that the IRA had used funds raised in the United States to buy guns and bombs for terrorist attacks. Sinn Fein was the political wing of the IRA, and Adams and other Sinn Fein leaders had a history of connections to IRA activities that put them on various lists of individuals who were regularly and routinely denied entry to the United States.

On the other side of the question were the president's national security advisor, Tony Lake, and his assistant, Nancy Soderberg. Both had been Clinton campaign aides during the New York primary when the candidate had made his promise to the Irish American community. Soderberg was a former staff assistant to Senator Kennedy. Her analysis early in 1994 was that the visa should be granted even if Adams had not yet fully endorsed the steps that were expected to follow the Downing Street agreement. If after his trip to the United States there was an IRA cease-fire, the administration could claim some credit for nudging Adams in the right direction. If Sinn Fein rejected the peace process and the IRA continued its terrorist attacks, the administration could tell the Irish American community that it had tried to promote peace and that Adams had failed to take advantage of the opportunity. It would then be easier to tighten enforcement of the counterterrorism measures Reno was supporting. Granting Adams a visa would be, Soderberg and Lake believed, "a win-win decision."

For Clinton this was "the first important issue on which my foreign policy advisors couldn't reach a consensus."[10] Christopher and Reno were not persuaded by Soderberg's arguments, and, as Soderberg reports in her oral history interview, FBI director Louis Freeh was "apoplectic" at the thought of allowing Adams to enter the country. In Britain, John Major made clear his strong opposition to an Adams visa.[11] The Irish taoiseach, who earlier had asked Clinton not to get involved in the Anglo-Irish negotiations, now urged the American president to approve an Adams visit. The president was getting the same message from Senators Kennedy, John F. Kerry, Christopher Dodd, and Daniel Patrick Moynihan and Senate Majority Leader George Mitchell, all of whom represented northeastern states with large Irish American constituencies. Members of the House of Representatives, labor leaders, and a variety of groups connected with the Irish American community were also lobbying in favor of the visa decision.

Just as Clinton was about to say yes, a bizarre news report led to a brief delay. Wire service stories from San Diego indicated that several British stores in California had been targeted with bomb scares by an organization calling itself the Southern California IRA. According to statements made by the southern California group, further trouble would occur if Gerry Adams was not allowed to visit the United States. No one in the federal government, and no one in Ireland, had ever heard of the Southern California IRA, but the FBI was taking these kinds of threats seriously after a major explosion in the parking garage of the World Trade Center in New York City in 1993. Any appearance that the administration was giving in to the demands of a terrorist organization, even a terrorist organization that no one had ever heard of, was problematic. Soderberg called Niall O'Dowd, an Irish American activist with close ties to Sinn Fein.[12] She asked O'Dowd to contact Gerry Adams and urge him to issue a public renunciation of the Southern California IRA. O'Dowd could hardly believe the strange request he was receiving, and Adams was even more surprised when he got a phone call in Belfast at 2 a.m. with the White House message. His initial reaction was to reject the request. "Does this mean I have to apologize every time an Irishman gets into a fight with an Englishman in a pub?" Adams reportedly asked O'Dowd.[13] When his American supporter persisted, the Sinn Fein leader duly issued a public condemnation of the California bomb threats. This was the occasion when Soderberg "realized that Adams had a sense of humor."

Clinton's visa approval went through just in time for Adams to catch the last trans-Atlantic flight that could take him to the New York conference. The media blitz that accompanied his visit included an appearance on *Larry King Live.* The world took notice.

The conference in New York was attended by Adams, Hume, and John Alderdice, three leading Catholic politicians in Northern Ireland, but unionist party leaders Ian Paisley and James Molyneaux boycotted it because Adams would be present. This was not the beginning of actual peace negotiations, but it was a signal that America took a new view of Sinn Fein.

Criticism of Clinton's decision in British newspapers and by British politicians was just as bad as Christopher and others had warned it would be. One member of Parliament said, "In the future, deaths in Northern Ireland will be Clinton deaths."[14] The *Daily Telegraph* saw the situation as "the worst rift [in U.S.-British relations] since Suez."[15] The bad press in Britain was accompanied by continued IRA violence, including a mortar attack on the runway at Heathrow international airport that led Senator Moynihan and others to question their earlier support for the Adams visit.[16] It took months for the IRA to announce a cease-fire and, in the end, it took another visa.

In August of 1994, Albert Reynolds made a second direct appeal to President Clinton asking for permission to allow Joe Cahill to visit the United States. At that time Cahill was seventy-four years old and had a long association with the IRA that included legal and illegal trips to the United States to raise money for the cause. As a young man he had been jailed for killing a British policeman and later was arrested for gun running on a ship that carried five tons of weapons from Libya. "Have you read this man's CV?" the president asked the Irish taoiseach.[17] Reynolds replied that the IRA was close to issuing a cease-fire announcement and wanted one of its oldest and most trusted members on hand in the United States to reassure American supporters that the cease-fire was genuine and that the IRA was united in taking this important step. The president, who was on vacation in Martha's Vineyard, reviewed the prospective cease-fire language and granted a second controversial visa. Joe Cahill, who had officially been barred from entry into the United States since 1971, was allowed to fly to New York. His visit got far less publicity than the earlier trip by Adams. All the press attention was focused on the IRA's announcement that military operations would cease and on the celebrations that announcement brought to the streets of Northern Ireland.

The IRA cease-fire was a significant breakthrough, but progress toward peace continued to be slow. It took six more weeks to achieve a reciprocal cease-fire from Northern Ireland's unionist paramilitary groups. That came in a remarkable public statement, which included an apology to the loved ones of all the innocent victims who had lost their lives in twenty-five years of armed struggle. Despite the twin cease-fire commitments, actual face-to-face negotiations between the parties continued to be delayed. The British government insisted that the IRA would have to do more than issue a statement; it would have to begin disarming as concrete proof that it was abandoning the path of violence. Without such proof, the IRA could easily resume its attacks at any time its members chose.

During the cease-fire period before formal negotiations could begin, the Clinton White House continued to promote peace in Northern Ireland with a variety of public gestures and symbolic actions. Gerry Adams was allowed to return to the United States twice. On the first trip he was entertained by members of Congress; on the second he was allowed to visit the White House for the annual St. Patrick's Day celebrations. More important than any travel by Adams was a decision by Clinton to visit Northern Ireland late in 1995 in the midst of budget battles with the Republican-led Congress. The trip was important. Presidents John F. Kennedy and Ronald Reagan had made highly publicized sentimental journeys to their ancestral hometowns in Ireland, but no sitting American president had ever been to Northern Ireland. Clinton's walk through the streets of communities that had experienced years of violence was acknowledgement of progress. Tony Lake remembers the trip as "the high point of the first term. . . . There were these huge crowds who so wanted peace, and were so enjoying the cease fire," that Lake became convinced that "the people are so far ahead of the parties that I don't think they can turn it back now."

The words the president spoke in Belfast and Londonderry were upbeat and inspirational. He quoted the Nobel Prize–winning poet Seamus Heaney about the possibility "for a great sea change on the far side of revenge." He shared the poet's hope "that a further shore is reachable from here,"[18] and urged his audience to

> build on the opportunity you have before you, to believe that the future can be better than the past, to work together because you have so much more to gain by working together than by drifting apart. Have the patience to work for a just and lasting peace. Reach for it. The United States will reach with you. The further shore of that peace is within your reach.[19]

When the president returned to Washington he was ecstatic about the trip. "I don't know if in my life I'll ever have a couple of days like that again," he said to his associates.[20]

Six weeks later, on February 9, an IRA bomb planted on Canary Wharf in the city of London exploded killing two and injuring over 100. The further shore got further away, and a new round of even more difficult negotiations would have to take place before the peace process was back on track.

Just before the president's trip to Northern Ireland, and perhaps because of pressure brought to bear on the British by the scheduling of that trip, John Major and Reynolds' successor in Dublin, John Bruton, announced an agreement to form an international group to reconsider the difficult issue of disarming or "decommissioning" the IRA and the unionist paramilitary groups.[21] The two prime ministers agreed that once an international group was established, all-party negotiations could begin by the end of February 1996. The chair of the international group would be George Mitchell. The recently retired senator from Maine had been a lawyer, a prosecutor, a judge, and a party leader in the increasingly partisan U.S. Senate. He had co-chaired the congressional investigation of the Iran-Contra scandal in the 1980s and had a reputation as a tough negotiator. When he stepped down as majority leader of the Senate, Clinton asked him to work on trade incentives and economic aid programs for Northern Ireland that could be implemented in the event of significant progress in the peace process. Later Mitchell took on additional responsibilities in the Irish negotiations without fully understanding how difficult they would be.[22]

Even before the early February breakdown of the IRA cease-fire, Sinn Fein's participation in the all-party talks was problematic. Adams and the other Sinn Fein leaders continued to resist the demand that the IRA and unionists disarm and voiced problems with other aspects of the Downing Street Declaration. They stayed out of the emerging negotiations even as some unionist party leaders threatened to walk out if Sinn Fein was ever brought in. The unionists did not like the appointment of an American to chair the sensitive discussions about decommissioning. Petty arguments about who would sit in which chairs in the meeting room, how Mitchell would be addressed, and who would set the agenda delayed any substantive discussions. Meanwhile, events outside the negotiations—IRA terrorist attacks such as the one on Canary Wharf, a subsequent explosion in Manchester, and provocative marches by unionist groups through Catholic neighborhoods in Northern Ireland—overshadowed anything the negotiators might say.

Mitchell eventually persuaded the other international members of his group that no real progress would be made so long as the insistence on prior decommissioning remained the ticket to Sinn Fein's admission to the peace process. Mitchell was convinced that Adams lacked the power to deliver IRA disarmament even if he wanted to do so.[23] In January of 1996, Mitchell's international committee issued a report proposing a parallel process. Actual disarmament of republican and unionist groups probably would not take place prior to progress on the complicated negotiations about a political future for Northern Ireland and a new set of relationships between the island's northern and southern political communities. The best that could be hoped for would be a decommissioning process that moved in tandem with the all-party political discussions. Mitchell's group went somewhat beyond its mandate and produced a list of political principles regarding democracy and nonviolence that could guide the subsequent talks.[24]

Mitchell's report was a series of recommendations, not decisions, and they received a mixed reception from the British government and various prospective participants in the peace process. In the climate of disappointment that accompanied the end of the IRA cease-fire, it was understandably difficult to find a next step that would initiate negotiations. That step eventually came from a suggestion made by David Trimble, a hard-line unionist politician who gained prominence after organizing one of the annual marches through Catholic sections of Belfast. Trimble's idea was to proceed with elections of representatives to the all-party talks with the presumption that the political groups that did well in the polling would eventually be allowed to send representatives to a new forum where the old issues could be taken up.[25] Sinn Fein campaigned in the elections and won 15 percent of the vote, a better showing than it usually achieved in local or parliamentary contests. But winning a respectable share of the vote in

Northern Ireland did not guarantee Sinn Fein access to the peace process. That would take another election, another round of high-level negotiations between Great Britain and Ireland, and another cease-fire.

John Major's conservative government held a narrow majority in Parliament that included unionist members from Northern Ireland. He was obviously constrained by that political reality and was frequently accused of tailoring his Irish initiatives to the unionist parties whose support he needed to remain in power. This was not a fair criticism. Major had taken real risks with the Downing Street Declaration and the appointment of the Mitchell group, but those risks had not paid off. He gambled again by endorsing early elections in Northern Ireland and allowing the all-party representatives to begin their deliberations, with Mitchell serving as mediator and without the prior disarmament of any of the terrorist or paramilitary groups.

In the British national elections held in May 1997, Major's opponent, Tony Blair, won a decisive parliamentary majority that brought the Labor Party to power for the first time since Margaret Thatcher's first election in 1979. Blair immediately turned his attention to Northern Ireland, believing that the early months after a landslide electoral victory would be the best time to press for progress in the peace process. He encouraged British and Irish officials to develop detailed proposals for the cross-border institutions that had been contemplated since the Downing Street Declaration. As for Sinn Fein, Blair announced that "the train was leaving the station," and the group would have to decide whether they were going to get on board or not.[26] By July of 1997, a new IRA cease-fire was in place and Gerry Adams had a seat at the all-party negotiations for the first time.

But progress in the peace process was still slow and erratic. Political reconciliation in Northern Ireland was a lot like traditional Irish dancing. Steps forward were invariably followed by an equal number of steps in the opposite direction. There was a lot of fancy footwork and a great deal of energy expended in the enterprise, but not much actual movement. Despite the efforts by Prime Ministers Major and Blair, no dramatic breakthroughs occurred in the meetings that Mitchell was chairing. When Adams finally got his seat at the table, Ian Paisley left. The frustrations of dealing with Northern Ireland began to wear on Mitchell. "They had talked for nearly two years" without success, Mitchell remembered in a 2001 televised interview. "These guys could talk for twenty years if given the opportunity."[27]

In December of 1997, violence again interrupted the slow-moving negotiations. A unionist paramilitary leader was killed in the infamous Maze prison by a group of inmates associated with the republican cause. A few days later, in an act of revenge, gunmen fired on a social club in Belfast. The victims of that attack came from both sides of the struggle, including relatives of Gerry Adams and David Ervine, a unionist politician.[28] A series of killings took place in Northern Ireland in the weeks that followed, creating a risk that the negotiations would collapse. In March, masked gunmen entered a bar in County Armagh and fired repeatedly at the customers lying on the floor. The dead included two young men, a Catholic and a Protestant, who were meeting to make plans for an upcoming wedding in which one was to be the groom and the other best man.[29] This was a human tragedy that everyone who heard the story clearly recognized. David Trimble, whose constituency included a portion of the neighborhood where the attack took place, joined with the Catholic representative from the adjoining district to visit the families of the victims. Their spontaneous act of common decency was televised in Ireland and the British Isles. Mitchell may have seen it as a good occasion for forcing the parties to an agreement. He announced a short but firm deadline. His services as mediator would end in two weeks, at the beginning of the Easter holidays in 1998.

Foot dragging finally gave way to a hectic round of serious deliberations. The controversial questions still involved decommissioning and the nature of the new institutions that would provide some political connections between north and south. Questions also had to be answered about the release of prisoners incarcerated for acts of political violence. On the eve of the deadline, Tony Blair called Bill Clinton and asked for his help in persuading Gerry Adams to accept a compromise on the timing for prisoner release. Clinton remembers talking to Adams twice before going to bed at 2:30 a.m. and again at 5 a.m. that morning, when Mitchell requested one more presidential intervention to seal the deal.[30] The president made other important phone calls to David Trimble and Bertie Ahern, the new Irish prime minister.[31] In the final hours, Adams accepted a two-year deadline for the release of political prisoners and the unionists were persuaded that the new north-south institutions would not compromise self-rule in Northern Ireland. Vague language on decommissioning was accepted by all but would continue to cause problems in the years that followed.

On April 10, 1998, the major political parties in Northern Ireland and the governments of Great Britain and the Republic of Ireland accepted the terms of what came to be known as the Good Friday Agreement. In May, large majorities, voting in referendums held in the north and south of Ireland, endorsed the negotiated agreements. The long years of violence appeared to be at an end. But as so often had happened, hopes for peace in Northern Ireland were short lived. Three months later, the largest terrorist attack in the region's modern history took place. A bomb blew up in the marketplace of the village of Omagh, killing twenty-nine shoppers, including nine children, and injuring more than 200. A death toll that size in the very small population of Northern Ireland was, by proportion, roughly twice as large as the loss of American lives on 9/11. A splinter group calling itself the Real IRA claimed responsibility for the bomb.

In September, a few days before special prosecutor Kenneth Starr released his official report about the relationship between the president and former White House intern Monica Lewinsky, Clinton made a second trip to Northern Ireland. This time he addressed the new assembly in Belfast and visited with the relatives of the Omagh victims. There was far less promise and poetry than there had been in the earlier presidential visit. The combination of the Good Friday Agreement and the senseless killing of innocent people living their everyday lives had provided the sobering message that peace in Northern Ireland had not yet been fully achieved. Still, the president went out of his way to emphasize the positive side of the ledger in Northern Ireland, reminding the audiences he spoke to about the progress they had made. Two years later, when Clinton made his third presidential visit just before leaving office, the message he delivered included the same mixture of praising the steps that had been taken, offering sympathy for victims of lingering incidents of political violence, and encouraging the various parties to implement Good Friday provisions that were not yet in effect.[32] The pace of movement toward peace in Northern Ireland remained painfully slow, but Clinton left office confident that a change in direction had taken place in Northern Ireland and that his administration had made a contribution to that change.

The Middle East

Clinton's efforts to bring peace to the Middle East were far more extensive than those he devoted to Northern Ireland. They were also less successful.

The administration began with clearly recognized opportunities for progress on the long-standing issues between Israel and her Arab neighbors. In 1991, the first Gulf War had involved both a decisive defeat of Saddam Hussein and remarkable Israeli restraint in response to Iraq's Scud missile attacks. The Jordanians and Palestinians who supported Hussein had emerged from the war in a weakened position. And at the international conference in Madrid that followed the war, Israeli and Palestinian representatives, for the first time, were seated together at a diplomatic forum devoted to discussions of the Middle East. Momentum in Madrid was modest, but the fact that the conference took place with most of the major players in attendance was a significant accomplishment. In addition, Yitzhak Rabin was elected prime minister of Israel in the same year that Clinton was elected president. Rabin had campaigned on a platform that included a reinvigorated peace process. The political stars in the Middle East appeared to be favorably aligned in the early 1990s.

In an unusual decision, the Clinton State Department retained the services of Dennis Ross, who had been Secretary of State James Baker's head of Policy Planning and an active advisor on Middle East issues. Ross was actually called out of his State Department going-away party to be offered a special appointment as the new administration's chief negotiator for the Arab-Israeli conflict.[33] Retaining Ross was an indication that the new administration wanted to build on what had been achieved in the Bush years, particularly in the months after the first Gulf War. According to Warren Christopher, "From almost the first day I was in office, President Clinton directed me to give priority attention to the Middle East." Christopher wanted the advantage of Ross's experience in order to give this matter both continuity and priority.

Two items were high on the Middle East agenda at the outset of the new administration. One was a continued dialogue between Israelis and Palestinians on the issues they faced regarding the future of the West Bank and Gaza. The other was the possibility of a separate agreement between Israel and Syria that, like the earlier treaty between Israel and Egypt, would end hostilities in exchange for restoring borders close to those that existed before the 1967 Arab-Israeli War.[34] During Clinton's first term, Christopher had numerous meetings with Syria's president Hafez al-Assad in the hope that he could broker a peace agreement. Christopher entered those negotiations with private assurances from Rabin that a full return of the Golan Heights to Syrian sovereignty was possible if Israel's security concerns could be effectively addressed. Although Christopher was criticized for the time and energy he devoted to what was ultimately a futile Israeli-Syrian peace project, he told his oral history interviewers that he had no regrets about the commitment he made to these endeavors.

A separate peace was achieved between Israel and Jordan when a declaration ending belligerency was signed in Washington in the summer of 1994 and then a final treaty was signed in the Middle East the following October. Clinton's trip to the region that fall included stops in Jordan, Israel, Egypt, Saudi Arabia, Kuwait, and Syria. He was the first president to visit Damascus in decades. There he encountered the caution that frustrated Christopher's negotiations with Assad. When the president, counseling boldness, urged the Syrian leader to follow Sadat's example and make a personal trip to Israel, he knew he was "beating a dead horse."[35] But the dead horse in Damascus was not the end of Clinton's efforts to make progress with Syria. There were additional trips to the Middle East by Christopher, Ross, and Madeleine Albright and additional meetings between Clinton and Assad. When Ehud Barak was elected as Israeli prime minister in 1999, he made the same calculation that Rabin had made earlier in the decade and tried to achieve a separate peace with Syria before seriously taking up the Palestinian issues. In January 2000, Clinton had his last high-level encounter with

Assad, this time in Geneva. The president presented what he thought was a generous offer from Barak, but Assad cut him off before all the details were even put on the table. Assad, who had dithered, now declined to follow Sadat in recovering lost territory in a peace agreement with Israel. The Syrian leader, then in ill health and worried about the anticipated succession of his son, would not even listen to what was being offered.

Whenever progress with Syria came to a dead end, both Israeli and American diplomats typically turned their attention to the other unsolvable problem in the region, the resolution of the outstanding issues between Israelis and Palestinians. Those efforts would be long, drawn out, and occasionally dramatic. And they would come tantalizingly close to success, succumbing to failure only in the final days of Clinton's presidency.

Like the negotiations between Israel and Egypt or between Israel and Syria, the Israeli negotiations with the Palestinians involved a seemingly simple formula: Israel would surrender control of territory taken in the 1967 war in exchange for a genuine recognition of Israel's right to exist and respect for its security interests in a region that had spawned multiple wars and frequent terrorist attacks. This was the formula embodied in widely endorsed UN resolutions and summarized by the simple slogan "land for peace." But the formula was never as simple as the slogan. Returning the West Bank and Gaza to Arab control was vastly more complicated than returning the Sinai Desert or the Golan Heights. Gaza was heavily populated and the West Bank included locations within the boundaries of biblical Jewish communities. Palestinian refugees displaced by the series of wars in the Middle East following the UN's 1947 partition of the territory under British mandate insisted on the right to return to their former homes, even if those homes no longer existed.

In addition, after the 1967 war the Israelis controlled Jerusalem, including the Muslim neighborhoods of East Jerusalem and sacred sites of enormous importance to Arabs, Jews, and Christians. Any contemplated compromises about the future of the city touched deeply held religious convictions and were bound to be highly controversial. The West Bank was the location of new Israeli settlements, many near the city of Jerusalem, that were so established that no Israeli political leader could seriously consider surrendering all of them. Although returning captured territory to Arab control would be an essential element of any peace agreement between Israel and the Palestinians, by the 1990s not all the territory taken in 1967 could realistically be returned. And any Palestinian state adjacent to Israel could not be allowed to be the launching point for new wars or steady streams of terrorist incursions. Palestinian control of territory on the West Bank and in Gaza would have to be conditioned on assurances that protected legitimate Israeli security concerns.

Land for peace was the formula, but which land and what kind of peace were extremely difficult to determine. It was on this cluster of issues—settlements, borders, security, sovereignty, the status of Jerusalem, and the right of return for Arab refugees—that the Israeli and Palestinian negotiators, with Clinton administration assistance, attempted to make progress in the ongoing Middle East peace process.

Dramatic breakthroughs came early. Without direct American participation, Israeli and Palestinian representatives met in Oslo and developed a plan for a gradual Israeli withdrawal from the territories taken in 1967 that would give Palestinians limited self-rule in sections of the West Bank and Gaza that could grow over time. If commitments to Israeli security were kept, additional withdrawals would take place. The Oslo Accords left some of the harder issues unresolved but set deadlines for a step-by-step transfer of authority that seemed promising.

Public acknowledgement of Oslo's success took place on the lawn of the White House in September of 1993 as President Clinton stage-managed a handshake between Yasser Arafat and Yitzhak Rabin that was watched the world over. The oral history interviews include observations from a number of participants about how complicated the logistics for the ceremony were and how anxious Rabin was about how the event would be conducted. Sandy Berger remembers Rabin agreeing to the handshake by saying, "Okay. But no kissing." Senior White House aides then practiced with Clinton a set of presidential movements that would prevent any Palestinian lips from touching Israeli or American cheeks.[36] Tony Lake remembers shaking hands with Arafat before the public events as a difficult thing to do but also observes that the public and private greeting of a former Palestinian terrorist on the South Lawn of the White House made it easier to justify a visa for Gerry Adams.[37]

Following the ceremonies at the White House, there was genuine optimism that real progress on the Israeli-Palestinian front would be made. That optimism was anchored in an unusually close relationship between President Clinton and Prime Minister Rabin, the world leader the president most admired. According to Lake, "Of all the foreign leaders who had influence on him [Clinton], and that he—I won't say 'liked' in this case, I'll say 'loved'—Yitzhak Rabin, was the first. . . . Rabin had a huge influence on him." On November 4, 1995, Rabin was killed. "The hardest thing I had to do," Lake remembers about his years of White House service, "was first to tell the President that Rabin had been wounded" and then to "tell him that his friend was dead." That death, Lake says, "had a huge, *huge* impact on the history of the Middle East." Berger recalls a conversation on the day of the assassination in which he talked to the president about Rabin's killer and sadly observed, "That young man knew what he was doing."[38]

Clinton and Rabin were an international odd couple who never allowed their differences in age, experience, and demeanor to interfere with candid conversation and calculated risk taking. They both wanted peace in the Middle East and the president who never wore a uniform formed a remarkably close bond with the soldier and statesman who served in every Israeli war and national emergency. The assassination of Rabin was a setback, and in hindsight perhaps an irreparable setback, to the Middle East peace process.

Even while Rabin was alive, implementing the Oslo principles that were agreed to on the White House lawn was difficult. Deadlines were missed, incidents of violence occurred in the region, and negotiations about the issues yet to be resolved stalled. After Rabin's funeral, Shimon Peres led a weaker Israeli government that in the wake of dramatic terrorist attacks lost an election to Benjamin Netanyahu and the Likud Party. Netanyahu's government observed the letter of the Oslo commitments but took full advantage of opportunities to delay new transfers of territory when Palestinians failed to keep promises. Instead of building trust with gradual transfers of authority, implementing the Oslo agreement was generating new sources of tension. Madeleine Albright observes that Middle East negotiations became much more complicated because "instead of having a lubricant, like Rabin, you had sandpaper like Netanyahu."

In 1998, the year of the Lewinsky scandal, the administration invited Israeli and Palestinian delegations to the Wye River Estate outside Washington for sustained face-to-face negotiations that were intended to put the Oslo process back on track. The Wye River talks involved intense presidential lobbying and a poignant visit from Jordan's King Hussein, who was in the United States for critical cancer treatment. When the negotiations succeeded, Sandy Berger observes that they included an ironic development. Hard-line Israeli insistence that the Palestinian National Council (PNC) reiterate its commitment to remove anti-Israeli provisions from the Palestinian covenant led to a suggestion that President Clinton attend a PNC meeting. Members of the Israeli delegation thought this was a good idea. It resulted in a dramatic presidential visit to the West Bank, where Clinton gave an important speech, dedicated the opening of a Palestinian airport, and met with Arafat. As in Northern Ireland, presidential travel was an important tool the Clinton White House used to draw attention to international issues and advance ongoing diplomatic efforts.[39]

In Israel, although the Knesset formally approved the Wye River Memorandum, it was unpopular on both the left, where there was concern that the negotiations were moving too slowly, and on the right, where there was criticism of continued concessions of territory. In the 1999 Israeli election, Netanyahu was defeated by Ehud Barak, the leader of the Labor Party, who had campaigned on a promise to resume the Rabin approach to the peace process. That commitment, together with a Palestinian threat to unilaterally seek recognition of independence from the United Nations, led to the Camp David summit. In the summer of 2000, when Clinton was in his final year in office, he held high-level negotiations on the most sensitive issues on the Israeli-Palestinian agenda without any prior assurances that progress was possible. Israeli and Palestinian delegations talked about borders, refugees, and the future of Jerusalem in detail and offered serious proposals for their final resolution. Although the summit began with very little movement from either side, in the end, Barak made concessions on Palestinian control of Arab neighborhoods in East Jerusalem, transfer of Israeli territory in exchange for the incorporation of selected settlements into the state of Israel, the right of Palestinian refugees to return to the new Palestinian state, and elaborate mechanisms for shared access and administration of Jerusalem's holy places. In making these offers, Barak risked much. There was no comparable flexibility from the Palestinians. Arafat declined to make an agreement and the Camp David summit ended in failure that was followed by complex recriminations about what had gone wrong.

According to Sandy Berger, "Camp David is a bit of a *Rashomon* event. There is the American Camp David, there is the Palestinian Camp David, and there is the Israeli Camp David, and they're all different. . . . It was an event that you could look at from many different perspectives." Berger's own perspective is that "Arafat failed to seize an extraordinary opportunity because he did not have the courage or the disposition or the will to risk taking on his own extremists." Madeleine Albright believes that Arafat might have accepted the deal were it not for the complicated provisions regarding the holy sites in Jerusalem, which were of great concern across the Arab world. "We were asking Arafat to make those decisions," Albright observes, "and he couldn't, because for that you needed approval of the other Arabs. Barak had not told us his bottom lines [before Camp David was well underway], we had not, to use Dennis [Ross]'s favorite word, 'conditioned' the Saudis or various people."

It is hard to say why Arafat declined an offer that contained far better provisions than any that had ever been made in serious negotiations. Clinton put enormous pressure on him to accept or at least counter the Israeli proposals. Berger described Clinton's personal diplomacy with Arafat as "Johnsonian." When the two leaders met for one of their one-on-one Camp David sessions, Berger, Albright, and Ross were in the next room listening attentively and watching the exchange through a door that was slightly ajar. Clinton's Johnsonian style, Berger recalls, was "a combination of persuasion and cajoling and intimidation. Arafat looked like he was ready to die. He just kept getting smaller and smaller as Clinton kept getting larger and larger and larger."

No matter how large he got, the president could not get Arafat to move, and Camp David ended without success and with heightened frustrations in the Middle East, where new violence broke out. When Likud politician Ariel Sharon made a controversial visit to the Temple Mount in September of 2000, the violence escalated further and became the second Intifada. In the final weeks of his presidency, Clinton tried again to get a commitment from Arafat and with Barak's approval put forward a set of parameters for resolving the outstanding issues between Israel and the Palestinians that was essentially the Camp David proposals with a few more details and Israeli concessions. Again, Arafat walked away. In 2001, when Deborah Sontag published an article in the *New York Times* that took a critical view of the U.S. and Israeli positions in the Middle East peace process,[40] Clinton called Ehud Barak and reportedly said:

> What the hell is this? Why is she turning the mistakes we made into the essence? The true story of Camp David was that for the first time in the history of the conflict the American president put on the table a proposal, based on UN Security Council resolutions 242 and 338, very close to the Palestinian demands, and Arafat refused even to accept it as a basis for negotiations, walked out of the room, and deliberately turned to terrorism. That's the real story—all the rest is gossip.[41]

The gossip has continued, but events in the Middle East since the end of the Clinton presidency have made it abundantly clear that if and when the peace process resumes in any serious fashion, it will almost certainly involve discussions that owe a debt to the proposals developed in the final months of the Clinton administration.

Conclusion

Critics of Clinton's efforts to contribute to the peace processes in Northern Ireland and the Middle East often speculate about his motives. Perhaps he made his commitment to a Gerry Adams visa in order to win votes in the 1992 New York primary. Maybe his final year push for a Middle East agreement was an effort to make amends for a second term that was dominated by scandal and impeachment.

Motives are hard to measure and assess; presidential activity is not. Bill Clinton spent many hours talking with foreign leaders and advisors about the prospects for peace in Northern Ireland and the Middle East. He learned the details of complicated negotiations in multiple venues and offered to help his highly qualified negotiators when they ran into difficulties. He did his homework. Sandy Berger remembers that when you "spread out a map of Jerusalem," Clinton knew all the neighborhoods "and where the various pockets of population were." And he took controversial trips. The president of the United States traveled to Belfast and Londonderry and to cities on the West Bank, putting his personal and presidential prestige on the line for peace processes that were not yet complete.

After Clinton's first and most famous trip to Northern Ireland, the IRA cease-fire broke down and a bomb went off in London's financial district. In the short run, the president's commitment to the Northern Ireland peace process looked like a mistake. There were often risks in Clinton's travel to trouble spots, and they were not the only risks he was willing to take. Clinton knowingly offended a major ally with the Adams visa decision and he willingly went to Wye River and Camp David without prior assurance that high-level meetings would produce positive results. Even after violence broke out in the Middle East following the failure to reach agreement at Camp David, Clinton continued to take chances and make commitments to further meetings in the region and in Washington in what turned out to be a futile effort to revive the languishing peace process. Clinton's reasons for engaging in Northern Ireland and the Middle East can be questioned, but the reality and the intensity of those engagements cannot.

Of course, presidential engagement, by itself, does not deliver peace. As the outside facilitator, or mediator, or cheerleader, Clinton's contributions to peace negotiations would always be secondary to the contributions of the principal players. The Nobel Peace Prizes went to the major party leaders, Hume and Trimble, in Northern Ireland after the Good Friday peace agreement and Rabin, Peres, and Arafat after Oslo. There was justice in those prize decisions. And there were important breakthroughs in the two peace processes to which the United States made little or no contribution. Oslo was accomplished by Israeli and Palestinian negotiators without any American participation, and long before Clinton became involved in Northern Ireland, important meetings took place between Irish and British diplomats and between Gerry Adams and John Hume that set the stage for the subsequent successes with the Downing Street Declaration and the Good Friday accords. Where he could, and when he could, Clinton was willing to make a contribution, but there was never any guarantee that presidential involvement would tip the scales on the side of progress. It did in Northern Ireland; it did not in the Middle East.

The failure to secure a negotiated solution to the long-standing disputes between Israel and the Palestinians was one of the great disappointments of the Clinton presidency.[42] The simple version of that failure was summarized by Dennis Ross, "You couldn't make peace with Yasser Arafat; and you couldn't make peace without him."[43] Clinton could never escape that central dilemma, but he cannot be faulted for not trying. He tried often, up to and including his final days in the White House. As he observed in his memoirs about the problematic prospects for the meetings at Wye River, "I always preferred failure in a worthy effort to inaction for fear of failure."[44] That is not a bad motto for any prospective presidential peacemaker.

Conclusion

CLINTON'S LEGACY FOR POLITICS AND GOVERNMENT

Sidney M. Milkis

The chapters of this volume shed valuable light on the complicated character and political times of America's forty-second president. Examining Bill Clinton's campaigns, his domestic and foreign policy record, and the challenges posed by the political environment of the 1990s, the authors make clear that both his successes and his failures were highly consequential. They differ considerably, however, in their interpretations of his legacy for American politics and government. As Russell Riley shows, Clinton himself struggled to make sense of his place in history, noting that "no president has courted Clio, the muse of history, more assiduously." Clinton was a man of great ambition who aspired to leave not just a record of change but also—like Washington, Jefferson, Jackson, Lincoln, and Franklin Roosevelt—an enduring transformation of the American political landscape. Indeed, Clinton's first important speech in his 1992 quest for the White House—a well-reasoned address in October 1991 at his alma mater, Georgetown University—proclaimed a "New Covenant" that would restore "opportunity, responsibility and community" to a nation that had been ravaged by the rapaciousness of Republicans and the maternalism of Democrats.[1]

Yet Clinton was resigned, Riley observes, to the possibility that the political climate of the 1990s might not allow for greatness. He "recognized that one of the most fundamental laws of American politics is that big presidencies typically follow from big moments. War or domestic crisis was the necessary predicate for the kinds of presidencies Clinton most admired." "Vexed by the constraints of tranquility," Clinton's settled on Theodore Roosevelt as his historical model, a strong leader who presided over peace and prosperity but still managed to earn a place next to Lincoln on Mount Rushmore. Just as TR earned his place among America's presidential immortals by identifying and seeking the first public remedies for the dislocations brought by the industrial revolution, so Clinton hoped to be the first president to take on the hard challenges posed by the global economy that had emerged at the twilight of the twentieth century.

During more realistic reflections, Clinton identified with Harry Truman, whose star rose considerably with the passage of time, a historical appreciation that was aided considerably by David McCulloch's hagiographic biography of Truman, which was published in 1992. Clinton believed that just as Truman led the nation from the uncertainties of the post–World War II era to the exalted mission of the Cold War, so he would direct the country to a new role in the world amid the chaos left by the collapse of the Soviet Union.

But Clinton's course seemed less purposeful than that of Roosevelt and Truman. TR established important precedents that Franklin Roosevelt would build on as he dedicated the national government to protecting individuals from the abuses of big business and the uncertainties of the marketplace. In contrast, even as Clinton promised major programmatic initiatives to ameliorate the disruptions caused by the global economy, he proclaimed—or acknowledged—that "the era of big government is over."[2] Similarly, Truman displayed determined leadership in mobilizing support for the Cold War, deftly mixing "soft" power with the Marshall Plan and military preparedness with the creation of the national security apparatus. In contrast, as Spencer Bakich shows, Clinton was skeptical if not indifferent to "grand strategy," believing that such "organizing principles" were "imposed after the fact."

Riley suggests that Clinton's defensive pragmatism followed from the limited possibilities for consequential action afforded the first president of the post–Cold War period. He thus sees strong parallels between the early Truman years—before the onset of the Cold War—and Clinton's two terms. In both cases, a "political *status quo antebellum*" restored political opposition and institutional torpor that weakened executive power. What Truman and Clinton experienced, Riley argues, was not anomalous but was rather a "commonplace for presidents who govern when a major war has ended." Clinton's unsteady efforts, then, should be viewed "as part of the larger, repeating pattern of postwar contraction of the presidency's standing in the political order"—the down side of a cycle that also plagued Andrew Johnson and Woodrow Wilson.

However, presidents are not always ensnared by their political times. Building on the foundation of the modern executive office his progressive forbears had constructed, Truman forged the national security apparatus—comprised of the Department of Defense, the Central Intelligence Agency, and the National Security Council and international organizations such as the North Atlantic

Treaty Organization (NATO)—that made the sort of "return to normalcy" previous postwar presidents had experienced less likely. Although Clinton did not "adopt a radical or innovative grand strategy," Bakich makes clear that he made a significant difference in world politics. "The end of the cold war signaled no 'holiday from history' for the United States," he writes. "The period from the fall of the Berlin Wall to the terrorist attacks on 9/11 was of tremendous historical importance, particularly in Europe, where core issues pertaining to U.S.-Russian relations and the continent's security architecture came to a head." After a slow start, Clinton's foreign policy team grasped its historical opportunity, combining sensitive diplomacy with Russia and forceful action with its NATO allies to halt the "serial aggressiveness" of Serbian president Slobodan Milosevic in Bosnia and Kosovo. The battle against ethnic cleansing in the former Yugoslavia marked, as National Security Advisor Sandy Berger noted, NATO's first war, one that severely tested its ability to expand its influence and membership in Eastern Europe.

The successful use of force in the Balkans, Bakich concludes, owed in large part to Clinton's pragmatism. The "inclusiveness and flexibility" of his foreign policy allowed him to manage effectively rather than become the victim of the post–Cold War milieu. The president's pluralism, according to Strobe Talbott, his friend and a member of the administration's State Department, expressed itself as "a ferocity of commitment" in peacemaking efforts in Ireland and the Middle East. Although the president was not completely successful in either of these endeavors—diplomatic efforts to work out an agreement between the Palestinians and Israel proved especially frustrating—he made extraordinary efforts under the most difficult of circumstances. As Robert Strong shows, Clinton's celebrated visits to the West Bank and Northern Ireland revealed how a modern president could play an important peacemaking role in world affairs—and thus pursue a lifelong devotion to reconciliation—even as his office was besieged by partisan rancor and impeachment at home.

Clinton's pragmatism in foreign affairs, although it was determined and consequential, was not the core of his New Covenant, which promised to restore what Arthur Schlesinger Jr. once called the "vital center" of the liberal political order.[3] Having witnessed the liberal regime forged by FDR and Lyndon Johnson being strongly challenged, if not fractured, by Ronald Reagan's two terms in office, Clinton and his allies in the Democratic Leadership Council, a think tank that incubated many of the ideas that informed his 1992 campaign, promised a new form of Democratic Party politics that would cure the ills brought on by the ideological and institutional conflicts that had plagued the party since the late 1960s. This "third way" alternative to orthodox conservatism and liberalism met its first challenge during Clinton's first year when his administration sought to restore strength to a faltering economy, as he promised to do during the campaign. As Brendan Doherty chronicles, during the campaign Clinton promoted a series of policies championed by Secretary of Labor Robert Reich that would provide relief for the middle class, including a middle-class tax cut and investments in education, job training, and other programs to enhance economic opportunity. This obeisance to Keynesian economics would be balanced by Clinton's promise, strongly advocated by Robert Rubin, the director of the newly formed National Economic Council, to cut the budget deficit in half in four years. Faced with a budget situation that was far worse than he and his economic team expected, however, Clinton was forced to rely much more than he wanted to on "Rubinomics." Doherty reports that some members of the administration, at least in hindsight, view the emphasis on deficit cutting as a corrective to the imbalances Reagan's supply-side economics had created. Yet as Clinton's domestic policy advisor William Galston observes, Clinton found the course he felt forced to take frustrating: "The President got so angry at being in this fiscal box that he exploded and said, 'God damn it, we're all Eisenhower Republicans now.' There was a lot of truth to that. Centrist Democrats had turned into what moderate Republicans used to be. What Republicans used to be had morphed into something unrecognizable."[4]

Hoping to reimagine the progressive tradition, Clinton thus found himself dwelling uncomfortably in Reagan's shadow. Just as Dwight Eisenhower's so-called Modern Republicanism, which triumphed in the presidential elections of 1952 and 1956, accepted and ensured bipartisan support for Roosevelt's New Deal, so Clinton's New Democratic principles appeared to signal the Democrats' full retreat in the face of a conservative political realignment. Eisenhower was a domestic political conservative who had no desire to innovate except in modest, incremental ways, but he believed that the New Deal had become a permanent part of modern American life. When his conservative brother Edgar, impatient with his sibling's compromises with liberalism, criticized him privately for carrying on liberal policies, the president replied bluntly, "Should any political party attempt to abolish social security and eliminate labor laws and farm programs, you should not hear of that party again in our political history."[5] "Above all else," historian Oscar Handlin wrote soon after Eisenhower left office, "Eisenhower made palatable to most Republicans the social welfare legislation of the preceding two decades."[6]

Clinton's presidency conceded much to the Reagan "revolution." As Michael Nelson argues in his chapter on welfare reform, his willingness to sign the 1996 welfare reform bill, eliminating the entitlement to Aid to Families with Dependent Children, abetted a rout of the party's liberal establishment. (On the final vote to replace AFDC in the Senate, only twenty-one Democrats voted against the measure.) Similarly, Clinton acquiesced to the general objectives of the

Republican program to balance the budget by the year 2002, an agreement that included the most significant tax cuts and spending restraints since the heady days of the Reagan revolution. The Clinton administration and Republicans in Congress also collaborated to enact the 1999 Gramm-Leach-Bliley bill, which repealed the Glass-Steagall Act, a New Deal law passed during the early days of the Roosevelt presidency that established a firewall between banking and speculation. Gramm-Leach-Bliley removed this barrier by allowing banks to merge with insurance companies and investment houses. In the wake of the Reagan "revolution," the restraint on banks' financial activity had come to be viewed as an impediment to economic growth, and there had been several attempts to remove it during the Reagan and George H. W. Bush presidencies. Clinton and Secretary of the Treasury Lawrence Summers, viewing the modernization of markets as consistent with New Democratic principles, formed an alliance with a Republican-controlled Congress to push a deregulatory bill through Congress, a capstone measure that appeared to bestow bipartisan legitimacy on conservatives' celebration of unfettered markets.

Still, Clinton was no Eisenhower. Ike was a military hero who came to the White House "to crown a reputation[,] not to make one."[7] As his love was not for power but for duty, Eisenhower was well suited to the task of bestowing legitimacy on the New Deal. In contrast, Clinton struck most Americans as a charming and talented but irresolute man on the make. Having failed to achieve reform that would guarantee all Americans a comprehensive package of health care benefits, he appeared all too eager to embrace the conservative mood that in 1994 ushered in the first Republican Congress since 1954. Then, sensing that Speaker Newt Gingrich and the Republicans had overreached, the president pounced on the Republican budget cuts, particularly in Medicare, and blocked their passage. Of Clinton and his relationship to the post–New Deal order, it can be said as historian Robert Blake wrote of Benjamin Disraeli: "He did not care which way he traveled providing he was in the driver's seat."[8] That Clinton committed a long train of private and political indiscretions only reinforced the serious doubts about his character. The spectacle of the Monica Lewinsky scandal, during which Clinton become the first elected president to be impeached by the House of Representatives, confirmed the public's disrespect for his personal morality. (Andrew Johnson, the only other president to be impeached, had succeeded to the office when Abraham Lincoln died.)

But no less remarkable than the House indictment and the Senate trial of Clinton was the president's popularity throughout the ordeal. As Andrew Rudalevige observes in his comprehensive discussion of the impeachment episode, Clinton's public approval rating in a Democratic poll taken immediately after the impeachment vote was 73 percent, the highest of his presidency. An even greater testament to Clinton's resilience in the face of scandal came in a January 2, 1999, Gallup poll, which reported that Clinton was the man most admired by Americans, beating out Pope John Paul II. The public thus distinguished between Clinton the man, whom they regarded as immoral and untrustworthy, and Clinton the chief executive, whose record of "peace, prosperity and moderation" they approved.[9]

In truth, Clinton's presidency displayed the virtues of his defects. Ideological promiscuity and volatility are the story of his political life. Indeed, both as governor of Arkansas and as president, Clinton's first two years in office were desperately unsuccessful. But this very unsteadiness may have suited Clinton's political time, an era of weak partisan loyalties, divided government, and widespread distrust of the political process. Al From, president of the Democratic Leadership Council, credits presidential scholar Stephen Skowronek for the most discerning analysis of third-way politics. Skowronek identified Clinton as a "preemptive" leader—a stance distinguished by a "mongrel politics" that aggressively resists prevailing doctrines. Previous presidents such as Woodrow Wilson and Richard Nixon had played this role; but Skowronek suggests that secular developments—the rhetorical and administrative powers of the modern presidency, the decline of party loyalties, the mystifying complexity of modern domestic and foreign policy—offered unprecedented opportunities for an unabashedly pragmatic president to govern effectively.[10] Thus, even as he was criticized by ardent liberals and militant conservatives for failing to provide a compelling vision of the nation's future, Clinton's extraordinary dexterity often served him well at a time when most Americans resisted the programmatic ambitions of both major political parties. As Skowronek puts it, "It might as well be said that slick and tricky men rise to power when the nation most wants them, when it is fed up with ideologies of all kinds and casting about for someone who is fast and loose enough in his commitments to generate the mixture it is yearning for."[11]

The two-tier politics that Michael Nelson describes in his chapter on Clinton's elections, characterized by a disjuncture between bitter partisanship in Washington and weakening partisan loyalties outside the beltway, gave Clinton, with his skill in combining doctrines, a certain appeal in the country. Although this eclecticism risked degenerating into rank opportunism, the popularity of programs such as AmeriCorps, the National Partnership for Reinventing Government, and the earned income tax credit suggests that Clinton's third way may have demonstrated, as Galson argues, that "there was indeed a serious governing agenda—that was neither the traditional Democratic agenda, nor movement Republican conservatism—which had an integrity of its own, and which could work."

Nonetheless, Clinton's third way suffered from political isolation that diminished his legacy. Al From, invoking Skowronek's analysis, observed, "Third Way presidents never have that hard-core support in their own party because they challenge too many of the orthodoxies of the party. So they don't have the kind of cadre of people that would fall on their sword for them. . . . But the opposition probably goes after them with more vehemence than they would a more partisan President because a Third Way President usurps some of the opposition's turf." Indeed, writing in 1997, Skowronek presciently observed that preemptive presidents have tended—either formally or informally—to be impeached.[12] In the absence of a political party and mass-based constituencies that could routinize his charisma, Clinton, although he survived the Republican assault on his presidency, could not withstand the rising tide of partisanship that arose in the 1980s and continued after Ronald Reagan left the White House. Instead of restoring the vital center of American politics, Clinton's two terms proved to be, as Sean Theriault, Patrick Hickey, and Megan Moeller argue, an "inflection point" that made partisan polarization a routine, intractable feature of political life in the United States. Ironically, Clinton's singular pragmatism unwittingly advanced a new form of politics that portended an immutable stalemate in Washington between liberals and conservatives.

The New Party System

Clinton's ascent to the White House and his tumultuous presidency must be understood within the context of a new form of partisanship that emerged during the 1970s and 1980s. Put simply, he won the 1992 presidential election because he presented himself as a New Democrat, an agent of change who offered the hope of an alternative to both traditional Democratic liberalism and traditional Republican conservatism. In truth, the third way (which Dick Morris branded as triangulation) was not created from whole cloth in 1995 by a desperate Clinton and a scheming Morris; it was there at the beginning of Clinton's quest for power.

Above all, Clinton's third-way politics sought to moderate the ideological and institutional confrontations that arose with the revitalization of partisanship during the 1980s. Since the 1970s, political scientists had been keeping a death watch for the American party system. Scholars and pundits lamented that reforms and the mass media had deprived political parties of their limited but significant influence in American politics, with little prospect of recovery. The declining influence of traditional decentralized, patronage-based party organizations was reflected not only in the presidential selection process but also in the political loyalties of the American people. Institutional changes that deemphasized partisan politics and governance, combined with television's emergence as the most important platform of political action, were "freeing more and more millions of Americans," as Theodore White wrote in 1973, "from unquestioning obedience to past tradition, . . . begetting what has been called the age of ticket-splitting."[13] Indeed, for all but four years in the period 1968–1992 (Jimmy Carter's term in the White House), the voters delivered a split verdict in national elections, handing control of the presidency to the Republicans and Congress and most state and local offices to the Democrats.

By the late 1980s, however, it seemed that the age of divided government had brought not the decline but rather the transformation of the American party system. Although partisan loyalties in the electorate declined during the late 1960s and 1970s, parties did not simply wither away. Indeed, during Reagan's presidency, the party system showed at least some signs of transformation and renewal. Reagan and his successor George Bush supported efforts by Republicans in the national committee and congressional campaign organizations to restore some of the importance of political parties by fashioning them into highly untraditional but politically potent national organizations. The Democrats lagged behind in party-building efforts, but the electoral losses they suffered in the 1980 elections encouraged them to modernize the national party machinery, openly imitating some of the devices employed by Republicans.[14]

Even as they became more national, programmatic organizations (the origins of which lay in the New Deal and the opposition it spawned), the Democratic and Republican Parties appeared to have lost their connection with the American people. Unlike the decentralized party system that had flourished in the nineteenth and early twentieth centuries, the politics of the 1960s and 1970s had spawned a form of partisanship centered on government rather than on the electorate. The Democrats and Republicans became parties of administration intent on using centralized administrative power in Washington to further the intractable demands of policy advocates. In addition, partisan disputes about rights had become increasingly associated with the expansion of national administrative power (even conservatives in the abortion dispute demanded governmental intervention to protect the rights of the unborn). The attempt to graft programmatic rights onto individual liberties further shifted partisan politics away from parties as associations that organize political sentiments into an electoral majority.[15]

A major (if not the main) forum for partisan conflict during the Reagan and Bush years was a sequence of investigations through which Democrats and Republicans sought to discredit one another. In part, enhanced legal scrutiny of public officials was a logical response to the Watergate scandal. But partisan maneuvering using investigations and scandalous revelations was institutionalized by the 1978 Ethics in Government Act, which provided for the appointment of independent counsels to investigate allegations of criminal activity by executive officials.[16] Not surprisingly, divided government encouraged the exploitation of the act for partisan purposes. In the 1980s, congressional Democrats found themselves in a position to demand criminal investigations and possible jail sentences for their Republican opponents. When Clinton became president, congressional Republicans turned the tables with a vengeance. Consequently, political disagreements were readily transformed into criminal charges. Investigations under the special prosecutor statute tended to deflect attention from legitimate constitutional and policy differences and to focus the attention of Congress, the press, and citizens on scandals.[17]

Democratic and Republican organizations raised large campaign war chests and fostered party discipline in Washington. Yet developments during the 1980s and 1990s—virulent institutional clashes between the executive and the legislature, the decline of public authority, and the impeachment of a popular president presiding over the most prosperous economy in three decades—raised serious doubts about the capacity of these emergent national parties to build popular support for political principles and programs.[18] Indeed, as fierce partisan battles were waged within the Washington Beltway, the influence of the Democrats and the Republicans on the perceptions and habits of the American people continued to decline. The weak partisan attachments of the electorate were exposed by the 1992 presidential campaign of H. Ross Perot, whose garnering of 19 percent of the popular vote was the most significant challenge to the two-party system since Theodore Roosevelt's Progressive Party campaign of 1912. Perot's campaign, which was dominated by 30-minute "infomercials" and hour-long appearances on television talk shows, set a new standard for direct, plebiscitary appeals that threatened to sound the death knell of the party campaign. "Perot hints broadly at an even bolder new order," the historian Alan Brinkley wrote in July 1992, "in which the president, checked only by direct expressions of popular desire, will roll up his sleeves and solve the nation's problems."[19]

The New Covenant

Much of Clinton's political success derived from his masterful exploitation of the American people's disdain for partisanship. Indeed, his third-way politics, originally dubbed the New Covenant, made Perotism respectable. Clinton dedicated his 1992 campaign to principles and policies that "transcended," he claimed, the exhausted debate between right and left that had afflicted the nation for two decades. More particularly, like his Democratic predecessor Jimmy Carter, Clinton's purpose was to move his party to the center and thus prepare it to compete more effectively at a time when the New Deal and the Great Society appeared to be losing support in the country. But Clinton seemed to pursue this objective with greater programmatic coherence than Carter had. In 1990, Clinton became the chairman of the Democratic Leadership Council (DLC), which developed many of the ideas that became the central themes of his run for the presidency. As Clinton declared frequently during the campaign, these ideas represented a new philosophy of government that would "honor middle class values, restore public trust, create a new sense of community and make America work again." He heralded "a new social contract," a "new covenant," one that would seek to constrain, in the name of responsibility and community, the demands for rights summoned by the Roosevelt revolution.[20] Invoking Roosevelt's 1932 Commonwealth Club address, in which FDR first outlined the "economic constitutional order" that became the principal aspiration of the New Deal, Clinton declared that the liberal commitment to guaranteeing economic security through entitlement programs such as Social Security, Medicare, Medicaid, and Aid to Families with Dependent Children had gone too far. The objective of the New Covenant was to correct the tendency of Americans to celebrate individual rights and government entitlement programs without any sense of the mutual obligations they had to each other and their country.[21]

Clinton's commitment to educational opportunity best exemplified the objective of restoring a balance between rights and responsibilities. Its central feature, a national service corps, was emblematic of the core New Covenant principle—national community. According to Clinton, a trust fund would be created from which any and all Americans could borrow money for a college education, so long as they paid it back either as a small percentage of their life's income or with two years of service as teachers, police officers, child care workers, or by participating in other activities that "our country desperately needs."[22] It was touted as a domestic GI Bill, which political scientist Suzanne Mettler has shown nurtured the sense of civic responsibility that animated the so-called greatest generation, and Clinton's "vow that he would institute a program" of national service was the most consistently popular applause line of the 1992 campaign."[23]

Clinton's New Democratic message appeared to work. As Deputy Domestic Policy Advisor Bruce Reed argues, his third-way approach

> made it possible to get out of the traditional left/right box that seemed like a zero-sum game within the party. The Democrats had run campaigns that were perceived as somewhat too far to the left. But understandably, people didn't want to just change labels or shift their principles. Then Clinton came along, and he was neither fish nor fowl. He had some liberal passions, but conservative governing values. He'd

also thought through the difficult issues in a way that others hadn't. We quickly realized that he was perfectly suited to bridge the divide [between liberals and moderates] in the Democratic Party because he was new and young and exciting, but had to govern in a tough, relatively conservative Southern state.

To be sure, Clinton's 43 percent share of the national popular vote was hardly a mandate. (Indeed, it was roughly the same percentage that losing Democratic candidates had received in the previous three elections.) But support for Clinton was impressively broad. He won a strong 370–168 Electoral College majority by sweeping thirty-two states, many of which had not voted Democratic since 1964. In the congressional elections, the Democrats preserved but did not increase their majorities in the House and the Senate. But more than 100 new members were elected to Congress in 1992, many of them willing to work cooperatively with the new president. Since 1968, the public's striking ambivalence about the parties had usually left the government divided between a Republican president and a Democratic Congress. In 1992, however, an exit poll revealed that 62 percent of the voters preferred to have the presidency and Congress controlled by the same party, in the hope that ideological polarization and institutional confrontation would come to an end.[24]

In truth, Clinton and his allies in the Democratic Leadership Council were ambivalent about party politics. Clinton—the first president of the baby-boom generation—had cut his political teeth during the late 1960s and 1970s when parties were under siege. He rose to national prominence as a luminary of the "new" politics that matured during the 1970s, in which those who had ambitions of higher office saw no reason to seek the support of old machines and regular party organizations. Instead, as a 1984 article celebrating Clinton and other practitioners of the new politics observed, they were "tough, outspoken champions of the movements they [stood] for." Eschewing party politics, they viewed politics as an "exercise in narrowcasting," seeking out people who "shared their vision."[25]

Clinton's disinclination to rely on party organization was reinforced by the tension between the Democratic Leadership Council and the regular party apparatus. "Bill Clinton ran, and won, on the basis of ideas that enjoyed widespread support in the country," Galston observes, "but much less widespread support within his own party. You can write the history of the first two years of the Clinton administration around that proposition." The Democratic Leadership Council was founded for the most part by elected Democratic officials who believed that the party's national committee and congressional caucus had become too responsive to liberal constituency groups. In fact, the council was divided between those who wanted to reform the party and those who preferred to build a new progressive coalition that would transcend parties entirely.[26] Clinton appeared to be torn between these two objectives. Even as he styled himself a "new" Democrat who would challenge the liberal orthodoxy of his party, he formed a campaign organization that included many traditional liberals and promised congressional Democrats that he would work in "harness" with them to pursue policies of mutual interest.[27] Clinton's artful fence mending enabled the Democrats to run a unified, effective campaign in 1992. At the same time, his campaign rhetoric was at odds with the majority of liberal activist groups and Democratic members of Congress. The difficulty of reconciling "new" Democratic principles and the traditional commitments of the party would be a constant source of trouble for Clinton, threatening to undermine his authority as a moral leader.

Clinton's words and actions during the early days of his presidency seemed to betray his campaign pledge to dedicate the Democratic Party to the new concept of justice he espoused. No sooner had he been inaugurated than Clinton announced his intention to lift the long-standing ban on homosexuals in the military. In the social climate that prevailed in the early 1990s, however, it was unrealistic to expect that such a divisive issue could be resolved by the stroke of a pen. To be sure, the development of the administrative presidency since the New Deal had given presidents more power to exercise domestic policy by executive fiat.[28] But as Reagan and Bush had discovered, with the expansion of national administration to issues that shaped the direction and character of American public life, this power often provoked opposition from Congress, interest groups, and the bureaucracy. Intense resistance from the respected head of the Joint Chiefs of Staff, Colin Powell, and the influential Democratic chair of the Senate Armed Services Committee, Sam Nunn of Georgia, forced Clinton to defer the executive order for six months while he sought a compromise solution. In the end, Clinton and the Congress reached an agreement—the "Don't Ask, Don't Tell" policy passed into law in 1993 that banned gays from serving openly in the military. The delay and the compromise aroused the ire of gay and lesbian activists who had given strong financial and organizational support to Clinton during the election. Most damaging for the new president was that the issue became a glaring benchmark of his inability to revitalize progressive politics as an instrument for redressing the economic insecurity and political alienation of the middle class.

The bitter partisan fight in the spring and summer of 1993 over the administration's budgetary program served only to reinforce doubts about Clinton's ability to lead the nation in a new, more harmonious direction. Even though Clinton's budget plan promised to reduce the deficit, it involved new taxes and an array of social programs that Republicans and moderate Democrats perceived as traditional tax-and-spend liberalism. The Republicans marched in lockstep opposition to Clinton's economic program, especially to his $16 billion stimulus package, which he offered as a partial antidote to the economic contraction that he feared deficit reduction would cause. In April 1993, Senate Republicans unanimously supported a filibuster that killed the stimulus package. Congress did enact a modified version of the president's budgetary plan a few months later, but by razor-thin margins and without any support from Republicans, who voted unanimously against it in the House and Senate. Clinton won this narrow, bruising victory only after promising moderate Democrats that he would put together another package of spending cuts in the fall. But this uneasy compromise failed to dispel the charge of his political opponents that Clinton was a wolf in sheep's clothing—a conventional liberal whose commitment to reform had expired at the end of the presidential campaign.[29]

As Brendan Doherty's chapter on Clinton's economic policy makes clear, the GOP's characterization of the president was not fair. In truth, his commitment to lower the deficit was the political equivalent of "root canal" politics. The term is Federal Reserve Board member Alan Blinder's, who insists that Clinton's fiscal restraint belied the president's reputation as a trimmer: "I really believe he decided to take this calculated risk because he thought it was good for the country. And, incidentally, if it proved to be good for the country, that would help him get reelected in '96. But that's the way you want a President to think. You do something that's good, four years later the good chickens come home to roost and you get reelected, and you don't worry much about four weeks later."

Nevertheless, Clinton never made a persuasive case to the country on the merits of the budgetary legislation that might have benefited foot soldiers such as Margaret Margolies-Mezvinsky, the Pennsylvania Democrat from a wealthy suburban district who cast the crucial vote for the economic package in the House. As From laments, Clinton spent too much time during his first two years wrestling with party and committee leaders in Congress: "He wasn't a good arm twister, but he was a good persuader. I think, by the time all that became really clear to him, we had probably lost a year or two in the Congress. At the worst point, he got his first budget done." Deputy Secretary of Treasury Roger Altman dramatically recounts how as Margolies-Mezvinsky made her famous walk to the well to cast her fate with the president, the Republicans serenaded her with "Bye, Bye Marjorie." As it turned out, that act proved to be the death knell not only of her reelection bid in 1994 but also of the Democratic congressional majority.

Clinton said and did little about a New Covenant during the first two years of his presidency. In a February 1993 address to Congress, in which he laid out his administration's goals, instead of trumpeting reciprocal obligations between citizens and their government, Clinton proposed a new set of entitlements in the form of job training, a college education, and health care. Clinton's proposal to make college loans available to all Americans did include the campaign-touted plan to form a national service corps. But news of the enactment of a scaled-down version of this educational reform program in August was lost amid Clinton's promises to expand the welfare state. In fact, the reciprocal obligation Clinton expected of the beneficiaries of college loans seemed almost apologetic. They would be able to pay the country back with a small percentage of their income, thereby avoiding national service. This alternative to public service, it seems, greatly diluted the concept of national community. Indeed, Clinton muddied the message of sacrifice by emphasizing the financial benefit of his reform program to college students.[30]

In this respect, AmeriCorps did not become an "earned entitlement," as the GI Bill had after World War II. "While millions benefitted from the GI Bill," journalist Steven Waldman lamented in the spring of 1999, "only about one percent of 18 year olds have had the AmeriCorps experience—hardly enough to transform a cultural ethos. While AmeriCorps has established the principle that at least some government benefits should be tied to giving something back to the community, almost all of college aid is still given out according to other criteria, primarily need and academic merit."[31] Former Democratic senator Harris Wofford, who headed the AmeriCorps initiative, gave Clinton a lot of credit for getting a program passed in the face of the indifference, if not avowed hostility, of his party. Still, he expressed disappointment that the president did not "take national citizen service from the periphery to the center," that he failed to embrace it, as he had during his campaign, as "the transcending idea" of the third way.

The Restoration of Divided Government

The apologetic stance Clinton displayed in the face of traditional liberal causes was, to a point, understandable; it was a logical response to the modern institutional separation between the presidency and the party. The moderate wing of the Democratic Party that he represented—including the members of the Democratic Leadership Council—was a minority wing. The majority of liberal interest-group activists and Democratic members of Congress still preferred entitlements to obligations and regulations to responsibilities. Only the unpopularity of liberal groups and the emphasis on candidate-centered campaigns in presidential politics made Clinton's nomination and election possible.

The media-driven caucuses and primaries that dominate the presidential nomination process gave Clinton an opportunity to seize the Democratic label as an outsider candidate but offered no means to effect a transformation of his party when he took office. Clinton's Democratic predecessor, Jimmy Carter, who intended to be fiercely independent and a scourge to traditional liberal approaches, faced nearly complete political isolation during his unhappy term in office. To bring about the new mission of progressivism that he advocated during the election, Clinton would have to risk a brutal confrontation with the major powers in the Democratic Party, a battle that might have left him even more vulnerable politically than Carter had been.[32] In truth, no president had risked such a confrontation with his party since Franklin Roosevelt's failed "purge" campaign of 1938.[33] It is not surprising, therefore, that Clinton's allies in the Democratic Leadership Council urged him to renew his "credentials as an outsider" by going over the heads of the party leadership in Congress and taking his message directly to the people. Most important, Democratic Leadership Council leaders argued that the president needed to take his New Covenant message directly to the large number of independents in the electorate who voted for Perot so as to forge "new and sometimes bipartisan coalitions around an agenda that moves beyond the polarized left-right debate."[34]

In the fall of 1993, Clinton took a page from his former political associates in his successful campaign to secure congressional approval of the North American Free Trade Agreement (NAFTA). The fight for NAFTA caused Clinton to defend global free enterprise ardently and to oppose the protectionism supported by labor unions, which still represented one of the most important constituencies in the national Democratic Party. Clinton's victory owed partly to the active support of the Republican congressional leadership. In fact, a majority of Republicans in the House and Senate supported the free trade agreement, while a majority of Democrats, including the House majority leader and the majority whip, opposed it. No less important, however, was the Clinton administration's mobilization of popular support. Indeed, the turning point in the struggle came when the administration challenged Perot, the leading opponent of NAFTA, to debate Vice President Gore on CNN's *Larry King Live*. Gore's optimistic defense of open markets was well received by the large television audience, rousing enough support to persuade a bare majority of legislatures in both houses of Congress to approve the trade agreement.[35]

With the success of the fight over NAFTA, moderate Democrats began to hope that Clinton had finally begun the task of dedicating his party to principles and policies he had espoused during the campaign. Besides national service, the signature third-way issue was welfare reform. During the 1992 campaign, Michael Nelson shows, Clinton departed from traditional Democratic commitments to poverty programs, famously and controversially promising, as he put it at the 1992 Democratic Convention, "an America where we end welfare as we know it. We will say to those on welfare: You will have, and you deserve, the opportunity, through training and education, through childcare and medical coverage, to liberate yourself. But then, when you can, you must work, because welfare should be a second chance, not a way of life."[36] The president had managed to insert an expanded earned income tax credit in the 1993 budget reconciliation—a measure that would provide economic relief to the working poor. But welfare reform, which was dedicated to placing the most economically disadvantaged Americans in jobs, was the most resonant third-way antipoverty program. As Reed notes, "Welfare was the best example of what Clinton would prove to be a master of, of taking an issue that Republicans had demagogued for years and turning it into an affirmative, political, and substantive agenda for Democrats. It was not without controversy."

No doubt the controversy of taking on a divisive but long-standing Democratic commitment played large in Clinton's decision to delay the overhaul of welfare and to make an ambitious health care program, which promised to "guarantee all Americans a comprehensive package of benefits over the course of an entire lifetime," the defining legislative battle of his administration's first two years.[37] For dramatic effect, Clinton brandished a red, white, and blue "health security card" in his September 1993 speech to Congress on health care reform, a symbol of his ambition to carry out the most important extension of social policy since the enactment of Social Security in 1935. To White House stewards of New Democratic principles such as Galston, this proved to be an unfortunate critical juncture of Clinton's presidency: "I will believe to my dying day that the decision to lead with healthcare rather than welfare was not a very well considered judgment, and certainly was ill judged. I don't think the gravity of that sequential decision was really understood at the time it was made, although some of us had strong feelings about it. But it was impossible to articulate those feelings, for obvious reasons."

The principal source of this forbearance was that health care reform became the major initiative of First Lady Hillary Rodham Clinton, who, as Barbara Perry writes, "established her unprecedented role in the White House from the day her husband took the presidential oath." She "became the first presidential spouse to have an office for herself and an extensive staff in the West Wing as well as the customary suite in the East Wing." Moreover, "Hillaryland," as the president's secretary Betty Currie dubbed the first lady's staff, became a critical beachhead in the Clinton administration for the advance of progressive causes favored by liberal advocacy groups and the Democratic congressional caucus. Just as welfare reform divided the party, so health care reform—the holy grail of liberals since the New Deal—promised to unify it. "Every Democrat had a different idea how to do it," Reed recalls, "but they all wanted to do it."

The first lady sought to avoid these disparate reform ambitions by setting up a highly insulated policy process, which seemed to violate New Democratic administrative principles and practices. The third-way remedy for bureaucratic torpor was its National Partnership for Reinventing Government. Originally championed by journalist David Osborne and former city manager Ted Gaebler, this initiative promised "a new customer service contract with the American people, a new guarantee of effective, efficient and responsive government."[38] The reinventing government program, which was announced with much fanfare in September 1993, was not, as many of its critics charged, merely hollow rhetoric. As political scientist Donald Kettl has written, "It energized employees, . . . attracted citizens, . . . drew media attention to government management . . . and made the point that management matters."[39] Curiously, however, the lessons of how to recast administration were disregarded in the development of the health care program. Indeed, the formulation of this program appeared to mark the apotheosis of New Deal administrative politics. It was designed behind closed doors by the Health Care Task Force, which was headed by the first lady and the president's longtime friend Ira Magaziner. Moreover, the health care proposal would have created a new government entitlement program and an administrative apparatus that would have signaled the revitalization rather than the reform of traditional social welfare state policy.[40]

Nelson's chapter on Clinton's elections cites media consultant Frank Greer warning the president that "he didn't get elected on health care." "You were elected on welfare reform," Greer admonished, "and you might have been better off if you started with that." Greer's forewarning proved prescient. "It was clear by the fall of 1994," Galston laments, "that the American people had decided that the Clinton campaign of '92 had been a bait-and-switch operation, and they didn't like it." In truth, the Clinton administration's proposal offered an alternative to more liberal and conservative plans. But the president's third way, which purported to both guarantee universal coverage and contain costs, resulted in a Rube Goldberg contraption that appeared to require an intolerable expansion of the federal bureaucracy. With its complexity (the bill was 1,342 pages long) and obtrusive bureaucratic framework, the Clinton proposal was an easy target for Republicans.[41]

Although the administration made conciliatory overtures to the plan's opponents, hoping to forge bipartisan cooperation on Capitol Hill and a broad consensus among the general public, the possibilities for comprehensive reform hinged on settling differences over the appropriate role of government that had divided the parties for the past two decades. In the end, this proved impractical. The health care bill died in the 103rd Congress when a compromise measure, negotiated between Senate Democratic leader George Mitchell of Maine and Republican Senator John Chafee of Rhode Island could not win enough Republican support to break a threatened filibuster.[42] By proposing such an ambitious health care reform bill, Clinton enraged conservatives. By failing to deliver on his promise to secure a major overhaul of the health care system, he dismayed the ardent liberals of his party. Most significant, the defeat of the president's health care program created the overwhelming impression that he had not lived up to his campaign promise to transcend the bitter philosophical and partisan battles of the Reagan and Bush years.

The president and his party paid dearly for these failures in the 1994 election. In taking control of the Congress, the Republicans gained fifty-two seats in the House and eight in the Senate. Moreover, they won dramatic victories at the state and local level. Republicans increased their share of governorships from nineteen to thirty, their first majority since 1970. They also reached near-parity in state legislatures, a status they had not enjoyed since 1968. The Republicans achieved this victory in an off-year campaign that was unusually ideological and partisan. The charged atmosphere of the campaign owed largely to House Minority Leader Gingrich. His party's choice to be the new speaker of the 104th Congress, Gingrich persuaded more than 300 House candidates to sign a Republican Contract with America, a conservative "covenant" with the nation that worked against Clinton's pledge to shore up the vital center. The Republican manifesto promised to restore limited government by eliminating programs, ameliorating regulatory burdens, and cutting taxes. Clinton's attack on the Republican program during the campaign seemed to backfire, serving only to abet Republicans in their effort to highlight the president's failure to fulfill his promise to reinvent government. Examining exit polls that suggested that a "massive anti-Clinton coalition came together" to produce the "revolution" of 1994, political analyst William Schneider characterized the voters' desire for change as deriving from the opinion that "if the Democrats can't make government work, maybe the Republicans can solve problems with less government."[43]

The Republican triumph was especially notable in the South. For the first time in more than a century, southern Republicans emerged from an election controlling a majority of the governorships, a majority of the seats in the Senate, and a majority of seats in the House. Republican also gained 119 state legislative seats in the South and captured control of three state legislative chambers, the Florida Senate, North Carolina House, and South Carolina House.[44] For the first time since Reconstruction, Republicans elected the speakers of two southern legislatures. Although white southerners had been rebelling against national Democratic politics since the 1950s, Democratic candidates in the South assumed they could insulate themselves from what southern voters regarded as the most unappealing aspects of the national party. From argues that the southern realignment in the South was inevitable: "What it meant was the Democratic advantage of incumbency and history in the South was gone. But that wasn't Clinton; that was going to happen." Nevertheless, Clinton's failure to provide a signpost of an alternative progressive program during his first two years as president played an important catalyzing role. "Clinton had earned praise as one of the brightest most agile governors in his region," Dan Balz and Ronald Brownstein wrote after the 1994 elections, "but, as President his policies, from his advocacy of ending discrimination against homosexuals in the military to his economic and health care programs that stressed big-government activism, often seemed like a stick in the eye of his native South."[45] Southerners had expressed a sense of betrayal in their reaction to the progressive policies of Lyndon Johnson and Jimmy Carter; with Clinton, however, their anger spilled over to Democrats in Congress and state government. White southerners' long resentment of the Civil War and Reconstruction had enabled the Democrats to control the Congress for most of the post–New Deal era, even as the South became estranged from the national Democratic Party. Now they identified with the Republican Party in roughly the same percentages as northern Protestants, the most loyal Republican constituency since the party was founded. As Galston observed in the wake of this dramatic partisan transformation, "the Civil War is finally over."[46]

The Republican triumph in the 1994 midterm elections led scholars and pundits to suggest that the nation might be on the threshold of another critical partisan realignment.[47] It remained to be seen, however, whether the New Deal and its aftermath had left room for another rendezvous with America's political destiny. The emphasis on rights advocacy and administrative politics that characterized contemporary political struggles seemed to belie the sort of collective partisan affiliations that had made full-scale party realignments possible in the past. To be sure, the Reagan years showed that party conflict had not withered away, that the New Deal and the opposition it spawned had brought a new blending of partisanship and administration that encouraged Democrats and Republicans to deploy administrative power for partisan objectives. But the American people had become alienated from these parties of administration by the 1990s, so much so that a renewal of partisan loyalties in the electorate, let alone a full-scale partisan transformation, seemed unlikely. Indeed, the 1994 elections attenuated the moderate wings of both parties, thus deepening this alienation. Just as the defeat of southern Democrats strengthened the influence of liberals within the party councils, so the expansion of Republican power in the South intensified the conservative tendencies of the GOP, particularly its commitment to social issues such as school prayer and abortion.

The new Republican majority in Congress and the states was not unmindful of these obstacles to forging a conservative majority. They promised to pursue a program dedicated to building a wall of separation between government and society and to cultivating a vital debate about the role of the state in promoting the general welfare. Significantly, the Contract with America was silent on the abortion issue. The failure to mention the "rights of the unborn" in this "covenant" with the electorate suggested that some Republican leaders were willing to approach controversial social issues more pragmatically. More to the point, this political strategy appeared to signify the determination of some conservatives to moderate programmatic ambitions that presupposed new uses of, rather than a fundamental challenge to, the centralized administrative power created in the aftermath of the New Deal realignment.

The determination of the new conservative majority to challenge the administrative state was also apparent in the sweeping changes that the new speaker and his allies made in the House's rules. House Republicans reduced the number of standing committees and their staffs, limited the tenure of committee chairs, and prohibited closed-door hearings and unrecorded votes. These reforms, conservative legislators promised, would restrain the institutions that had encouraged the House to focus excessively on management of the executive at the expense of serious public debate about major issues of national policy. Indeed, Speaker Gingrich pledged to Democrats and moderate Republicans a renewed emphasis on legislative debate that would "promote competition between differing political philosophies."[48]

Although the members of the new Republican majority promised to rededicate the government to principles of limited government and states' rights, they were hardly unreconstructed Jeffersonians. The Republican contract proposed to strengthen national defense in a form that would require the expansion rather than the rolling back of the central government's responsibilities, and the GOP's proposals to reduce entitlements for the poor and to get government off the back of business demanded the creation of alternative national welfare and regulatory standards.[49] Finally, during the campaign, the Republican Party was reluctant to challenge middle class entitlements such as Social Security and Medicare, which dwarfed the spending on programs that guaranteed a minimum standard of living to the destitute. The Contract with America thus failed to establish a platform for a serious reexamination of the core assumptions of the New Deal.[50]

In the absence of a meaningful debate about conservative and liberal principles, the first session of the 104th Congress degenerated into the same sort of administrative politics that had corroded the legitimacy of political institutions since the presidency of Richard Nixon. This time, however, the struggle between the branches assumed a novel form: institutional confrontation between a Democratic White House and a Republican Congress. The Republican victory in the 1994 elections, as Nelson puts it, "redivided government." Theriault and his colleagues explain how this new stage of divided government locked in place a more polarized form of institutional combat. The Senate especially, they show, animated by Republicans who were "graduates" of the Gingrich "revolution" in the House, exploited all the obstructive tactics the upper chamber afforded them—especially the filibuster—not only to kill legislation but also to block nominations to the executive branch and the courts. Even before the 1994 election, in fact, Republican Senate leader Robert Dole regularly resorted to the filibuster as a tool of partisan opposition.

Still, the perception that Clinton was an enfeebled president who was thwarted at every turn by fierce Republican opposition and unsteady Democratic support was belied by his aggressive use of the administrative presidency. Beginning in 1995, the president issued a blizzard of executive orders, regulations, proclamations, and other decrees on matters such as tobacco regulation, labor policy, and environmental protection to achieve his goals, with or without the blessing of Congress. Clinton's use of force in the Balkans also defied opposition in Congress. Although the House defeated a resolution in May 1999 that endorsed the administration's bombing campaign in Kosovo, the president's persistence eventually forced Serb leader Slobodan Milosevic to accept a peace settlement. Unlike his initiative on gays in the military, some of these executive actions were well received. But Clinton's actions encouraged the Republican Congress to torment him with investigations and try to micromanage domestic and foreign policy, just as Democratic Congresses had assaulted the presidency during the Nixon, Reagan, and Bush years.[51] Indeed, Clinton's two terms marked a new, more Manichean phase of the institutional combat that Democrats and Republicans had waged for more than two decades.

Clinton's Resurrection

The battle between Clinton and Congress became especially fierce in a contest over legislation to balance the budget. More than any other idea celebrated in the GOP's Contract with America, Republicans believed that a balanced budget would give them their best opportunity to control Congress for years to come. But their proposal for a constitutional amendment to require a balanced budget died in the Senate, where, facing stiff resistance from the president and his Democratic allies, it failed by one vote to get the necessary two-thirds support.

After the defeat of the proposed constitutional amendment, Republicans in the House and Senate put their faith in a bold legislative plan to balance the budget by 2002. The most controversial part of this program was a proposal to scale back the growth of Medicare by encouraging beneficiaries to enroll in health maintenance organizations and other private managed health care systems. Rallied by their militant partisan colleagues in the House, Republican leaders sought to pressure Clinton to accept their priorities on the budget by inviting the president to veto their appropriations bill—a tactic that would lead to the shutting down of government offices and, more ominously, risk forcing the Treasury Department into default. These confrontational tactics backfired. Refusing to back down, Clinton vetoed the sweeping budget bill in December 1995, which not only would have overhauled Medicare but also would have remade decades of federal social policy. Most important, Clinton's stand on the budget, which signaled his growing willingness to draw sharp differences between his priorities and those of the Republican Congress, appeared to preserve the major programs of the New Deal and its successor, the Great Society. In attacking Medicare and social policies such as environmental and education programs, the Republicans' militant assault on programmatic liberalism went beyond what was promised by the Contract with America, thus giving Clinton the opportunity to take a political stand that most of the country supported. He persuaded most of the country that Gingrich, Dole, and the Republican Congress were responsible for the two federal government shutdowns that began in late 1995 in the absence of a budget agreement.

When Congress returned for the second session of the 104th Congress in January 1996, it was not to Speaker Gingrich's agenda of reducing the role of Washington in the society and economy but to the measured tones of Clinton's third State of the Union message. The president addressed many of the themes of his Republican opponents, boldly declaring, "The era of big government is over."[52] This line was not a mere rhetorical flourish. Clinton withstood furious criticism from liberal members of his party and signed welfare reform legislation in August that replaced the existing entitlement to cash payments for low-income mothers and their dependent children with temporary assistance and a strict work requirement.[53]

As Reed, the custodian of the White House welfare reform initiative, attests, the president agonized over whether to sign the act. Clinton conceded that the welfare legislation was flawed, cutting too deeply into nutritional support for low-income working people and denying support unfairly to legal immigrants. It thus failed to live up to Clinton's pledge during the 1992 campaign to tie the elimination of the existing welfare system to increased funding for jobs, training, and child care. New Democrats shared with conservatives a commitment to replacing the legal entitlement to welfare with a reciprocal compact that linked public assistance to work. But conservative Republicans, disdaining the notion of reinventing welfare as a 1990s version of Harry Hopkins's Works Progress Administration, incorporated budget savings and strict time limits on adults' receipt of cash assistance into the welfare legislation. Nevertheless, deeply committed to the core tenet of the Democratic Leadership Council and knowing that his reelection might hinge on signing the welfare reform bill, Clinton insisted that by forcing welfare recipients to take jobs, the legislation, flawed as it was, served the fundamental principle he had championed in the 1992 campaign: "recreating the Nation's social bargain with the poor."[54] By standing for a program that not only required work but also enabled the poor to find decent employment, Clinton and his New Democratic allies claimed the high ground in the welfare debate. As Nelson shows, Clinton absolved himself of responsibility for the more draconian Republican-sponsored measures of the legislation by taking credit for successfully championing the earned income tax credit and for fending off Republican efforts to scale back support for the working poor during the debate over welfare reform. Characteristically, Clinton tried to have it both ways: he simultaneously appealed to conservatives and moderates by claiming credit for "ending welfare as we know it" while promising liberals that if reelected he would "fix" the flaws in the welfare law.[55]

Indeed, even as Clinton proclaimed the end of big government, his 1996 State of the Union address called for a halt to Republican assaults on basic liberal programs dedicated to providing economic security, educational opportunity, and environmental protection.[56] Using Democratic National Committee funds, the White House had orchestrated a national media blitz toward the end of 1995 that excoriated the Republicans' program to reform Medicare and presented the president as a figure of national reconciliation who favored welfare reform and a balanced budget but who also would protect middle-class entitlements, education, and the environment.[57] Clinton's carefully modulated State of the Union message underscored this media campaign, revealing the president as a would-be healer eager to bring all sides together.[58]

Throughout the 1996 election campaign, Clinton held firmly to the centrist ground he had staked out after the 1994 election, campaigning on the same New Democratic themes of "opportunity, responsibility, and community" that had served him well during his first run for White House. He won 49 percent of the popular vote to Dole's 41 percent and Perot's 8 percent, and 379 Electoral College votes to Dole's 159.

Clinton thus became the first Democratic president to be elected to a second term since FDR. But his candidate-centered campaign, abetted by a strong economy, did little to help his party. The Democrats lost two seats in the Senate and gained only a modest nine seats in the House, thus failing to regain control of either legislative chamber. In truth, Clinton's campaign testified to the fragility of the nationalized party system that arose during the 1980s. The president's remarkable political comeback in 1995 was supported by so-called soft money that was designated for party-building activities and thus was not restricted by campaign finance laws.[59] But these expenditures were used overwhelmingly to mount television advertising campaigns, such as the media blast of the Republicans during the 1995 budget battles, that championed the president's independence from partisan squabbles. Indeed, Clinton scarcely endorsed the election of a Democratic Congress and his fund-raising efforts for the party did not support congressional candidates until late in the campaign. Adding insult to injury, the administration's questionable fund-raising methods led to revelations during the final days of the election that may have reduced Clinton's margin of victory and undermined the Democrats' effort to retake the House.[60]

Balanced Budgets, Impeachment Politics, and the Limits of the Third Way

Clinton staked his success as president on forging a third way between Republican conservatism and Democratic liberalism. In the wake of the 1994 election, he relied on campaign advisor Dick Morris, a Republican political strategist whom he had often consulted as governor of Arkansas, to translate his message into a political strategy. Morris urged the president to "triangulate"—to embrace, and thereby neutralize, Republican issues such as crime, taxes, welfare, the budget, and faith in markets. To the dismay of New Democratic advisors such as Reed and Galston, triangulation, which often lacked policy substance, subordinated third-way objectives such as national service and welfare reform to crude transactional politics. Galson expressed his disappointment about the post-1994 correction:

> My deepest regret about that period is that it created the impression that the reform strategy of New Democrats was essentially a political tactic and not a governing agenda. We had worked for years creating a governing agenda (that I still believe in) to rebut that charge. It was a charge made by the opponents of the New Democratic movement from day one: This is a political tactic, it's unprincipled. Then here comes this politically androgynous advisor. It was our worst nightmare, because it was impossible to dispel the impression that the President had embraced this way of thinking as a tactic, and that's all it was.

In their careful examination of triangulation, Bruce Nesmith and Paul Quirk argue that Clinton's "centrism had idealistic principled roots as well as politically calculating ones." Clearly, Clinton paid careful attention to polls and looked for opportunities to score political points. Yet to do so required standing apart from powerful partisan advocacy in the capital that championed political positions and policies that were far removed from the "median voter." Moreover, "mongrel politics," as Skowronek characterizes third-way politics, might not simply express itself in a president opportunistically supporting Democratic and Republican policies that are popular.[61] Nesmith and Quirk argue that a policy wonk such as Clinton may also have recognized in certain instances that artful compromise yields "general substantive benefits." Presidential triangulation, they conclude, "can amount to sinking beneath ideology or rising above it."

In part, Clinton's remarkable popularity—his resilience in the face of scandal and a hostile Congress—followed from his ability to rise above the conventional left-right political spectrum. This gift for forging compromise was perhaps best displayed in May 1997, when the White House and the Republican leadership reached a tentative plan to balance the budget by 2002. Ostensibly, this deal was struck on Republican terms. The most dramatic measures in the budget—the first net tax cut in sixteen years, the largest Medicare savings ever enacted into law, and constraints on discretionary spending below the expected rate of inflation over five years—decidedly shifted priorities in a Republican direction.[62] While many liberal Democrats felt betrayed by the president's negotiated settlement, a number of Republicans acknowledged that Clinton had played a principal part in enacting a conservative policy, one that would have been far more difficult to achieve with one of their own in the White House.[63]

Nonetheless, Clinton exacted some important concessions from the Republicans, enough to persuade a majority of Democrats in Congress to support the plan. Most significantly, the Balanced Budget Act of 1997 ameliorated, although it did not fix, the tough remedies of the welfare reform bill. It provided substantial additional funding for immigrant benefits and food stamps. It also included $16 billion in spending for a new federally funded State Children's Health Insurance Program (SCHIP) for low-income working families who were not eligible for Medicaid.[64] Clinton thus accepted certain Republican budgetary priorities but stood his ground on partial fulfillment of his promise to renegotiate a fair new social contract with the poor.[65]

To be sure, this uneasy agreement between the White House and the Republican-controlled Congress was made possible by a revenue windfall from a robust economy, which enabled Clinton and GOP leaders to avoid the sort of hard choices over program cuts and taxes that had animated the bitter struggles of the 104th Congress.[66] Those hard choices would still have to be made if long-term entitlement reform was to be achieved. Even so, this rapprochement, which brought about the first balanced budget in three decades, testifies to the potential of modern presidents to advance principles and pursue policies that defy the sharp cleavages that are characteristic of the "new" party system.

The balanced budget agreement appeared to vindicate Clinton's invocation of scripture in his second inaugural address, in which he urged Democrats and

Republicans—divided into institutional partisan camps—"to be repairers of the breach and to move on with America's mission."[67] Yet, as Rudalevige's tale of the House impeachment and Senate trial of Clinton reveals, the president echoed this faith "that God can change us and make us strong in broken places" the morning the Starr report became public—this time seeking redemption for a sin that his aides feared was "resignation material." But Clinton's confession, although it aroused a strong sense of betrayal among his aides and members of his cabinet, did not unite Democrats and Republicans in condemnation of the president's breach of the public trust. Rather, it quickly gave way to an extraordinary episode of interbranch conflict that made it impossible for the center to hold. "Far from repairing the breach," Rudalevige writes, "Clinton and his enemies made it deeper."

Just as the Reagan and Bush presidencies were plagued by independent counsels who investigated abuses in their administrations, Clinton's troubles began with the Ethics in Government Act. Republicans had long opposed reauthorization of the independent prosecutor statue, considering it an unconstitutional infringement on the executive's prosecutorial authority. But their resistance to Democratic efforts to reauthorize the statute came to an end in 1993, when the Whitewater scandal emerged.[68] In early January 1998, independent counsel Kenneth Starr was authorized to expand the scope of the Whitewater inquiry to pursue allegations that the president had had an affair with White House intern Monica Lewinsky and that his friend Vernon Jordan had encouraged her to lie under oath about it.

Unlike the celebrated episodes of interbranch combat that played out in the Watergate and Iran-Contra affairs, which were moderated by bipartisan concerns about constitutional indiscretions, partisan loyalties almost completely trumped institutional affiliations in the Lewinsky scandal. Hillary Clinton famously framed this partisan contretemps by dismissing the allegations against her husband as a "vast right-wing conspiracy." This phrase, "one of the scandal's enduring gifts," Rudalevige observes, was "more evocative than strictly accurate. A 'fairly small (but very intense) right-wing collaboration' would have been closer to the truth." Indeed, the remarkable expression of overwhelming approval of Clinton's performance as the scandal unfolded in 1998 reflected not only approbation for the president's third-way policy positions and his management of the economy but also general disapproval of Starr's tenacious investigation into Clinton's peccadilloes and the eagerness with which the Republican-controlled Congress exploited the results.

During the Reagan and Bush administrations, scholars and pundits fretted that the development of a national programmatic party system atop a constitutional structure that discouraged party government made it more likely that the judiciary and the legal system would become a prime instrument of partisan warfare. What distinguished the Lewinsky conflict, Rudalevige shows, was the highly personal nature of the battle: "The parties were polarized not just over policy preferences but over their opponents' very legitimacy. One side's 'vast criminal conspiracy' ran up against the other's 'vast right-wing conspiracy' in self-reinforcing self-righteousness."

In the final analysis, it was Clinton's highly personalized third-way politics that abetted and ultimately became the victim of this moral passion play. At first, few Democrats came to the president's defense, which underscores the fact that while Clinton may have had allies in Congress, he had few close friends there. Most Democrats did oppose an impeachment inquiry, but this stance represented their disdain for the Republican majority rather than support for a president who appeared indifferent to their programmatic commitments and election prospects. In fact, as the *New York Times* reported, "it is the people who know [Clinton] best—from his own former aides to his wary fellow Democrats in Congress—who have been most disappointed and angry about his handling of the Monica Lewinsky matter, and who have held it against him more harshly than a detached and distant public."[69]

With the decline of Clinton's personal stature and political support, nearly every political expert predicted that the Republicans would emerge from the 1998 elections with a tighter grip on Congress and, by implication, on the president's political fate.[70] But having been preoccupied by the Lewinsky scandal for the entire year, the Republicans were left without an appealing campaign issue. Indeed, anxious to skewer Clinton as a libertine, Speaker Gingrich encouraged the caucus to quickly pass the fiscal 2000 budget, which, according to the president's director of legislative affairs, Lawrence Stein, made many policy concessions to the White House.[71] But this only seemed to confirm the Clintons' claim that the Republicans fiddled in character assassination while the president went "back to work for the American people."[72] The Republicans were unable to increase their 55–45 margin in the Senate and lost five seats in the House, leaving them a slim 223–211 majority. Clinton was the first Democrat since FDR to be reelected; he now became the first president since Roosevelt to see his party gain seats in a midterm election. Bitterly disappointed by the results, the Republicans descended into soul searching and recriminations. Ironically, it was Gingrich, the hero of their 1994 ascent to power, and not Clinton, who was forced from office. After the elections, Gingrich announced that he was giving up not only his leadership position but also his seat in Congress. Clinton's supporters felt it was poetic justice that Gingrich's fall from grace was abetted by his admission during the impeachment hearings that he, too, had engaged in an extramarital affair.

The 1998 elections and their aftermath appeared to take the steam out of the House's impeachment inquiry. But as the president gathered with friends and aides to celebrate what seemed to be another remarkable political resurrection, the Republicans prepared to move forward with the impeachment inquiry. A centrist, poll-sensitive politician, Clinton, like most pundits, underestimated the willingness of Republicans in Congress to defy the survey-tested will of the people.[73] In truth, as Rudalevige points out, Republicans represented districts that were far more supportive of impeachment than national polls indicated. In December, after a year of dramatic and tawdry politics on both sides, Clinton was impeached on charges of perjury and obstruction of justice by a bitterly divided House of Representatives, which recommended virtually along party lines that the Senate remove the nation's forty-second president.

Even impeachment, however, did not undermine the president's popular support. Soon after the House's historic action, large majorities of Americans expressed approval of Clinton's handling of his job, opposed a Senate trial, and proclaimed that Republican members of Congress were "out of touch with most Americans."[74] The public's support of the president and the small Republican majority in the Senate encouraged discussion among senators about the possibility of substituting a motion of censure for a protracted, agonizing impeachment trial. But Republican leaders were determined not to abort the constitutional process, even though acquittal of the president on the articles of impeachment seemed foreordained. After a five-week Senate trial, the president's accusers failed to gain even a majority for either of the charges against Clinton. On February 12, 1999, the Senate rejected the charge of perjury, 55–45, with ten Republicans voting against conviction; and then, with five Republicans breaking ranks, the Senate split 50–50 on a second article accusing the president of obstruction of justice. Clinton's job was safe. Moreover, the trial and tribulations of the impeachment process encouraged bipartisan opposition to the Ethic in Government Act, which Congress failed to reauthorize when its authority lapsed in the summer of 1999.

Still, whatever moral authority Clinton may have had at the beginning of his administration to establish a new covenant of rights and responsibilities between citizens and their government was shattered by the public disrespect for his morality. Indeed, the virulent partisanship that characterized the impeachment process forced Clinton to seek refuge once again among his fellow Democrats in Congress, thus short-circuiting plans to pursue entitlement reform as the capstone of his presidency.[75] In the wake of the impeachment debacle, Clinton positioned himself as the champion of Social Security and Medicare, urging Congress to invest a significant share of the mounting budget surplus in the salvation of these traditional liberal programs.[76] Clinton's extraordinary resiliency, it seemed, was achieved at the cost of failure to fulfill his promise to correct and renew the progressive tradition. As Galston grieves:

> I get sick every time I think about it. I believe that the most serious, long-term domestic problem facing the country is how we're going to sustain the safety-net promises we've made to ourselves. Before the scandal broke, the President was teeing up that issue for serious discussion in the second term. Through heroic efforts of political self-restraint which cost the President very dearly, we had rolled the fiscal rock all the way back up the mountain, and we finally had—for the first time in a generation—the opportunity and the resources to address the problem of the long-term stabilization of these entitlement programs. The transfer of the Presidency into the hands of someone [George W. Bush] with a very different agenda meant in extremely short order that everything we had worked for in that area was swept away as though it were a sand castle on the edge of a beach.

Conclusion: Clinton and the Politics of Fear

The most straightforward conclusion to draw from the chapters in this volume is that Clinton's passion for reconciliation failed. His two successors—Republican George W. Bush and Democrat Barack Obama—both pledged to transcend red and blue America, but their administrations also were pulled into the vortex of partisan warfare. As Rudalevige concludes, "Outrage remained the main trope of American political discourse." Evidence is mounting that mutual contempt between Democrats and Republicans, once confined to intramural beltway battles, has leaked out to the state capitals and into public opinion. The "only thing we have to fear," quips political scientist Alan Abramowitz, "is the other party."[77]

In the face of partisan polarization in which each side condemns not just the principles but also the motivations of the other, many scholars and pundits have cast a nostalgic eye on the Clinton years and expressed yearning for his pragmatic flair. Since leaving office, Clinton has once again become the most popular politician in America and the former first lady has gone on to serve in the Senate and the State Department. Having narrowly lost a heated contest to Obama for the 2008 Democratic nomination, Hillary Rodham Clinton emerged as the overwhelming favorite to gain the party's nod in 2016. For all the baggage the Clintons carry—a load made heavier by the highly influential and controversial Clinton Foundation[78]—there is considerable discussion of them forming the latest dynasty in American politics. It remains to be seen, however, whether

Secretary Clinton's quest for the White House will reach to the center or seek, as Obama has done, especially since 2010, to expand the progressive base. The latter strategy will be hard to resist at a time when partisanship has increased in the electorate, even as an unprecedented number of men and women self-identify as independents. Indeed, Clinton's strongest challenger, Senator Bernie Sanders of Vermont, preached a democratic socialist message that pressured Hillary to invoke fundamental liberal principles that her husband eschewed as president.

Bill Clinton's third-way politics was the midwife of the contemporary state of strong partisanship and weak parties. The wayward path of new democracy reveals how the third way can all too easily degenerate into a plebiscitary form of democracy in which citizens directly invest their support in an individual leader, then all too often withdraw it. As a leading political strategist for George W. Bush said during Bush's second term, "Both parties' organizing force has focused on President Bush—the Republicans in defense of his leadership; the Democrats in opposition—hostility—to it."[79] The same was true during the Obama administrations. That both the president's supporters and enemies referred to his signature achievement as "Obamacare" reveals how personal—and presidency-centered—American politics has become.

Just as surely, Clinton's tainted success sheds light on the love-hate relationship that Americans have formed with the national state forged by the New Deal and the Great Society. As Hugh Heclo has shown, the cultural, political, and institutional changes wrought in the 1960s yielded a new civics that taught individuals "so far as the governing system is concerned . . . to expect more and trust less than ever before."[80] Rather than healing this breach, Clinton's third way left the American people in a profound state of uneasy ambivalence. Even as liberalism became a discredited doctrine, the Reagan revolution failed to roll back many of its programmatic achievements. Republicans won dramatic electoral victories, most notably in 1980, 1994, 2010, and 2014, by promising to get government off the backs of the people, and yet the public's persistent commitment to middle-class entitlements, such as Social Security and Medicare, environmental and consumer protection, and health and safety measures raises doubts about Clinton's claim that "the era of big government is over." Even as Obama became the center of the most polarizing administration in the history of modern polling, he was able to get a major health care reform bill through Congress that went far to fulfill the vision of "Hillarycare"—the signature progressive proposal that did not comport with the new Democratic programmatic vision. Although most Americans were offended by the bureaucratic pathologies that initially afflicted "Obamacare," the benefits it provided soon were woven into the fabric of the American welfare state—so much so that the Republicans have not been able to fulfill their promise to repeal it.

The entire 2016 Republican presidential field supported repeal of the Patient Protection and Affordable Care Act. Yet the program's entanglement in American life through subsidies for the lower middle class and regulations that protect the public against abuses of insurance companies will make eliminating it a monumental political task.

Most Americans hope that the national government can provide them with programs they support without the centralized administration they have long been taught to shun and fear and with benefits that secure the general welfare without destroying individual responsibility. These are not necessarily incompatible goals, but they are unlikely to be reconciled without the renewal of principles and institutions that foster a sense of collective obligation. In calling for reciprocal responsibility and in slouching toward the reform of entitlements, Clinton "ingeniously addressed the political liabilities of the Democratic party," noted one of his close advisors. "But 'new' Democratic politics were crafted to serve Clinton's own political ambition; the Third Way did little to help the party's strength in Congress and the States."[81] It was Clinton-style pragmatism, which failed to build organizational support for a third way, that gave rise to the redividing of American politics that Nelson describes in his chapter on Clinton's elections.

One does not have to be a devotee of contemporary partisanship or a member of the shrinking core of party loyalists to find some aspects of the third way deeply troubling. In relying on personal charm and a presidency-centered organization to advance new Democratic principles and in subordinating the collective mission of his party to his personal political fortunes, Clinton may have further weakened, rather than invigorated, civic life in the United States. In the final analysis, a meaningful reinvention of government can emerge only from a great contest of opinion, after a painful but necessary struggle over the relative merits of the Democratic and Republican understandings of constitutional government. Clinton's view that the debate between these two understandings failed to provide for a meaningful sense of civic responsibility did not excuse him from partisan engagement; rather, such a position demanded the remaking of the Democratic Party. All previous political transformations have required extraordinary partisan leadership in which reform presidents have played a principal part by forming a new party or remaking an existing one.[82] But developments since the Progressive Era—the direct primary, campaign finance laws, the expansion of national administrative power, and the rise of the mass media—have encouraged presidents to seek office and govern as the heads of organizations they have created in their own image. At the end of the day, the Democratic Leadership Council, although an impressive incubator of third-way policies, was never able to mobilize a collective effort that could endure beyond the Clinton presidency. Indeed, the New Democratic think tank closed its doors in February 2011.

Although Bill Clinton exploited what Woodrow Wilson once termed the "extraordinary isolation" of the modern presidency to become perhaps the most popular politician of his time, artful triangulation might have deprived him of an opportunity to make a lasting mark on the nation.[83] The successes and failures of third-way politics thus shed light on the imposing power yet fragile authority of the modern presidency—and the unsteady ground under the third-way politics described in this volume.

Appendix 1

INTERVIEWEES FOR THE WILLIAM J. CLINTON PRESIDENTIAL HISTORY PROJECT

Madeleine K. Albright, *U.S. Ambassador to the United Nations; Secretary of State*

Roger Altman, *Deputy Secretary of Treasury*

Joan N. Baggett, *Assistant to the President for Political Affairs*

Charlene Barshefsky, *U.S. Trade Representative*

Eileen Baumgartner, *Staff Director, U.S. House Committee on the Budget*

Samuel R. Berger, *Deputy Assistant to the President for National Security Affairs; National Security Advisor*

Alan Blinder, *Vice Chairman of the Board of Governors of the Federal Reserve System; member of Council of Economic Advisers*

Sidney Blumenthal, *Assistant to the President*

Charles Brain, *Director of Legislative Affairs*

Warren Christopher, *Secretary of State*

Henry Cisneros, *Secretary of Housing and Urban Development*

Betty Currie, *Personal Secretary to the President*

David Cutler, *economist, Council of Economic Advisers and National Economic Council*

Thomas Daschle, *U.S. Senator*

James Dyer, *Majority Staff Director of U.S. House of Representatives Committee on Appropriations*

Peter Edelman, *Assistant Secretary for Planning and Evaluation; Counselor to the Secretary of Health and Human Services*

Kris Engskov, *Trip Coordinator in White House travel office; Assistant Press Secretary; Personal Assistant to the President*

Alphonso Michael Espy, *Secretary of Agriculture*

Al From, *Domestic Policy Advisor to the Clinton Transition, founder and CEO of the Democratic Leadership Council*

William Galston, *Deputy Assistant to the President for Domestic Policy*

John Gibbons, *Assistant to the President for Science and Technology*

Ben Goddard, *Co-founder, Goddard-Claussen*

Stanley Greenberg, *Pollster*

Frank Greer, *Media consultant*

Patrick J. Griffin, *Assistant to the President for Legislative Affairs*

Marcia Hale, *Assistant to the President; Director of Intergovernmental Affairs*

Vaclav Havel, *President of Czechoslovakia; President of the Czech Republic*

John Hilley, *Director of Legislative Affairs*

Chris Jennings, *Deputy Assistant to the President for Health Policy*

Lionel Johns, *Associate Director of the White House Office of Science and Technology Policy*

Kim Dae-jung, *President of South Korea*

Michael (Mickey) Kantor, *U.S. Trade Representative; Secretary of Commerce*

Peter Knight, *Deputy Director for the Presidential Transition; Campaign Manager, Clinton-Gore 1996 Reelection Committee*

David Kusnet, *Chief Speechwriter*

Anthony Lake, *National Security Advisor*

Jeanne Lambrew, *Associate Director, Office of Management and Budget; Senior Health Analyst, National Economic Council*

Joseph Lockhart, *Press Secretary*

Marjorie Margolies, *Member of the U.S. House of Representatives*

Thomas "Mack" McLarty, III, *White House Chief of Staff*

Abner Mikva, *White House Counsel*

George Mitchell, *U.S. Senator*

Roy M. Neel, *Gore's 1992 Campaign Manager; Chief of Staff to the Vice-President; Deputy White House Chief of Staff*

Bernard Nussbaum, *White House Counsel*

Leon Panetta, *Director of the Office of Management and Budget; Chief of Staff*

William Perry, *Deputy Secretary of Defense; Secretary of Defense*

Bruce Reed, *Domestic Policy Advisor*

Richard W. Riley, *Secretary of Education*

Alice Rivlin, *Director of Office of Management and Budget*

Charles Robb, *Governor of Virginia; U.S. Senator*

Robert Rubin, *Director of National Economic Council; Secretary of Treasury*

Eli Jay Segal, *Chief of Staff for Clinton's 1992 Campaign; CEO of AmeriCorps*

Donna Shalala, *Secretary of Health and Human Services*

John Shalikashvili, *Chairman of Joint Chiefs of Staff*

(Henry) Hugh Shelton, *Chairman of Joint Chiefs of Staff*

Alan Simpson, *U.S. Senator*

Nancy Soderberg, *Foreign Policy Director for the Clinton/Gore 1992 Campaign; Deputy Assistant to the President for National Security Affairs; Alternate Representative to the United Nations*

Lawrence Stein, *Director of Legislative Affairs*

James Steinberg, *Director of Policy Planning (State Department); Deputy National Security Advisor*

Strobe Talbott, *Ambassador-at-Large to the former Soviet Republics and Deputy Secretary of State*

Susan Thomases, *Personal Advisor; Chief Campaign Scheduler*

Harris Wofford, *U.S. Senator; CEO of AmeriCorps*

R. James Woolsey, *Director of Central Intelligence*

INTERVIEWERS FOR
THE WILLIAM J. CLINTON
PRESIDENTIAL HISTORY PROJECT

Interviewer	Affiliation*
Nancy Baker	New Mexico State University
Alan Beckenstein	Darden Business School, University of Virginia
Edward Berkowitz	George Washington University
MaryAnne Borrelli	Connecticut College
Gary Burtless	Brookings Institution
Jeffrey Cason	Middlebury College
Richard Conley	University of Florida
Jeffrey Cohen	Fordham University
Byron Daynes	Brigham Young University
I.M. "Mac" Destler	University of Maryland
Matthew Dickinson	Middlebury College
Kathryn Dunn Tenpas	University of Pennsylvania
Kimberly Elliott	Peterson Institute for International Economics
Daniel Ernst	Georgetown University School of Law
C. Lawrence Evans	College of William & Mary
Paul Freedman	University of Virginia
John Gilmour	College of William & Mary
Marie Gottschalk	University of Pennsylvania
Erwin Hargrove	Vanderbilt University
Randall Henning	American University
Karen M. Hult	Virginia Tech University

Charles O. Jones	University of Wisconsin-Madison; Brookings Institution
Nancy Kassop	SUNY New Paltz
Patrick McGuinn	Colby College
John Anthony Maltese	University of Georgia
Benjamin Marquez	University of Wisconsin-Madison
Daniel Meador	University of Virginia School of Law
Michael Nelson	Rhodes College
Don Oberdorfer	Johns Hopkins University
John Owen IV	University of Virginia
Daniel Palazzolo	University of Richmond
Eric Patashnik	University of Virginia
Barbara Perry	Sweet Briar College
James Pfiffner	George Mason University
Joseph Pika	University of Delaware
Nelson W. Polsby	University of California, Berkeley
Andrew L. Ross	University of New Mexico
James Savage	University of Virginia
Colleen Shogan	George Mason University
Kathy Smith	Wake Forest University
Robert Strong	Washington and Lee University
Glen Sussman	Old Dominion University
Norman Vig	Carleton College
Charles E. Walcott	Virginia Tech University
Stephen J. Wayne	Georgetown University
Steven Weatherford	University of California-Santa Barbara

* Interviewers' affiliations are from date of interview

Miller Center Interviewers

Jill Abraham
Duane Adamson
Jeff Chidester
Kent Germany
Stephen Knott
Paul Martin
Sidney Milkis
Darby Morrisroe
Timothy Naftali

Russell Riley
Marc Selverstone
James Young
Philip Zelikow

Total number of participating scholars: 59
Total number of institutions represented: 35

Notes

BILL CLINTON'S ROAD TO THE WHITE HOUSE

1. Hillary Rodham Clinton, *Living History* (New York: Simon and Schuster, 203), 247–48.
2. This brief biography relies on three main sources: the oral history interviews compiled for the William J. Clinton Presidential History Project; Bill Clinton's memoir, *My Life* (New York: Alfred A. Knopf, 2004); and David Maraniss, *First in His Class: The Biography of Bill Clinton* (New York: Simon & Schuster, 1995).
3. Clinton, *My Life*, 375.

INTRODUCTION: HISTORY AND BILL CLINTON

1. All quotations in this chapter relating to the Clinton presidency are from William J. Clinton Presidential History Project interviews unless otherwise noted. The interviews are available online at the Miller Center Web site: http://millercenter.org/president/clinton/oralhistory.
2. Bob Woodward, *The Choice: How Clinton Won* (New York: Simon & Schuster, 1996), 65; Maraniss, "First and Last," *Washington Post Magazine*, October 27, 1996, 13; John Kenneth White, *Still Seeing Red: How the Cold War Still Shapes the New American Politics* (Boulder, Colo.: Westview Press, 1997), 256.
3. "My Election Will Be Overwhelmingly Focused on the Future," *Washington Post*, August 25, 1996, A19, http://www.washingtonpost.com/wp-srv/national/longterm/inaug/players/cinterview.htm, accessed March 24, 2015. Clinton's reasoning is repeated in the short book he wrote to buttress his reelection bid, *Between Hope and History: Meeting America's Challenges for the 21st Century* (New York: Random House, 1996), 12–18.
4. David Von Drehle, "Clinton Aims to Shape New Century: His Model Is T. Roosevelt, but His Style Is More like McKinley's," *Washington Post*, January 20, 1997, A1, http://www.washingtonpost.com/wp-srv/national/longterm/inaug/mon/century.htm, accessed March 24, 2015.
5. Kathleen M. Dalton, "President Clinton, You're No Teddy Roosevelt," *Los Angeles Times*, January 26, 1997, http://articles.latimes.com/1997-01-26/opinion/op-22191_1_president-clinton, accessed March 24, 2015; Edmund Morris, "The Rough Rider and the Easy One," *New York Times*, October 6, 1996, http://www.nytimes.com/1996/10/06/opinion/the-rough-rider-and-the-easy-one.html, accessed March 24, 2105.
6. David McCullough, *Truman* (New York: Simon & Schuster, 1992).
7. For example, an article from the 1992 campaign trail by Jack Germond and Jules Witcover observed of Bush that "he seems to think that if he compares himself often enough to Harry Truman, the voters will begin to believe it." See "Now, Perot Is Making Bush, Clinton Nervous," *Baltimore Sun*, October 23, 1992, http://articles.baltimoresun.com/1992-10-23/news/1992297227_1_perot-bush-clinton, accessed March 24, 2015.
8. Donovan, *Conflict and Crisis: The Presidency of Harry S Truman, 1945–1948* (New York: W.W. Norton, 1977), 107.
9. This subject is the main topic of my current book project, tentatively entitled *American Regicide: Presidents and the Bitter Politics of Postwar Demobilization, from Washington to Clinton.*

10. Clinton Rossiter, *Constitutional Dictatorship: Crisis Government in the Modern De-mocracies* (New York: Harcourt, Brace & World, 1948). The book was republished after 9/11 by Transaction.

11. See Warren G. Harding's "return to normalcy" speech, Boston, Massachusetts, May 14, 1920, http://livefromthetrail.com/about-the-book/speeches/chapter-3/senator-warren-g-harding, accessed March 24, 2015.

12. David Runciman, "Will We Be All Right in the End?" *London Review of Books*, Janu-ary 5, 2012, 3–5, http://www.lrb.co.uk/v34/n01/david-runciman/will-we-be-all-right-in-the-end, accessed March 24, 2015.

13. Some added residue of presidential power may well survive the effort to right-size the institution when war is over, especially in the form of legal precedents—which cannot be destroyed—that survive for use by an entrepreneurial White House seeking sanction for aggressive executive action. For an argument about this up-and-down ratcheting of presidential power, focused more on that residual growth than on the postwar contrac-tion, see Robert Higgs, *Crisis and Leviathan: Critical Episodes in the Growth of American Government* (New York: Oxford University Press, 1987).

14. See Stephen G. Calibresi and Christopher S. Yoo, *The Unitary Executive: Presiden-tial Power from Washington to Bush* (New Haven, Conn.: Yale University Press, 2008), 179–87.

15. The impeachment articles may be found at http://law2.umkc.edu/faculty/projects/ftrials/impeach/articles.html, accessed March 24, 2015.

16. On the Wade-Davis bill and the Wade-Davis Manifesto, see David Herbert Don-ald, *Lincoln* (New York: Simon & Schuster, 1995), 509–37. The text of the manifesto can be seen at http://www.let.rug.nl/usa/documents/1851-1875/the-wade-davis-manifesto-august-5-1864.php, accessed January 9, 2016.

17. Woodrow Wilson, "An Appeal for a Democratic Congress," in *The Papers of Wood-row Wilson*, edited by Arthur S. Link, vol. 51 (Princeton, N.J.: Princeton University Press, 1985), 381–82.

18. See Higgs, *Crisis and Leviathan*, 123–58.

19. C.P. Trussell, "Congress Shifts Back to a Peacetime Basis: Home Front Problems and Politics Will Hold Attention From Now On," *New York Times*, September 9, 1945, 78.

20. Quoted in Donovan, *Conflict and Crisis*, chapter 13.

21. See "Special Message to the Congress Presenting a 21-Point Program for the Re-conversion Period," September 6, 1945, available at http://www.presidency.ucsb.edu/ws/?pid=12359, accessed March 31, 2015. Notably, Truman, who had only recently moved to the executive branch from the legislative, strongly praised Congress at the beginning of this message for its role in the military victory over Japan.

22. Arthur Krock, "The President: A New Portrait," *New York Times*, April 7, 1946, 96.

23. Roger Davidson, "The Advent of the Modern Congress: The Legislative Reorgani-zation Act of 1946," *Legislative Studies Quarterly* 15, no. 3 (1990): 357, 360.

24. Quoted in McCullough, *Truman*, 531.

25. Personal notes of remarks made by David Gray Adler at the conference "William Jefferson Clinton: The 'New Democrat' from Hope," Hofstra University, Hempstead, New York, November 10, 2005. The other panelists on this session about Clinton and the Con-stitution echoed Adler's assessment.

26. Interview with Sigmund Rogich, March 8–9, 2001,George H. W. Bush Oral His-tory, http://millercenter.org/president/bush/oralhistory/sigmund-rogich, accessed March 26, 2015.

27. White, *Still Seeing Red*, 202, 330.

28. Author's calculations in "Percentage of Nomination Acceptance Addresses Devoted to Foreign Affairs," unpublished typescript, September 2011.

29. These forces are more fully explored in Russell L. Riley, "History and George Bush," in *41: Inside the Presidency of George H. W. Bush*, edited by Michael Nelson and Barbara A. Perry (Ithaca, N.Y.: Cornell University Press, 2014).

30. Interview with Michael Boskin, July 30–31, 2001, George H. W. Bush Oral History, http://millercenter.org/president/bush/oralhistory/michael-boskin, accessed March 26, 2015.

31. Joseph S. Nye Jr., "Why the Gulf War Served the National Interest," *Atlantic Monthly*, July 1991, 60.

32. Frederick T. Steeper, "1992 Presidential Campaign: The Churchill Parallel, Memorandum to Robert Teeter," December 18, 1991, typescript provided to the author by Steeper.

33. Randolph Bourne's quote is taken from an unpublished manuscript entitled "The State," originally written in 1918, available at http://fair-use.org/randolph-bourne/the-state/, accessed March 24, 2015.

34. Data taken from tables in Higgs, *Crisis and Leviathan*, 22–23.

35. See "Historical Tables," Office of Management and Budget, Table 1.1, https://www.whitehouse.gov/omb/budget/Historicals.

36. See Table 3.1, ibid.

37. Defense secretary William Perry reports in his oral history that the actual annual savings adjusted for inflation from the Cold War high equaled about $100 billion by 1997.

38. The other two are the midterm elections of 1826 (during the administration of John Quincy Adams) and 1894 (during the administration of Grover Cleveland) For an argument about 2006 as a postwar case see Russell L. Riley, "Divided We Stand," *Politico*, January 30, 2007.

39. Terry Peterson in the Interview with Richard W. Riley, August 30–31, 2004, William J. Clinton Presidential History Project, http://millercenter.org/oralhistory/interview/richard-w-riley, accessed January 10, 2016.

40. In his survey of the literature on electoral trends, David R. Mayhew has noticed that elections with "durable realigning effects" tend to follow significant wars, citing the presidential election years of 1868, 1920, 1948, and 1972, among others, to sustain the point. He is critical of realignment theorists for not doing more with this correlation. Mayhew, *Electoral Realignments: A Critique of an American Genre* (New Haven, Conn.: Yale University Press, 2002), 142.

41. See the text of Clinton's April 18, 1995 news conference, when he said, "The Constitution gives me relevance. The power of our ideas gives me relevance. The record we have built up over the last 2 years and the things we're trying to do to implement it give it relevance. The President is relevant here, especially an activist President." See "The President's News Conference," April 18, 1995, American Presidency Project, http://www.presidency.ucsb.edu/ws/?pid=51237, accessed March 24, 2015.

42. Professor Robert Strong voices this interpretation during the course of his participation in the Madeleine Albright oral history interview.

43. "A Damaging Arms Control Defeat," *New York Times*, October 14, 1999; "It's Over: Treaty Defeat Marks End of Clinton's Effectiveness," *Newsday*, October 16, 1999.

44. John F. Harris, *The Survivor: Bill Clinton in the White House* (New York: Random House, 2005).

45. Kenneth W. Starr, *Referral from Independent Counsel Kenneth W. Starr in Conformity with the Requirements of Title 28, United States Code, Section 595(c): Communication from Kenneth W. Starr, Independent Counsel, Transmitting a Referral to the United States House of Representatives Filed in Conformity with the Requirements of Title 28, United States Code, Section 595(c)* (New York: PublicAffairs, 1998). This is commonly known as the Starr Report.

46. *Clinton v. Jones*, 520 U.S. 681 (1997), https://www.nationalcenter.org/Clintonv Jones.html, accessed December 11, 2015.

47. The definitive account to date of these tangled developments is Ken Gormley's *The Death of American Virtue: Clinton vs. Starr* (New York: Crown, 2010).

48. Susan Webber Wright, "Memorandum Opinion and Order," *Jones v. Clinton*, December 28, 1994, http://www.lectlaw.com/files/cas02.htm, accessed January 9, 2016. The Nixon case cited here and in the following paragraphs is *Nixon v. Fitzgerald*, https://supreme.justia.com/cases/federal/us/457/731/, accessed December 11, 2015.

49. Breyer's concurring opinion in *Clinton v. Jones* is found at https://www.national center.org/ClintonvJones.html.

50. His own review showed that the Court's "key paragraph, explaining why the President enjoys an absolute immunity rather than a qualified immunity, contains seven sentences, four of which focus primarily upon time and energy *distraction* and three of which focus primarily upon official decision *distortion*." *Clinton v. Jones*, https://www.national center.org/ClintonvJones.html.

51. Ibid.

52. "Thatcher Meets With President, Reasserts Falklands Sovereignty," "Israeli Forces Strike Anew At Syrians, PLO in Lebanon," "Mideast Paradox: Gains Now, Trouble Later for U.S.," "Arafat's Dilemma: A Martyr's Death or Banishment," "Nuclear Freeze Backed in House Committee Vote," "U.S. Raid Ends Mutiny Aboard Foreign Ship; 24 Arrested," *Washington Post*, June 24, 1982, A1; "The Riadys Persistent Pursuit of Influence: Perception of DNC Donors' Pipeline Into Oval Office Boosted Lippo Group in Indonesia, China," "For Yeltsin, Business Prospects Outweighed NATO Threat," *Washington Post*, May, 27, 1997, A1. On that latter date, an additional article headed "Koreas Agree on Food Aid to the North" made brief comment inside the paper about U.S. foreign policy interests.

53. See Dugald McConnell and Brian Todd, "Nuclear Launch Card Was Missing for Months, New Book Says," CNN, October 22, 2010, http://www.cnn.com/2010/POLITICS/10/21/shelton.clinton.nuclear.codes/, accessed March 24, 2015.

54. *Jones v. Clinton*, 72 F.3d 1354, Court of Appeals (8th Cir. 1996), https://scholar.google.com/scholar_case?case=4655029432138828272&hl=en&as_sdt=6&as_vis=1&oi=scholar.

55. *Jones v. Clinton*, F.3d (8th Cir. 1996), http://caselaw.findlaw.com/us-8th-circuit/1344449.html. In later years, Justice Stevens defended his ruling by asserting that even had the Court accepted the path Justice Breyer outlined, it would have made no difference in the political outcome because the president would still have had to record his testimony. "The likelihood that *any* decision would have let him get off without even a deposition being taken was about one chance in a million." Quoted in Gormley, *The Death of American Virtue*, 253. The existence of Judge Ross's opinion suggests that Stevens's bookmaking was perhaps tilted. But even if we concede the accuracy of his assessment in the times in which he served, my basic argument is that under conditions such as those that produced the *Nixon* decision, we could expect the courts' application of the Constitution to look much more like the *Nixon* ruling in the case that all agree is most like *Jones*. It is worth noting in this regard that some scholars have argued that the constitutional logic is actually stronger for limited immunity than for the total immunity granted Nixon. See Akhil Reed Amar and Neal Kumar Katyal, "Executive Privileges & Immunities: The Nixon and Clinton Cases," 108 *Harvard Law Review* (1995), http://digitalcommons.law.yale.edu/fss_papers/990, accessed March 25, 2015.

56. *Jones v. Clinton*, F.3d (8th Cir. 1996).

57. Richard Nixon avoided impeachment by resigning. This occurred in the aftermath of the peace settlement in Vietnam.

58. For a summary of the Sienna College Survey results, see http://www.usnews.com/news/articles/2010/07/02/survey-ranks-obama-15th-best-president-bush-among-worst, accessed January 10, 2016.

CHAPTER 1: REDIVIDING GOVERNMENT

1. An earlier version of this chapter appeared in the June 2016 issue of *Presidential Studies Quarterly*. I am grateful to the journal and its politics and history editor, Richard J. Ellis, for the opportunity to draw from it in this volume and for his very helpful comments on the manuscript.

2. Quoted in "Power and Geography Taking Root," *USA Today*, November 7, 1996.

3. For a defense of oral history as a tool in historical research, see the opening pages of chapter 6 in this volume.

4. On the 1968 election and its aftermath, see Michael Nelson, *Resilient America: Electing Nixon in 1968, Channeling Dissent, and Dividing Government* (Lawrence: University Press of Kansas, 2014).

5. Unless otherwise indicated, quotations in this chapter relating to the Clinton presidency and the 1992 and 1996 Clinton campaigns are from interviews with the following individuals conducted as part of the Miller Center's William J. Clinton Presidential History Project: Al From, William Galston, Stanley Greenberg, Frank Greer, Mickey Kantor, David Kusnet, Roy Neel, Bruce Reed, and Eli Segal, The interviews are available at the Miller Center website: http://millercenter.org/president/clinton/oralhistory.

6. See Michael Nelson, "Constitutional Aspects of the Election," in *The Elections of 1988*, ed. Michael Nelson (Washington, D.C.: CQ Press, 1989), 181–209.

7. Gary C. Jacobson, "Congress: Unusual Year, Unusual Election," in *The Elections of 1992*, ed. Michael Nelson (Washington, D.C.: CQ Press, 1993), 155.

8. The best book on Clinton's pre-presidential life and career is David Maraniss, *First in His Class: A Biography of Bill Clinton* (New York: Simon and Shuster, 1995).

9. Both quotes in Patrick J. Maney, *Bill Clinton: New Gilded Age President* (Lawrence: University Press of Kansas, 2016), 24.

10. Clinton discusses his work with the National Governors Association in Clinton, *My Life* (New York: Alfred A. Knopf, 2004), 313–50. On the DLC, see Kenneth S. Baer, *Reinventing Democrats: The Politics of Liberalism from Reagan to Clinton* (Lawrence: University Press of Kansas, 2000).

11. Robert Reich, *The Work of Nations: Preparing Ourselves for 21st Century Capitalism* (New York: Alfred A. Knopf, 1991).

12. On Hart's withdrawal, see Matt Bai, *All the Truth Is Out: The Week Politics Went Tabloid* (New York: Alfred A. Knopf, 2014).

13. Interview with Gloria Cabe, April 22 and June 15, 1993, 1992 Clinton Presidential Campaign Interviews, Diane D. Blair Papers, http://pryorcenter.uark.edu/projects/Diane%20D.%20Blair/CABE-Gloria/transcripts/CABE-Gloria-Blair-19930422and19930615-FINAL.pdf.

14. "Announcement Speech" http://www.4president.org/speeches/billclinton1992announcement.htm.

15. Interview with George Robert Stephanopoulos, December 11, 1992, 1992 Clinton Presidential Campaign Interviews, Diane D. Blair Papers, http://pryorcenter.uark.edu/projects/Diane%20D.%20Blair/STEPHANOPOULOS-George/transcripts/STEPHANOPOULOS-George-Robert-Blair-19921211-FINAL.pdf.

16. Interview with John T. Monahan, November 5, 1992, 1992 Clinton Presidential Campaign Interviews, Diane D. Blair Papers, http://pryorcenter.uark.edu/projects/

Diane%20D.%20Blair/MONAHAN-John-T/transcripts/MONAHAN-John-T-Blair-19921105-FINAL.PDF.

17. Interview with David Wilhelm, December 12, 1992, 1992 Clinton Presidential Campaign Interviews, Diane D. Blair Papers, http://pryorcenter.uark.edu/projects/Diane%20D.%20Blair/WILHELM-David/transcripts/WILHELM-David-Blair-19921212-FINAL.pdf.

18. Quoted in Jack W. Germond and Jules Witcover, *Mad as Hell: Revolt at the Ballot Box, 1992* (New York: Warner Books, 1993), 169.

19. Quoted in ibid., 186.

20. Interview with Stanley Bernard Greenberg, December 10, 1992, 1992 Clinton Presidential Campaign Interviews, Diane D. Blair Papers, http://pryorcenter.uark.edu/projects/Diane%20D.%20Blair/GREENBERG-Stanley-Bernard/transcripts/GREENBERG-Stanley-Bernard-Blair-19921210-FINAL.pdf.

21. Interview with Robert O. (Bob) Boorstin, November 19, 1992, 1992 Clinton Presidential Campaign Interviews, Diane D. Blair Papers, http://pryorcenter.uark.edu/projects/Diane%20D.%20Blair/BOORSTIN-Robert-O/transcripts/BOORSTIN-Robert-O-nBob-Blair-19921119-FINAL.pdf.

22. Interview with Paul Begala, February 2, 1993, 1992 Clinton Presidential Campaign Interviews, Diane D. Blair Papers, http://pryorcenter.uark.edu/projects/Diane%20D.%20Blair/BEGALA-Paul/transcripts/BEGALA-Paul-Blair-19930202-FINAL.pdf.

23. "Interview with Dan Balz—National Political Correspondent for *The Washington Post*," The Election of 2004, ed. Michael Nelson, Center for Presidential History, Southern Methodist University: http://cphcmp.smu.edu/2004election/dan-balz/.

24. Quoted in Bill Thompson, "Perot Used, Betrayed Followers," *Fort Worth Star-Telegram*, July 23, 1992.

25. Interview with Stanley Bernard Greenberg, 1992 Clinton Presidential Campaign Interviews, Diane D. Blair Papers.

26. Interview with Mandy Grunwald, December 20, 1992, 1992 Clinton Presidential Campaign Interviews, Diane D. Blair Papers, http://pryorcenter.uark.edu/projects/Diane%20D.%20Blair/GRUNWALD-Mandy/transcripts/GRUNWALD-Mandy-Blair-19921220-FINAL.pdf.

27. "Polls," *National Journal*, August 8, 1992, 1862.

28. Jon Meacham, *Destiny and Power: The American Odyssey of George Herbert Walker Bush* (New York: Random House, 2015), 508–9.

29. Quoted in Germond and Witcover, *Mad as Hell*, 371.

30. Quoted in ibid., 410.

31. Interview with Paul Begala, February 2, 1993, 1992 Clinton Presidential Campaign Interviews, Diane D. Blair Papers.

32. Interview with Mandy Grunwald, December 20, 1992, 1992 Clinton Presidential Campaign Interviews, Diane D. Blair Papers.

33. Interview with Nancy E. McFadden, October 21, 1992, 1992 Clinton Presidential Campaign Interviews, Diane D. Blair Papers, http://pryorcenter.uark.edu/projects/Diane%20D.%20Blair/MCFADDEN-Nancy-E/transcripts/MCFADDEN-Nancy-Blair-19921021-FINAL.pdf.

34. Quoted in Michael Duffy and Dan Goodgame, *Marching in Place: The Status Quo Presidency of George Bush* (New York: Simon and Schuster, 1992), 82.

35. Ibid., 83, 285.

36. Interview with Robert O. (Bob) Boorstin.

37. Interview with Mandy Grunwald, December 20, 1992, 1992 Clinton Presidential Campaign Interviews, Diane D. Blair Papers.

38. Michael Nelson, "The Elections: Turbulence and Tranquility in Contemporary American Politics," in *The Elections of 1996*, ed. Michael Nelson (Washington, D.C.: CQ Press, 1997), 44–80.

39. Dick Morris, *Behind the Oval Office: Winning the Presidency in the Nineties* (New York: Random House, 1997).

40. Quoted in "Victory March," *Newsweek*, November 18, 1996, 48.

41. Bob Woodward, *The Choice* (New York: Simon and Schuster, 1996), 368.

42. "A Bridge Too Far," *New York Times*, October 16, 1996.

43. Gerald M. Pomper, "The Presidential Election," in *The Election of 1996: Reports and Interpretations*, ed. Gerald M. Pomper (Chatham, N.J.: Chatham House, 1997), 198.

44. "Clinton Buoys His Party in Capitol Hill Visit," *New York Times*, September 27, 1996.

45. "Dole, in 3-Prong Effort, Seeks to Add Spark to His Campaign," *New York Times*, September 11, 1996.

46. Nelson, "The Elections: Turbulence and Tranquility in Contemporary American Politics."

47. The elections that set the stage from dramatic changes in public policy (1912, 1932, 1964, and 1980) all shared these ingredients, along with a landslide victory for the winning presidential candidate. Erwin C. Hargrove and Michael Nelson, *Presidents, Politics, and Policy* (Baltimore, Md.: Johns Hopkins University Press, 1984), chapter 3.

48. Daniel J. Galvin, *Presidential Party Building: Dwight D. Eisenhower to George W. Bush* (Princeton, N.J.: Princeton University Press, 2010), 225.

49. On the disadvantages for Democratic congressional candidates that are traceable in large part to "inefficiency," see Gary C. Jacobson, "It's Nothing Personal: The Decline of the Incumbency Advantage in US House Elections," *Journal of Politics* 77 (July 2015): 861–73. Jacobson points out that although Obama outpolled his Republican opponent, Mitt Romney, by 5 million popular votes, Romney carried 226 congressional districts to Obama's 209.

50. Arthur M. Schlesinger Jr., "The Turn of the Cycle," *New Yorker*, November 16, 1992, 46–54.

CHAPTER 2: TRIANGULATION

1. John Wagner, "O'Malley Serves Notice to Wall Street Ahead of Possible Presidential Bid," *Washington Post*, February 28, 2015, https://www.washingtonpost.com/news/post-politics/wp/2015/02/28/omalley-serves-notice-to-wall-street-ahead-of-possible-presidential-bid/.

2. All quotations in this chapter relating to the Clinton presidency are from interviews conducted for the William J. Clinton Presidential History Project unless otherwise noted. The interviews are available online at the Miller Center Web site: http://millercenter.org/president/clinton/oralhistory.

3. Lawrence R. Jacobs and Robert Y. Shapiro, *Politicians Don't Pander: Political Manipulation and the Loss of Democratic Responsiveness* (Chicago: University of Chicago Press, 2000); Brandice Canes-Wrone, *Who Leads Whom? : Presidents, Policy and the Public* (Chicago: University of Chicago Press, 2006); J. Cummins, "State of the Union Addresses and Presidential Position Taking: Do Presidents Back Their Rhetoric in the Legislative Arena?" *The Social Science Journal* 45, no. 3 (2008): 365–81; B. W. Marshall and B. C. Prins, "Strategic Position Taking and Presidential Influence in Congress," *Legislative Studies Quarterly* 32, no. 2 (2007): 257–84; Steven A. Shull and T. C. Shaw, "Determinants of Presidential Position Taking in Congress, 1949–1995," *The Social Science Journal* 41, no. 4 (2004): 587–604.

4. David R. Mayhew, *Congress: The Electoral Connection* (New Haven, Conn.: Yale University Press, 1974).

5. For example, Mayhew, *Congress*; Morris P. Fiorina, *Congress: Keystone of the Washington Establishment* (New Haven, Conn.: Yale University Press, 1977); Kenneth A. Shepsle and Barry R. Weingast, "The Institutional Foundations of Committee Power," *American Political Science Review* 81, no. 1 (1987): 85–104; Susanne Lohmann and Sharyn O'Halloran, "Divided Government and U.S. Trade Policy: Theory and Evidence," *International Organization* 48, no. 4 (1994): 595–632.

6. Richard F. Fenno Jr., *Home Style: House Members in Their Districts* (Boston: Little, Brown, 1978); Gary W. Cox and Mathew D. McCubbins, *Setting the Agenda: Responsible Party Government in the House of Representatives* (New York: Cambridge University Press, 2005).

7. Spatial models of collective decision making (for example, in legislatures) assume that actors have policy preferences, without regard for where the preferences come from. Works that assume good-policy or ideological motivation in explicit contradistinction to electoral or political motivation are very rare.

8. In one such work, one of us criticized single-motive, election-seeking theories of legislators and offered evidence of public interest seeking, or autonomous, policymaking in congressional voting on economic deregulation of the trucking industry. See Martha Derthick and Paul J. Quirk, *The Politics of Deregulation* (Washington: Brookings, 1985); see also Paul J. Quirk, "Evaluating Congressional Reform: Deregulation Revisited," *Journal of Policy Analysis and Management* 10, no. 3 (1991): 407–25.

9. J. Roland Pennock, *Democratic Political Theory* (Princeton, N.J.: Princeton University Press, 1979); Arthur Maass, *Congress and the Common Good* (New York: Basic Books, 1983); Joseph M. Bessette, "Is Congress a Deliberative Body?" in *The United States Congress*, ed. Dennis Hale (Chestnut Hill, Mass.: Boston College Press, 1982); Jane Mansbridge, *Beyond Adversary Democracy* (Chicago: University of Chicago Press, 1983).

10. Jacobs and Shapiro, *Politicians Don't Pander.*

11. Paul J. Quirk, "Politicians Do Pander: Mass Opinion, Polarization, and Lawmaking," *The Forum* 7, no. 4 (2009): Article 10. See also Paul J. Quirk, "Polarized Populism: Masses, Elites and Partisan Conflict," *The Forum* 9, no. 1 (2011): Article 5.

12. Quirk, "Politicians Do Pander, 5."

13. Canes-Wrone, *Who Leads Whom?*

14. For analysts' perceptions of uncertainties surrounding electoral outcomes, see James E. Campbell, "Forecasting the 2012 American National Elections—Editor's Introduction," *PS: Political Science & Politics* 45, no. 4 (October 2012): 610–13, and the other articles in the symposium.

15. Morris P. Fiorina, *Retrospective Voting in American National Elections* (New Haven, Conn.: Yale University Press, 1981).

16. In psychological experiments, people change their opinions to conform to statements they are induced to make by the experimenter. See Leon Festinger and James M. Carlsmith, "Cognitive Consequences of Forced Compliance," *Journal of Abnormal and Social Psychology* 58, no. 2 (1959): 203–10. For recent related work, see Susan T. Fiske and Shelley E. Taylor, *Social Cognition: From Brains to Culture* (London: Sage, 2013).

17. M. Stephen Weatherford, *Nixon's Business: Authority and Power in Presidential Politics* (College Station: Texas A&M University Press, 2005).

18. Charles O. Jones, *The Trusteeship Presidency: Jimmy Carter and the United States Congress* (Baton Rouge: Louisiana State University Press, 1988).

19. Sheldon D. Pollack, *Refinancing America: The Republican Antitax Agenda* (Albany: State University of New York Press, 2003).

20. Paul J. Quirk and Bruce Nesmith, "Divided Government and Policy Making: Negotiating the Laws," in *The Presidency and the Political System*, 8th ed., ed. Michael Nelson (Washington: CQ Press, 2005), 508–32; Paul J. Quirk and Bruce Nesmith, "Explaining Deadlock: Domestic Policymaking in the Bush Presidency," in *New Perspectives on American Politics*, ed. Lawrence C. Dodd and Calvin Jillson (Washington: CQ Press, 1994), 191–211.

21. David R. Mayhew, *Divided We Govern: Party Control, Lawmaking, and Investigations, 1946–1990* (New Haven, Conn.: Yale University Press, 1991); E. Scott Adler and John D. Wilkerson, "Intended Consequences: Jurisdictional Reform and Issue Control in the U.S. House of Representatives," *Legislative Studies Quarterly* 33, no. 1 (2008): 85–112.

22. The fourth kind of challenge in our larger study concerns resolving conflicts between two or more powerful constituencies, each with substantial and presumably legitimate interests at stake. Such cases do not present a simple distinction between principled decisions and pandering. We therefore omit cases that deal with conflict resolution from the current study.

23. Note that although we use terms such as "principled" and "pandering" that literally characterize the actor's beliefs or intentions, we do not have evidence or make claims about any actor's actual state of mind. We know whether a policy has a strong rationale in terms of policy objectives or satisfies powerful constituency demands. On the issues we deal with, no policy does both, because we choose policies marked by conflict between predominant constituency demands and reputable policy thinking.

24. See William C. Berman, *From the Center to the Edge: The Politics and Policies of the Clinton Presidency* (Lanham, Md.: Rowman & Littlefield, 2001), ch. 3; Graham K. Wilson, "Clinton in Comparative Perspective," in *The Clinton Legacy*, ed. Colin Campbell and Bert A. Rockman (New York: Chatham House/Seven Bridges, 2000), 258–60; Charles O. Jones, *Clinton and Congress, 1993–1996: Risk, Restoration, and Reelection* (Norman: University of Oklahoma Press, 1999), 143–44.

25. "Health-Care Reform Begins in Budget Bill," *Congressional Quarterly Almanac* 49 (1993): 366–69.

26. Pietro S. Nivola and Robert W. Crandall, *The Extra Mile: Rethinking Energy Policy for Automotive Transportation* (Washington: Brookings Institution, 1995), 86–87, 105–6; Alan S. Miller, "Energy Policy from Nixon to Clinton: From Grand Provider to Market Facilitator," *Environmental Law* 25, no. 3 (1995): 721; Walter A. Rosenbaum, *Energy, Politics and Public Policy*, 2nd ed. (Washington: CQ Press, 1987), 197. Commentators are ambivalent about a tax based on Btu content, as it treats all energy sources equally regardless of their scarcity or pollution, thus defeating the purpose of the policy; see Nivola and Crandall, *The Extra Mile*, 20.

27. "Lawmakers Enact $30.2-Billion Anti-Crime Bill," *Congressional Quarterly Almanac* 50 (1994): 273–94; Joan Petersilia, "A Crime Control Rationale for Reinvesting in Community Corrections," *Prison Journal* 75, no. 4 (December 1995): 479; Daniel Krislov, "Ideology and American Crime Policy, 1966–1996: An Explanatory Essay," in *The Crime Conundrum: Essays on Criminal Justice*, ed. Lawrence M. Friedman and George Fisher (Boulder, Colo.: Westview Press, 1997), 116–17; Eva Bertram, Morris Blackman, Kenneth Sharpe, and Peter Andreas, *Drug War Politics: The Price of Denial* (Berkeley: University of California Press, 1996), 122–24.

28. "Lawmakers Renew and Revamp 1965 Education Act," *Congressional Quarterly Almanac* 50 (1994): 383–96.

29. Bertram, Blackman, Sharpe, and Andreas, *Drug War Politics*, 121.

30. Michael Wines, "Plan Sounding Less Monumental," *New York Times*, March 26, 1993, A16; R. W. Apple Jr., "Clinton Plan to Remake the Economy Seeks to Tax Energy

and Big Incomes," *New York Times*, February 18, 1993, A1; "Clinton Throws Down the Gauntlet," *Congressional Quarterly Almanac* 49 (1993): 85–89.

31. "Overhaul of Mining Law Advances," *Congressional Almanac* 49 (1993), 262.

32. Jeanne Nienaber Clarke and Daniel C. McCool, *Staking Out the Terrain: Power and Performance among Natural Resource Agencies*, 2nd ed. (Albany: State University of New York Press, 1996), 174; "Rewrite of 1872 Mining Law Fails," *Congressional Quarterly Almanac* 50 (1994): 236–37.

33. *Tax Notes*, March 21, 1994, 1487; *Tax Notes*, June 20, 1994, 1531; *Tax Notes*, July 25, 1994, 428.

34. See George C. Edwards III, "Strategic Assessments: Evaluating Opportunities and Strategies in the Obama Presidency," in *The Obama Presidency: Appraisals and Prospects*, ed. Bert A. Rockman, Andrew Rudalevige, and Colin Campbell (Washington: CQ Press, 2012), 37–66.

35. Barbara Sinclair, "The President as Legislative Leader," in *The Clinton Legacy,* ed. Colin Campbell and Bert A. Rockman (New York: Chatham House/Seven Bridges, 2000), 83–86.

36. "Plan to Cut Farm Programs Stalls," *Congressional Quarterly Almanac* 51 (1995): 50.

37. David Hosansky, "Farm Policy on the Brink of a New Direction," *Congressional Quarterly Weekly Report*, March 23, 1996, 786.

38. "Regulatory Overhaul Effort Generates Little Enthusiasm," *Congressional Quarterly Almanac* 54 (1998): 22; "Pesticide Rewrite Draws Wide Support," *Congressional Quarterly Almanac* 52 (1996): 27.

39. "Senate Filibuster Derails Efforts to Limit Federal Regulations," *Congressional Quarterly Almanac* 51 (1995): 3–13; Marianne Lavelle, "Some Costs Benefit Companies," *National Law Journal*, November 27, 1995, A1, 21; "A Risky Business, Writing Regulations," *Science News*, March 11, 1995, 159; Cass R. Sunnstein, "Congress, Constitutional Moments and the Cost-Benefit State," *Stanford Law Review* 48, no. 2 (1996): 274–82.

40. Peter Passell, "A New Move to Cut the Costs of Federal Regulations," *New York Times*, July 17, 1997, C2.

41. George Hager and Eric Pianin, *Mirage: Why Neither Democrats nor Republicans Can Balance the Budget, End the Deficit, and Satisfy the Public* (New York: Times Books, 1997), 29–35, 233–80.

42. Jonathan Rauch, "Ducking the Challenge," *National Journal*, February 8, 1997, 265–66.

43. "Cuts Prompt Veto of VA-HUD Bill," *Congressional Quarterly Almanac* 51 (1995): 83–91.

44. "Tough Talk, Little Progress on GOP's Crime Agenda," *Congressional Quarterly Almanac* 51 (1995): 8; Petersilia, "A Crime Control Rationale," 479.

45. "Tough Talk, Little Progress," 3–6.

46. "Lawmakers Aim to Consolidate Job Training Programs," *Congressional Quarterly Almanac* 51 (1995): 3–5; "Support Collapses for Job Training," *Congressional Quarterly Almanac* 52 (1996): 11; Kirk Victor, "New Jobs for Old," *National Journal*, January 1, 1994, 6–10.

47. Charles Pope, "Political Ground May Be Shifting Under Mine Operations," *Congressional Quarterly Weekly Report*, September 11, 1999, 2111–13; Charles Pope, "Conferees Agree on Interior Bill After Knocking Off Policy Riders Opposed by the White House," *Congressional Quarterly Weekly Report*, November 20, 1999, 2783.

48. "GOP Offers Party-Defining Tax Cut Proposal; Clinton Responds With Veto," *Congressional Quarterly Almanac* 55 (1999): 7–23. For a critique of supply-side economic assumptions, see Herbert Stein, *Presidential Economics: The Making of Economic Policy from*

Roosevelt to Reagan and Beyond, 2nd rev. ed. (Washington, D.C.: American Enterprise Institute, 1988), chapters 7–8.

49. *Congressional Quarterly Almanac* 53 (1997): 3–7; "Gun Control Agreement Eludes Conferees, Derails Juvenile Crime Legislation," *Congressional Quarterly Almanac* 55 (1999): 3–26; "Juvenile Justice Bill Gets Hung Up on Dispute over Gun Control," *Congressional Quarterly Almanac* 56 (2000): 15–18.

50. *Congressional Quarterly Almanac* 55 (1998): 3–12; H. Wayne Moyer and Tim Josling, *Agricultural Policy Reform: Politics and Process in the EC and the USA* (Ames: Iowa State University Press, 2002); Adam D. Sheingate, *The Rise of the Agricultural Welfare State: Institutions and Interest Group Power in the United States, France, and Japan* (Princeton, N.J.: Princeton University Press, 2003), 210.

51. Rauch, "Ducking the Challenge," 260–61; Peter Passell, "Long-Term Effects of Deal Have Economists Concerned," *New York Times*, August 1, 1997, A11.

52. Peter Passell, "The Budget Deficit Problem Will Be Back, With a Vengeance," *New York Times*, May 8, 1997, C2.

53. Mark Trumbull, "Power Deregulation Draws Critics," *Christian Science Monitor*, June 18, 1991, 8; "Energy Bill Surges Toward Enactment," *Congressional Quarterly Almanac* 48 (1992): 233. It was also opposed by some consumer and environmental groups, which feared that the absence of regulation would affect access, prices, and the environment.

54. Charles Pope, "House Subcommittee Moves Electricity Deregulation Bill with Big Issues Unresolved," *Congressional Quarterly Weekly Report*, September 11, 1999, 2599.

55. James C. Benton, "Electricity Bill Short-Circuits," *Congressional Quarterly Weekly Report*, June 17, 2000, 1739.

56. "Ocean Shipping Deregulation Dies in the Senate," *Congressional Quarterly Almanac* 52 (1996): 38–39.

57. "Other Transportation Issues Considered in 1997," *Congressional Quarterly Almanac* 53 (1997): 30–31.

58. "Eleventh Hour Dealing Clears Way for Passage of New Dairy Pricing Plan," *Congressional Quarterly Almanac* 55 (1999): 6–9.

59. Comptroller General David Walker called Bush "the most fiscally irresponsible president in American history"; quoted in Morton Kondracke, "Will Obama Match Bush for Fiscal Irresponsibility?" *Roll Call*, March 26, 2009, http://www.rollcall.com/issues/54_109/-33520-1.html. See also Bruce Bartlett, *Imposter: How George W. Bush Bankrupted America and Betrayed the Reagan Legacy* (New York: Doubleday, 2006).

60. Thomas E. Mann and Norman Ornstein, *It's Even Worse than It Looks* (New York: Basic Books, 2012); Jonathan Weisman, "U.S. Economic Primacy Is Seen as Ebbing," *New York Times*, April 17, 2015.

61. Quirk and Nesmith, "Divided Government and Policymaking"; Sean M. Theriault, *Party Polarization in Congress* (New York: Cambridge University Press, 2008).

CHAPTER 3: COMPROMISE AND CONFRONTATION

1. George C. Edwards III, *Presidential Influence in Congress* (San Francisco: W. H. Freeman & Company, 1980); George C. Edwards III, *At the Margins: Presidential Leadership of Congress* (New Haven, Conn.: Yale University Press, 1989); Jon R. Bond and Richard Fleisher, "The Limits of Presidential Popularity as a Source of Influence in the U.S. House," *Legislative Studies Quarterly* 5, no. 1 (1980): 69–78; Jon R. Bond and Richard Fleisher, "Presidential Popularity and Congressional Voting: A Reexamination of Public Opinion as a Source of Influence in Congress," *Western Political Quarterly* 37, no. 2 (1984): 291–306; and Jon R. Bond and Richard Fleisher, *The President in the Legislative Arena* (Chicago: University of Chicago Press, 1990).

2. Matthew Eshbaugh-Soha, "The Politics of Presidential Agendas," *Political Research Quarterly* 58, no. 2 (2005): 257–68.

3. George C. Edwards III, "Presidential Influence in the House: Presidential Prestige as a Source of Presidential Power," *American Political Science Review* 70, no. 1 (1976): 101–113; George C. Edwards III, "Presidential Electoral Performance as a Source of Presidential Power," *American Journal of Political Science* 22, no. 1 (1978): 152–68; Edwards, *Presidential Influence in Congress*; George C. Edwards III, "Aligning Tests with Theory: Presidential Approval as a Source of Presidential Power," *Congress and the Presidency* 24, no. 2 (1997): 113–130; Charles W. Ostrom Jr. and Dennis M. Simon, "Promise and Performance: A Dynamic Model of Presidential Popularity," *American Political Science Review* 79, no. 2 (1985): 334–58; Douglas Rivers and Nancy L. Rose, "Passing the President's Program: Public Opinion and Presidential Influence in Congress," *American Journal of Political Science* 29, no. 2 (1985): 183–196; Paul Brace and Barbara Hinckley, *Follow the Leader: Opinion Polls and the Modern Presidents* (New York: Basic Books, 1992); Brandice Canes-Wrone and Scott de Marchi, "Presidential Approval and Legislative Success," *Journal of Politics* 64, no. 2 (2002): 491–509; and Andrew W. Barrett and Matthew Eshbaugh-Soha, "Presidential Success on the Substance of Legislation," *Political Research Quarterly* 60, no. 1 (2007): 100–12.

4. Paul Gronke, Jeffrey Koch, and J. Matthew Wilson, "Follow the Leader? Presidential Approval, Presidential Support, and Representatives' Electoral Fortunes," *Journal of Politics* 65, no. 3 (2003): 785–808; and Patrick T. Hickey, "Beyond Pivotal Politics: Constituencies, Electoral Incentives, and Veto Override Attempts," *Presidential Studies Quarterly* 44, no. 4 (2014): 577–601.

5. Samuel Kernell, *Going Public: New Strategies of Presidential Leadership* (Washington, D.C.: Congressional Quarterly Press, 1986).

6. George C. Edwards III, *On Deaf Ears: The Limits of the Bully Pulpit* (New Haven, Conn.: Yale University Press, 2003).

7. Brandice Canes-Wrone, *Who Leads Whom? Presidents, Policy, and the Public* (Chicago: University of Chicago Press, 2005).

8. Christopher Berry, Barry Burden, and William Howell, "The President and the Distribution of Federal Spending," *American Political Science Review* 104, no. 4 (2010): 783–99.

9. Unless otherwise noted, all quotations in this chapter relating to the Clinton presidency are from interviews conducted for the William J. Clinton Presidential History Project. The interviews are available online at the Miller Center Web site: http://millercenter.org/president/clinton/oralhistory.

10. Richard Conley, "Divided Government and Democratic Presidents: Truman and Clinton Compared," *Presidential Studies Quarterly* 30, no. 2 (2000): 222–44.

11. Melody Rose, "Losing Control: The Intraparty Consequences of Divided Government," *Presidential Studies Quarterly* 31, no. 4 (2001): 679–98.

12. Jeffrey Cohen, "The Polls: Change and Stability in Public Assessments of Personal Traits, Bill Clinton, 1993–99," *Presidential Studies Quarterly* 31, no. 4 (2001): 733–41; Brian Newman, "Integrity and Presidential Approval, 1980–2000," *Public Opinion Quarterly* 67, no. 3 (2003): 335–67; and Brian Newman, "The Polls: Presidential Traits and Job Approval: Some Aggregate-Level Evidence," *Presidential Studies Quarterly* 34, no. 2 (2004): 437–48.

13. Shoon Kathleen Murray and Peter Howard, "Variation in White House Polling Operations: Carter to Clinton," *Public Opinion Quarterly* 6, no. 4 (2002): 527–58; Kathryn Dunn Tenpas and James McCann, "Testing the Permanence of the Permanent Campaign: An Analysis of Presidential Polling Expenditures, 1977–2002," *Public Opinion Quarterly* 71, no. 3 (2007): 349–66.

14. Diane Heith, "The Polls: Polling for a Defense: The White House Public Opinion Apparatus and the Clinton Impeachment," *Presidential Studies Quarterly* 30, no. 4 (2000): 783–90.

15. David Lanoue and Craig Emmert, "Voting in the Glare of the Spotlight: Representatives' Votes on the Impeachment of President Clinton," *Polity* 32, no. 2 (1999): 253–69.

16. Diana Owen and Richard Davis, "Presidential Communication in the Internet Era," *Presidential Studies Quarterly* 38, no. 4 (2008): 658–73.

17. Ronald Heifetz, "Some Strategic Implications of William Clinton's Strengths and Weaknesses," *Political Psychology* 15, no. 4 (1994): 763–68; and Fred I. Greenstein, "The Qualities of Effective Presidents: An Overview from FDR to Bill Clinton," *Presidential Studies Quarterly* 30, no. 1 (2000): 178–85; and Fred I. Greenstein, *The Presidential Difference: Leadership Style from FDR to Barack Obama* (Princeton, N.J.: Princeton University Press, 2009).

18. Dan Wood, "Presidential Rhetoric and Economic Leadership," *Presidential Studies Quarterly* 34, no. 3 (2004): 573–606.

19. Brandice Canes-Wrone, "The President's Legislative Influence from Public Appeals," *American Journal of Political Science* 45, no. 2 (2001): 313–29.

20. Franco Mattei, "The Gender Gap in Presidential Evaluations: Assessments of Clinton's Performance in 1996," *Polity* 33, no. 2 (2000): 199–228.

21. *Congressional Quarterly Almanac* (Washington, D.C.: CQ Press, 2013), B-10.

22. See also Richard Fleisher and Jon Bond, "The President in a More Partisan Legislative Arena," *Political Research Quarterly* 49 (December 1996): 729–48.

23. Donna R. Hoffman and Alison D. Howard, *Addressing the State of the Union: The Evolution and Impact of the President's Big Speech* (Boulder, Colo.: Lynne Rienner Publishers, 2006).

24. Of course, a newly elected president is incapable of delivering a State of Union Address. Because the new president is newly inaugurated and because the last State of the Union Address at the end of an administration happens weeks before the president leaves office, Hoffman and Howard, *Addressing the State of the Union,* examine the newly elected president's Address to the Nation and do not include the almost-retired president's State of the Union address in their analysis.

25. Although their graphic from the *New York Times* editorial includes all of the G. H. W. Bush years and Obama's first term, the more rigorous analysis from their book only goes through G. H. W. Bush's first two years. Hoffman and Howard, *Addressing the State of the Union.*

26. David R. Mayhew, *Divided We Govern: Party Control, Lawmaking, and Investigations: 1946–2005,* 2nd ed. (New Haven, Conn.: Yale University Press, 2005).

27. George C. Edwards III, Andrew Barrett, and Jeffrey Peake, "The Legislative Impact of Divided Government," *American Journal of Political Science* 41, no. 2 (1997): 545–63; and George C. Edwards III and Andrew Barrett, "Presidential Agenda Setting in Congress," in *Polarized Politics: Congress and the President in a Partisan Era,* ed. John R. Bond and Richard Fleischer (Washington, D.C.: CQ Press, 2000).

28. Sarah A. Binder and Forrest Maltzman, *Advice and Dissent: The Struggle to Shape the Federal Judiciary* (Washington, D.C.: Brookings Institution Press, 2009); and Jon R. Bond, Richard Fleisher, and Glen S. Krutz, "Malign Neglect: Evidence that Delay Has Become the Primary Method of Defeating Presidential Appointments," *Congress and the Presidency* 36, no. 3 (2009): 226–43.

29. Binder and Maltzman, *Advice and Dissent.*

30. Bond, Fleisher, and Krutz, "Malign Neglect."

31. Sean M. Theriault, *The Gingrich Senators: The Roots of Partisan Warfare in Congress* (New York: Oxford University Press, 2013).

32. Polarization Scores are based upon Keith Poole and Howard Rosenthal's DW-NOMINATE statistical procedures; see http://voteview.com/dwnl.htm (accessed on January 11, 2015).

33. For the Coats quote, see Ceci Connolly, "Health: Panel Recommends Elders, Approves Three Bills," *CQ Weekly*, July 31, 1993, 2068. For Gregg's opposition, see Nancy Mathis, "Panel Approves Elders/Nominee Awaits Full Senate Vote," *Houston Chronicle*, July 31, 1993, 8. An extensive search of the other two no votes—Strom Thurmond and Orrin Hatch—did not reveal any public statement, comment, or quote.

34. The difference in the voting patterns of the Gingrich senators and the other Republicans is statistically significant ($p = 0.042$).

35. The difference in the voting patterns of the Gingrich senators and the other Republicans is statistically significant ($p = 0.0$).

36. The difference in the voting patterns of the Gingrich senators and the other Republicans is statistically significant ($p = 0.0$).

37. Richard Neustadt, *Presidential Power and the Modern Presidents: The Politics of Leadership from Roosevelt to Reagan* (New York: Free Press, 1990), 28.

CHAPTER 4: ROOT CANAL POLITICS

1. Unless otherwise indicated, all quotations in this chapter relating to the Clinton presidency are from interviews conducted as part of the William J. Clinton Presidential History Project. The interviews are available at the Miller Center website: http://millercenter.org/president/clinton/oralhistory.

2. Alan Fram, "Bush's Budget Shows Deficit Increase," *Associated Press*, January 6, 1993.

3. Ezra Klein, "Bill Clinton: Wonk-in-Chief," *Washington Post*, September 6, 2012, http://www.washingtonpost.com/blogs/wonkblog/wp/2012/09/06/bill-clinton-wonk-in-chief/.

4. Office of the Clerk of the U.S. House of Representatives, "Party Divisions of the House of Representatives (1789 to Present)," History, Art & Archives, http://artandhistory.house.gov/house_history/partyDiv.aspx, accessed October 14, 2014; U.S. Senate Historical Office, "Party Division in the Senate, 1789–Present," United States Senate, http://senate.gov/pagelayout/history/one_item_and_teasers/partydiv.htm, accessed October 14, 2014.

5. Karen Tumulty, "Clinton and Congress: A Bad Marriage," *Time*, September 28, 1998, http://www.cnn.com/ALLPOLITICS/time/1998/09/21/clinton.congress.html.

6. "Election of 1992," The American Presidency Project, http://www.presidency.ucsb.edu/showelection.php?year=1992, accessed March 19, 2015.

7. "Election of 1992."

8. Quoted in Karen Tumulty, "Bob Dole Is Back on Top of Hill," *Los Angeles Times*, May 2, 1993, http://articles.latimes.com/1993-05-02/news/mn-30329_1_bob-dole.

9. Douglas Jehl, "Clinton Names Bentsen, Panetta to Economic Team," *Los Angeles Times*, December 11, 1992, http://articles.latimes.com/1992-12-11/news/mn-1762_1_wall-street-s-respect.

10. "Clinton Administration Economic Policy," November 14, 2014, http://www.c-span.org/video/?322629-3/discussion-economic-policy-clinton-administration.

11. John Greenwald, "Greenspan's Rates of Wrath," *Time*, November 28, 1994, http://content.time.com/time/magazine/article/0,9171,981879,00.html.

12. Karen Tumulty and William J. Eaton, "Clinton Budget Triumphs, 51–50 : Gore Casts a Tie-Breaking Vote in the Senate," *Los Angeles Times*, August 7, 1993, http://articles.latimes.com/1993-08-07/news/mn-21325_1_deficit-reduction-plan.

13. Ibid.

14. "Clinton Administration Economic Policy."

15. In Panetta's 2003 interview for the Miller Center's William J. Clinton Presidential History Project, he describes this discussion as taking place during the 1993 budget battle.

Years later, in his memoir *Worthy Fights: A Memoir of Leadership in War and Peace* (New York: Penguin Books, 2014, 144–45), he describes the conversation as occurring during the debate over the 1994 Crime Bill. While these accounts conflict, the story is included in this chapter because it was part of Panetta's earlier recollection of the fight to pass the 1993 budget bill.

16. Bill Clinton, *My Life* (New York: Alfred A. Knopf, 2004), 536.

17. Marjorie Margolies, "Democrats: Vote Your Conscience on Health Care," *Washington Post*, March 18, 2010, http://www.washingtonpost.com/wp-dyn/content/article/2010/03/17/AR2010031701496.html?wpisrc=nl_politics.

18. Leslie Klein Funk, "No Promises on Taxation from Fox, Mezvinsky, Miller," *The Morning Call*, October 26, 1992, http://articles.mcall.com/1992-10-26/news/2890356_1_tax-increase-taxes-or-user-fees-property-tax.

19. Ibid.

20. Tumulty and Eaton, "Clinton Budget Triumphs, 51–50."

21. "Clinton Administration Economic Policy."

22. Tumulty and Eaton, "Clinton Budget Triumphs, 51–50."

23. "The Clinton Presidency: Historic Economic Growth," http://clinton5.nara.gov/WH/Accomplishments/eightyears-03.html, accessed April 2, 2015.

CHAPTER 5: THE BROKEN PLACES

1. *Referral from Independent Counsel Kenneth W. Starr in Conformity with the Requirements of Title 28, United States Code, Section 595(c)*, 105th Congress, 2nd session, H. Doc. 105-310 (Washington, D.C.: Government Printing Office,).See also appendices at H. Doc. 105-311 and supplemental materials at H. Doc. 105-316 and H. Doc. 105-317. In this chapter references are to the version published as *The Starr Report: The Findings of Independent Counsel Kenneth W. Starr on President Clinton and the Lewinsky Affair, with Analysis by the Staff of the Washington Post* (New York: PublicAffairs, 1998).

2. Ken Gormley, *The Death of American Virtue: Clinton vs. Starr* (New York: Crown Publishers, 2010), 574.

3. Quoted in Bob Woodward, *Shadow: Five Presidents and the Legacy of Watergate* (Random House, 2000), 386. See http://www.drudgereport.com for the site's current iteration, which is little different in appearance than it was in 1998.

4. Lawrence Stein oral history. Unless otherwise attributed, all quotations in this chapter relating to the Clinton presidency are from interviews conducted as part of the William J. Clinton Presidential History Project. The interviews are available at the Miller Center website: http://millercenter.org/president/clinton/oralhistory.

5. "Remarks at a Breakfast with Religious Leaders," September 11, 1998, American Presidency Project, http://www.presidency.ucsb.edu/ws/index.php?pid=54886&st=&st1=. This and other presidential statements cited in this chapter are drawn from the on-line version of the *Public Papers of the Presidents* made available by The American Presidency Project at the University of California-Santa Barbara, curated by Gerhard Peters and John T. Woolley.

6. Isaiah 58:12.

7. Ernest Hemingway, *A Farewell to Arms* (New York: Charles Scribner's Sons, 1929), 267.

8. John F. Harris, *The Survivor: Bill Clinton in the White House* (New York: Random House, 2005), 334.

9. Gormley, *The Death of American Virtue* is the indispensable single volume here. Bringing to bear a wealth of new documentary evidence and interviews with most of the principals, it covers the chronological and topical spans of three excellent earlier treatments: for the Whitewater "prequel," James B. Stewart, *Blood Sport: The President*

and His Adversaries (New York: Simon & Schuster, 1996); for the Starr investigation, Jeffrey Toobin, *A Vast Conspiracy* (New York: Touchstone, 2000); and for the impeachment and subsequent Senate trial, Peter Baker, *The Breach: Inside the Impeachment and Trial of William Jefferson Clinton* (New York: Berkley Books, 2001). Susan Schmidt and Michael Weisskopf, *Truth at Any Cost: Ken Starr and the Unmaking of Bill Clinton* (New York: HarperCollins, 2000), emphasizes the Starr/OIC side of the narrative. Taylor Branch, *The Clinton Tapes: Wrestling History with the President* (New York: Simon & Schuster, 2009), provides accounts of contemporaneous conversations with the president, while Clinton biographer David Maraniss, *The Clinton Enigma: A Four-and-a-Half Minute Speech Reveals This President's Entire Life* (New York: Simon & Schuster, 1998), uses the August 17, 1998, speech as his fulcrum.

Participant memoirs include Bill Clinton, *My Life* (New York: Knopf, 2004); Hillary Rodham Clinton, *Living History* (New York: Simon & Schuster, 2003); Lanny Davis, *Truth to Tell: Notes from My White House Education* (New York: Free Press, 1999); Michael Isikoff, *Uncovering Clinton: A Reporter's Story* (New York: Crown, 1999); Monica Lewinsky, "Shame and Survival," *Vanity Fair*, June 2014; Andrew Morton, *Monica's Story* (New York: St. Martin's Press, 1999); and George Stephanopoulos, *All Too Human: A Political Education* (Boston: Little, Brown: 1999).

Republican memoirs focus on the House impeachment process: see Bob Barr, *The Meaning of Is: The Squandered Impeachment and Wasted Legacy of William Jefferson Clinton* (Atlanta: Stroud & Hall, 2004); James E. Rogan, *Catching Our Flag: Behind the Scenes of a Presidential Impeachment* (Washington, D.C.: WND Books, 2011); David P. Schippers with Alan P. Henry, *Sellout: The Inside Story of President Clinton's Impeachment* (Washington, D.C.: Regnery, 2000); and K. Alan Snyder, *Mission: Impeachable* (Vienna, Va.: Allegiance Press, 2001). Additional conservative commentary can be found in William Bennett, *The Death of Outrage: Bill Clinton and the Assault on American Ideals* (New York: Free Press, 1999); and Barbara Olson, *Hell to Pay* (Washington, D.C.: Regnery, 1999).

Political science accounts of impeachment and the Clinton presidency include Colin Campbell and Bert A. Rockman, eds., *The Clinton Legacy* (Chatham, N.J.: Chatham House, 2000); Nancy Kassop, "The Clinton Impeachment: Untangling the Web of Conflicting Considerations," *Presidential Studies Quarterly* 30 (June 2000): 359–73; Irwin Morris, *Votes, Money, and the Clinton Impeachment* (Boulder, Colo.: Westview Press, 2002); Rosanna Perotti, ed., *The Clinton Presidency and the Constitutional System* (College Station: Texas A&M Press, 2012); Nicol C. Rae and Colton C. Campbell, *Impeaching Clinton: Partisan Strife on Capitol Hill* (Lawrence: University Press of Kansas, 2004); and Mark Rozell and Clyde Wilcox, eds., *The Clinton Scandal and the Future of American Government* (Washington, D.C.: Georgetown University Press, 2000).

For legal approaches see, e.g., David Gray Adler and Michael A. Genovese, eds., *The Presidency and the Law: The Clinton Legacy* (Lawrence: University Press of Kansas, 2002); Richard A. Posner, *An Affair of State: The Investigation, Impeachment, and Trial of President Clinton* (Cambridge, Mass.: Harvard University Press, 1999). For analyses of the scandals' impact on journalism, see, inter alia, Marvin Kalb, *One Scandalous Story* (New York: Free Press, 2001); Woodward, *Shadow*; Steven Brill, "Pressgate," *Brill's Content* 1 (August 1998); and Bill Kovach and Tom Rosenstiel, *Warp Speed* (New York: Century Foundation, 1999). Finally, there is a volume of feminist theory inspired by the matter, perhaps most notable for its embrace of content from which the Starr Report itself might have shied away. See Lauren Berlant and Lisa Duggan, eds., *Our Monica, Ourselves: The Clinton Affair and the National Interest* (New York: New York University Press, 2001.)

10. Apparently he told Monica Lewinsky that in Arkansas "he had had 'hundreds of affairs.'" Quoted in Isikoff, *Uncovering Clinton*, 350. See also *The Starr Report*, 83; Gormley, *The Death of American Virtue*, 320; and Woodward, *Shadow*.

11. Gary Hart had already been forced to withdraw from the 1988 campaign for similar reasons. Maraniss, *The Clinton Enigma*, 56–57, 95–99; Gormley, *The Death of American Virtue*, 10, 543; Bruce Reed oral history.

12. Clinton, *My Life*, 384–87. See also Gennifer Flowers, *Passion and Betrayal* (New York: Emery Dalton, 1995).

13. Jeff Gerth, "Clintons Joined S&L Operator in an Ozark Real Estate Venture," *New York Times*, March 8, 1992, A1; see also Toobin, *A Vast Conspiracy*, 61–63.

14. In a memoir he drafted while in prison, Jim McDougal wrote that "the Whitewater case unfolded because I wanted Bill Clinton to feel my pain." Quoted in Gormley, *The Death of American Virtue*, 61.

15. Clinton, *My Life*, 391.

16. Altman oral history; *Wall Street Journal* editorial quoted in Harris, *The Survivor*, 104.

17. Harris, *The Survivor*, 278; Branch, *The Clinton Tapes*, 364–65.

18. Thomas L. Friedman, "Haircut Grounded Clinton While the Price Took Off," *New York Times*, May 20, 1993, A10; press briefing by George Stephanopoulos, May 20, 1993, The American Presidency Project, http://www.presidency.ucsb.edu/ws/?pid=60158, accessed March 16, 2015.

19. Quoted in Gormley, *The Death of American Virtue*, 86. See 75–91 on the Foster suicide generally and its aftermath.

20. *Final Report of the Special Committee to Investigate Whitewater Development Corporation and Related Matters* (Senate Report 104–280), June 17, 1996.

21. Toobin, *A Vast Conspiracy*, 87–88; Gormley, *The Death of American Virtue*, 188–91.

22. Quoted in Gormley, *The Death of American Virtue*, 91.

23. Patrick Griffin, then the head of Clinton's office of legislative affairs, recalls: "There's a little explosion here on Trooper-gate that everybody thought was containable, but it was the seeds of this Whitewater thing that would eventually really overwhelm us in that year, or overwhelm a lot of initiatives," notably health care.

24. David Brock, "His Cheatin' Heart," *The American Spectator*, January 1994, 26. See also Toobin, *A Vast Conspiracy*, 3–4, 17–24; and, on the editing error, Gormley, *The Death of American Virtue*, 117.

25. Daschle oral history; Rogan, *Catching Our Flag*, 24.

26. Paula Corbin was engaged to Steve Jones in May 1991, at the time of the alleged harassment. Steve Jones despised Clinton generally and became an aggressive protagonist of pushing the lawsuit forward. Paula's agreement to do so was therefore a boon to marital harmony.

27. Clinton noted later that Jones claimed she only wanted to clear her name and that he was happy to agree with her that nothing untoward had occurred in May 1991. See Gormley, *The Death of American Virtue*, 170.

28. Clinton's personal lawyer, Washington uber-attorney Robert Bennett, said nude photos of Jones could emerge at trial, while Jones's attorneys suggested that Jones could testify to "distinguishing characteristics in Clinton's genital area." Toobin, *A Vast Conspiracy*, 44–47.

29. *Clinton v. Jones*, 520 U.S. 681 (1997).

30. Patrick Griffin oral history.

31. Quoted in Gormley, *The Death of American Virtue*, 94. Hillary Clinton also argued against appointing a prosecutor, and in 1998 Clinton told historian Taylor Branch that ignoring this advice had been his biggest mistake; *The Clinton Tapes*, 511.

32. Quoted in Gormley, *The Death of American Virtue*, 110. See also Barr, *Meaning of Is*, 115.

33. Public Law 103-270, signed June 30, 1994.

34. Quoted in Gormley, *The Death of American Virtue*, 111, 151. Starr was certainly regarded as more reliably conservative than Fiske (who had worked for both Jimmy Carter and Gerald Ford). He had argued in favor of Paula Jones's right to bring suit while the president was in office—another reason his appointment set off White House alarm bells.

35. David Maraniss, "The Hearings End Much as They Began," *Washington Post*, June 19, 1996.

36. *The Starr Report*, 50.

37. Karen Breslau and Mark Hosenball, "Odyssey of a California Girl," *Newsweek*, February 2, 1998, 38.

38. Quoted in Woodward, *Shadow*, 259; see also Toobin, *A Vast Conspiracy*, 167. Susan Thomases' oral history is intriguing on this point: in 1992, she says, "I told him if I found him having sex on the campaign, he was dead, that I was leaving and taking everybody with me. I said, 'You're stupid enough to blow this whole Presidential thing over your dick. And if that turns out to be true, buddy, I'm going home, and I'm taking people with me. If you don't have enough self-control to keep yourself straight, then it's just dumb.'"

39. Quoted in Toobin, *A Vast Conspiracy*, 222.

40. Quoted in *Starr Report*, 64; see also Panetta's oral history: "Evelyn Lieberman came to me and said, 'She's hanging around, we need to . . .' I said, "Get rid of her." And she said, 'Yes. We will.'"

41. *Starr Report*, 50–62.

42. Ibid., 77–81.

43. See Baker, *The Breach*, 127, 395–96; Kathleen Willey, *Target: Caught in the Crosshairs of Bill and Hillary Clinton* (Washington, DC: WND Books, 2007).

44. Goldberg's son Jonah later told Marvin Kalb, "My mom was the only one who was absolutely truthful. She never made any secret of the fact that she really disliked Clinton." Quoted in Kalb, *One Scandalous Story*, 127.

45. In what Gormley terms "a burst of candor," conservative activist Ann Coulter said that settling the case "was contrary to our purpose of bringing down the President"; quoted in *The Death of American Virtue*, 259. Since Clinton had lied to his attorneys about his actions with Lewinsky and others, they did not realize they should push for a settlement either, even though Judge Susan Webber Wright told the parties in early January 1998 that the case "just *screams* for settlement"; quoted in ibid. 319.

46. Ibid., 228; Toobin, *A Vast Conspiracy*, 163–66.

47. On the Whitewater decision, see Gormley, *The Death of American Virtue*, 277. Gormley notes that the OIC's investigation began to take a new turn toward Clinton's past womanizing in the spring of 1997—coincidentally or not, soon after Starr announced that he would leave his post to move to Pepperdine University and then, under intense co-partisan fire in the media, changed his mind. For instance, William Safire, in his *New York Times* column, called Starr "a wimp" whose planned resignation brought "shame to the legal profession." Quoted in Gormley, *The Death of American Virtue*, 246; on the shift of emphasis in the OIC investigation, see pp. 247–49.

48. Specifically with regard to Hillary Clinton's old law partner Webster Hubbell, who had come to Washington to join the Justice Department but was convicted of embezzlement back in Little Rock. More broadly, Starr concluded that he should not have allowed his office to expand its investigation. "It had to be investigated," he told Ken Gormley much later. "But I was a poor choice to do it." Quoted in Gormley, *The Death of American Virtue*, 431.

49. This was sent to the OIC by the Jones lawyers, according to Toobin, *A Vast Conspiracy*, 199–200. But it seems they—and thus the OIC—somehow got a copy of the affidavit *before* it was ever formally filed with the district court in Arkansas, meaning that no crime had actually been committed by Lewinsky at the time the OIC threatened her

with perjury and obstruction of justice charges; Gormley, *The Death of American Virtue*, 313, 674.

50. Gormley, *The Death of American Virtue*, chapter 28. On the Department of Justice report, which was completed in December 2000 but not released publicly until the autumn of 2014, see Rosalind Helderman, "Lewinsky Mistreated by Authorities in Investigation of Clinton, Report Says," *Washington Post*, October 23, 2014. The full *Report of the Special Counsel Concerning Allegations of Professional Misconduct by the Office of Independent Counsel in Connection with the Encounter with Monica Lewinsky on January 16, 1998*, is available at http://www.washingtonpost.com/r/2010-2019/Washington Post/2014/10/23/National-Politics/Graphics/specialcounselreport.pdf, accessed October 9, 2015.

51. For more details and the quoted testimony, see Toobin, *A Vast Conspiracy*, 216–27; Gormley, *The Death of American Virtue*, 380–90; and Harris, *The Survivor*, 300–303.

52. The media's role as protagonist in, as well as chronicler of, these events is important but beyond the scope of this chapter. The threat of a *Newsweek* story on Tripp and Lewinsky, for instance—Tripp was talking to *Newsweek* reporter Michael Isikoff as well as to the Jones lawyers and the OIC—pushed the OIC to react faster than good judgment dictated in pursuing Lewinsky. The Drudge Report received a stream of information from Tripp's literary agent, Lucianne Goldberg, because she feared Isikoff would not publish it because of pressure from Starr's office not to do so and in the face of doubts from his editors. See Isikoff, *Uncovering Clinton*; Kalb, *One Scandalous Story*.

53. Harris, *The Survivor*, 306–7.

54. "Remarks on the After-School Child Care Initiative," January 26, 1998. American Presidency Project, http://www.presidency.ucsb.edu/ws/index.php?pid=56257&st=&st1=.

55. Quoted in Harris, *The Survivor*, 307–8; see also Toobin, *A Vast Conspiracy*, 243–44.

56. Quoted in Toobin, *A Vast Conspiracy*, 254–56.

57. Ibid., 244.

58. Clinton, *My Life*, 776

59. See Harris, *The Survivor*, 314; and Kalb, *One Scandalous Story*, especially the chapter entitled "Stampede." Kalb notes that the OIC was passing along tidbits to the press that its own investigation would later fail to confirm.

60. Harris, *The Survivor*, 342. Press secretary Joe Lockhart, in his oral history, agreed: "I do believe that if what he said, say, at the prayer breakfast a year later was said that day—even if it was said with that much sincerity and that much grief—he probably wouldn't have survived."

61. Gormley, *The Death of American Virtue*, 476.

62. Brill, "Pressgate."

63. Secret Service director Lew Merletti claimed that an FBI agent falsely told him—presumably hoping it would get back to the president and encourage him to lie in his grand jury testimony—that the FBI lab results for DNA had revealed nothing; Gormley, *The Death of American Virtue*, 524–26. Note that in negotiations with the OIC, Clinton succeeded in having the subpoena formally withdrawn. Thus his cooperation was, technically, voluntary.

64. Gormley interview with Sol Wisenberg, quoted in *The Death of American Virtue*, 551.

65. Quotes in this section are from the *Starr Report*, various; see also Gormley, *The Death of American Virtue*, 546–51.

66. However, they never went as far as anti-Clinton hardliners on the OIC staff had urged prior to the session. For instance, OIC prosecutor Brett Kavanaugh (who would be named by George W. Bush to the D.C. Circuit Court of Appeals in 2006), pushed hard in a memo for a far tougher line. "The President has disgraced his Office, the legal system, and the American people . . . ," he wrote. Thus, he should be asked brutally direct questions

about oral sex, ejaculation, and masturbation. Memo quoted (far more explicitly) in Gormley, *The Death of American Virtue*, 541.

67. Jokes based on this answer extended even to his wife's career: blogger Robert Matson referred to the flap over how Hillary Clinton had stored the e-mails she generated as secretary of state from 2009 to 2013 as "a refresher course in Clintonian semantics," generating the joke "It depends on what the meaning of the word 'ISP' is." See Robert Matson, "A Refresher Course in Clintonian Semantics," March 13, 2015, *Roll Call*, http:// blogs.rollcall.com/capitol-ink/a-refresher-course-on-clintonian-semantics/?dcz=emaila lert, accessed October 9, 2015.

68. Jackie Bennett and Starr quoted in Gormley, *The Death of American Virtue*, 551.

69. "Address to the Nation on Testimony before the Independent Counsel's Grand Jury," August 17, 1998, American Presidency Project, http://www.presidency.ucsb.edu/ws/ index.php?pid=54794&st=&st1=.

70. Betty Currie was the main target here, and in her oral history Currie strongly backed up Clinton: "The many, many, many times I went up there and every time they would ask me whether, when I talked to the President, he was influencing my thoughts. I tried to tell them, in the best way I knew how, that he wasn't. . . . From that day to this, there was no coaching."

71. Rogan, *Catching Our Flag*, 99–102; Dan Balz, "Hill Democrats See Speech as a Failure," *Washington Post*, August 20, 1998, A1. An elder statesman of the Washington press corps, David Broder, went so far as to call Clinton "truly Nixonian." Quoted in Maraniss, *The Clinton Enigma*, 63.

72. This paragraph and its predecessor are drawn from Maraniss, *The Clinton Enigma* (which uses the speech as the backbone of an entire short book); Toobin, *A Vast Conspiracy*, 310–12, 316–20; Baker, *The Breach*, 24–26, 32–34; Harris, *The Survivor*, 342–44; Gormley, *The Death of American Virtue*, 552–54; Clinton, *My Life*, 802–3; Clinton, *Living History*, 465. Those in favor of an aggressive speech included lawyers Kantor and Kendall, White House aide and former journalist Sidney Blumenthal, and family friend Harry Thomason; those against included Paul Begala (whom Bowles originally asked to write the speech), Rahm Emanuel, John Podesta, and Doug Sosnik (the source of the Carville quote.)

73. Mikva oral history; see also Woodward, *Shadow*, 274, 277–80.

74. Hillary Clinton was, unsurprisingly, furious both at the affair and at having been deceived. Her close friend and advisor Susan Thomases later said in her oral history "That's the only time in this whole thing that I have felt there was a near crisis in their relationship." See also Kate Andersen Brower, "The Secret Lives of Hillary and Bill in the White House," *Politico Magazine*, April 2015.

75. Baker, *The Breach*, 37–40; Harris, *The Survivor*, 314–15. In his oral history, Deputy Chief of Staff Roy Neel adds, "Like a lot of people, I was very angry with the President. He put the party and the White House at risk for such stupid behavior."

76. Gormley, *The Death of American Virtue*, 557.

77. Baker, *The Breach*, 36.

78. Lockhart argues, though, that this divergence was not as frequent or as fierce as was often assumed in the press at the time.

79. Baker, *The Breach*, 36–37.

80. One of the few items relevant to impeachment available from the Clinton Library as of this writing is the title of an e-mail chain: "Monica Lewinsky Drinking Game." The contents of the e-mails remain redacted.

81. Quoted in Gormley, *The Death of American Virtue*, 582.

82. Kalb, *One Scandalous Story*, 221; see also Harris, *The Survivor*, 326. Speechwriter David Kusnet said in his oral history that "Clinton was less distracted by all the

scandal-mongering than most politicians would have been. He was such a multitasker that you had a sense that he was so intellectually adventurous that he was always doing more than one thing at the same time."

83. The head of the World Bank, James Wolfensohn, told a White House aide that "it's like he isn't there." Quoted in Baker, *The Breach*, 36.

84. John Harris, "The Last Chance Presidency," *Washington Post Magazine,* September 10, 2000. Clinton himself told Representative Peter King (R-N.Y.) that "just because I come to work every day and keep my head up doesn't mean this isn't tearing me apart." Quoted in Baker, *The Breach*, 201. See also Gormley, *The Death of American Virtue*, 605–6.

85. Quoted in Harris, *The Survivor*, 327.

86. See, e.g., Barr, *The Meaning of Is*.

87. Rogan, *Catching Our Flag*, 57, emphasis in original.

88. Schippers with Henry, *Sellout*, 6. On Schippers, see Toobin, *A Vast Conspiracy*, 327; and Baker, *The Breach*, 84–85.

89. From Rogan's diary, quoted in *Catching Our Flag*, 80.

90. Baker, *The Breach*, 68. At the end of Judiciary Committee hearings, Hyde "was forced to add an awkward footnote. 'I was referring to the two-thirds requirement in the Senate,' he said at the end of the inquiry. 'I never really expected a lot of bipartisanship here.'" Quoted in David Hosansky and Andrew Taylor, "Judiciary's 'Fateful Leap,'" CQ Weekly, December 12, 1998, 3294.

91. Quoted in Baker, *The Breach*, 164.

92. 28 U.S.C. 595(c) required Starr to provide the House with "any substantial and credible information" that might constitute grounds for impeachment. Gormley, *The Death of American Virtue*, 566–69.

93. Joel Achenbach, "Dreary Prose, Silly Plot—Can't Put It Down," reprinted in *The Starr Report*, xlvii, xlvi.

94. Ibid., xlvi, xlvii. In fact some Republicans recognized the danger of this. According to James Rogan, Speaker Newt Gingrich told him in an angry private conversation on the House floor that Starr had "dumped it" (his report) on the House, an action Gingrich characterized as "unprofessional and total horseshit." Quoted in *Catching Our Flag*, 110.

95. Rogan, *Catching Our Flag*, 130.

96. Richard Pious, "The Clinton Impeachment: Politics and Public Law," in *The Clinton Presidency and the Constitutional System,* ed. Rosanna Perotti (College Station: Texas A&M Press, 2012), 184.

97. Quoted in Rae and Campbell, *Impeaching Clinton*, 63. In the roll call vote about whether to begin the inquiry, all 227 Republicans and 31 Democrats voted in favor. As noted below, far fewer Democrats would vote for impeachment itself.

98. See Morris, *Votes, Money, and the Clinton Impeachment*, chapter 3. Clinton's approval rating during this time surpassed public approval of Congress by as much as 25 percentage points.

99. From Rogan's diary entry for September 19, 1998. See Rogan, *Catching Our Flag*, 134.

100. This came as a surprise even to Democrats. Despite the good poll numbers, Lawrence Stein recalls, "the argument had been made rather frequently by good people that he was hurting the party. . . . Democrats didn't always believe the poll numbers." But "I believed the poll numbers implicitly. They were absolutely unmistakable. They were detailed, the cross tabs were clear. It wasn't as though it was a bubble or superficial. It was quite real. People understood. This was not an issue that people had trouble understanding. It wasn't like when they got the next dimension of this and delved down below the surface they were suddenly going to come to the conclusion that he was in fact guilty and

that he ought to be removed. They understood it. They knew it, they banked it. Many of them had understood this stuff about him before, I think. But many Democrats were unable to accept it because they thought it affected them. Maybe they thought that with his charisma he was able to escape his own culpability, but they couldn't." Clinton himself claimed Republican ads boasting of impeachment caused a seven- to fifteen- point swing toward the Democrats. For what Taylor Branch calls Clinton's "fountain of ecstatic detail" in a post-election conversation, see *The Clinton Tapes*, 518–20.

101. Quoted in Rogan, *Catching Our Flag*, 167.

102. Baker, *The Breach*, 165–66. Jones received $850,000 from Clinton (before legal fees), a far cry from the $5,000 her lawyer first sought. But she received no apology or admission. Clinton told Gormley (*American Virtue*, 589) that he agreed to settle, despite the summary judgment, to prevent further demands on his time and interference with his presidency—and in fact *because* of the summary judgment, since it showed the case had no legal merit and thus proved that the settlement was not a tacit admission of guilt. Taylor Branch says that Clinton asked what he thought history's verdict would be on such a large payment; *The Clinton Tapes*, 461–62.

103. Rogan, *Catching Our Flag*, 196, 199. See also Dan Carney, "Hyde Leads Impeachment Drive in Growing Isolation," *CQ Weekly Report*, December 5, 1998, 3247.

104. Quoted in Rae and Campbell, *Impeaching Clinton*, 23. See more broadly Posner, *An Affair of State*, chapter 3.

105. Merrill McLoughlin, ed., *The Impeachment and Trial of President Clinton: The Official Transcripts, from the House Judiciary Committee Hearings to the Senate Trial* (New York: Times Books/Random House, 1999), 71, 81 (see, generally, 67-85.) Owens thought the charges were equivalent to an article of impeachment charging President Nixon with tax fraud that the Watergate-era Judiciary Committee had rejected.

106. Posner, *An Affair of State*, 45–48. Basically, Clinton argued that she had had sexual relations with him but that he had not had them with her (and thus, his testimony was technically truthful.) A related piece of parsing that received intermittent attention was the fact that neither Clinton nor Lewinsky apparently considered oral sex to be "sex."

107. Quoted in McLoughlin, *The Impeachment and Trial of President Clinton*, 88–90, 93–94.

108. Representative Bob Inglis (R-S.C.), quoted in ibid., 96.

109. McCollum quoted in Toobin, *A Vast Conspiracy*, 355. Rogan, *Catching Our Flag*, 201–5, also touts these witnesses, but Toobin is significantly less impressed: he notes that both of them had actually initiated the court proceedings under the false pretenses for which they were later prosecuted for perjury.

110. See Gormley, *The Death of American Virtue*, 595–99; Baker, *The Breach*, 169–74; Rogan, *Catching Our Flag*, 190–94.

111. One Republican voted against Article II (perjury in the Jones deposition), resulting in a 20–17 vote in favor.

112. Baker, *The Breach*, 233–36. Referring to the new movie *Wag the Dog*, Lawrence Stein remembers that when he heard the news, "I said the obvious thing: the wag-the-dog scenario is going to be inescapable. To be honest with you, that was probably the worst moment among many bad ones that I had at the White House." He adds: "We heard the next day DeLay was going ahead [with impeachment] on Saturday. I tell that for anyone who believed that they weren't hell bent to do this. They were doing it, they were working the votes, and they were going to break the elbows of anyone who was going to oppose it."

113. The quotes below are drawn from Baker, *Breach*, 240ff; *Impeachment and Trial*, 168ff.

114. Oral histories. See also Baker, *The Breach*, 245–46. Bill Clinton had told Taylor Branch earlier that the GOP attacks on his infidelity during the 1998 midterms had the unintended effect of making Hillary Clinton extremely popular; *The Clinton Tapes*, 519.

115. Baker, *The Breach*, 246–47. Hyde quoted in Rogan, *Catching Our Flag*, 249. The publisher of *Hustler* magazine, Larry Flynt, had offered cash awards to anyone giving him information confirming what he saw as hypocrisy on sexual matters, leading to the "Flynt-ing" of a number of GOP leaders. In the wake of Livingston's departure, House deputy whip Dennis Hastert (R-Ill.) won the speakership in January 1999.

116. The parliamentary motion allowing a censure substitute failed with 204 votes in favor and 230 opposed. Article I passed, 228–206; Article II failed, 205–229; Article III passed, 221–212; and Article IV failed, 148–285.

117. As Stein's hesitance suggests, many people on the White House staff had doubts. Engskov, for instance, thought "the rallying team thing probably wasn't necessarily the right thing to do."

118. Some scholars, notably Bruce Ackerman of Yale, argued that an impeachment voted in one Congress (the 105th, 1997–98) was not valid in the next (the 106th, 1999–2000), but this never became a serious impediment to moving forward with the trial.

119. Quoted in Baker, *The Breach*, 289, 291. See also Carroll J. Doherty, "Senate's Uncertain Course," *CQ Weekly Report*, December 22, 1998, 3326.

120. Quoted in Gormley, *The Death of American Virtue*, 628–29.

121. Stein oral history. See also Baker, *The Breach*, 316, who discusses the White House's "don't-irritate-Byrd strategy."

122. Schippers with Henry, *Sellout*, 7, and see 24.

123. Gormley, *The Death of American Virtue*, 617. In the end, it took twenty-one days.

124. Rogan, *Catching Our Flag*, 308.

125. Quoted in Baker, *The Breach*, 294–95.

126. Quoted in Rae and Campbell, *Impeaching Clinton*, 130.

127. Baker, *The Breach*, 319; James Bennet, "Unbowed, Clinton Presses Social Security Plan," *New York Times*, January 20, 1999, A1.

128. Quotes are from McLoughlin, *The Impeachment and Trial of President Clinton*, Part III.

129. A GOP Senate lawyer would call Lewinsky, ruefully, "the best witness I ever saw." Quoted in Baker, *The Breach*, 373; Baker makes clear that GOP senators generally thought the managers did a poor job in deposing the witnesses (pp. 372–76, 385.)

130. Quoted in ibid., 332–33.

131. Quoted in ibid., 323.

132. Rae and Campbell, *Impeaching Clinton*, 140–42; Gormley, *The Death of American Virtue*, 644; Baker, *The Breach*, 380–88.

133. Quoted in Baker, *The Breach*, 397.

134. Interview with John Hilley and Lawrence Stein. See also Joe Lockhart quoted in Baker, *The Breach*, 388; and Clinton, "Remarks on the Conclusion of the Senate Impeachment Trial and an Exchange with Reporters," February 12, 1999. American Presidency Project, http://www.presidency.ucsb.edu/ws/index.php?pid=56912&st=&st1=.

135. From conversations with OIC staff and with Clinton, Gormley concludes that "President Clinton would never fully grasp how close he came to being indicted." *The Death of American Virtue*, 669, and on Judge Wright, 649–50.

136. Gormley, *The Death of American Virtue*, 642.

137. Toobin, *A Vast Conspiracy*, 8.

138. James Madison, Federalist #51.

139. Paul Quirk, "Scandal Time," in *The Clinton Scandal and the Future of American Government*, ed. Mark Rozell and Clyde Wilcox (Washington, D.C.: Georgetown University Press, 2000), 121.

140. Toobin, *A Vast Conspiracy*; and see more generally Martha Derthick, *Up in Smoke: From Legislation to Litigation in Tobacco Politics*, 3rd ed. (Washington, D.C.: CQ Press, 2011).

141. Kalb, *One Scandalous Story*.

142. Rae and Campbell, *Impeaching Clinton*, 156.

143. Morris, *Votes, Money, and the Clinton Impeachment*, 19 and 59–82.

144. Branch, *The Clinton Tapes*, 529.

145. He adds: "Moreover, many of them hated Hillary. And when I use hate, I use that advisedly. I've experienced those attacks from literally hundreds of people." Oral history of Roy Neel.

146. Rogan, *Catching Our Flag*, 134; see also his long subsequent recitation of Clinton's wrongdoings, culminating with "my question . . . for the two-thirds of you out there in America who tolerated, enabled, and rewarded this behavior: *Why didn't you care?*" (p. 187, emphasis in original). This is also the theme of Bennett, *The Death of Outrage*.

147. Waters quoted in Morris, *Votes, Money, and the Clinton Impeachment*, 10.

148. McLoughlin, *The Impeachment and Trial of President Clinton*, 432.

149. "Remarks and a Question and Answer Session with the American Society of Newspaper Editors," April 13, 2000. American Presidency Project, http://www.presidency. ucsb.edu/ws/index.php?pid=58369&st=&st1=. Bernard Nussbaum likewise said in his oral history, based on a conversation with Hillary Clinton, that "she looks at Watergate as a constitutional impeachment and this impeachment—the Lewinsky impeachment—as an unconstitutional impeachment."

150. Nearby, small panels complain of legal fees generated by "fruitless hearings and depositions," and the "numerous allegations" in Arkansas that "failed to unearth any credible information." Whitewater receives three sentences, the longest of which notes the length and cost of the investigation. (Library/museum exhibits quoted from photographs taken by author, reflecting their presentation as of November 2014.) Interestingly, talking to the American Society of Newspaper Editors in April 2000, Clinton was asked whether there would "be a wing in your presidential library to your impeachment trial?," to which he replied, "I will deal with it—we'll have to deal with it. It's an important part of it." "Remarks and a Question and Answer Session with the American Society of Newspaper Editors."

151. Susan Collins, "Incivility and Hyper-Partisanship: Is Washington a Symptom or a Cause?" Margaret Chase Smith Public Affairs Lecture, University of Maine at Orono, March 31, 2015, http://www.collins.senate.gov/newsroom/senator-collins-addresses-hyperpartisanship-washington-delivers-keynote-lecture-university, accessed October 9, 2015.

CHAPTER 6: CLINTON AND WELFARE REFORM

1. An earlier version of this chapter appeared in the September–December 2015 issue of *Congress and the Presidency*. The work originated as an unpublished background paper for the 2015 Presidential Leadership Scholars program. I am grateful to the journal and its editor, James Thurber, as well as to Mike Hemphill and others at the program, for the opportunity to draw from it in this volume.

2. Dick Morris, *Behind the Oval Office: Winning the Presidency in the Nineties* (New York: Random House, 1997), 300.

3. Robert B. Reich, *Locked in the Cabinet* (New York: Alfred A. Knopf, 1997), 320.

4. Leon Panetta, with Jim Newton, *Worthy Fights: A Memoir of Leadership in War and Peace* (New York: Penguin, 2014), 175.

5. George Stephanopoulos, *All Too Human: A Political Education* (Boston: Little, Brown, 1999), 421.

6. Peter Edelman, *So Rich, So Poor: Why It's So Hard to End Poverty in America* (New York: The New Press, 2014), 86–87.

7. Unless otherwise indicated, the quotations in this chapter relating to the Clinton presidency are from interviews conducted for the William J. Clinton Presidential History

Project. The interviews are available online at the Miller Center Web site: http://miller center.org/president/clinton/oralhistory.

8. Philip Zelikow, "Foreword," in *41: Inside the Presidency of George H.W. Bush*, ed. Michael Nelson and Barbara A. Perry (Ithaca, N.Y.: Cornell University Press, 2014), vii–xi.

9. Russell L. Riley, "Presidential Oral History: The Clinton Presidential History Project," *Oral History Review* 34: 81–106.

10. The best published accounts of welfare reform are R. Kent Weaver, *Ending Welfare as We Know It* (Washington, D.C.: Brookings Institution Press, 2000); Jason DeParle, *American Dream: Three Women, Ten Kids, and a Nation's Drive to End Welfare* (New York: Viking, 2004); and, from a congressional Republican perspective, Ron Haskins, *Work over Welfare: The Inside Story of the 1996 Welfare Reform Law* (Washington, D.C.: Brookings Institution Press, 2006).

11. David T. Ellwood, *Poor Support: Poverty in the American Family* (New York: Basic Books, 1988).

12. Bill Clinton, *My Life* (New York: Alfred A. Knopf, 2004), 330.

13. Ibid.

14. Bill Clinton, "Remarks at the Symposium on the Clinton Administration," Clinton Presidential Center, Little Rock, Arkansas, November 14, 2014, author's transcription.

15. Hillary Rodham Clinton, *Living History* (New York: Simon and Schuster, 2003), 366.

16. Bill Clinton, "The New Covenant: Responsibility and Rebuilding the American Community," Remarks at Georgetown University, October 23, 1991, http://www.c-span. org/video/?23518-1/clinton-campaign-speech:October 23.

17. Clinton, *My Life*, 494.

18. Marian Wright Edelman, "Say No to This Welfare 'Reform,'" *Washington Post*, November 3. 1995.

19. Clinton, "Remarks at the Symposium on the Clinton Administration."

20. Ibid.

21. Ibid.

22. Clinton, *My Life*, 720.

23. Bill Clinton, "Remarks on Welfare Reform Legislation and an Exchange with Reporters," July 31, 1006, http://www.gpo.gov/fdsys/pkg/WCPD 1996-08-05/pdf/WCPD-1996-08-05-Pg1379.pdf.

24. Peter Edelman, "The Worst Thing Bill Clinton Has Done," *Atlantic Monthly* (March 1997), 43–58.

25. Clinton, "Remarks at the Symposium on the Clinton Administration."

26. Ibid.

27. See, for example, Philip A. Klinkner and Rogers M. Smith, *The Unsteady March: The Rise and Decline of Racial Equality in America* (Chicago: University of Chicago Press, 2002); and Mimi Abramovitz, "Welfare Reform in the United States: Gender, Race, and Class Matter," *Critical Social Policy* 26 (May 2006): 336–64.

28. Edelman, *So Rich, So Poor*.

29. Peter A. Hall, "Social Policy-Making for the Long Term," *PS: Political Science & Politics* 48 (April 2015): 290; Sharon Hays, *Flat Broke with Children: Women in the Age of Welfare Reform* (New York: Oxford University Press, 2003).

CHAPTER 7: HILLARY RODHAM CLINTON

1. Hillary Rodham Clinton, *Living History* (New York: Simon and Schuster, 203), 180–81.

2. Unless otherwise indicated, all quotations in this chapter relating to the Clinton presidency are from interviews conducted as part of the William J. Clinton Presidential

History Project. The interviews are available at the Miller Center website: http://miller center.org/president/clinton/oralhistory. Peter Baker and Amy Chozick, "Hillary Clinton's History as First Lady: Powerful, but Not Always Deft," *New York Times*, December 5, 2014, http://www.nytimes.com/2014/12/06/us/politics/hillary-clintons-history-as-first-lady-powerful-but-not-always-deft.html?_r=0, is a superb guide to and analysis of the observations about Mrs. Clinton contained in interviews conducted for the Clinton Presidential History Project.

3. For an excellent analysis of first ladies' roles see Robert P. Watson, *The Presidents' Wives: The Office of First Lady in U.S. Politics*, 2nd ed. (Boulder, Colo.: Lynne Rienner Publishers, 2014).

4. David Maraniss, *First in His Class: A Biography of Bill Clinton* (New York: Simon and Schuster, 1995), 249–52; Betty Boyd Caroli, *First Ladies* (New York: Oxford University Press), 288–308.

5. Clinton, *Living History*, 31; Maraniss, *First in His Class*, 252–57.

6. Miriam Horn, *Rebels in White Gloves: Coming of Age with Hillary's Class—Wellesley '69* (New York: Anchor Books, 2000), xiii.

7. Clinton, *Living History*, 36–41; Maraniss, *First in His Class*, 257–59.

8. "The Man from Hope," Clinton Campaign Video, Democratic National Committee, 1992; Clinton, *Living History*, 44–53; Bill Clinton, *My Life* (New York: Knopf), 181–82.

9. Clinton, *Living History*, 91–92.

10. Ibid.

11. Ibid., 69–78.

12. Clinton, *My Life*, chapters 20–21; Clinton, *Living History*, 79–84.

13. Gil Troy, *Mr. & Mrs. President: From the Trumans to the Clintons* (Lawrence: University Press of Kansas, 2000), 349; Clinton, *Living History*, 91–95; Clinton, *My Life*, 308–11.

14. Maraniss, *First in His Class*, 428–29.

15. Clinton, *Living History*, 101–5.

16. Ibid., 106–7; Clinton, *My Life*, 385–87.

17. "The Clinton Years," *Frontline*, PBS, Chapters: The Campaign, http://www.pbs.org/wgbh/pages/frontline/shows/clinton/chapters/1.html. The Flowers accusations were later proven partially true.

18. Clinton, *Living History*, 109; and Clinton, *My Story*, 397. These impatient, sometimes angry, replies to legitimate questions in 1992 foreshadowed the tone of Mrs. Clinton's initial responses to members of Congress and the press about the 2012 Benghazi tragedy and the controversy over her e-mail protocols while she served as secretary of state from 2009 to 2013.

19. Clinton, *Living History*, 110.

20. Ibid.

21. George J. Church, "Bill Clinton: The Long Road," *Time*, November 2, 1992, 38.

22. Quoted in ibid.

23. David Maraniss, "President Clinton," *Washington Post*, January 20, 1993, F21.

24. Jessica Lee, "First Lady's Staff Carries Clout," *USA Today*, January 20, 1993, 4A.

25. Elizabeth Drew, *On the Edge: The Clinton Presidency* (New York: Simon and Schuster, 1994).

26. Lee, "First Lady's Staff Carries Clout," 4A; Clinton, *Living History*, 135.

27. Betty Monkman, *The White House: Its Historic Furnishings and First Families* (New York: White House Historical Association and Abbeville Press, 2000), 261; Clinton, *Living History*, 449.

28. Clinton, *Living History*, 134.

29. Drew, *On the Edge*, 93.

30. Clinton, *Living History*, 136.

31. See Barbara A. Perry, *Jacqueline Kennedy: First Lady of the New Frontier* (Lawrence: University Press of Kansas, 2004).

32. Clinton, *Living History*, 138.

33. Ibid., 144.

34. Drew, *On the Edge*, 103.

35. Ibid, 194.

36. Ibid., 192.

37. *The President's Health Security Plan* (New York: Times Books, 1993).

38. Clinton, *Living History*, 247–48.

39. Peter Maas, "I Think We've Learned a Lot," *Parade Magazine*, February 19, 1995, 4.

40. Hillary Rodham Clinton, *It Takes a Village: And Other Lessons Children Teach Us* (New York: Touchstone, 1996).

41. "Clinton Says She 'Misspoke' About Sniper Fire," CNN, March 25, 2008, http://www.cnn.com/2008/POLITICS/03/25/campaign.wrap/index.html?iref=hpmostpop.

42. Bill Turque, "Hillary Shores Up a Shaky Base for '96," *Newsweek*, June 5, 1995, 29.

43. Clinton, *My Life*, 776; Gary Wills, "Inside Hillary's Head," *Washington Post*, January 21, 1996, C1.

44. Clinton, *Living History*, 466, 471.

45. Fred I. Greenstein, *The Presidential Difference: Leadership Style from FDR to George W. Bush*, 2nd ed. (Princeton, N.J.: Princeton University Press, 2004), 184; Robert P. Watson, *The Presidents' Wives: Reassessing the Office of First Lady* (Boulder, Colo.: Lynne Rienner, 2000), 179; Barry C. Burden and Anthony Mughan, "Public Opinion and Hillary Rodham Clinton," *Public Opinion Quarterly* 63, no. 2 (1999): 239.

46. Andrea Bernstein, "Hillary Clinton's 'Smaller Steps': Big Thinking Is Out, Celebrity-Style Touring Is In, for This U.S. Senate Campaign," *The Nation*, September 6, 1999, 16; Roxanne Roberts, "The Double Life of Hillary Clinton: Is the First Lady Abandoning Her Role or Redefining It?" *Washington Post*, February 8, 2000, C1.

47. Late Show with David Letterman, CBS, May 12, 2015.

48. Nancy Beck Young, *Lou Henry Hoover: Activist First Lady* (Lawrence: University Press of Kansas, 2004).

49. Jim VandeHei, "First Lady's Initiative Aimed at Providing Stability for Youths," *Washington Post*, March 8, 2005, A4.

50. Quoted in *Newsweek*, January 1, 1962, 35, emphasis in original.

CHAPTER 8: THE RELUCTANT GRAND STRATEGIST AT WAR

1. Charles Krauthammer, "History Will Judge," *Washington Post*, September 19, 2008, A19.

2. Stephen Sestanovich, *Maximalist: America in the World from Truman to Obama* (New York: Knopf, 2014), 263.

3. Henry R. Nau, *Conservative Internationalism: Armed Diplomacy under Jefferson, Polk, Truman, and Reagan* (Princeton, N.J.: Princeton University Press, 2013), 68–69.

4. See Strobe Talbott's assessment of these three factors in the Christopher and Talbott interview. All quotations in this chapter relating to the Clinton presidency are from interviews conducted for the William J. Clinton Presidential History Project unless otherwise noted. The interviews are available online at the Miller Center Web site: http://millercenter.org/president/clinton/oralhistory.

5. Richard K. Betts, *American Force: Dangers, Delusions, and Dilemmas in National Security* (New York: Columbia University Press, 2012), 266–67.

6. Laura Silber and Allan Little, *Yugoslavia: Death of a Nation* (New York: Penguin, 1997), 287–88.

7. Anthony Lake, *6 Nightmares: Real Threats in a Dangerous World and How American Can Meet Them* (New York: Little, Brown, 2000), 143–44; Madeleine Albright with Bill Woodward, *Madam Secretary: A Memoir* (New York: Harper Perennial, 2013), 178–83.

8. Perry interview.

9. Ivo H. Daalder, *Getting to Dayton: The Making of America's Bosnia Policy* (Washington, D.C.: Brookings Institution Press, 2000), 7, 31.

10. Derek Chollet and James Goldgeier, *American between the Wars: From 11/9–9/11* (New York: PublicAffairs, 2008), 66–72; James M. Goldgeier and Michael McFaul, *Power and Purpose: U.S. Policy toward Russia after the Cold War* (Washington, D.C.: Brookings Institution Press, 2003), 87–119. In both the Lake and Berger interviews, NATO expansion is referenced as being core to the Clinton administration's agenda early on.

11. Colin Dueck, *Reluctant Crusaders: Power, Culture, and Change in American Grand Strategy* (Princeton, N.J.: Princeton University Press, 2006), chapter 5.

12. Berger interview.

13. Strobe Talbott, *The Russia Hand: A Memoir of Presidential Diplomacy* (New York: Random House, 2002), 133–34.

14. Quoted in Hal Brands, *What Good Is Grand Strategy? Power and Purpose in American Statecraft from Harry S. Truman to George W. Bush* (Ithaca, N.Y.: Cornell University Press, 2014), 146–47.

15. As detailed in the Steinberg interview, the grand strategy of enlargement did have strong support in the working levels of the administration.

16. Shalikashvili interview and Perry interview.

17. Chollet and Goldgeier, *American between the Wars*, 122–25.

18. Stuart J. Kaufman, *Modern Hatreds: The Symbolic Politics of Ethnic War* (Ithaca, N.Y.: Cornell University Press, 2001), 165–201.

19. Albright interview.

20. David Mitchell, "Does Context Matter? Advisory Systems and the Management of the Foreign Policy Decision-Making Process," *Presidential Studies Quarterly* 40, no. 1 (2010): 655.

21. David J. Rothkopf, *Running the World: The Inside Story of the National Security Council and the Architects of American Power* (New York: PublicAffairs, 2004), 311–12.

22. I.M. Destler, Leslie H. Gelb, and Anthony Lake, *Our Own Worst Enemy: The Unmaking of American Foreign Policy* (New York: Simon and Schuster, 1984), 279.

23. "Organization of the National Security Council," Presidential Decision Directive/NSC-2, January 20, 1993, http://clinton.presidentiallibraries.us/items/show/12736, accessed 21 January 2015.

24. Spencer D. Bakich, *Success and Failure in Limited War: Information and Strategy in the Korean, Vietnam, Persian Gulf, and Iraq Wars* (Chicago: University of Chicago Press, 2014), 28–41.

25. Ivo H. Daalder and I.M. Destler, *In the Shadow of the Oval Office: Profiles of the National Security Advisers and the President they Served—From JFK to George W. Bush* (New York: Simon and Schuster, 2009), 216–18.

26. On national security advisors as "strategists in chief," see Steven Metz's contribution to *H-Diplo/ISSF Roundtable* 7, no. 2 (2014), http://issforum.org/ISSF/PDF/ISSF-Roundtable-7-2.pdf.

27. Regional Intelligence, "Bosnian Thunder: And Now Something Completely Different: Brcko," *Transitions Online*, May 9, 1994, http://www.tol.org/client/article/15772-bosnian-thunder-and-now-something-completely-different-brcko.html, accessed January 21, 2015.

28. Daalder, *Getting to Dayton*, chapter 2.

29. Derek Chollet, *The Road to the Dayton Accords: A Study of American Statecraft* (New York: Palgrave MacMillan, 2005), 11–16.

30. Richard Holbrooke, *To End a War*, rev. ed. (New York: Modern Library, 1999), 65–68; Daalder, *Getting to Dayton*, 46–48; Chollet, *The Road to the Dayton Accords*, 22–24.

31. Lake interview.

32. Steven L. Burg and Paul S. Shoup, *The War in Bosnia-Herzegovina: Ethnic Conflict and International Intervention* (New York: M. E. Sharpe, 2000), 316.

33. Lake interview.

34. Daalder and Destler, *In the Shadow of the Oval Office*, 231–33.

35. Quoted in John P. Burke, "The National Security Advisor and Staff: Transition Challenges," *Presidential Studies Quarterly* 39, no. 2 (2009): 297.

36. Bob Woodward, *The Choice* (New York: Simon and Schuster, 1996), 257–58; and Rothkopf, *Running the World*, 367.

37. However, domestic political factors had much less salience than international events in this case. Mitchell, "Does Context Matter?" 657.

38. Daalder, *Getting to Dayton*, 163; Chollet, *The Road to the Dayton Accords*, 184. On the Croatian military offensive, see John Ashbrook and Spencer D. Bakich, "Storming to Partition: Croatia, the United States, and the Krajina in the Yugoslav War," *Small Wars & Insurgencies* 21, no. 4 (2010), 544–46.

39. Steinberg interview.

40. Daalder, *Getting to Dayton*, 84; Woodward, *The Choice*, 253.

41. On the overall process of rethinking America's Bosnia policy, see Steinberg interview.

42. Chollet, *The Road to the Dayton Accords*, 20.

43. Rothkopf, *Running the World*, 367–68.

44. Woodward, *The Choice*, 253.

45. Chollet, *The Road to the Dayton Accords*, 18.

46. Ibid., 22.

47. Bill Clinton, *My Life* (New York: Knopf, 2004), 666.

48. It also forced the hand of Chairman of the Joint Chiefs of Staff John Shalikashvili; David Halberstam, *War in a Time of Peace: Bush, Clinton, and the Generals* (New York: Touchstone, 2001), 326–27.

49. Quoted in Chollet, *The Road to the Dayton Accords*, 26.

50. Lake interview.

51. Ashbrook and Bakich, "Storming to Partition," 546–50; Clinton, *My Life*, 667.

52. Quoted in Chollet, *The Road to the Dayton Accords*, 39.

53. Ibid., 31–35.

54. Ibid., 41.

55. Ibid., 187–88.

56. Tim Judah, *Kosovo: War and Revenge*, 2nd ed. (New Haven, Conn.: Yale University Press, 2002), 124–26.

57. "The Crisis in Kosovo," *Human Rights Watch* 12, no. 1 (2000), http://www.hrw.org/reports/2000/nato/Natbm200-01.htm#P153_32943, accessed January 21, 2015.

58. Misha Glenny, "Motives for a Massacre," *New York Times*, January 20, 1999, A31.

59. Ivo H. Daalder and Michael E. O'Hanlon, *Winning Ugly: NATO's War to Save Kosovo* (Washington, D.C.: Brookings Institution Press, 2000), 77–84.

60. Timothy W. Crawford, "Pivotal Deterrence and the Kosovo War: Why the Holbrooke Agreement Failed," *Political Science Quarterly* 116, no. 4 (2001–2002): 519–22.

61. John Norris, *Collision Course: NATO, Russia, and Kosovo* (Westport, Conn.: Praeger, 2005), 189.

62. Stephen T. Hosmer, *The Conflict over Kosovo: Why Milosevic Decided to Settle When He Did* (Santa Monica, Calif.: RAND, 2001), 91–120.

63. For a critical assessment of the role of air power in affecting the outcome of the war, see Frederick W. Kagan, *Finding the Target: The Transformation of American Military Policy* (New York: Encounter Books, 2006), 190–97.

64. Secretary of State Madeleine K. Albright, "Building a Europe Whole and Free" (Remarks at Event Sponsored by the Bohemia Foundation, Prague, Czech Republic, March 7, 2000). http://1997-2001.state.gov/www/statements/2000/000307.html, accessed December 31, 2015.

65. Michael Ignatieff, "Chains of Command," *New York Review of Books* 48, no. 12 (2001): 18.

66. Robert J. Art, *A Grand Strategy for America* (Ithaca, N.Y.: Cornell University Press, 2003), 154–56.

67. Norris, *Collision Course*, 115.

68. Goldgeier and McFaul, *Power and Purpose*, 251. Albright maintains that her expectations of a short war were always cast in relative terms—that is, compared to Vietnam. Albright interview.

69. Steven B. Redd, "The Influence of Advisers and Decision Strategies on Foreign Policy Choices: President Clinton's Decision to Use Force in Kosovo," *International Studies Perspectives* 6, no. 1 (2005): 139.

70. Patricia A. Weitsman, *Waging War: Alliances, Coalitions, and Institutions of Interstate Violence* (Stanford, Calif.: Stanford University Press, 2014), 89–93.

71. David L. Phillips, *Liberating Kosovo: Coercive Diplomacy and U.S. Intervention* (Cambridge: MIT Press, 2012), 105–6.

72. Benjamin S. Lambeth, *NATO's Air War for Kosovo: A Strategic and Operational Assessment* (Santa Monica, Calif.: Rand Corporation, 2001), 9.

73. Dag Henriksen, *NATO's Gamble: Combining Diplomacy and Airpower in the Kosovo Crisis, 1998–1999* (Annapolis, Md.: Naval Institute Press, 2007), 166.

74. Goldgeier and McFaul, *Power and Purpose*, 255–56.

75. Talbott, *Russia Hand*, 311.

76. Domestic political costs stemming from congressional oversight—or obstructionism—proved to be illusory. In April 1999, for example, the House passed a bill precluding the administration from using funds designated for the Department of Defense to deploy American ground troops to Kosovo without prior congressional authorization. Yet shortly thereafter, Congress passed an appropriations bill that funded American operations in the Balkans at a substantially higher level than the White House had requested. William G. Howell and Jon C. Pevehouse, "When Congress Stops Wars: Partisan Politics and Presidential Power," *Foreign Affairs* 86, no. 5 (2007): 104. For the most part, Congress served as the forum for debate on the meaning of the conflict in Kosovo and its implications for American national security, a debate in which the Clinton administration was an active participant. Roland Paris, "Kosovo and the Metaphor War," *Political Science Quarterly* 117, no. 3 (2002), 438–47.

77. Daalder and O'Hanlon, *Winning Ugly*, 126–27.

78. Bill Clinton, "Statement on Kosovo," March 24, 1999, Miller Center, http://miller center.org/president/speeches/speech-3932, accessed January 21, 2015.

79. Wesley K. Clark, *Waging Modern War: Bosnia, Kosovo, and the Future of Conflict* (New York: PublicAffairs, 2002), 268–69; Albright, *Madam Secretary*, 414–16.

80. Norris, *Collision Course*, 49.

81. Albright, *Madam Secretary*, 415–17.

82. Daalder and O'Hanlon, *Winning Ugly*, 141.

83. Clinton told Shelton privately that "I hardly know the man [Clark]; you need to understand that. I don't want any military officer to get hurt because of his association with me, one way or the other."

84. Rothkopf, *Running the World*, 379.

85. Quoted in Daalder and O'Hanlon, *Winning Ugly*, 170. This statement comes from a NATO press release following the meeting of the North Atlantic Council on April 13–24.

86. Ibid., 169–71.

87. Talbott, *Russia Hand*, 319, 326.

88. Vladimir Baranovsky, "Russia: Reassessing National Interests," in *Kosovo and the Challenge of Humanitarian Intervention: Selective Indignation, Collective Action, and International Citizenship*, ed. Albrecht Schnabel and Ramesh Thakur (New York: United Nations University Press, 2000), 104–5.

89. Quoted in Norris, *Collision Course*, 98–105.

90. Talbott, *Russia Hand*, 315.

91. Ibid., 317.

92. Norris, *Collision Course*, 58.

93. Clark, *Waging Modern War*, 268.

94. Ibid., 282.

95. Ibid., 309–15.

96. Albright interview.

97. Norris, *Collision Course*, 117.

98. Dana Priest, *The Mission: Waging War and Keeping Peace with America's Military* (New York: W. W. Norton, 2003), 96.

99. Norris, *Collision Course*, 190.

100. Nau, *Conservative Internationalism*, 69.

101. Bakich, *Success and Failure in Limited War*, chapter 5.

102. Sten Rynning, *NATO in Afghanistan: The Liberal Disconnect* (Stanford, Calif.: Stanford University Press, 2012), 39.

103. Allen C. Lynch, *Vladimir Putin and Russian Statecraft* (Washington, D.C.: Potomac Books, 2011), 45.

CHAPTER 9: PEACEMAKER'S PROGRESS

1. Ezer Weizman, *The Battle for Peace* (New York, 1981), 382.

2. All quotations in this chapter relating to the Clinton presidency are from interviews conducted for the Miller Center's William J. Clinton Presidential History Project unless otherwise noted. The interview transcripts are available at: http://millercenter.org/president/clinton/oralhistory

3. Portions of this account of the peace process in Northern Ireland were previously published. Copyright 2005, from *Decisions and Dilemmas: Case Studies in Presidential Foreign Policy Making since 1945*, 2nd ed. by Robert A. Strong. Reproduced by permission of Taylor and Francis Group, LLC, a division of Informa plc.

4. Bill Clinton, *My Life* (New York: Knopf, 2004), 401.

5. In some reports of this event, Nancy Soderberg, one of Clinton's 1992 foreign policy advisors is said to be present. In her Miller Center transcript, she makes it clear that she was not.

6. Quoted in Conor O'Clery, *Daring Diplomacy: Clinton's Secret Search for Peace in Ireland* (Boulder, CO: Roberts Rinehart Publishers, 1997), 16.

7. Ibid., 47.

8. For the text of the declaration, see "Joint Declaration on Peace: The Downing Street Declaration, Wednesday 15 December 1993," CAIN Web Service, http://cain.ulst.ac.uk/events/peace/docs/dsd151293.htm.

9. The Miller Center oral history interview with Nancy Soderberg describes the internal deliberations of the Clinton administration on the visa issue. A brief version is also found in Nancy Soderberg, *The Superpower Myth* (Hoboken, New Jersey, 2005), 69-72.

10. Clinton, *My Life*, 579.

11. John Major, *The Autobiography* (New York: Harper Collins, 1999), 456.

12. This strange episode with the Southern California IRA has been described in a number of books and articles, but the Soderberg oral history account is one of the best.

13. Gerry Adams, *A Farther Shore* (New York: Random House, 2003), 155.

14. Quoted in ibid., 156.

15. Quoted in O'Clery, *Daring Diplomacy*, 122.

16. Ibid., 131.

17. "Endgame in Ireland," Frontline Special, Public Broadcasting System, 2001. Originally broadcast by the BBC in June/July, 2001 and rebroadcast in the United States as part of the Frontline series in December, 2001.

18. "Remarks to the community in Londonderry, Northern Ireland, November 30, 1995," in *Public Papers of the Presidents of the United States: William J. Clinton, 1995* (Washington, D.C.: Government Printing Office, 1996), 1810.

19. Ibid., 1810–11.

20. Quoted in O'Clery, *Daring Diplomacy*, 244.

21. Tony Lake in his transcript says that the administration used the forthcoming presidential trip to Northern Ireland to "blackmail" the Brits into concessions. This is almost certainly the concession he is referring to.

22. The Miller Center oral history interview with George Mitchell unfortunately does not cover his time as a mediator in Northern Ireland.

23. "Endgame in Ireland."

24. George Mitchell, *Making Peace* (New York: Knopf, 1999), 35–38.

25. Major, *Autobiography*, 480.

26. "Endgame in Ireland."

27. Ibid.

28. Deaglam de Breadun, *The Far Side of Revenge: Making Peace in Northern Ireland* (Cork: The Collins Press, 2001), 94.

29. "Endgame in Ireland."

30. Clinton, *My Life*, 784.

31. Michael Cox, "The War That Came in from the Cold: Clinton and the Irish Question," *World Policy Journal* 16, no. 1 (1999), 73–84.

32. "Remarks to the People of Northern Ireland in Belfast," December 13, 2000, *Public Papers of the Presidents of the United States, Bill Clinton, 2000* (Washington, D.C.: Government Printing Office), 2691–95.

33. Dennis Ross, *The Missing Peace* (New York: Farrar Straus and Giroux, 2004), 97.

34. Which pre-1967 borders would turn out to be a complicated question in the negotiations between Israel and Syria in the 1990s, and although the differences between alternative boundaries were relatively small, they were never fully resolved.

35. Clinton, *My Life*, 626.

36. Clinton also provides an account of these events in his memoirs. Ibid., 543.

37. Discussing the Adams visa, Lake notes, "After all, Yasser Arafat had had involvement in terrorism and he's been on the South Lawn."

38. "Clinton Administration Foreign Policy," panel discussion at the Clinton Presidential Center, November 14, 2014, http://www.c-span.org/video/?322629-1/discussion-foreign-policy-clinton-administration. John Harris reports the same conversation between

Berger and Clinton, but in his version it is Clinton who says "That young man sure knew what he was doing." John F. Harris, *The Survivor* (New York: Random House, 2005), 217.

39. Clinton is reported to be the president who made more international trips than any other. Emily O. Goldman and Larry Berman, "Engaging the World: First Impressions of the Clinton Foreign Policy Legacy," in *The Clinton Legacy*, ed. Colin Campbell and Bert A. Rockman (New York: Chatham House, 2000), 228.

40. Deborah Sontag, "And Yet So Far: A Special Report/Quest for Mideast Peace: How and Why It Failed," *New York Times*, July 26, 2001.

41. Quoted in Benny Morris, "Camp David and After: An Exchange (1. Interview with Ehud Barak)," *New York Review of Books*, June 13, 2002.

42. For a balanced assessment of the president's efforts in the Middle East, see William B. Quandt, "Clinton and the Arab-Israeli Conflict: The Limits of Incrementalism," *Journal of Palestinian Studies* 30, no. 2 (2001), 26–40.

43. Dennis Ross, "Diplomacy in the Middle East," lecture at Washington and Lee University, October 29, 2007.

44. Clinton, *My Life*, 815.

CONCLUSION: CLINTON'S LEGACY FOR POLITICS AND GOVERNMENT

1. William Clinton, "The New Covenant: Responsibility and Rebuilding the American Community, Georgetown University, Washington, D.C., October 23, 1991," http://www.c-span.org/video/?23518-1/clinton-campaign-speech.

2. "Bill Clinton's Third State of the Union Address," in Michael Nelson, ed. *The Evolving Presidency: Landmark Documents, 1787–2010,* 4th edition, 269–73.

3. Arthur M. Schlesinger Jr., *The Vital Center: The Politics of Freedom* (Boston: Houghton Mifflin, 1949).

4. Clinton's outburst was first reported in Bob Woodward, *The Agenda: Inside the Clinton White House* (New York: Simon and Schuster, 1994), 165.

5. Quoted in William Leuchtenburg, *In the Shadow of FDR: From Harry Truman to Ronald Reagan*, rev. ed. (Ithaca, NY.: Cornell University Press, 1985), 49.

6. Oscar Handlin, "A Self Portrait," *Atlantic Monthly*, November 1963, 68.

7. Richard Neustadt, *Presidential Power and the Modern Presidents: The Politics of Leadership Roosevelt to Reagan*, 4th ed. (New York: Free Press, 1990), 139.

8. Robert Blake, *Disraeli* (New York: St. Martin's Press, 1967), 477.

9. John R. Zaller, "Monica Lewinsky's Contribution to Political Science," *PS: Political Science & Politics* 31 (June 1998): 182–89.

10. Stephen Skowronek, *The Politics Presidents Make: From John Adams to Bill Clinton* (Cambridge, Mass.: Harvard University Press, 1997), 447–66.

11. Ibid, 462.

12. Ibid, 44.

13. Theodore White, *America In Search of Itself: The Making of the President, 1956–1980* (New York: Harper and Row, 1982), 124.

14. Daniel Galvin argues that recent Republican presidents, viewing themselves as part of a minority, invested more effort and resources in party building than their Democratic counterparts. See Galvin, *Presidential Party-Building: From Dwight Eisenhower to George W. Bush* (Princeton, N.J.: Princeton University Press, 2009).

15. I make this argument more fully in Sidney M. Milkis, *The President and the Party: The Transformation of the Party System since the New Deal* (New York: Oxford University Press, 1993). For a view of parties as platforms for group demands, see Kathleen Bawn, Martin Cohen, David Karol, Seth Masket, Hans Noel, and John Zaller, "A Theory of Political Parties: Groups, Policy Demands and Nominations in American Politics," *Perspectives on Politics* 10, no. 3 (2012): 571–97.

16. Benjamin Ginsberg and Marin Shefter, *Politics by Other Means: Politicians, Prosecutors, and the Press form Watergate to Whitewater*, rev. and updated ed. (New York: W. W. Norton, 1999), 41.

17. Linda Greenhouse, "Ethics in Government: The Price of Good Intentions," *New York Times*, February 1, 1988; and Cass R. Sunnstein, "Unchecked and Unbalanced: Why the Independent Counsel Act Must Go," *The American Prospect* (May–June 1998): 20–27.

18. For a more complete treatment of the "new" party system, see Sidney M. Milkis, *Political Parties and Constitutional Government: Remaking American Democracy* (Baltimore, Md.: Johns Hopkins University Press, 1999), chapter 6; and Sidney M. Milkis, Jesse Rhodes, and Emily Charnock, "What Happened to Post-Partisanship? Barack Obama and the New American Party System," *Perspectives on Politics* 20, no. 1 (2012): 57–76.

19. Alan Brinkley, "Roots," *New Republic*, July 27, 1992, 45.

20. Clinton, "The New Covenant." This speech marked the first pronouncement of these "sacred principles." From then on, Clinton repeated them at every defining moment of his journey to the White House: the announcement of Senator Albert Gore, who shared his ideas, as his running mate; the party platform; his acceptance speech at the Democratic National Convention in New York; and his victory remarks in Little Rock on election night.

21. Ibid.

22. Similar ideas and attendant policy proposals are spelled out in detail in Will Marshall and Martin Schramm, eds., *Mandate for Change* (New York: Berkeley Books, 1993).

23. Suzanne Metter, *Soldiers to Citizens: The GI Bill and the Making of the Greatest Generation* (New York: Oxford, 2007); Clinton, "The New Covenant"; Steven Waldman, *The Bill: How the Adventures of Clinton's National Service Bill Reveal What is Corrupt, Comic, Cynical—and Noble—about Washington* (New York: Penguin Books, 1995), 2.

24. William Schneider, "A Loud Vote for Change," *National Journal*, November 7, 1992, 2544.

25. Phillip Moffitt, "Champions of the People," *Esquire*, December, 1984, 447.

26. Author's interview, Will Marshall, President, Progressive Policy Institute, and Al From, President, Democratic Leadership Council, May 20, 1997.

27. Dan Balz, "Democrats' Perennial Rising Star Wants to Put a New Face on the Party," *Washington Post*, June 25, 1991, A4; E. J. Dionne, "Democratic Hopefuls Play for Solidarity, *Washington Post*, March 15, 1992, A21; Helen Dewar and Kenneth Cooper, "Clinton Seeks Partnership for Change on Hill," *Washington Post*, April 30, 1992, A16; and David Von Drehle, "Clinton's Movers and Shakers," *Washington Post*, March 23, 1992, A1.

28. Richard Nathan, *The Administrative Presidency* (New York: John Wiley, 1983).

29. Sidney Blumenthal, "Bob Dole's First Strike," *New Yorker*, May 3, 1993, 40–46; Douglas Jehl, "Rejoicing Is Muted for the President in Budget Victory," *New York Times*, August 8, 1993, 1, 23; David Shribman, "Budget Battle a Hollow One for President," *Boston Globe*, August 8, 1993, 1, 24.

30. William Clinton, "Address before a Joint Session of Congress on Administration Goals," *Weekly Compilation of Presidential Documents*, February 17, 1993, 215–24; Jill Zuckerman, "Pared Funding Speeds Passage of National Service," *Congressional Quarterly Weekly Report*, August 7, 1993, 2160–2161. The story of the creation of AmeriCorps is told in Steven Waldman, *The Bill*.

31. Steven Waldman, "Nationalize National Service," *Blueprint*, Spring 1999, 20.

32. Indeed, during the early days of his presidency, Clinton sought to identify with his party's leadership in Congress and the national committee—partly, one suspects, to avoid the political isolation from which Carter suffered. Whereas Carter kept party leaders in Congress and the national committee at arm's length, Clinton sought both to embrace and empower the national organization. The White House lobbying efforts on Capitol Hill focused almost exclusively on the Democratic caucus, and the administration relied

heavily on the Democratic National Committee to marshal public support for its domestic programs. Author's interviews with White House staffer, November 3, 1994, not for attribution; David Wilhelm, chairman, Democratic National Committee, October 18, 1993; and Craig Smith, political director, Democratic National Committee, October 19, 1993. Also see Rhodes Cook, "DNC under Wilhelm Seeking a New Role," *Congressional Quarterly Weekly Report*, March 13, 1993, 634.

33. On the 1938 "purge" campaign, see Milkis, *The President and the Parties*, chapter 4.

34. Al From and Will Marshall, *The Road to Realignment: Democrats and the Perot Voters* (Washington, D.C.: Democratic Leadership Council, July 1, 1993), 3–5.

35. David Shribman, "A New Brand of D.C. Politics," *Boston Globe*, November 18, 1993, 15; Gwen Ifill, "56 Long Days of Coordinated Persuasion," *New York Times*, November 19, 1993, A27.

36. William J. Clinton, "Address Accepting the Presidential Nomination at the Democratic Convention in New York," July 16, 1992, The American Presidency Project, http://www.presidency.ucsb.edu/ws/?pid=25958.

37. William Clinton, "Address to Congress on Health Care Plan," *Congressional Quarterly Weekly Report*, September 25, 1993, 2582–86.

38. Al Gore, *From Red Tape to Results: Creating a Government that Works Better and Costs Less*, Report of the National Performance Review, September 10, 1993, i.

39. Donald F. Kettl, *Reinventing Government? Appraising the National Performance Review* (Washington, D.C.: Brookings, 1994), ix.

40. Clinton, "Address to Congress on Health Care Plan"; Robin Toner, "Alliance to Buy Health Care: Bureaucrat or Public Servant," *New York Times*, December 5, 1993, 1, 38.

41. For a fuller account of the health care reform battle, see Haynes Johnson and David S. Broder, *The System: The American Way of Politics at the Breaking Point* (Boston: Little, Brown, 1996); and Theda Skocpol, *Boomerang: Clinton's Health Security Effort and the Turn against Government* (New York: W.W. Norton, 1996).

42. Adam Clymer, "National Health Program, President's Greatest Goal, Declared Dead in Congress," *New York Times*, September 27, 1994, A1, B10. For a sound and interesting case study of the Clinton health care program, see Cathie Jo Martin, "Mandating Social Change within Corporate America," paper presented at the annual meeting of the American Political Science Association, September 1–4, 1994, New York, New York. Martin's study shows that health care reform became the victim of a battle between "radically different world views about the state and corporation in modern society."

43. William Schneider, "Clinton: The Reason Why," *National Journal*, November 12, 1994, 2630–32. Schneider cites a nationwide poll by Voter News Service that revealed that 82 percent voters who approved of the job Clinton was doing as president (44 percent of all those who voted) cast their ballots for Democrats in House elections. Eighty-three percent of those who disapproved of his performance (51 percent of all who voted) chose Republicans.

44. Dan Balz and Ronald Brownstein, *Storming the Gates: Protest Politics and the Republican Revival* (Boston: Little Brown, 1996), 205–6.

45. Ibid., 207.

46. Remarks of William Galston, Forum on the 1994 Election, Harvard University, December 2, 1994.

47. Steven Gettinger, "'94 Elections: Real Revolution or Blip on Political Radar?" *Congressional Quarterly Weekly Report*, November 5, 1994, 3127–32; Richard L. Berke, "Epic Political Realignments Often Aren't," *New York Times*, January 1, 1995, Section 4, 3.

48. Michael Wines, "Republicans Seek Sweeping Changes in the House's Rules," *New York Times*, December 8, 1994, A1, B21; Michael Wines, "Moderate Republicans Seek an Identity for Gingrich Era," *New York Times*, December 26, 1994, 1, 22.

49. Republicans disagreed about whether federalism or national conservative policy is the appropriate path to a conservative revolution. With respect to reforming the Aid to Families with Dependent Children program, for example, the Republican Contract with America proposed to expand the flexibility of the states, allowing them to design their own work programs and determine who participates in those programs. In fact, states would have been able to opt out of the AFDC program and convert their share of AFDC payments into fixed annual block grants, thus removing federal control over the program. For states that chose to stay in the program, however, the so-called contract called for national standards to determine eligibility, attack illegitimacy and teen pregnancy, and establish work requirements. As John J. Dilulio and Donald Kettl argue in their analysis of the Contract with America, "every relevant study indicates that nationally initiated contract-style welfare reforms can be achieved only where significant resource increases are made in the government bureaucracies." *Fine Print: The Contract With America, Devolution, and the Administrative Realities of American Federalism* (Washington, D.C.: Brookings Institution, 1995), 49. Similarly, with respect to regulatory policy, the Contract envisioned strengthening federalism by ending the practice of imposing unfunded federal mandates on state and local governments. At the same time, it called for the protection of property rights against "takings" in a form that would greatly reduce the discretion of states and localities to control land use. See Richard A. Harris and Sidney M. Milkis, *The Politics of Regulatory Change: A Tale of Two Agencies*, 2nd ed. (New York: Oxford University Press, 1996), chapter 7.

50. Although many pundits were quick to view the 1994 election results as the end of the New Deal, neither Democrats nor Republicans proposed making changes to the largest entitlement program, Social Security, or ending the entitlement status of Medicare. See Robert Pear, "Welfare Debate Will Re-Examine Core Assumptions," *New York Times*, January 2, 1995, 1, 9.

51. Peter Baker and John F. Harris, "Clinton Seeks to Shift Focus by Using Executive Powers," *Washington Post*, April 11, 1997, A1; John H. Cushman, "Clinton Sharply Tightens Air Pollution Regulations Despite Concerns over Costs," *New York Times*, A1; Allan Freedman, "Oversight: Lack of Focus Leaves GOP Stuck in the Learning Curve," *Congressional Quarterly Weekly Report*, November 1, 1997, 2649–55; Robert Pear, "The Presidential Pen Is Still Mightier than the Sword," *New York Times*, June 28, 1998.

52. William Clinton, "Address before a Joint Session of Congress on the State of the Union," January 23, 1996, *Congressional Quarterly Weekly Report*, January 27, 1996, 258–62.

53. As R. Shep Melnick has noted, many public officials and journalists claimed that the new law put an end to "a sixty-one year old entitlement to welfare." In truth, the Aid to Families with Dependent Children program never existed as an entitlement in the sense that Social Security and Medicare did. The program only guaranteed federal matching funds to states that established AFDC programs. See Melnick, "The Unexplained Resilience of Means-Tested Programs," paper delivered at the annual meeting of the American Political Science Association, Boston, Massachusetts, September 3–6, 1998.

54. William Clinton, "Remarks on Signing the Personal Responsibility and Opportunity Reconciliation Act," August 22, 1996, *Weekly Compilation of Presidential Documents*, August 26, 1996, vol. 34, no. 34, 1484–89.

55. R. Kent Weaver, "Ending Welfare as We Know It," in *The Social Divide: Political Parties and the Future of Activist Government*, ed. Margaret Weir (Washington, D.C.: Brookings), 396.

56. Bill Clinton, "State of the Union Address," January 23, 1996, Miller Center, http://millercenter.org/president/clinton/speeches/speech-5494.

57. Bob Woodward, *The Choice* (New York: Simon and Schuster, 1996), 344.

58. Not surprisingly, Clinton's speech received praise from the Democratic Leadership Council's president, Al From, who celebrated it as an attempt "to speak to the main concerns of the millions of disaffected voters in the political center" who were estranged from the ideological and institutional combat between liberal and conservatives and "were likely to be the margin of difference in the 1996 election." From, "More than a Good Speech: The State of the Union Address Could Have Marked a Turning Point in History," *New Democrat*, March–April, 1996, 35–36.

59. Anthony Corrado, "Financing the 1996 Elections," in *The Elections of 1996*, ed. Gerald Pomper (Chatham, N.J.: Chatham House, 1997). "Soft money" was provided for in the 1979 amendments to the campaign finance legislation of 1974, as part of the broader effort to strengthen national party organizations. By 1992, both Democrats and Republicans had come to depend on it to finance the expensive media campaigns that dominated national elections. As such, the parties violated the spirit of the 1979 amendments, which were dedicated to increasing party spending on traditional grassroots boosterism and get-out-the-vote drives rather than on mass media campaigns. More to the point, the institutional separation between the president and parties allowed, indeed encouraged, presidential candidates to exploit these funds. See Beth Donovan, "Much-Maligned 'Soft Money' Is Precious to Both Parties," *National Journal*, May 15, 1993, 1195–1200. In 2002, the McCain-Feingold Act banned soft money contributions to political parties.

60. Michael Nelson, "The Election: Turbulence and Tranquility in Contemporary American Politics," in *The Elections of 1996*, ed. Michael Nelson (Washington, D.C.: Congressional Quarterly Press, 1997), 52; and Gary Jacobson, "The 105th Congress: Unprecedented and Unsurprising," in *The Elections of 1996*, 161.

61. Skowronek, *The Politics Presidents Make*, 449.

62. Daniel J. Palazzolo, *Done Deal? The Politics of the 1997 Budget Agreement* (Chatham, N.J.: Chatham House, 1999), 189.

63. "Can you imagine what they would be doing to us if this was a Republican-only plan?" asked one GOP Budget Committee member. "They would be killing us. Clinton gave us the cover to do some things. I think this is better than if Dole were president." Quoted in Palazzolo, *Done Deal*, 100. For the Democratic reaction to the budget package, see Alison Mitchell, "Despite Angry Colleagues, Clinton United His Party," *New York Times*, May 6, 1997, A12.

64. States are given flexibility in designing SCHIP eligibility programs and policies within broad federal guidelines.

65. Weaver, "Ending Welfare As We Know It," 397.

66. Richard Stevenson, "After Year of Wrangling, Accord Is Reached on Plan to Balance the Budget by 2002," *New York Times*, May 3, 1997, 1.

67. Bill Clinton, "Second Inaugural, January 20, 1997," Miller Center, http://miller center.org/president/clinton/speeches/speech-3443.

68. Kathy Hariger, "Independent Justice: The Office of the Independent Counsel," in *Government Lawyers: The Federal Bureaucracy and Presidential Politics*, ed. Cornell W. Clayton (Lawrence: University Press of Kansas, 1995), 86.

69. Adam Clymer, "Under Attack, Clinton Gets No Cover from His Party," *New York Times*, March 16, 1997, 1; Todd S. Purdum, "Clinton Most Charming at a Distance," *New York Times*, September 17, 1998, 18. One Clinton official who knew the president well acknowledged that even as he went into the administration eagerly, his enthusiasm was tempered by "Clinton's lack of firm attachment to any principles and his undisciplined nature.... Clinton is a talented leader, but his major influence is one of effect—there is no moral compass or sense of direction." Author's interview with Clinton official, not for attribution, May 28, 1998.

70. Janny Scott, "Talking Heads Post-Mortem: All Wrong, All the Time," *New York Times*, November 8, 1998, A22.

71. Stein interview.

72. Bill Clinton, Response to the Lewinsky Allegations, January 26, 1998, http://millercenter.org/president/speeches/speech-3930.

73. Richard L. Berke, John M. Broder, and Don Van Natta Jr., "How Republican Determination Upset Clinton's Backing at the Polls," *New York Times*, December 28, 1998.

74. "Early Views After Impeachment: The Public Supports Clinton," *New York Times*, December 21, 1998.

75. Author's interview with Will Marshall, president, Progressive Policy Institute, June 14, 1999.

76. David E. Rosenbaum, "Surplus a Salve for Clinton and Congress," *New York Times*, June 29, 1999.

77. Alan I. Abramowitz, *The Disappearing Center: Engaged Citizens, Polarization and American Democracy* (New Haven, Conn.: Yale University Press, 2011); and "The Only Thing We Have to Fear Is the Other Party: How Negative Partisanship Is Dividing Americans and Shaping the Behavior of the 2016 Election," Sabato's Crystal Ball, June 4, 2015, http://www.centerforpolitics.org/crystalball/articles/the-only-thing-we-have-to-fear-is-the-other-party/.

78. David A. Fahrenhold, Tom Hamburger and Rosalind S. Helderman, "Results and Repercussions: How the Clintons Built a $2 Billion Global Charity, and How It Became a Problem for Hillary," *New York Times*, June 3, 2015, A1, 10–12.

79. Personal interview with Matthew Dowd, Chief Campaign Strategist, 2004 Bush-Cheney Campaign, July 26, 2004.

80. Hugh Heclo, "Sixties Civic," in *The Great Society and the High Tide of Liberalism*, ed. Sidney M. Milkis and Jerome Mileur (Amherst: University of Massachusetts Press, 2005), 54.

81. Author's interview with Democratic Party official, not for attribution, July 12, 1999.

82. On this point, see Marc Landy and Sidney M. Milkis, *Presidential Greatness* (Lawrence: Kansas University Press, 2000).

83. Woodrow Wilson, *Constitutional Government in the United States* (New York: Columbia University Press, 1908), 69.

Contributors

Spencer D. Bakich is a visiting lecturer in the Department of Political Science at the University of Richmond. He is the author of *Success and Failure in Limited War: Information and Strategy in the Korean, Vietnam, Persian Gulf, and Iraq Wars* and has published articles on the relationship between force and diplomacy in the Balkans, the Vietnam War, and maritime East Asia.

Brendan J. Doherty is associate professor of political science at the United States Naval Academy and the author of *The Rise of the President's Permanent Campaign.* His other published work has examined presidential travel and fund-raising, Senate leadership, and the targeting of Spanish-speaking voters in presidential elections, among other topics.

Patrick T. Hickey is assistant professor of political science at West Virginia University. His research examines the interaction between Congress, the president, and the people and has been published in *Presidential Studies Quarterly.*

Elaine Kamarck is a senior fellow and founding director at the Brookings Institution's Center for Effective Public Management in Washington D.C. where she conducts research on government and politics. She is also faculty chair at Harvard's Emerging Leaders Executive Education Program, and is the author of *Primary Politics: Everything You Want to Know about How America Nominates Its Presidents.*

Sidney M. Milkis is the White Burkett Miller Professor of Politics and faculty associate at the Miller Center at the University of Virginia. His most recent books are *The American Presidency: Origins and Development, 1776–2014*, with Michael Nelson; and *Theodore Roosevelt, the Progressive Party, and the Transformation of American Democracy.* His articles have been published in *Perspectives on Politics, Studies in American Political Development*, and other journals.

Megan Moeller is a PhD candidate in the Department of Government at the University of Texas at Austin.

Michael Nelson is Fulmer Professor of Political Science at Rhodes College, a senior fellow at the University of Virginia's Miller Center, and senior contributing editor and book editor of the *Cook Political Report.* His book *Resilient America: Electing Nixon in 1968, Channeling Dissent, and Dividing Government* won the

Richard E. Neustadt Award for best book on the presidency, and his coauthored book *How the South Joined the Gambling Nation: The Politics of State Policy Innovation* won the V. O. Key Award for Outstanding Book on Southern Politics.

Bruce F. Nesmith is Joan and Abbott Lipsky Professor of Political Science at Coe College. He is author of *The New Republican Coalition: The Reagan Campaigns and White Evangelicals*. He is working with Paul Quirk on a book-length study of the presidency, Congress, and policy making.

Barbara A. Perry is the White Burkett Miller Professor of Ethics and Institutions at the University of Virginia's Miller Center, where she directs the Institute of Presidential Studies and co-chairs the Presidential Oral History Program.

Paul J. Quirk holds the Phil Lind Chair in U.S. Politics and Representation at the University of British Columbia. He has published widely on the presidency, Congress, public opinion, and public policy and won the best book award of the (U.S.) National Academy of Public Administration and the Enduring Achievement Award of the Public Policy Section of the American Political Science Association.

Russell L. Riley co-chairs the Presidential Oral History Program at the University of Virginia's Miller Center. He is the author of *The Presidency and the Politics of Racial Inequality: Nation Keeping from 1831 to 1965* and the editor a forthcoming oral history–based book on the Clinton presidency.

Andrew Rudalevige is Thomas Brackett Reed Professor of Government at Bowdoin College and a former city councilor in Massachusetts. Rudalevige's books include *Managing the President's Program: Presidential Leadership and Legislative Policy Formulation*, which won the Richard E. Neustadt Award for best book on the presidency, and *The New Imperial Presidency: Renewing Presidential Power after Watergate*. He is a contributor to the Monkey Cage blog on the *Washington Post* website.

Robert A. Strong has been a teacher of international relations, the presidency, and American foreign policy at Tulane University and at Washington and Lee University, where he recently served as interim provost. He is the author of books on Henry Kissinger and Jimmy Carter. His writing for newspapers and popular publications can be found at http://www.huffingtonpost.com/robert-strong/.

Sean M. Theriault is a professor of government and University Distinguished Teaching Professor at the University of Texas at Austin. In addition to his three books on Congress (most recently, *The Gingrich Senators*), Theriault's research has been published in the *Journal of Politics* and *Legislative Studies Quarterly*.

Index

Note: *t* indicates tables